African Studies

The African Studies series, founded in 1968, publishes research monographs by emerging and senior scholars that feature innovative analyses in the fields of history, political science, anthropology, economics and environmental studies. The series also produces mature, paradigm-shifting syntheses that seek to reinterpret and revitalize the scholarly literature in these fields.

A list of books in this series will be found at the end of this volume.

Political Thought and the Public Sphere in Tanzania

Freedom, Democracy and Citizenship in the Era of Decolonization

EMMA HUNTER

University of Edinburgh

 CAMBRIDGE
UNIVERSITY PRESS

CAMBRIDGE
UNIVERSITY PRESS

University Printing House, Cambridge CB2 8BS, United Kingdom

One Liberty Plaza, 20th Floor, New York, NY 10006, USA

477 Williamstown Road, Port Melbourne, VIC 3207, Australia

4843/24, 2nd Floor, Ansari Road, Daryaganj, Delhi - 110002, India

79 Anson Road, #06-04/06, Singapore 079906

Cambridge University Press is part of the University of Cambridge.

It furthers the University's mission by disseminating knowledge in the pursuit of education, learning and research at the highest international levels of excellence.

www.cambridge.org
Information on this title: www.cambridge.org/9781107458628

First published 2015
First paperback edition 2017

A catalogue record for this publication is available from the British Library

Library of Congress Cataloging in Publication data
Hunter, Emma
Political thought and the public sphere in Tanzania : freedom, democracy and citizenship in the era of decolonization / Emma Hunter.
pages   cm. – (African studies)
Includes bibliographical references and index.
ISBN 978-1-107-08817-7 (hardback)
1. Political participation – Tanzania.   2. Democracy – Tanzania.   I. Title.
JQ3519.A15H87   2015
323´.04209678–dc23   2014044902

ISBN 978-1-107-08817-7 Hardback
ISBN 978-1-107-45862-8 Paperback

Contents

Acknowledgements

This book has been written over many years, in many places, and with the help of many people. The questions I explore in this book were ones I began to ask more than a decade ago in dialogue with John Lonsdale, who first introduced me to African history and supervised the PhD thesis which followed. Although this research has taken many twists and turns since then, this book remains profoundly shaped by his supervision.

The research for this book was supported by the Arts and Humanities Research Council, the British Academy, the Smuts Memorial Fund and Gonville and Caius College. I am very grateful to all of these institutions for their assistance, which has enabled me to travel to archives and libraries across Europe, Africa and the United States.

The book is based in large part on research conducted in Tanzania in 2005–2006 and 2009–2010. I am grateful to the Tanzanian Commission for Science and Technology (COSTECH) for granting research permission for those two periods, and to the officials, archivists and librarians in Tanzania who made this research possible. I am very grateful to archivists at the Tanzania National Archives, particularly Selina H. Macha and Moshi Omari Mwinyimvua in Dar es Salaam and Herman Rwechungura in the regional office in Mwanza, as well as to Geoffrey M. Chelelo at the Chama cha Mapinduzi Archives in Dodoma and to Jane Matowo, archivist at the Evangelical Lutheran Church of Tanzania Archives in Moshi. I would like to thank Nestor Luanda and Bertram Mapunda at the University of Dar es Salaam who offered helpful guidance and advice, and made it possible for me to use the East Africana Collection in the library of the University of Dar es Salaam, which has a wonderful collection of Swahili-language texts and newspapers.

Research for this book has also taken me to the Library of Congress in Washington, DC; the United States National Archives in College Park, Maryland; the University of Leipzig library; and, within the United Kingdom, to the National Archives at Kew, the British Library and the newspaper library at Colindale, the School of Oriental and African Studies (SOAS) library and archives in London and Rhodes House library in Oxford. I am very grateful to all the librarians and archivists of those institutions. In Cambridge, the staff of the University Library, particularly librarians in the Rare Books Room, which houses the Royal Commonwealth Society collection, and the Commonwealth Room, have been enormously helpful, as have Marilyn Glanfield and Rachel Malkin in the African Studies Library.

This book was written during the years I spent as a Fellow and Lecturer in History at Gonville and Caius College and Newton Trust Lecturer at the Centre of African Studies in Cambridge. Cambridge provided a fantastic environment in which to write this book, and the ideas developed here were worked out in dialogue with students and with colleagues. I am enormously grateful to undergraduate students in world history and M.Phil. students in African studies and the history of political thought whose probing questions forced me to articulate my ideas more clearly. The research which my doctoral students, Catherine Porter, Eva Namusoke, Louisa Cantwell, Donald Fraser, Naomi Parkinson and Katherine Bruce-Lockhart, have conducted across the African continent and beyond has in turn provoked new questions for me.

Friends and colleagues in the World History subject group of the Faculty of History and in the Centre of African Studies were a constant source of inspiration and new ideas, including Andrew Arsan, Chris Bayly, Felicitas Becker, Florence Brisset-Foucault, Joya Chatterji, Leigh Denault, Harri Englund, Tim Gibbs, Tim Harper, David Maxwell, Megan Vaughan and Ruth Watson. At Gonville and Caius, I benefitted from the wisdom, insights and, most importantly, fellowship of a group of historians whose commitment and energy have created the most wonderful intellectual environment in which to think, teach and write. Conversations with David Abulafia, Andrew Bell, Annabel Brett, Melissa Calaresu, Peter Mandler, Robert Priest and Sujit Sivasundaram have helped to shape this book, and have also made it a far more pleasant experience to write than it otherwise would have been.

Parts of this book have been presented in many different forums over the last six years and I am very grateful for all the comments and suggestions received. Particular thanks are due to the participants in the

American Historical Association Decolonization Seminar in Washington, DC, in July 2008 for engaging with an early attempt to articulate the core arguments of the book; to Cherry Leonardi, Chris Vaughan and Justin Willis for an invitation to Durham which provided a first attempt to think through the material which is now in Chapter 7; and to colleagues in the African Print Cultures network, particularly Derek Peterson, Stephanie Newell, Karin Barber and David Pratten, for many discussions on matters newspaper-related. Leigh Denault, Harri Englund, Leslie James and Derek Peterson read draft chapters and I thank them for their comments. I am particularly indebted to Peter Mandler and Megan Vaughan for heroically reading the full manuscript and for their insightful comments and suggestions.

This book has been shaped by my own historical and political education, growing up in Scotland in the years immediately leading up to devolution and the establishment of a Scottish Parliament in 1999, and I am grateful to my parents, Penny and Frank, and my brother, Euan, for their role in introducing me to the universal political questions which are explored here.

Finally, this book owes a great deal to my partner, Charles West. Few historians of medieval Europe are called on to read and comment on multiple iterations of draft chapters packed with untranslated Swahili. Fewer still find themselves spending a Christmas vacation attempting to translate a Latin treatise in the back of a minibus bumping along untarmacked roads or dodging mosquitos in the guesthouses of southern Tanzania. My thanks to him for all this, and much more.

Map of Tanzania

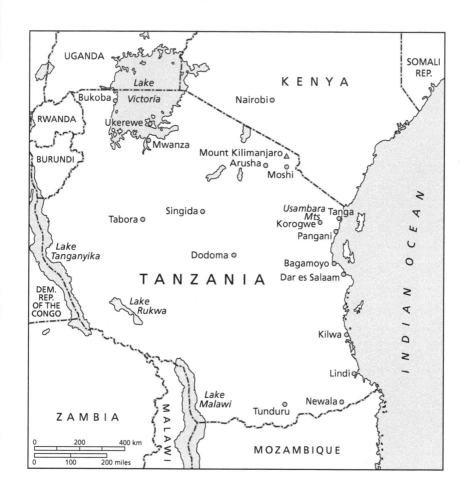

Abbreviations

AMNUT	All-Muslim National Union of Tanganyika
ANC	African National Congress
CCM	Chama Cha Mapinduzi Archives, Dodoma
CDP	Chagga Democratic Party
KCCU	Kilimanjaro Chagga Citizens Union
RHO	Rhodes House Oxford
TANU	Tanganyika African National Union
TNA	Tanzania National Archives
TNA UK	The National Archives of the United Kingdom
UNTC	United Nations Trusteeship Council
UTP	United Tanganyika Party

Introduction

In the late 1960s, the nationalist politician Lameck Bogohe set out to record his role in Tanzania's nationalist movement and to reflect on the changes which had happened since independence in 1961. In a text which straddles the genres of autobiography, nationalist history and political treatise, he considered the relative advantages of alternative political systems, the nature of government, the importance of law and the meaning of citizenship. Had political independence made a difference, or had one group of illegitimate rulers simply been replaced by another?[1]

By this point, Bogohe had suffered arrest, and had, he believed, been deprived of political office by the postcolonial Tanzanian state. He might have had good reason for adopting a critical tone. Yet Bogohe remained optimistic. While all governments, he believed, had a tendency towards oppressing their citizens, such oppression was less likely in an independent African state than in a colonial African state. For although colonial officials might forget the suffering of poor villagers struggling to make a living, African politicians would not. They might live in the capital, far from the trials and tribulations of poor harvests and overzealous tax collectors, but they had relatives in the countryside who would alert them to the injustices of government, remind them of their duties to kin and locality and, in doing so, hold them to account.

Bogohe was asking questions about the nature of politics, the concept of freedom and the meaning of citizenship. It is the contention of

---

[1] Lameck Bogohe, *Historia ya TANU*, CCM Archives, Acc 5/686. The text will be referred to as Bogohe, *Historia ya TANU* although no title page was found when the file was consulted in November 2005.

this book that such questions were being debated across the decolonizing world of the mid-twentieth century, but that the richness of these arguments has been masked by a still dominant grand narrative of decolonization. The questions posed by African politicians and African writers engaging in the public sphere were prompted by the intersection of the deep politics of the locality and the global political ruptures and realignments of a decolonizing world. The answers that they developed similarly drew on and engaged with global discourses to provide locally meaningful political narratives. The arguments and discussions that took place within the United Nations Trusteeship Territory of Tanganyika between 1945 and the Arusha Declaration of 1967 serve as a good example of this process, and it is these arguments and discussions that this book explores.

HISTORIES OF DECOLONIZATION

The conflict between two opposing forces, imperialism and nationalism, once seemed to define the history of the colonial and postcolonial world in the mid-twentieth century. Early accounts of the passage from colonial state to postcolony took this clash of forces as their starting point. While some accounts told the story from the perspective of imperial powers facing the loss of their empires, others took the opposite perspective and documented the rise of the new mass nationalist parties charged with leading new nation-states into the modern world.[2]

In the past decade our understanding of the era of decolonization has begun to change radically. Frederick Cooper's groundbreaking work has reframed our understanding of both the motor of decolonization and the breadth of options open to the political thinkers of the mid-twentieth century.[3] The imperative of development drove political reform and sparked a conversation between European colonial powers, the new international institutions of the post-1945 era, and African political thinkers and activists. In forums such as the French Parliament or the Trade Union movement, certain shared fundamental assumptions permitted a

---

[2] Thomas Hodgkin, *Nationalism in Colonial Africa* (New York: New York University Press, 1957); Ruth Schachter Morgenthau, *Political Parties in French-Speaking West Africa* (Oxford: Clarendon Press, 1964).

[3] Frederick Cooper and Randall Packard (eds.), *International Development and the Social Sciences: Essays on the History and Politics of Knowledge* (Berkeley: University of California Press, 1997); Frederick Cooper, *Citizenship between Empire and Nation: Remaking France and French Africa, 1945–1960* (Princeton, NJ: Princeton University Press, 2014).

space for debate, and the lines of alliance and conflict were not always those of colony versus metropole.[4] The final outcome remained radically uncertain until the second half of the 1950s, and was the result of a 'messy give-and-take process between people with different expectations and objectives'.[5] Within a wide spectrum of political possibilities, '[n]ationalism was part of the repertoire of political opposition, but not necessarily the most important one'.[6]

If the process of decolonization was far more open than was once assumed, so too was twentieth-century nationalism. When nationalists wrote their histories, they imposed uniformity on intellectual, social and political movements that were in reality wide-ranging and often mutually contradictory. This formed part of their own claim to legitimate authority. Reading events through the lens of modernization theory, nationalist histories privileged the role of Western-educated elites and squeezed out those aspects of the story which did not fit a narrative of secular, modernist progress.[7] This narrative was reinforced by later interpretations. In Benedict Anderson's still powerful account, new conceptions of nationhood were first thought out in Latin America, then exported back to Europe, and from there to the rest of the world.[8] But as Partha Chatterjee asked, 'If nationalisms in the rest of the world have to choose their imagined community from certain 'modular' forms already made available to them by Europe and the Americas, what do they have left to imagine?'[9]

In fact, as new work has shown, the nationalisms of the late colonial era incorporated a wide range of competing perspectives and ways of imagining the nation. In India, the spectrum of nationalist thinking ranged from the conservative Hindu cultural nationalism of Vallabhai Patel on the right to M. N. Roy's Indian Communist party on the left.

---

[4] Frederick Cooper, 'Possibility and Constraint: African Independence in Historical Perspective', *Journal of African History*, 49 (2008), 167–196; Frederick Cooper, *Decolonisation and African Society: The Labour Question in French and British Africa* (Cambridge: Cambridge University Press, 1996).

[5] Ryan Irwin, *Gordian Knot: Apartheid and the Unmaking of the Liberal World Order* (Oxford: Oxford University Press, 2012), p. 10.

[6] Frederick Cooper, *Colonialism in Question: Theory, Knowledge, History* (Berkeley and London: University of California Press, 2005), p. 156.

[7] George McTurnan Kahin, *Nationalism and Revolution in Indonesia* (Ithaca, NY: Cornell University Press, 1952).

[8] Benedict Anderson, *Imagined Communities: Reflections on the Origin and Spread of Nationalism* (London: Verso, 1991); Benedict Anderson, *Spectre of Comparison: Nationalism, South East Asia and the World* (London: Verso, 1998).

[9] Cited in Ziad Fahmy, *Ordinary Egyptians: Creating the Modern Nation through Popular Culture* (Stanford: Stanford University Press, 2011), p. 11.

As Maria Misra writes, 'Gandhi had mixed a compound national vision that was either startlingly radical or deeply conservative, depending on the political proclivities of the beholder. However, despite his determination to eclipse enemies left and right, rival ideologies flourished on both flanks, invoking visions of the nation wholly at odds with Gandhi's ashramite utopia'.[10]

A new body of literature now shows that where once nationalism seemed unitary, the creation of elites who then mobilized a mass movement, it was in fact far more disparate. There was not one nationalism but many nationalisms.[11] And nationalism could divide as much as it could unite. Taken together, these new histories of decolonization and postnationalist histories of nationalism have reminded us that the narrative of a smooth path from colonial dependency to independent state conceals lively intellectual debate. More fundamentally, they remind us that not everyone who engaged in political thinking was a nationalist, and that there were many different types of nationalism.[12]

But we can go further. As we begin to probe beneath the meta-narrative of decolonization, we find a rich vein of political thinking to which familiar accounts of the mid-twentieth century fail to do justice. What did freedom mean, and was it a universal good? What forms of political engagement were open to late colonial subjects or postcolonial citizens? What did democracy mean, in theory and in practice? These fundamental questions of political theory were debated not only by colonial or nationalist elites, but by all those who engaged in colonial and postcolonial public spheres. And while the answers they gave to these questions may have engaged with and been shaped by global discourses, they also drew on local experience and responded to local circumstances. This book traces the history of some of these debates in the United Nations Trusteeship Territory of Tanganyika which, after 1964, joined with Zanzibar to create Tanzania.[13]

---

[10] Maria Misra, *Vishnu's Crowded Temple: India since the Great Rebellion* (London: Allen Lane, 2007), p. 154.

[11] See, e.g., Israel Gershoni and James Jankowski (eds.), *Rethinking Nationalism in the Arab Middle East* (New York: Columbia University Press, 1997).

[12] For example., Gregory Mann, *Native Sons: West African Veterans and France in the Twentieth Century* (Durham, NC: Duke University Press, 2006). Timothy Parsons argues in a similar vein that the 'political influence of East African veterans has been largely overstated.' Timothy Parsons, *The African Rank-and-File: Social Implications of Colonial Military Service in the King's African Rifles, 1902–1964* (Oxford: James Currey, 1999), p. 260.

[13] In accordance with general usage, I shall use the term 'Tanganyika' when referring specifically to the colonial period, and otherwise will use the term 'Tanzania' or 'mainland Tanzania'.

HISTORIES OF EAST AFRICA BETWEEN
THE LOCAL AND THE GLOBAL

To explore these arguments, this book builds on recent local histories which have radically transformed our understanding of colonial Africa and the intellectual currents operating at the grassroots in the locality. The impression was often given, both by nationalist leaders recalling their path to power and by the first generation of historians who analysed that rise to power, that peasants had little interest in politics until 'awakened' by their leaders. As Paul Landau explained in his study of popular politics in South Africa between 1400 and 1948: 'Quite often in historical literature, Africans are depicted as pre-political or as politically naive, mired in irrational beliefs, and they are imagined to have stayed that way until modern nationalism began to pull them free.'[14] But the development of African social history has demonstrated very clearly that the intellectual and political cultures of rural and urban Africa were far from those imagined by nationalist leaders and their historians.

Building on this tradition of Africanist social history, intellectual historians have demonstrated that local idioms, often demonstrating significant continuity over time, provided a means of critiquing illegitimate power and holding leaders to account. In Steven Feierman's study of the Shambaa kingdom in north-eastern Tanzania, political battles dismissed by colonial authorities as anticolonial agitation or resistance to progress become part of a long running contest over political authority in the region, in which the right to rule depends on the balance struck between healing and harming the land. Feierman traced arguments over the meaning of terms like freedom and slavery and uncovered the salience of the term 'democracy' in mid-twentieth-century Usambara, meanings and terms picked up by national leaders like Julius Nyerere.[15] While Feierman's focus is specifically on the local politics of the Usambara Region, the point that peasants in the locality and nationalists operating at the centre were connected has wider significance.

This scholarship has taken on board the attention paid by social historians of Africa to cleavages of gender and generation within African society, and integrated these dynamics into local political histories.[16] It

---

[14] Paul Landau, *Popular Politics in the History of South Africa, 1400–1948* (Cambridge: Cambridge University Press, 2010), p. xii.

[15] Steven Feierman, *Peasant Intellectuals: Anthropology and History in Tanzania* (Madison, WI: University of Wisconsin Press, 1990).

[16] Derek Peterson, *Ethnic Patriotism and the East African Revival: A History of Dissent, c. 1935–1972* (Cambridge: Cambridge University Press, 2012); Derek Peterson, *Creative Writing: Translation, Bookkeeping, and the Work of Imagination in Colonial*

has explored the duties which the young owe to the old and the old to the young, as well as the centrality of gendered identities to local politics. Attempts by elder men to control women's sexuality and defend their right to make decisions about women's bodies against interference from younger men, colonial officials or missionaries is shown not to have been a straightforward battle between the forces of tradition and the forces of modernity, but an arena in which political ideas were fought out. This work stresses that such concerns are not separate from the true domain of 'political' history, but are central to it, and when political historians ignore them or relegate them to a separate sphere of social or gender history, they do so at the expense of impoverishing their understanding of African political history.[17]

More generally, this scholarship has shown that colonial regimes were not strong enough to impose their political philosophies on Africa. They shaped struggles over power and authority, but they did not end those struggles.[18] Nor did nationalist parties silence debate. Nationalist parties succeeded when they could enter into and shape local conflicts over power and authority.[19] They did not, and could not, end these debates, which were at once local and particular, and national and universal. Political debates were local, in the sense that they attacked corrupt chiefs, tax collectors who enriched themselves, district officers who imprisoned unjustly, or denied aspirant politicians a voice. Yet they were also universal, because these were debates about the nature of authority, including political authority, and the relationship between individual and community.

Kenya (Portsmouth, NH: Heinemann, 2004); John Lonsdale, 'Authority, Gender and Violence: The War within Mau Mau's Fight for Land and Freedom', in John Lonsdale and E. S. Atieno Odhiambo (eds.), *Mau Mau and Nationhood: Arms, Authority and Narration* (Oxford: James Currey, 2003), pp. 46–75; John Lonsdale, 'The Moral Economy of Mau Mau: Wealth, Poverty and Civic Virtue in Kikuyu Political Thought', in John Lonsdale and Bruce Berman (eds.), *Unhappy Valley: Conflict in Kenya and Africa. Book Two: Violence and Ethnicity* (Oxford: James Currey, 1992), pp. 315–504.

[17] This is not unique to African history. There is a tendency more broadly to assume that questions of morality or ethics belong in the 'private sphere' and are secondary to more classically 'political' concerns. See Saba Mahmood, *Politics of Piety: The Islamic Revival and the Feminist Subject* (Princeton, NJ: Princeton University Press, 2005), p. 32.

[18] On which see Sara Berry, 'Hegemony on a Shoestring: Indirect Rule and Access to Agricultural Land', *Africa*, 62 (1992), 327–355; Frederick Cooper, 'Conflict and Connection: Rethinking Colonial African History', *The American Historical Review*, 99 (1994), 1516–1545; Benjamin Lawrance, Emily Lynn Osborn and Richard L. Roberts (eds.), *Intermediaries, Interpreters and Clerks: African Employees in the Making of Colonial Africa* (Madison, WI: University of Wisconsin Press, 2006).

[19] Gregory Maddox and James Giblin (eds.), *In Search of a Nation: Histories of Authority and Dissidence in Tanzania* (Oxford: James Currey, 2005).

This strand of research, which we might term 'intellectual history from below', has reinvigorated the intellectual history of twentieth-century Africa by opening up new perspectives. Yet it has remained largely separate from the concerns which animate political historians and social scientists such as, crucially, the political transition from colony to independent state and questions of political legitimacy within these two state formations. More broadly, because it privileges research in the locality, where possible conducted in the vernacular, it is necessarily self-limiting in terms of the potential for broader comparative research.[20]

Alongside these localized studies, Tanzania also benefits from a rich secondary literature detailing its twentieth-century political history. In the early 1960s, the History Department at the University of Dar es Salaam was home to a dynamic group of historians setting the agenda for a new postcolonial African history. One result of that productive period was John Iliffe's magisterial *A Modern History of Tanganyika* published in 1979, making Tanzania one of very few countries in sub-Saharan Africa to have a thoroughly researched political and social history covering the period from 1800 until independence.[21] In recent years, scholars such as James Giblin, James Brennan and Paul Bjerk have built on this foundation to revise further the history of nationalism and begin writing the history of the early postcolonial state in Tanzania, offering perspectives from below, revisionist accounts of the importance of race in nationalist thought and new accounts of Julius Nyerere's leadership.[22] For the first decade of independence, there is also a substantial body of work written at the time. A great many researchers were drawn to Tanzania by the personal charisma of Julius Nyerere and his ambitious development ideas, and their work provides a rich seam of evidence collected on the

---

[20] For example, Peter Pels, 'Creolization in Secret: The Birth of Nationalism in Late-Colonial Uluguru, Tanzania', *Africa* 72 (2002), 1–28.

[21] John Iliffe, *A Modern History of Tanganyika* (Cambridge: Cambridge University Press, 1979).

[22] James Giblin, *A History of the Excluded: Making Family a Refuge from State in Twentieth-Century Tanzania* (Oxford: James Currey, 2004); James Brennan, *Taifa: Making Nation and Race in Urban Tanzania* (Athens, OH: Ohio University Press, 2012); James Brennan, 'The Short History of Political Opposition and Multi-party Democracy in Tanganyika, 1958–1964', in Gregory Maddox and James Giblin (eds.), *In Search of a Nation: Histories of Authority and Dissidence in Tanzania* (Oxford: James Currey, 2005), pp. 250–276; Ronald Aminzade, *Race, Nation, and Citizenship in Post-Colonial Tanzania* (Cambridge: Cambridge University Press, 2013); R. Aminzade, 'The Politics of Race and Nation: Citizenship and Africanization in Tanganyika', *Political Power and Social Theory*, 14, 2000, pp. 53–90; Paul K. Bjerk, *Julius Nyerere and the Establishment of Sovereignty in Tanganyika*. Unpublished PhD thesis, University of Wisconsin (2008).

ground in the 1960s.[23] As enthusiasm for Nyerere's policies later turned
to disillusionment in some quarters, this prompted revisionist accounts
which have further contributed to our knowledge of the period.[24]

The combination of these two bodies of literature, intellectual history
from below on the one hand and the rich secondary literature relating to
Tanzania on the other, provides an important basis for this book, which
builds on existing scholarship but moves in a new direction by going back
to the core political concepts which were at issue in the mid-twentieth
century. It explores these concepts as they were debated in Tanzania's
sphere of public debate, debates which were often, though not exclusively, conducted in the Swahili language which increasingly served as a
shared *lingua franca* for an emerging literate elite, and which were situated at the cross-section of wider currents.

CONCEPTS OF POLITICS

For a long time, historians interested in exploring the ways in which colonized peoples reflected on and engaged with shifting intellectual trends
focussed on how leading thinkers in the colonial world thought about
the challenges posed by the growth of European power. For Robert July,
writing in 1968, the challenge was to understand a 'fundamental con-
frontation of two ways of life', of Europe and of Africa. He approached
this question through a study of great men and their writings, and his
reading of the encounter he perceived was situated firmly within the
framework of 1960s assumptions about trajectories of modernization.[25]
Similar studies of other parts of the world were also concerned with great
men and their thought. While Albert Hourani's classic study of political

---

[23] For a helpful review of the literature, see Paul Bjerk, 'Sovereignty and Socialism in
Tanzania: The Historiography of an African State', *History in Africa* 37 (2010),
275–319. Within this literature, see in particular Cranford Pratt, *The Critical Phase in
Tanzania, 1945–1968* (Cambridge: Cambridge University Press, 1976); Lionel Cliffe
(ed.), *One Party Democracy: The 1965 Tanzania General Elections* (Nairobi: East
African Publishing House, 1967); Henry Bienen, *Tanzania: Party Transformation and
Economic Development* (Princeton, NJ: Princeton University Press, 1967).

[24] Leander Schneider, 'Colonial Legacies and Postcolonial Authoritarianism in Tanzania,'
African Studies Review 49 (2006), 93–118; James C. Scott, *Seeing Like a State: How
Certain Schemes to Improve the Human Condition Have Failed* (New Haven, CT: Yale
University Press, 1998); Priya Lal, 'Self-reliance and the State: The Multiple Meanings of
Development in Early Post-colonial Tanzania', *Africa*, 82 (2012), 212–234.

[25] Robert W. July, *The Origins of Modern African Thought: Its Development in West Africa
during the Nineteenth and Twentieth Centuries* (London: Faber and Faber, 1968), p. 19.

thought in the Arab world was less tied to a theory of modernization, it similarly focussed on the thought of leading intellectuals, particularly on their development of theories of nationalism – religious, territorial and ethno-linguistic.[26] But if limited to longer texts written by known authors, we find ourselves with a very narrow view indeed of Africa's mid-twentieth-century intellectual history.

An alternative route into the intellectual history of the colonial and postcolonial world is to turn instead to a wider corpus of texts, and to trace continuities and change in political languages within that corpus. By doing so we are able to explore a broader swathe of society than we would otherwise reach.[27] As C. A. Bayly explained in his 2007 Wiles Lectures, '[f]rom the elite to the poor, colonized people argued and debated, trying to understand their world and to improve it.'[28] In Tanzania, the pages of Swahili-language newspapers and other texts allow us access to these debates among people far below the governing elite.[29] In this way, working with corpora of texts and the voices of often unnamed and unknowable authors enables us, even given the relatively small proportions of colonial and postcolonial populations who were literate and who engaged in the public sphere through their writing, to move beyond an intellectual history limited to elites.

Through these texts we can trace individual words which travel the world and take on new meanings in different contexts, as well as broader political languages of freedom or democracy. This offers us a path towards elucidating vernacular understandings of fundamental political concepts. Historians have increasingly found that a focus on political concepts is a productive route into the intellectual history of the colonial and postcolonial world.[30] As Sudipta Kaviraj has argued with respect to

---

[26] Albert Hourani, *Arabic Thought in the Liberal Age, 1798–1939* (Cambridge: Cambridge University Press, 1983), pp. 342–343.

[27] Iain Hampsher-Monk, 'Speech Acts, Languages or Conceptual History?' in Iain Hampsher-Monk, Karin Tilmans and Frank van Vree (eds.), *History of Concepts: Comparative Perspectives* (Amsterdam: Amsterdam University Press, 1998), pp. 37–50, p. 59.

[28] C. A. Bayly, 'South Asian Liberalism under Strain', *Wiles Lecture 4*, p. 25.

[29] Working with newspapers presents its own specific problems, dealt with in the text that follows and in Chapter 1.

[30] Reinhard Koselleck, '*Begriffsgeschichte* and Social History' in Reinhard Koselleck, *Futures Past: On the Semantics of Historical Time* (New York: Columbia University Press, 2004), pp. 75–92, p. 81; Keith Tribe, 'Translator's Introduction' in Reinhard Koselleck, *Futures Past: On the Semantics of Historical Time* (New York: Columbia University Press, 2004), pp. vii–xx, p. xvi. Melvin Richter, *The History of Social and Political Concepts: A Critical Introduction* (Oxford: Oxford University Press, 1995),

nineteenth-century India, this approach is preferable to alternative modes of doing intellectual history because it focuses 'less on theoretical constructs, more on practical meanings of individual concepts', allowing us to write intellectual history about times and places where 'there is no self-conscious tradition of social theorizing in the Western sense'.[31]

Studying political languages and, through those languages, political concepts, also enables us to see the interaction of the global and the local. Work by A. C. Milner on the 'invention of politics' in Malaya, by Rhoderick Chalmers on the concept of *unnati* in the Nepali public sphere, by C. A. Bayly on liberalism in India and by Benjamin Zachariah on development discourse in India has reminded us of the entangled nature of the history of political thinking in the twentieth century. Indeed, as C. A. Bayly has argued, '[all] modern political languages have mixed together global and local discourses.'[32]

In the mid-twentieth century, political concepts often appeared universal and claimed universality. But apparent uniformity and homogeneity of concepts and discourses can mask significant local divergences and debates. Not only did words and concepts change as they moved from one context to another, the ambiguity which characterizes all concepts by their very nature ensured they experienced friction and provoked argument within local contexts.[33] In this respect, this book draws inspiration from a recent book edited by Carol Gluck and Anna Lowenhaupt Tsing which explores the ways in which words travel. Their volume offers a cogent case for a greater attention to the movement of words and the reconfiguration of key concepts in the global twentieth century.[34]

This book is an intellectual history, which means that a full account of the underlying political processes and the messy cut and thrust of day to day politics would go far beyond its purposes. But revisiting the debates around core political concepts also allows us to reinterpret and

---

p. 10; Terence Ball, 'Conceptual History and the History of Political Thought' in Iain Hampsher-Monk, Karin Tilmans and Frank van Vree, *History of Concepts: Comparative Perspectives* (Amsterdam: Amsterdam University Press, 1998), pp. 75–86, p. 8.

[31] Sudipta Kaviraj, 'Ideas of Freedom in Modern India' in Robert Taylor (ed.), *The Idea of Freedom in Asia and Africa* (Stanford, CA: Stanford University Press, 2002), pp. 97–142, especially pp. 98–99.

[32] C.A. Bayly, *Recovering Liberties: Indian Thought in the Age of Liberalism and Empire* (Cambridge: Cambridge University Press, 2012), p. 8.

[33] Koselleck, '*Begriffsgeschichte* and Social History', p. 85.

[34] Carol Gluck, 'Words in Motion', in Carol Gluck and Anna Lowenhaupt Tsing, *Words in Motion: Toward a Global Lexicon* (London and Durham, NC: Duke University Press, 2009), pp. 3–10, p. 4.

reimagine key moments of political history. A better understanding of the intellectual history of mid-twentieth-century Tanzania and indeed Africa more broadly, built on a locally rooted understanding of African history, allows us to understand the discursive possibilities open to political actors as they sought to construct new political narratives and new political institutions.[35] In this way, the book is divided between chapters which focus on elaborating the intellectual history of the period through detailed examination of political concepts, and chapters which also explore political practice through case studies. While this might seem to set up a tension between language and the world, we should remember that politics itself takes place through language, and the construction of a compelling narrative by political actors is integral to mobilizing constituencies of support.

FREEDOM IN SOCIETY

The concept of freedom has long framed our reading of decolonization, and for good reason. Implicit in narratives of decolonization, both the stories that our historical actors told at the time and those constructed by historians since, is the idea that the desire for autonomy is part of a universal human condition. Demonstrating that colonialism constituted a denial of autonomy and that political independence was its antidote was central to nationalist projects across the colonial world. When Julius Nyerere published his collected speeches and writings, all three volumes included the word freedom in the title. The very terminology points to the Cold War moment at which independence occurred, and the liberal tradition which framed contemporary global thinking.

But if a language of freedom seemed to define the 1940s and 1950s in Tanzania as elsewhere around the postcolonial world, so the immediate aftermath of independence seemed to be characterized by new limits on freedom. As postcolonial states introduced coercive measures such as preventive detention of political opponents, discussion turned to the question of whether limits on individual freedoms were justified in the cause of postcolonial state building. At the same time, neo-colonial critiques suggested that independence had been more apparent than real, and that while political independence might have been achieved,

---

[35] Patrick Chabal, 'Introduction: Thinking about Politics in Africa', in Patrick Chabal (ed.), *Political Domination in Africa: Reflections on the Limits of Power* (Cambridge: Cambridge University Press, 1986), pp. 1–16, p. 1.

economic dependence made that political freedom of minimal import. More recently, it is the extent of state power in the postcolony that has dominated scholarly analysis, as in James C. Scott's *Seeing Like a State* which presents Julius Nyerere's Tanzania as an example of high-modernist authoritarianism.[36]

But how universal is the concept of freedom which underpins much scholarly analysis? When we look closely at the political arguments of the 1940s and 1950s in Tanganyika, we find a neglected set of political languages which were more concerned with relationships than with individual autonomy. Africans engaged in the public sphere reflected on how to balance progress, *maendeleo*, with the construction and reconstruction of social bonds. They sought new political relationships, with neo-traditionalist chiefs, European and West Indian lawyers, or nationalist politicians, which would enable them to gain a voice or to make claims. At the same time as Africans sought to free themselves from the bonds that tied them to an increasingly illegitimate colonial state, they sought to create new relationships which were as likely to have been dependent and unequal as to have been based on the principles of individual rights and equality.

In his study of contemporary rural Malawi, the anthropologist Harri Englund discovered a similar set of arguments which at first appeared to present a paradox. To his surprise, he found a group of villagers using an international human rights discourse, translated into the Chichewa language as the idea of 'birth freedoms', to demand the institution of a headman over their village. At first sight, this seemed to be a misuse of the concept of human rights and a language of freedom. Why were villagers claiming that they had achieved freedom from slavery by instituting a new relationship of dependence with a headman? But as Englund shows, '[w]hat the villagers were claiming was the freedom to be the subjects of the authority they had chosen themselves' and this stemmed from an understanding of freedom whereby 'subjects have rights in so far as they have relationships'.[37]

Englund's analysis draws on an extremely productive strand of feminist critical scholarship. In her 2005 book *The Politics of Piety* the

[36] James C. Scott, *Seeing Like a State: How Certain Schemes to Improve the Human Condition Have Failed*, New Haven, CT: Yale University Press, 1998, pp. 223–261.

[37] Harri Englund, 'Human Rights and Village Headmen in Malawi: Translation beyond Vernacularisation', in Julia Eckert, Brian Donahoe, Christan Strümpell and Zerrin Özlem Biner (eds.), *Law against the State: Ethnographic Forays into Law's Transformations* (Cambridge: Cambridge University Press, 2012), pp. 70–93, p. 75, p. 90.

anthropologist Saba Mahmood asked why Egyptian women joined religious groups which were founded on principles of inequality and sought to deny freedom, in the sense of personal autonomy, to women.[38] Her conclusions directly challenge liberal assumptions about the innate desire of individuals in all places and at all times to seek freedom as defined in terms of personal autonomy. She argued that for the women concerned, freedom came through membership rather than through autonomy, and that obedience did not equate to the absence of agency.

Historians of Africa should not be surprised by this line of analysis. In precolonial Africa, state building was extremely difficult. In a continent where land was plentiful and populations were sparse, attempts by aspirant state builders to exploit their populations through demands for tax, labour or military service often failed, as it was all too easy for subjects to leave and set up an alternative polity elsewhere. Precolonial Africa was a mobile continent in which authority was always at risk of slipping away.[39] To establish political authority, chiefs had bound people to them through multiple forms of dependence which included slavery. In return for labour they offered protection, whether from enemies or from food shortage. Relationships were reciprocal though unequal, and the worst fate which could befall an individual was to be left without networks of kinship of any kind. In this context, we should not assume that freedom was understood in terms of autonomy and the absence of relationships. Rather, as Suzanne Miers and Igor Kopytoff argue, '[i]n most African societies, 'freedom' lay not in a withdrawal into a meaningless and dangerous autonomy but in attachment to a kin group, to a patron, to power – an attachment that occurred within a well-defined hierarchical framework.'[40]

We shall not understand freedom in the Tanzanian public sphere if we simply understand it in terms of search for autonomy. Freedom was

---

[38] Mahmood, *Politics of Piety: The Islamic Revival and the Feminist Subject*, p. 5.

[39] John Lonsdale, 'States and Social Processes in Africa: A Historiographical Survey', *African Studies Review*, 24 (1981), 139–225; Megan Vaughan, 'Africa and the Birth of the Modern World', *Transactions of the Royal Historical Society*, 16 (2006), 143–162, p. 152.

[40] Igor Kopytoff and Suzanne Miers, 'African 'Slavery' as an Institution of Marginality' in Suzanne Miers and Igor Kopytoff (eds.), *Slavery in Africa: Historical and Anthropological Perspectives* (Madison, WI: University of Wisconsin Press, 1977), pp. 3–85, p. 17; Frederick Cooper, 'Review: The Problem of Slavery in African Societies', *Journal of African History*, 20, 1979, 103–125; Marcia Wright, *Strategies of Slaves and Women: Life-Stories from East/Central Africa* (London: James Currey, 1993).

realized through the reworking of relationships as much as through the rejection of them, and it was within these parameters that arguments over the meaning of political membership – citizenship, or more broadly political subjecthood – and the best way of choosing leaders took place. These concerns crossed apparent divides between types of political organization in twentieth-century Africa, such as between 'traditional' and 'modern' politics, or between 'ethnic' or 'national' political projects.[41]

LANGUAGES OF DEMOCRACY AND CITIZENSHIP

This point in turn leads us to revisit some of the central categories which mid-twentieth-century politicians and intellectuals employed in thinking about their world. While radical projects of emancipation have often attracted attention, those political projects which sought to reconfigure social and political relationships are just as important. Some political thinkers embraced egalitarianism; others sought the renewal and remaking of older hierarchies. Although the latter set of languages was increasingly difficult to deploy effectively by the late 1950s, these languages did not go away and indeed served as the basis for a defence of chiefship in Tanzania in the early 1960s.

This raises important questions about political subjecthood and citizenship in the mid-twentieth century. Arguments over the boundaries of belonging and who could be a member of which political community intersected with arguments over the rights and duties which political membership entailed. Cutting through these arguments was the growing power of a political language which had long existed but which was reformulated in new ways in the mid-twentieth century, the language of democracy. What did it mean to conceive of the authority of government as coming from the people, and what practical systems could be instituted to make this possible? What kinds of intermediaries might serve to represent the people to government, and who had the right to speak for which people? As we shall see, there were no straightforward answers to these questions, but in tracing the ways in which they were argued over in public and the arguments mobilized on both sides we can better understand how new political systems were ultimately authorized.

---

[41] There are interesting parallels here with Felicitas Becker's explanation of the forces motivating conversion to Islam in southern Tanzania. Felicitas Becker, *Becoming Muslim in Mainland Tanzania, 1890–2000* (Oxford: Oxford University Press, 2008), p. 7.

TRACING A GENEALOGY OF THE POLITICAL

This is a book about the mid-twentieth century. It argues that the mid-twentieth century was a pivot point in the history of Tanzania, but also of East Africa and the colonial world, and a crucial moment in the formulation and reformulation of the concepts that are explored in what follows. Against the backdrop of world war, the birth of new international institutions and a growing conflict between West and East, as European empires unravelled and new nations were born, political ideas were debated with a striking urgency and intensity.[42]

But this does not mean that the intersection of vernacular and global political languages was a new phenomenon in Eastern Africa, or that the questions being asked were entirely new. East Africa had long formed part of an Indian Ocean trading zone, and textual and archaeological records show the extent of exchange of peoples, ideas and objects. Moreover, as already stated, Africa has always been a mobile continent.[43] People did not only move across seas and oceans, they moved across land and lakes, and as people moved they brought new ideas to their new homes.

The histories of Christianity and Islam in East Africa constitute one element of a long-term history of vernacular engagement with global ideas. In some periods, ideas and goods associated with distant lands were prized, at other times their perceived importance faded. On the Islamized coast, connections across the Islamic world, literacy in Arabic and claims to close association with Arabia were particularly prized in the late nineteenth century, whereas at other times it was the Swahili culture of the coast that defined what it meant to be 'civilized'.[44] Inland, as

---

[42] Christopher J. Lee (ed.), *Making a World after Empire: The Bandung Moment and Its Political Afterlives* (Athens, OH: Ohio University Press, 2010).

[43] In his 1987 edited volume Igor Kopytoff summarized the lessons of Africanist scholarship as having demonstrated that '[c]ontrary to a previously widespread stereotype as a continent mired in timeless immobility, its history has emerged to be one of ceaseless flux among populations that, in comparison to other continents, are relatively recent occupants of their present habitat.' Igor Kopytoff, 'The Internal African Frontier: The Making of African Political Culture' in Igor Kopytoff (ed.), *The African Frontier: The Reproduction of Traditional African Societies* (Bloomington: Indiana University Press, 1987), pp. 3–84, p. 7; A recent scholarly literature has complemented recent work on connections across oceans by showing the importance of connections across land. See in particular: Judith Scheele, *Smugglers and Saints of the Sahara: Regional Connectivity in the Twentieth Century* (Cambridge: Cambridge University Press, 2012); Ghislaine Lydon, *On Trans-Saharan Trails: Islamic Law, Trade Networks, and Cross-Cultural Exchange in Nineteenth-Century Western Africa* (Cambridge: Cambridge University Press, 2009).

[44] Randall L. Pouwels, *Horn and Crescent: Cultural Change and Traditional Islam on the East African Coast, 800–1900* (Cambridge: Cambridge University Press, 1987), p. 129.

Felicitas Becker has shown, '[f]ew people were unambiguously "local"' and the story of the expansion of Islam in the southeast of the country in the twentieth century is in part a story of villagers seeking new ideas and resources in 'overcoming a heritage of exploitative social relations and reconstituting the field for the negotiation of dependency and control.'[45] In the Usambara Mountains to the north, as we have already seen, an apparently constant political idiom of healing the land and harming the land in fact shifted in dialogue with wider processes of historical change.[46]

There is therefore a long history of East Africans thinking about politics and employing new ideological resources in order to reflect on and seek to change the political order. But the era of the mid-twentieth century was nevertheless distinctive. It was characterized by the coming into being of a distinctive 'political sphere'. Whereas religious, social and political spheres of life had been inseparably intertwined, 'the political' was now coming to be conceived of as something separable.[47] As Anthony Milner has argued for colonial Malaya, the late colonial period was not only a period of nationalism, it was also the time when the distinctive category of the political and the character of the *homo politicus* came into being.[48] This book is in part a contribution to the tracing of a similar process in East Africa through the case study of Tanzania.

POLITICAL OUTLINE

It is worth briefly setting out the outline of Tanzania's political history as a background for what follows. German colonial rule began formally in 1885 when the German chancellor, Otto von Bismarck, agreed to support the territorial claims made in the region by the German explorer Carl Peters and the German East African Company.[49] This led to the establishment of German rule over the area which is now mainland Tanzania, plus modern day Rwanda and Burundi. After the First World War, German colonial rule was succeeded by British rule under mandate from the League of Nations.

---

[45] Becker, *Becoming Muslim in Mainland Tanzania, 1890–2000*, pp. 23, 7.

[46] Feierman, *Peasant intellectuals: Anthropology and History in Tanzania*, p. 6.

[47] Gregory Maddox, 'African Theology and the Search for the Universal' in Thomas Spear and Isaria N. Kimambo (eds.), *East African Expressions of Christianity* (Oxford: James Currey, 1999), pp. 25–36, p. 31.

[48] Anthony Milner, *The Invention of Politics in Colonial Malaya: Contesting Nationalism and the Expansion of the Public Sphere* (Cambridge: Cambridge University Press, 1994), pp. 1–2.

[49] Iliffe, *A Modern History of Tanganyika*, pp. 88–91.

After 1945, Tanganyika followed other League of Nations Mandates in becoming a Trust of the United Nations. As elsewhere in Africa, a period of rapid political reform followed. In 1945 the first African representatives were appointed to Tanganyika's Legislative Council, the consultative body which was the only representative structure operating at a territorial level and from which Africans had, since its creation in 1926, been excluded. New structures of local government were developed which incorporated non-chiefly African representation, first nominated then elected.

The nationalist party the Tanganyika African National Union (TANU) was formed in 1954. Four years later, the first national elections were held which the governor, Edward Twining, hoped would block TANU and further his preferred policy of multiracialism. But TANU succeeded in winning a sweeping majority, turning Twining's system in which each constituency would be represented by one African, one Asian and one European, with each voter voting for each representative, to its own advantage. In the first set of elections in February 1958 which covered five of Tanganyika's ten constituencies, TANU won all five African seats while eight out of the ten European and Asian seats were won by candidates publicly supportive of TANU.[50] Twining was replaced in July 1958 by a new governor, Richard Turnbull, who quickly saw the advantages of working with TANU and its leader, Julius Nyerere, rather than against them, particularly faced with a deteriorating security situation in parts of the country. After an even stronger showing for TANU in the second set of elections in February 1959, Tanganyika moved rapidly first to a further general election without the tripartite voting system and then to internal self-government in October 1960. Independence followed on 9 December 1961 with Julius Nyerere as prime minister, and the following year Tanganyika became a Republic with Nyerere as president.

Yet as recent research has shown, even as TANU seemed to carry all before it in 1958–59, support for TANU was never unanimous. When in January 1958 TANU committed itself to fighting the 1958–59 elections under the multiracial tripartite voting system, TANU's organizing secretary Zuberi Mtemvu broke away to form the African National Congress (ANC) to argue against multiracialism.[51] Although the ANC

[50] John Iliffe, 'Breaking the Chain at Its Weakest Link: TANU and the Colonial Office', in Gregory Maddox and James Giblin (eds.), *In Search of a Nation: Histories of Authority and Dissidence in Tanzania* (Oxford: James Currey, 2005), pp. 168–197, p. 182.
[51] Brennan, 'The Short History of Political Opposition and Multi-party Democracy in Tanganyika, 1958–1964', p. 252.

never succeeded in posing a serious electoral challenge to TANU, and Mtemvu himself rejoined TANU in January 1963, the party's opposition to multiracialism echoed the feelings of many of TANU's supporters and activists at the grassroots. In the early 1960s as Tanzania moved towards a single-party system, the ANC argued strongly in favour of political pluralism and against the suppression of political parties.[52]

The All-Muslim National Union of Tanganyika (AMNUT), formed in July 1959, was also the result of a secession from TANU. In this case the split came because its leaders felt that Muslims were being sidelined within TANU in favour of younger Christians.[53] Their stated aim was to promote Muslim interests in Tanganyika but they also strongly opposed Nyerere's leadership, describing him as a 'dictator'.[54] As with the African National Congress, they achieved little electoral success but, like the ANC, they argued against the creation of a one-party state after independence.[55]

There were also tensions within TANU. Nyerere struggled to control grassroots activists and other TANU leaders whose public pronouncements were far more radical than the public line he advocated at the centre.[56] His relationship with his close ally, Oscar Kambona, was one of rivalry as much as one of cooperation. Already in 1960, Kambona was envisioning a post-TANU future after independence in which TANU would be replaced by a Tanganyika Socialist Party in which he would have a leading role.[57] Kambona remained a thorn in Nyerere's side until his departure into exile in 1967. After independence, opposition came both from those on the left who thought TANU was moving too slowly towards socialism, and from those who thought TANU's policies to be too radical.

The result was that Nyerere's position often looked insecure in the years immediately after independence, never more so than when army mutinies across East Africa in January 1964 saw the government briefly

---

[52] Ibid, p. 264.

[53] Ibid., p. 261, Governor, Dar es Salaam, to Secretary of State for the Colonies, 'All Muslim National Union of Tanganyika', 12 December 1960, TNA UK, CO 822/2130, f. 31.

[54] Governor, Dar es Salaam, to Secretary of State for the Colonies, 'All Muslim National Union of Tanganyika', 12 December 1960, TNA UK, CO 822/2130, f. 31.

[55] David Westerlund, *Ujamaa na Dini: A Study of Some Aspects of Society and Religion in Tanzania, 1961–1977* (Stockholm: Almquist and Wiksell International, 1980), p. 94.

[56] Iliffe, 'Breaking the Chain at Its Weakest Link: TANU and the Colonial Office', p. 191.

[57] I. V. Carrel, S. L. O. Tanganyika to Permanent Secretary, Ministry of Security and Immigration, 'Oscar Kambona', TNA UK, FCO 141/17768, f. 8A.

lose control of the capital.[58] Next door, Zanzibar became a focus of Cold War tensions after its revolution in January 1964, and the shotgun marriage between Tanganyika and Zanzibar which created the new state of Tanzania in April of that year further complicated Nyerere's attempts to lead Tanzania along a path of moderate socialism at home and non-alignment abroad.[59] However, as discussed in Chapter 8, the Arusha Declaration of February 1967 helped put Nyerere back in control, enabling him both to resolve the question of how a nationalist party becomes a party of postcolonial government by committing TANU to a clear ideological position, and to sideline his political rivals.

TANZANIA: UNITY IN DIVERSITY

A long history of mobility within Africa and interaction with places and peoples far from Eastern Africa's shores means that the borders of Tanganyika, and after 1964 mainland Tanzania, contained a myriad of local political cultures, from the decentralized authority which characterized the south to the strong centralized power of Bukoba district in the north-west.[60] Social structures were correspondingly diverse, sharply hierarchical in some places, flatter in others. Tanzania was also, and remains, religiously diverse. Both Christianity and Islam expanded rapidly in the twentieth century. At independence in December 1961, approximately 20 to 25 per cent of the population was Muslim and approximately the same proportion were Christian, while the remainder of the population of nine million followed African religions.[61] Christian groups broke down further between Protestants and Catholics, Lutherans and Seventh-Day Adventists, with differences of doctrine and culture promoting contrasting approaches to authority and ideas about the present, the past and the future.

---

[58] Brennan, 'The Short History of Political Opposition and Multi-party Democracy in Tanganyika, 1958–1964', p. 267.

[59] Ian Speller, 'An African Cuba? Britain and the Zanzibar Revolution', *Journal of Imperial and Commonwealth History*, 35 (2007), 283–302.

[60] There are many local studies which taken together convey the diversity of precolonial Tanzanian society and the ways in which this was sustained into the colonial period. See, e.g., J. Gus Liebenow, *Colonial Rule and Political Development in Tanzania: The Case of the Makonde* (Evanston, IL: Northwestern University Press, 1971); Isaria N. Kimambo, *A Political History of the Pare of Tanzania, c. 1500–1900* (Nairobi: East African Publishing House, 1969); Göran Hydén, *Political Development in Rural Tanzania: TANU yajenga nchi* (Nairobi: East African Publishing House, 1969).

[61] Frieder Ludwig, *Church and State in Tanzania: Aspects of Changing Relationships, 1961–1994* (Leiden: Brill, 1999), p. 53.

In the nineteenth century, economic and political power was concentrated on the coast. The coastal region had long formed an important part of the trading world of the Indian Ocean, and was further invigorated by Omani rule and the expansion of long-distance trade over the course of the nineteenth century.[62] The relationship between inland areas and the coast was a complicated and ambiguous one.[63] On the one hand, the coast could stand for wealth and power, and peoples of the interior were attracted to the cosmopolitan culture of the coastal towns. Yet the coast was also associated with the disruptive slave and ivory trades. Urban townsmen were known to adopt a pose of haughty exclusivity in their relationships with people from the interior. Members of the coastal elite defined their status in opposition to the *washenzi* of the interior, the word *washenzi* or 'barbarians' denoting the absence of the civilization which the coastal elite believed themselves exclusively to possess.[64]

In the twentieth century, the economic balance of power shifted away from the coast. As the networks of power associated with coastal dominance declined, new social dynamics emerged. In the southeast, as Felicitas Becker has shown, many converted to Islam as it changed from being a religion 'instrumentalized by nineteenth-century slave owners as a means of social exclusion into a creed of free commoners.'[65] In the same period, European colonial rule saw economic power move north, towards the cash crop growing areas of the northeast and northwest. Literacy was concentrated in those areas which benefited from cash crop wealth and where the rapid growth of Christianity led to the emergence of new schools, and many of these legacies continued deep into the twentieth century.

The second British governor of Tanganyika, Donald Cameron, came to Tanganyika in 1925 bringing with him from Nigeria a conviction of the merits of 'indirect rule', an approach which was increasingly attractive to interwar colonial governments as they sought to combine colonial rule on the cheap with a coherent philosophy aiming ultimately

---

[62] Pouwels, *Horn and Crescent: Cultural Change and Traditional Islam on the East African Coast, 800–1900*, p. 114. For an introduction to the Indian Ocean world, see K. N. Chaudhuri, *Trade and Civilisation in the Indian Ocean: An Economic History from the Rise of Islam to 1750* (Cambridge: Cambridge University Press, 1985) and for the later period Sugata Bose, *A Hundred Horizons: The Indian Ocean in the Age of Global Empire* (London and Cambridge, MA: Harvard University Press, 2006).

[63] Becker, *Becoming Muslim in Mainland Tanzania, 1890–2000*, p. 4.

[64] Inter-Territorial Language Committee, *A Standard Swahili-English Dictionary* (London: Oxford University Press, 1951), p. 419.

[65] Becker, *Becoming Muslim in Mainland Tanzania, 1890–2000*, p. 23.

at self-government which could be defended in front of the League of Nations in Geneva.[66] Although never as coherent on the ground as it might appear on the pages of Lord Lugard's *The Dual Mandate*, the adoption of indirect rule as a governing policy meant that Tanzania's political diversity was to some extent sustained.[67]

Political, economic and religious diversity were thus important dimensions of mid-twentieth-century Tanzania. But alongside this diversity were two unifying factors which make mainland Tanzania relatively unusual in mid-twentieth-century Africa, and which help make this investigation possible.

The first element which made Tanganyika unusual was its international supervision, first by the League of Nations and then by the United Nations. As a Trusteeship Territory, Tanganyika was the subject of annual discussion at the Trusteeship Council in New York, and every three years received a Visiting Mission sent by the Trusteeship Council to inspect the Territory.[68] Tanzania was thus in the spotlight of attempts by international and colonial officials to think through what sort of political structures were fitting to modern Africa. The texts produced by colonial and international officials, in Swahili and English, reflected these debates, and their attempts to impose new definitions of concepts such as democracy or citizenship. But while they believed that politics had to be 'taught' to Africa, in practice new concepts and new modes of political organization fed into existing ways of reflecting on political society and existing political concepts, which themselves drew on both memories of the past and comparative lessons from the global present.[69] The political culture and political discourses which developed were a product of that interaction.

Second, over the course of the twentieth century the development of a Swahili-language press in Tanzania saw the emergence of a public sphere which connected multiple local publics. The Swahili-language press was not a free press, but nevertheless constituted a space connecting vernacular, colonial (and later postcolonial) and global languages of politics, in which global concepts acquired local definitions. Tanzania's Swahiliphone

---

[66] Iliffe, *A Modern History of Tanganyika*, pp. 318–341.

[67] Frederick Lugard, *The Dual Mandate in British Tropical Africa* (London: Frank Cass, 1965).

[68] Ullrich Lohrmann, *Voices from Tanganyika: Great Britain, the United Nations and the Decolonization of a Trust Territory, 1946–1961* (Berlin: Lit., 2007).

[69] Andrew Ivaska's excellent recent study of culture in postcolonial Dar es Salaam serves as a powerful reminder of the importance of the transnational in defining postcolonial orders. Andrew Ivaska, *Cultured States: Youth, Gender and Modern Style in 1960s Dar es Salaam* (Durham, NC: Duke University Press, 2011).

public sphere, the contours of which we shall trace in Chapter 1, was a space for public debate which crossed regions and religions, and was shaped by a colonial state which ruled over all the diverse peoples under its authority. Crucially, debate was conducted in a shared African language, rather than a colonial language or localized vernaculars, as was the case elsewhere.

Exploring a shared public sphere entails paying less attention to Tanzania's diversity than would be the case in a different type of study. Yet while it is true that by focussing on literate local elites we hear more Christian voices than Muslim voices and more from the rich north than from the relatively poorer south, voices from the south are not entirely absent, and appear particularly in the records of local council minutes from the south-east for the late colonial and early postcolonial period.[70] At the same time, this book incorporates recognition of Tanzania's diversity by moving between analysis of the territory-wide public sphere and its local variants and more in-depth analysis of one particular locality, Moshi District in north-eastern Tanzania, now part of Kilimanjaro Region. Kilimanjaro is a relatively rich cash-crop growing area whose mid-twentieth-century wealth was built on coffee grown on the slopes of Kilimanjaro. The land was fertile and the climate attractive to European settlers who came from Germany, Britain and South Africa. As the African population grew over the twentieth century, land was in increasingly short supply and this helped give rise to a local politics which was at times explosive. The district was predominantly, though not exclusively, Christian, and those who were most politically active were Lutheran, though the Catholic Church was also strong in the District.

SOURCES AND METHOD

Newspapers are at the heart of this book. While colonial East Africa never had an independent African-owned newspaper culture to rival that of West Africa, nevertheless the range of government and church-sponsored newspapers and monthly periodicals, as well as occasional independent newspapers, amount to a sizable textual corpus and constituted spaces

---

[70] Becker, *Becoming Muslim in Mainland Tanzania, 1890–2000*. On the marginalization of Muslims after independence, see Ludwig, *Church and State*, p. 40; Westerlund, *Ujamaa na Dini: A Study of Some Aspects of Society and Religion in Tanzania, 1961–1977*, pp. 94–95; Mohamed Said, *The Life and Times of Abdulwahid Sykes: The Untold Story of the Muslim Struggle against British Colonialism in Tanganyika* (London: Minerva Press, 1998).

in which new identities and new political formations were imagined and critiqued.[71] The colonial press had to operate within the discursive parameters of strict colonial censorship laws, but after 1957 a more open and critical nationalist press began to appear. In the early years after independence, newspapers such as *Uhuru* which were closely linked to the nationalist party TANU coexisted with other newspapers who maintained the voice of a critical friend of TANU, notably *Kiongozi*, the newspaper of the Catholic Church in Tanzania, and *Ngurumo*.[72] Newspapers varied dramatically – some were one- or two-page mimeographed sheets, others were full-scale broadsheets. Some, such as the Catholic *Kiongozi*, devoted considerable space to religious matters, others focussed more on news from around the world. But almost all had an editorial and a letters' page, which offer rich insights into political thinking in mid-twentieth-century Tanzania.

The Swahili language press, both provincial and territorial, thus offers us a way into the arguments and debates taking place in rural areas among those who were literate but who were not necessarily members of a governing elite. It connects the centre of power in Dar es Salaam both with localities within Tanzania and with international sites of both discursive and institutional power. In doing so, it provides both a new perspective on the history of Tanzania and an African perspective on global political change. In this book this press is read alongside a published literature in Swahili and English consisting of histories as well as didactic texts on the subjects of citizenship and good governance. A close reading of this literature allows us to trace changing political ideologies and their discussion and dissemination in the public sphere.

The term 'public sphere' is used loosely here. Historians of the world beyond Europe were once reluctant to use concepts like the 'public sphere', either for the colonial period or the early postcolonial era of the one-party state. If the essence of a public sphere lay in being able to

---

[71] This issue is discussed at greater length in Emma Hunter, '"Our Common Humanity": Print, Power and the Colonial Press in Interwar Tanganyika and French Cameroun', *Journal of Global History* 7, 2012, 279–301. See also Isabel Hofmeyr, Preben Kaarsholm and Bodil Folke Frederiksen, 'Introduction: Print Cultures, Nationalisms and Publics of the Indian Ocean', *Africa*, 81 (2011), 1–22; James Brennan, 'Politics and Business in the Indian Newspapers of Colonial Tanganyika', *Africa*, 81 (2011), 42–67. The authoritative guide to Tanzania's newspaper history can be found in Martin Sturmer, *The Media History of Tanzania* (Ndanda: Ndanda Mission Press, 1998). See also James F. Scotton, 'Tanganyika's African Press, 1937–1960: A Nearly Forgotten Pre-independence Forum', *African Studies Review*, 21 (1978), 1–18.

[72] Ivaska, *Cultured States: Youth, Gender, and Modern Style in 1960s Dar es Salaam*, p. 30.

come together and engage rationally and critically with government, then such possibilities did not exist in colonial settings and very often did not exist in postcolonial settings either. Yet used more loosely to describe a sphere of public debate and reflection, recognizing the constraints under which debate took place and the power dynamics at play, this term helpfully directs us towards a space in which we can hear the voices of men and women who were mostly not leading intellectuals and who have often left little other trace in the historical record. In it we can trace their thinking about the political and social change they saw around them and which, through their public reflection, they contributed to shaping.[73]

In approaching Tanganyika's public sphere in this way, I am departing from previous approaches to the press in mainland Tanganyika, which were once characterized by neglect and which more recently have been marked by a focus on urban and Indian Ocean influences. The reasons for initial neglect are easy to understand. Both in terms of book and newspaper publication, print culture in Tanganyika was and remained until a late stage less widespread than in neighbouring territories. Bookshops were hard to find and often expensive. When in 1959 the missionaries of the Africa Inland Mission in the Lake Province of north-west Tanganyika opened a bookshop to compete with the Catholic White Fathers missionary bookshop, they felt compelled to distribute free sweets to old and young alike to encourage custom.[74] Low wages and poor communications, as well as relatively strict censorship laws, all limited the circulation of ideas through print.[75] But more important still was the nature of the press and other publications. For an earlier generation of historians, seeking to understand the roots of anticolonial nationalism in colonial Africa, the Tanganyikan press offered slim rewards. Where in other parts of Africa there was an extensive African-owned press which was often critical of government, in Tanganyika the press tended to be funded and, at first, edited by Europeans – whether working for missionary organizations or the government. In interwar Kenya and Uganda,

---

[73] Jürgen Habermas, *The Structural Transformation of the Public Sphere: An Inquiry into a Category of Bourgeois Society* (Cambridge: Polity, 1992); Stephanie Newell, 'Articulating Empire: Newspaper Readerships in Colonial West Africa', *New Formations*, 73 (2011), 26–42.

[74] Travel of Principal Officer to Western and Lake Provinces, 26 February 1959, p. 8. 778.00/2-2659. U.S. National Archives, College Park, Maryland.

[75] Note though that this comparative West African advantage was itself only relative. Even in the late 1960s Africa had the lowest circulation of daily newspapers in the world. William Hachten calculated that in 1968–69 only 179 of the world's 6,861 daily newspapers were published in Africa. William Hachten, *Muffled Drums: The News Media in Africa* (Ames: Iowa State University Press, 1971), p. 24.

in contrast, there was a lively and often vociferously anticolonial press, published in the vernacular.[76] It was not surprising that the title of the single article-length study of the Tanganyikan press to appear before the recent resurgence of interest described the Tanganyikan press as a 'nearly forgotten pre-independence forum'.[77]

More recently, however, following a growing trend among historians to explore African writing from the colonial era, historians have returned to the Swahili-language press, and have argued that it constitutes a resource with which to explore African political thinking, at the intersection of the East African and Indian Ocean worlds.[78] Jonathon Glassman's recent work on Tanganyika's neighbour, Zanzibar, has illuminated in masterly fashion the ways in which Zanzibari thinking about race, nationalism and politics developed over the twentieth century through the writings of Zanzibari intellectuals in Zanzibar's Swahili-language newspapers.[79] Back on the mainland, James Brennan has effectively used Swahili-language newspapers to trace the development of African racial thought in the 1920s and to shed new light on the nationalist thought of the 1950s and 1960s.[80] This work has shown that in Africa, as elsewhere, print culture provided a space in which to reflect on global processes in

---

[76] On Uganda see James F. Scotton, 'The First African Press in East Africa: Protest and Nationalism in Uganda in the 1920s', *The International Journal of African Historical Studies*, 6 (1973), 211–228. At greater length see James R. Scotton, *Growth of the Vernacular Press in Colonial East Africa: Patterns of Government Control*. Unpublished PhD thesis, University of Wisconsin (1971). For an important study of Jomo Kenyatta's Kikuyu newspaper *Muigwithania*, see John Lonsdale, '"Listen while I read": Patriotic Christianity among the Young Gikuyu' in Toyin Falola (ed.), *Christianity and Social Change in Africa* (Durham, NC: Carolina Academic Press, 2005), pp. 563–593. On the Kikuyu press after WW2, see Bodil Folke Frederiksen, '"The Present Battle Is the Brain Battle": Writing and Publishing a Kikuyu Newspaper in the Pre-Mau Mau Period in Kenya', in Karin Barber (ed.), *Africa's Hidden Histories: Everyday Literacy and Making the Self* (Bloomington: Indiana University Press, 2006), pp. 278–313 and Wangaria Muoria-Sal et al. (eds.), *Writing for Kenya: The Life and Works of Henry Muoria* (Leiden: Brill, 2009).

[77] James F. Scotton, 'Tanganyika's African Press, 1937–1960: A Nearly Forgotten Pre-independence Forum', *African Studies Review*, 21 (1978), 1–18.

[78] Karin Barber, 'Introduction' in Karin Barber (ed.), *Africa's Hidden Histories: Everyday Literacy and Making the Self* (Bloomington: Indiana University Press, 2006), p. 7; Hofmeyr et al., 'Introduction: Print Cultures, Nationalisms and Publics of the Indian Ocean', p. 10.

[79] Jonathon Glassman, *War of Words, War of Stones: Racial Thought and Violence in Colonial Zanzibar* (Bloomington: Indiana University Press, 2010).

[80] James R. Brennan, 'Realizing Civilization through Patrilineal Descent: African Intellectuals and the Making of an African Racial Nationalism in Tanzania, 1920–50', *Social Identities*, 12 (2006), 405–423; James Brennan, 'Blood Enemies: Exploitation and Urban Citizenship in the Nationalist Political Thought of Tanzania, 1958–75', *Journal of African History*, 47 (2006), 389–413.

ways which were locally specific and which cannot be termed 'derivative' in any straightforward sense.[81]

But the newspapers explored for the colonial period in this book are slightly different, in that they were mostly produced either by the territorial or local arms of the colonial state, or by the Catholic or Lutheran missions. In taking such publications seriously, publications operating under conditions of clear, if sometimes arm's-length, European direction, I take my cue from studies of other parts of the colonial world, similarly without an independent press. In interwar Nepal, Rhoderick Chalmers found a government newspaper very similar to those found in interwar colonial Tanganyika, and to some extent after 1945 as well. Until 1935 this was the only newspaper available in Nepal, and while it offered a vehicle for the government to transmit its own messages, it also displayed 'several of the features that would mark the role of journals within the Nepali public sphere.' In particular, Chalmers draws attention to the way in which this newspaper's 'brief news reports from across the country … provided a basic representation to the print community of the geographical extent and variety of the country', while 'the complementing of local news with reports from India and around the world initiated a new means of siting Nepalis within a regional and global context and providing information, however limited, by which readers might compare their situation with that of other peoples and countries'.[82] In Nepal, and in other colonial public spheres, the concerns which animated correspondents often tended towards the moral more than the overtly political, but through their pages we learn a great deal about contemporary moral and political arguments.[83] Even in the absence of an independent and politically oppositional press, then, there is much that newspapers can tell us.

The same is true for the early postcolonial period. After long-running attempts first by the African Association and later by TANU to establish a party newspaper, TANU eventually began to put out a largely English-language newssheet called *Sauti ya TANU* in 1957.[84] From 1959 its

---

[81] Leigh Denault, *Publicising Family in Colonial North India, c. 1780–1930.* Unpublished PhD thesis, University of Cambridge (2008), pp. 9–10.

[82] Rhoderick Chalmers, *"We Nepalis": Language, Literature and the Formation of a Nepali Public Sphere in India, 1914–1940.* Unpublished PhD thesis, SOAS (2003), pp. 113–114.

[83] Shawn Frederick McHale, *Print and Power: Confucianism, Communism and Buddhism in the Making of Modern Vietnam* (Honolulu: University of Hawai'i Press, 2003).

[84] On efforts to establish an African Association newspaper see file 'Gazeti la African Association', TNA 571/AA/17, especially 'Minutes of the African Association Dodoma Meeting held on 28.6.47 in the S. W. C. – Dodoma', TNA 571/AA/17, f. 04. On *Sauti ya TANU*, Sturmer, *The Media History of Tanzania*, p. 66.

polemical articles drew equally polemical rebuttals from the colonial state in their own occasional newssheet, *Sauti ya Kweli* or 'The Voice of Truth'.[85] The late 1950s also saw an independent nationalist press briefly flourish in Tanzania. The newspaper *Mwafrika*, founded in September 1957, played a key role in disseminating TANU's message and served as a forum in which letter-writers debated the meaning of democracy and self-government.[86] Other newspapers, such as *Tanganyika Mpya*, published by E. R. Munseri, who had once been so reliably loyal to the colonial government that his local newspapers had been exempted from the requirement to pay a bond, began adopting a pro-TANU line from early 1957, as did the Dar es Salaam newspaper *Zuhra*. Colonial officials quickly surmized that mentioning TANU or Nyerere in headlines helped to sell papers.[87]

This flourishing of the press did not last, and there was a rapid shrinking of the number of newspapers after independence in 1961. Many local newspapers closed, particularly those in vernacular languages, and the TANU party newspapers *Uhuru* and *The Nationalist* became increasingly important, alongside the long-standing English-language daily *The Standard*. By 1967, *Uhuru* was estimated to have 100,000 readers which would have made it the most widely read of Tanzania's Swahili-language newspapers.[88] The dominance of party newspapers gave Tanzania's public sphere a distinct character, but as in the colonial period it continued to serve as an important site for the working and reworking of political concepts, as we shall see in Chapter 8. More broadly, it is the contention of this book that even in periods when the public sphere was tightly controlled by colonial and postcolonial governments, it is possible to trace continuity and change in the ways in which those who participated in that public sphere conceptualized society and politics.

The second major set of sources used in this book is archival records. For the colonial period, the Tanzanian National Archives in Dar es Salaam contain a rich seam of correspondence, much of it in Swahili, between African politicians and colonial officials. In addition to letters, there are

---

[85] Government of Tanganyika, *Annual Report of the Public Relations Department, 1959*, Dar es Salaam: Government of Tanganyika, 1960, p. 6.

[86] Sturmer, *The Media History of Tanzania*, p. 67.

[87] Commissioner of Police to Chief Secretary, 'Publication: Tanganyika Mpya', 11 February 1957, TNA UK, FCO 141/17949, f. 1; Commissioner of Police to Chief Secretary, 'Zuhra', 11 July 1957, TNA UK, FCO 141/17949, f. 21.

[88] James C. Condon, 'Nation Building and Image Building in the Tanzanian Press', *The Journal of Modern African Studies*, 5 (1967), 335–354, pp. 336–337. The newspaper *Ngurumo* had an estimated readership of 50,000 but a larger daily print run, of 14,000 as compared with 11,000 for *Uhuru*.

requests for permission to hold meetings, circulars and announcements. For the later 1950s, there are also minutes of local council meetings and subcommittees, again generally recorded in Swahili though sometimes also in English. For the early postcolonial period, up to around 1967, there is far more material than has yet been appreciated, largely in district files. In a number of cases, local council minutes continue beyond independence, along with correspondence between different levels of the nationalist party bureaucracy and between political and administrative leaders. From outside party and state structures, there are petitions requesting jobs or other preferment, complaints, and handwritten histories of TANU. I have also used the regional archives in Mwanza and the Chama cha Mapinduzi (CCM) party archives in Dodoma, as well as church archives in Moshi and at Makumira in Northern Tanzania.

There is also valuable material, some of it only relatively recently released, in the Colonial Office and Commonwealth Relations Office Archives held at the U.K. National Archives at Kew, notably the so-called 'migrated archives' or Hanslope Park Files, and in the U.S. National Archives at College Park in Maryland.[89] Finally, the records of the United Nations Trusteeship Council in New York provide insights into the debates taking place at the international level in the 1940s and 1950s. In this sense, this book draws on the insights of a new body of international history which has redirected our attention to international institutions in general and the League of Nations and the United Nations in particular.[90]

In taking this archival and published material seriously, this study builds on the recent 'textual turn' within African history.[91] Historians of Africa have discovered a far greater textual record than was once believed

---

[89] David M. Anderson, 'Mau Mau in the High Court and the 'Lost' British Empire Archives: Colonial Conspiracy or Bureaucratic Bungle', *The Journal of Imperial and Commonwealth History*, 39 (2011), 699–716.

[90] Peter Dumbuya, *Tanganyika under International Mandate* (London: University Press of America, 1995); Michael D. Callahan, *Mandates and Empire: the League of Nations and Africa, 1914–1931* (Brighton: Sussex Academic Press, 1999); Michael D. Callahan, *A Sacred Trust: the League of Nations and Africa, 1929–1946* (Brighton: Sussex Academic Press, 2004). For a recent historiographical review of the League of Nations and the Mandates system, see Susan Pedersen, 'Back to the League of Nations', *American Historical Review*, 112 (2007), 1091–1117; Mark Mazower, *No Enchanted Palace: The End of Empire and the Ideological Origins of the United Nations* (Princeton, NJ: Princeton University Press, 2009); Roland Burke, *Decolonization and the Evolution of Human Rights* (Philadelphia: University of Pennsylvania Press, 2010); Irwin, *Gordian Knot: Apartheid and the Unmaking of the Liberal World Order*, e.g., pp. 51–71.

[91] Karin Barber, *Africa's Hidden Histories: Everyday Literacy and Making the Self* (Bloomington: Indiana University Press, 2006).

to exist as they have become ever more resourceful both in seeking out new sources and in using old sources in innovative ways. The streams of letters sent off to colonial officials were dismissed as 'agitation' by weary colonial states, yet both the fact of their existence in written form, mirroring, as Derek Peterson has argued, the bureaucratic practices of the colonial state, and the content of these letters provides enormously important material if we are to reach into political thinking outside the Legislative Council and the nationalist memoir.[92]

The Swahili language connected people across mainland Tanzania and was a language which growing numbers of people could read and write. It nevertheless remains the case that in focussing on a textual corpus, we are engaging with the political thinking of a literate elite which remained relatively small up to the end of colonial rule. In 1961 it was estimated that around sixteen per cent of adults were literate.[93] This elite was also largely, though not exclusively, male. In the south of Tanzania, excluding women from access to the Swahili language had served as a means of keeping them away from the realm of long-distance trade, and cultural injunctions against the acquisition of Swahili remained long into the twentieth century.[94] Elsewhere, in many parts of the country women were less likely to go to school and thus less likely to acquire literacy in Swahili.[95] This book explores political concepts on the printed page, but as we journey into this world on the page we must always remember that there was a world beyond the printed page. The ideas explored here did not exist in a vacuum, they emerged in dialogue with other discussions carried out in the vernacular, and were in turn re-translated into the vernacular, and there is much that we do not and cannot know about this world beyond the printed page.[96]

---

[92] Peterson, *Creative writing: Translation, Bookkeeping, and the Work of Imagination in Colonial Kenya*, p. 139. Though in fact relatively little work has been done on the political debates which are preserved, in the Tanzanian case, in Hansard. For an excellent discussion of the challenges of writing postcolonial African history, see Jean Allman, 'Phantoms of the Archive: Kwame Nkrumah, a Nazi Pilot Named Hanna, and the Contingencies of Postcolonial History Writing', *American Historical Review*, 118 (2013), 104–129.

[93] Iliffe, *A Modern History of Tanganyika*, p. 574.

[94] Becker, *Becoming Muslim in Mainland Tanzania, 1890–2000*, p. 44.

[95] Iliffe, *A Modern History of Tanganyika*, p. 531.

[96] When I conducted interviews in Mwanza Region in 2005, elderly men who remembered the growth of the nationalist movement in the 1950s recalled that while Julius Nyerere would address crowds in Swahili, many of his auditors would not understand what was said, and for the majority small group discussions held in the Sukuma language afterwards were more important than public rallies in shaping local understandings.

The public sphere which we explore here was also distinguished from other areas of mid-twentieth-century Tanzanian life by its approach to religion. Religion is both everywhere and nowhere in the story which follows. In the pages of the government periodical *Mambo Leo*, direct discussion of religion was explicitly banned. As a result, many of the old coastal Islamic elite were forced out of the pages of *Mambo Leo*, but the voices of Muslims who separated religion from public engagement and wrote in roman-script Swahili as opposed to the Arabic script continued to be heard. Engaging in the pages of *Mambo Leo* meant adhering to a separation of religion and public life.

Yet this anxiety to preserve a position of religious neutrality coexisted with a commitment by the colonial state to religion, broadly defined, within public life, a commitment that persisted into the postcolonial period.[97] The practice of starting meetings with a prayer in which both Christians and Muslims could take part was sufficiently embedded in local practice as to be adopted by the new political organizations of the 1950s, such as the Kilimanjaro Chagga Citizens Union which we trace in Chapter 4. The same practice was adopted by the postcolonial state, when the parliamentary prayer was devised so as to be acceptable to adherents of Tanzania's two dominant monotheistic faiths.[98] If religion played an important role in buttressing authority, it also informed public debate. The voices heard in this book drew on religious teaching and were informed by the ethical dimensions of religious faith. At other times we peer into an explicitly religious domain, as when we explore the pages of the Catholic newspaper *Kiongozi*.

This distinctive blend of secularism and civil religion, identified by David Westerlund for the postcolonial period, emerged from the local history of colonial rule in mainland Tanzania.[99] As a result, as Gregory

[97] On the development of a policy of 'religious neutrality' in nineteenth-century India, see Andrew Porter, *Religion versus Empire? British Protestant Missionaries and Overseas Expansion, 1700–1914* (Manchester, U.K.: Manchester University Press, 2004). For a discussion of the evolution of 'secularism' in colonial contexts, see Nandini Chatterjee, *The Making of Indian Secularism: Empire, Law and Christianity, 1830–1960* (Basingstoke, U.K.: Palgrave Macmillan, 2011), pp. 8–11.

[98] Westerlund, *Ujamaa na dini: A Study of Some Aspects of Society and Religion in Tanzania, 1961–1977*, p. 68.

[99] Westerlund, *Ujamaa na dini: A Study of Some Aspects of Society and Religion in Tanzania, 1961–1977*, p. 75. For a comparative study of secularism in a post-colonial Zambian context, see Marja Hinfelaar, 'Debating the Secular in Zambia: the Response of the Catholic Church to Scientific Socialism and Christian Nation, 1976–2006' in Harri Englund (ed.), *Christianity and Public Culture in Africa* (Athens, OH: Ohio University Press, 2011), pp. 50–66.

Maddox has argued, although Tanzanian society is divided between Christians and Muslims, 'the fault line is not absolute' and 'a sort of rough civil society has been created across Tanzania'. Those excluded are those on the margins and thus, Maddox continues, 'religious radicalism, both Pentecostal movements and Islamic renewal movements, have tended to appeal to the socially alienated, with the Islamic version seemingly more political.'[100] It is the domain of this 'rough civil society' that is explored in this book.

STRUCTURE OF THE BOOK

The first chapter sets out the contours of thinking about politics and society in Tanzania's public sphere in the 1940s and 1950s in a transnational context. It does so by showing that over the first decades of the twentieth century, a public sphere developed in Tanzania which was relatively unusual in its openness and breadth. It provided a space in which to think comparatively and reflexively about social and political change and what it meant to take one's place in the modern world, a discussion framed, particularly after 1945, in terms of *maendeleo*, progress or development.

Chapter 2 explores the transnational language of 'democracy' as it developed after 1945. It traces the new importance of this language across the world and reflects on the ways in which uniformity of language did not entail consensus. Underlying the universal language of democracy were sharply contrasting conceptions of the political subject, with important implications for the ways in which political reform was conceptualized in post-1945 Tanganyika.

Chapter 3 shifts the focus to the discussion of political reform in the Swahiliphone public sphere and argues that we need to take the concept of representation seriously. The 1920s and 1930s in Tanganyika were characterized by important shifts in the conceptualization of political society and development of new conceptions of political subjecthood which can in part be traced through the changing use of the word *raia*, subject or citizen, but theories of representation remained underdeveloped as the colonial state expected chiefs to be the legitimate representatives of their people. In contrast, the political reform era after 1945 saw 'representation' become a central point of debate.

---

[100] Gregory Maddox, 'The Church and Cigogo: Father Stephen Mlundi and Christianity in central Tanzania', in Thomas Spear and Isaria N. Kimambo (eds.), *East African Expressions of Christianity* (Oxford: James Currey, 1999), pp. 150–166, p. 163.

Chapter 4 moves to the local level and explores one local organization founded in the late 1940s to campaign for an elected paramount chief, the Kilimanjaro Chagga Citizens Union (KCCU). It argues that the KCCU used the new opportunities brought by political reform and new languages of politics rhetorically to create a new political community. This was a vision of a political community which offered the people a greater voice and freedom from oppression by unjust rulers. But it also sought to balance *maendeleo* with strengthened social relations, so that the rich would help the poor, and the strong would help the weak. This conservative vision was briefly attractive to a wide constituency, but ultimately could not sustain political support.

Chapter 5 tracks the term *uhuru* as a 'word in motion' in twentieth-century Tanzania. Recent studies of South Asia and Indonesia have reminded us of the variety of vocabularies of freedom which existed in colonial settings in the twentieth century. The term 'freedom' was powerful because it was broad enough to carry meaning both at the high political level and at the very personal level. But it was also a sphere of contestation. Nationalists disagreed among themselves as to its meaning, as did those listening to them. But this did not mean a discursive free-for-all, rather new languages of freedom took on particular meaning in local settings.

Chapter 6 builds on this analysis by exploring the arguments over the position of Kilimanjaro's paramount chief and the rise of the nationalist party, TANU. TANU emerged into very specific intellectual and political contexts, and to win support in particular localities it had to engage with local debates. Just as the KCCU had sought to create a new type of political community under its leadership in which justice could be attained and *maendeleo* achieved, with the Union serving as an intermediary with power, so too did TANU. Yet TANU and its local allies also brought novelty, particularly through its more powerful language of freedom, framed in terms of rights and democracy. This chapter considers the rise of TANU in Kilimanjaro, and explores why and how TANU was able to construct a compelling narrative in which it was briefly able to monopolize discourses of *maendeleo* and democracy for itself.

Chapter 7 moves to the postcolonial period. The closing down of political space in postcolonial states is often understood in terms of the challenges they faced from within as they failed to meet the expectations of independence, and from without as they struggled to sustain their independence in a challenging world order. But postcolonial states were rarely strong enough to impose such a shift on their citizens. This chapter argues that the move to one-party democracy was the outcome of a struggle over what political membership means – defined from above in one way, in which all are citizens, and from below in another – linking political membership to party membership and the act of being a patriotic citizen, and that the one-party structure was not simply imposed from above but was authorized through debate in mainland Tanzania's increasingly restricted public sphere.

In the Arusha Declaration of 1967, Julius Nyerere declared that Tanzania's course henceforth would be defined by the idea of *Ujamaa*, literally 'familyhood' but more often translated as 'African socialism'. This decisive turn in his political thinking from leading a national party of *all* Tanzanians to defining TANU as a party committed to a specific set of objectives has dominated narratives of Tanzania's post-independence history. Chapter 8 explores the concept of *ujamaa* in its wider discursive context, and shows that its power lay in its ability to engage with themes current in political discourse since 1945 and earlier.

I

Concepts of Progress in
Mid-Twentieth-Century Tanzania

In 1955, the latest in a long line of newspapers and other printed ephemera which had appeared (and often quickly disappeared) in Tanganyika over the preceding sixty years was printed in Marangu, a small chiefdom on the slopes of Kilimanjaro in Northern Tanzania. The newspaper may have consisted of only two pages, but its title, *Makusaro* or *Thoughts*, gives a sense of its purpose. The concerns of *Makusaro* were, in some ways, very limited. The newspaper offered a mechanism by which young Lutherans from the district might communicate when studying away from home and appeal for news of their friends and fellow church members. But it also provided a space in which larger questions were raised. One article called on Africans to defend their own civilization and copy only the good habits of Europeans, not the bad. The author suggested that: '[t]hey have taught us much, but we have good things to teach them too', such as the habit of greeting strangers in the street. He encouraged readers to greet Europeans in this way. While they might begin by ignoring the greeting, they would eventually learn to reply. Ultimately, this writer argued, 'They are in our country and therefore we should accustom them to our ways – [the ways] of Marangu, of the Chagga and of Africa!'[1]

Historians and literary scholars have recently come to realize the importance of printed ephemera such as *Makusaro* and of the colonial public spaces that such newspapers helped to create, spaces in which political and social thinking ranged far beyond narrow questions of self-rule and nationhood.[2] Although not overtly oppositional, these public spaces

[1] 'Salaam kwetu Marangu na Uchaggani', *Makusaro*, March 1955, p. 1.
[2] Stephanie Newell, *The Power to Name: A History of Anonymity in Colonial West Africa* (Athens, OH: Ohio University Press, 2013), p. 47; Karin Barber, 'Translation, Publics,

can reveal a great deal about the changing languages of politics and political thinking. Accordingly, this chapter argues that the colonial press in Tanganyika from the 1940s and 1950s constituted the development of two sides of a narrative about progress, one side representing a particular kind of liberalism defined by self-help, association and global comparison, and the other characterized by uncertainty and even fear as to what the implications of social and political change might be. The often anonymous voices of this colonial public spoke in the context of dominant discourses but did not simply reproduce them. An understanding of the discourses at work here provides an essential context for the arguments that are examined in later chapters.

The narrative about progress discussed here served as a space in which to reflect on and argue about modernity, a term which has recently come to assume an importance which, as Frederick Cooper has argued, would have surprised anyone who had lived through the rise and fall of modernization theory.[3] 'Modernity' has come to play not one but many analytic roles, adopted by scholars from a range of theoretical standpoints. For some, it is a concrete process closely linked to the rise of capitalism and the colonial state. For Bruce Berman, writing in 2006, '[i]ndustrial capitalism, the nation-state, and the culture of modernity came to Africa and the rest of the non-Western world primarily through the forceful imposition of Western hegemony'.[4] Modernity, then, was something done to Africa, a negative force which was 'experienced as a crisis of moral economy, a challenge to indigenous understandings of the legitimate bases of inequalities of wealth and power, authority and obedience, and the reciprocities and loyalties of social relations.'[5] For others, modernity is a broader cultural construct, formed in Europe and then exported through the European colonial project, associated not just with new economic and social relations but also with the creation of new forms of subjectivity.[6]

---

and the Vernacular Press in 1920s Lagos', in Toyin Falola (ed.), *Christianity and Social Change in Africa: Essays in Honour of J. D. Y. Peel* (Durham, NC: Carolina Academic Press, 2005), pp. 187–208.

[3] Frederick Cooper, *Colonialism in Question* (Berkeley: University of California Press, 2005), p. 117.

[4] Bruce Berman, 'The Ordeal of Modernity in an Age of Terror', *African Studies Review*, 491 (2006), 1–14, p. 7.

[5] Ibid., p. 9.

[6] John Comaroff, 'Governmentality, Materiality, Legality, Modernity: on the Colonial State in Africa', in Jan-Georg Deutsch, Peter Probst and Heike Schmidt (eds.), *African Modernities: Entangled Meanings in Current Debate* (Oxford: James Currey, 2002), pp. 107–134.

As an analytic category through which to understand the twentieth century, neither usage is particularly helpful. The effects of the concrete processes gathered under the label of 'modernity' were uneven and appropriated in diverse ways. It is far from apparent that there is a sharp and all-pervasive break in European history which can be described as the onset of modernity, and even less clear that a concerted effort was ever made to export such a phenomenon to the colonial world. However, as Frederick Cooper has also shown, 'modernity' has another function, as what he terms a 'native's category'.[7] For as a number of scholars have shown, a concept of modernity and of what it meant to be modern was enormously important as a means of claim-making, of aspiring to a better future and of worrying about the dangers posed by social and economic change.[8] The term 'modernity' is far more helpful, then, if our concern is not with these processes of social and political change themselves but rather with the ways in which change was reflected on by those engaging in public debate.

Studying such changes through the medium of public debate requires that we move beyond the literal translation of 'modern' and instead think of the vernacular terms used to express a concept of change towards a position of equality within the world. As Richard Rathbone pointed out for nineteenth- and early twentieth-century West Africa, the terms used tended not to be 'modernity' or 'modernization' but rather 'progress' and later 'development'.[9] In Tanzania in the 1940s and 1950s, as we shall see, the term most frequently used in Swahili-language writings was *maendeleo*.[10] This term is sometimes straightforwardly translated as 'modernity'. As will become clear, I think this is too simple, but the term *maendeleo* was a site at which modernity could be argued over.

To make this case, this chapter begins by setting out the newspaper landscape in colonial Tanganyika. In the second part, I consider the ways in which dominant discourses within this arena can be seen to constitute an example of colonial liberalism, and in the third part, I explore the concerns exhibited about the relations between individual and community, men and women and young and old, and the boundaries of community,

---

[7] Cooper, *Colonialism in Question*, p. 113.

[8] Ibid., p. 118.

[9] Richard Rathbone, 'West Africa: Modernity and Modernization' in Jan-Georg Deutsch, Peter Probst and Heike Schmidt (eds.), *African Modernities: Entangled Meanings in Current Debate* (Oxford: James Currey, 2002), pp. 18–30, p. 25.

[10] Todd Sanders, *Beyond Bodies: Rainmaking and Sense Making in Tanzania* (Toronto: University of Toronto Press, 2008), p. 101.

often couched in terms which revealed a fear that progress might go backwards as well as forwards.

NEWSPAPERS IN COLONIAL TANGANYIKA

Before 1914, four newspapers competed with each other in the colony of German East Africa, three published by missions and one by the German government school at Tanga, subsidized by the German government.[11] After the First World War, the titles of the newspapers changed but the number of newspapers remained fairly steady during the interwar period. A few African-owned and edited newspapers tentatively began to appear, first *Anga la Tanganyika*, which appeared in March 1932 and then promptly disappeared, and Erica Fiah's *Kwetu*, which first appeared in November 1937 and lasted rather longer.[12] The most important newspaper of the interwar years, however, was *Mambo Leo*, produced by the Education Department from 1923.[13] After 1945, even as new government newspapers emerged, the circulation of *Mambo Leo* continued to grow, so that by 1952 it had reached 52,000.[14]

Even more importantly, a number of local newspapers were set up. Some were independent, such as Ewald Munseri's *Bukya na Gandi*,

---

[11] The circulation of all four (*Kiongozi*, *Habari za Mwezi*, *Rafiki Yangu* and *Pwani na Bara*) was small but grew steadily. In the case of *Kiongozi*, it was originally intended for former pupils of the government school in Tanga, but by the end of its life it had expanded beyond that relatively narrow base. Circulation averaged around 2000 per newspaper by 1914. See Martin Sturmer, *The Media History of Tanzania* (Ndanda: Ndanda Mission Press, 1998); Hilda Lemke, *Die Suaheli-Zeitungen und Zeitschriften in Deutsch-Ostafrika*. Unpublished PhD dissertation, Leipzig University (1929).

[12] N. J. Westcott, 'An East African Radical: The life of Erica Fiah', *Journal of African History*, 22 (1981), 85–101, p. 92. Fiah avoided the strictures of the Newspaper Ordinance by publishing every eighteen days. On *Anga la Tanganyika* see TNA 20705.

[13] Thomas Geider, 'The Paper Memory of East Africa: Ethnohistories and Biographies Written in Swahili', in Axel Harneit-Sievers (ed.), *A Place in the World: New Local Historiographies from Africa and South Asia* (Leiden: Brill, 2002), pp. 255–288, p. 264. On *Mambo Leo* in the interwar period, see also Katrin Bromber '*Ustaarabu*: A Conceptual Change in Tanganyika Newspaper Discourse in the 1920s', in R. Loimeier and R. Seesemann (eds.), *The Global Worlds of the Swahili* (Berlin: Lit Verlag, 2006), pp. 67–81; James R. Brennan, 'Realizing Civilization through Patrilineal Descent: African Intellectuals and the Making of an African Racial Nationalism in Tanzania, 1920–50', *Social Identities*, 12 (2006), 405–423.

[14] James F. Scotton, 'Tanganyika's African Press, 1937–1960: A Nearly Forgotten Pre-independence Forum', *African Studies Review*, 21 (1978), 1–18, p. 7. Though it increasingly changed its character and became more focussed on the transmission of government information as alternative outlets developed. Geider, 'The Paper Memory of East Africa: Ethnohistories and Biographies Written in Swahili', p. 267.

published in English, Swahili and Kihaya.[15] Others were tied to mass education efforts. For example, the Pare newspaper *Habari za Upare* was established in 1951 by the Social Development Officer to complement the government's literacy campaign.[16] Later, the Pare Council took over and employed an editor and team of local reporters, and by 1956 it had grown to twelve pages with a circulation of around 3,000 per month.[17] Whereas most district newspapers were printed on a much smaller scale, sometimes consisting of only a couple of typed sheets, the combined circulation of the district newspapers in 1953 was around 27,000.[18] There were also a number of newspapers produced by missionaries, such as the Lutheran *Ufalme wa Mungu* of the interwar period and then later *Umoja* and *Bendera ya Kikristo* as well as the Catholic newspaper *Kiongozi*, which, confusingly for historians, adopted the name of the pre-1914 German government newspaper when it began publication in 1950.[19]

Because of the tight censorship which was practised, there was relatively little that might be termed overt 'political' debate.[20] Political commentary tended to be restricted to factual reports or encouragement to obey colonial laws. But far more interesting were the reflections on social change contained in letters to the editors and news from the regions. Newspapers also contributed to new geographical imaginaries among readers and correspondents. A year after it began publication in 1904, the German government-sponsored newspaper *Kiongozi* had forty-seven

[15] Martin Sturmer notes that *Bukya na Gandi* succeeded in avoiding paying the bond which was normally required of newspaper proprietors because it 'did by no means oppose the Government's policies.' Sturmer, *The Media History of Tanzania*, p. 62. *Bukya na Gandi*'s editor, Ewald R. Munseri, had previously worked in the Information Office in Uganda and been assistant editor of *Mambo Leo* and *Habari za Leo*. Godfrey Mwakikagile, *Life in Tanganyika in the Fifties* (Grand Rapids, MI: Continental Press, 2006), p. 69.

[16] 'Notes and News', *Africa*, 26 (1956), 187–194, p. 190. Horace Mason, 'Pare News and other publications of the Pare mass literacy and community development scheme', in UNESCO, *Reports and Papers on Mass Communication: Periodicals for New Literates: Seven Case Histories*, Vol. 24, 1957, pp. 19–23.

[17] 'Notes and News', p. 190; Scotton, 'Tanganyika's African Press, 1937–1960: A Nearly Forgotten Pre-independence Forum', p. 8.

[18] Scotton, ibid., p. 7.

[19] There seem not to have been Islamic equivalents to the Lutheran and Catholic newspapers in mainland Tanganyika, aimed at an African rather than an Asian audience. Sturmer, *The Media History of Tanzania*, pp. 73, 85. *Kiongozi* had an exceptionally high circulation, more than 25,000 by the late 1950s. Scotton, 'Tanganyika's African Press, 1937–1960: A Nearly Forgotten Pre-independence Forum', p. 2.

[20] On legislation regarding the press, see Sturmer, *The Media History of Tanzania*, pp. 54, 73.

correspondents writing with news from thirty different places.[21] After 1923, *Mambo Leo* similarly attracted regular correspondents from across the territory. Their contributions were crucial in ensuring that demand constantly outstripped supply, and the government's acting chief secretary wrote in 1933 that it was local news and 'the correspondence columns that sell the paper.'[22]

In contrast to other parts of East Africa, the language of public writing was overwhelmingly Swahili, and this had implications for the nature of the press. In Kenya and Uganda, there was far more publishing in languages identified with a particular ethnic or regional group, such as Kikuyu or Luganda.[23] Vernacular newspapers were often concerned with the problems of a particular people, and were dominated by the patriarchal concerns of how to control women and younger men. Perceived problems of prostitution and female independence loomed large. But in Tanganyika the vernacular press was much smaller, and even when local newspapers began to appear in Tanganyika from the 1950s, they tended to be published either entirely or in large part in Swahili, a consequence of Tanganyika's distinctive colonial language policy.[24] The implicit audience was broader, and harder to pin down, and as a result the tenor of debate seemed to be more open. In the case of national newspapers, when very local issues were discussed in the pages of *Mambo Leo*, the discussions were read by others across the territory, and specific local political

---

[21] In the German period too there seems to have been a degree of enthusiasm for writing personal letters, and letters to newspapers. Lemke, *Die Suaheli-Zeitungen und Zeitschriften in Deutsch-Ostafrika*, p. 66.

[22] Acting Chief Secretary to Hon. Director of Education, Dar es Salaam, 9 April 1934, TNA 12871, f. 238.

[23] John Lonsdale, '"Listen while I read": Orality, Literacy and Christianity in the Young Kenyatta's Making of the Kikuyu' in Louise de la Gorgendière, Kenneth King and Sarah Vaughan (eds.), *Ethnicity in Africa: Roots, Meanings and Implications* (Edinburgh: Centre of African Studies, 1996), pp. 17-53, James F. Scotton, 'The First African Press in East Africa: Protest and Nationalism in Uganda in the 1920s', *The International Journal of African Historical Studies*, 6 (1973), 211–228, pp. 211–212.

[24] Thomas Geider, "Swahilisprachige Ethnographien (ca. 1890-heute): Produktionsbedingungen und Autoreninteressen', in Heike Behrend and Thomas Geider (eds.), *Afrikaner Schreiben Zurück: Texte und Bilder afrikanischer Ethnographien* (Köln, Rüdiger Koeppe Verlag Köln, 1998), pp. 41–71, p. 56. See also Geider, 'The Paper Memory of East Africa: Ethnohistories and Biographies Written in Swahili', p. 267. On colonial language policy see, among others, Marcia Wright, 'Swahili Language Policy, 1890–1940', *Swahili*, 35 (1965), 40–48; Derek Peterson, 'Language Work and Colonial Politics in Eastern Africa: The Making of Standard Swahili and "School Kikuyu", in D. Hoyt and K. Oslund (eds.), *The Study of Language and the Politics of Community in Global Context* (Lanham, MD: Lexington Books, 2006), pp. 185–214. There were a number of vernacular language publications – see Sturmer, *The Media History of Tanzania* for more details.

debates were often explicitly identified as having lessons for 'the whole of Tanganyika' as well as the individual area in question.[25] The same terminology, particularly key phrases such as 'unity is strength' or *umoja ni nguvu*, appeared in letters and articles from across the territory.

This relative openness was reflected in the oft-repeated emphasis on newspapers being open to all. Frequently, questions sent to the 'questions and answers' section of *Mambo Leo* asked whether anyone could write to *Mambo Leo* and have his or, less frequently, her letters published. The editor's response was always the same: *Mambo Leo* was a public forum open to anyone. In an answer to K. H. Yusufu of Kigomba the editor wrote: 'If you bring suitable news it will be published if we have space, whether you are poor or rich ... it is all the same to us.'[26]

Mambo Leo was also understood as providing a direct line to the colonial government, particularly for those who might not otherwise gain a hearing. As a result, *Mambo Leo* quickly came to be understood by readers as a means by which Africans could engage directly with the state, at a time when they were expected to express their grievances via the intermediaries of their chiefs or district officials.[27] Their understanding seems to have been justified, for letters sent to *Mambo Leo*'s editor were investigated. A letter sent in 1934 warning of food shortage and a risk of starvation in the sub-chiefdom of Ngote, Ihangiro prompted a tour and further enquiries by the district officer, and a report reassuring the chief secretary, passed on to *Mambo Leo*, that all was well.[28] Other letters were dismissed out of hand, but some, on further investigation, were found to be true.[29]

Yet these newspapers were also exclusive, though in a different way from the vernacular press, the exclusivity of which was based on language and ethnic belonging. Here exclusivity was defined by literacy and the material means to buy or access newspapers.[30] Their constituency was limited to the small minority who could read and who could afford to

[25] Letter from E. R. Munseri, 'Mkifikiri Mema Yatendeni', *Mambo Leo*, November 1946, p. 122.

[26] Editor, 'Majibu kwa Waandikaji', *Mambo Leo*, February 1945, p. 21. The implicit contrast is between the new newspaper as a printed *baraza* or public forum and those public meetings in which the right to speak was closely policed.

[27] John Iliffe, *A Modern History of Tanganyika* (Cambridge: Cambridge University Press, 1979), pp. 318–325.

[28] Letter from T. John Batamzi, 'Hatari za njaa'; TNA 12871/II, ff. 255–257, Acting Provincial Commissioner, Bukoba to Chief Secretary, 8 October 1934.

[29] J. M. Mwigulila, 'Lawama na chuki juu ya watoza kodi ya kichwa', TNA 12871/II, ff. 242–243.

[30] As mentioned in the introduction, at independence in 1961 around 16 percent of the population was literate. Iliffe, *A Modern History of Tanganyika*, p. 574.

subscribe or who knew someone who could read to them. Reading books and newspapers was therefore, as in other parts of the world, understood as a way of embracing modernity, a way, in the words of one of the Nepali intellectuals studied by Rhoderick Chalmers, to 'stand up like men in today's world'.[31] Although the number of people who formed part of this world grew steadily over the century, this group remained a minority of the population and had a strong sense of its own distinctiveness. Those who wrote to newspapers often described the newspapers as a *chama* or association, access to which was understood to be, in a sense at least, limited to its members.[32]

These newspapers were thus distinctive, in comparison both to those of neighbouring countries and to those which came later. They cannot be understood either as a space in which colonial officials imposed their view of the world on their readers, or as a space in which Africans could debate purely among themselves. Rather, as we begin to explore the debates and arguments which animated these newspapers in the period between 1945 and the rise of an independent press after 1957, we must remember that we are dealing with an intellectual environment shared among colonial officials, missionaries, and the growing number of Africans who could read and write in Swahili. What they shared was a concern with progress: what it was, how it might be achieved and what its pitfalls were. It is this concern that we now move on to explore.

LIBERALISM AND PROGRESS

Concepts of progress were part of a broader discursive nexus which we can term liberalism, but the term is a notoriously tricky one to deal with.[33] In a memorable phrase, Raymond Geuss suggests liberalism is 'more like Christianity than like the state', inasmuch as it is 'a complex of doctrines, ideals, suggestions for implementing those ideals, beliefs,

---

[31] Rhoderick Chalmers, *We Nepalis: Language, Literature and the Formation of a Nepali Public Sphere in India, 1914–1940*. Unpublished PhD thesis, SOAS, (2003).

[32] In 1952 the teacher M. B. Salim wrote to the Usambara newspaper *Maendeleo ya Shambalai* to ask how many members the newspaper had and how much they paid each month. The editor professed not to understand the question, stating that newspapers could not have members. But Salim's question spoke to a wider truth as to how newspapers were perceived. Maswali na majibu, *Maendeleo ya Shambalai*, October 1952, p. 3.

[33] For a useful discussion of the history of liberalism, see Alan Ryan, 'Newer than What? Older than What?' in Ellen Frankel Paul et al. (eds.), *Liberalism Old and New* (Cambridge: Cambridge University Press, 2007), pp. 1–15, p. 1.

and informal patterns of habitual actions and thought.'[34] The difficulties of pinning down anything that might be termed a philosophy or a doctrine of liberalism is itself only amplified once we look beyond Britain or Europe and towards its development in the wider world. Recent work on the translation and development of liberalism beyond Europe has made this very clear. Thus Douglas Howland has shown that in Japan, far from a liberal moment giving way to conservative reaction after 1884 as was once thought, in fact Japanese liberals consistently defined liberalism in terms which owed 'more to an elite republicanism than to populist democracy and more to law and order than to personal freedoms and rights.'[35] In India, C. A. Bayly has shown that not only did Indian liberals rework Western ideas and use them against their rulers, they also debated and disagreed both among each other and with liberal thinkers elsewhere about 'projects of political representation, the obligations of the state', and 'the basic meaning of the Good Life.'[36]

Moreover, when dealing with imperialism, we encounter a fundamental difficulty. If liberal thought is commonly associated with a concern with rights and freedoms, what are we to do when we encounter professed liberals arguing in favour of the denial of rights and freedoms constituted by colonial rule? Are we to accept, as Uday Singh Mehta asked in his 1999 book *Liberalism and Empire*, that we have encountered a contradiction between liberal thought and practice, or are we rather to seek, as he does, an explanation for this apparent contradiction?[37] Mehta shows convincingly that there is a contradiction only if we ignore the fact that within liberal universalism there was a space for liberal exclusion, on the grounds that not all were born with or yet enjoyed the dispositions which were an essential basis for liberal inclusion.[38] If not all were yet fit to enjoy the liberties of self-government, how were they to reach this stage? Here, the concept of progress assumed an enormous importance. 'History and progress' were, Mehta argues, 'an unremitting

---

[34] Raymond Geuss, *History and Illusion in Politics* (Cambridge: Cambridge University Press, 2001), p. 69.

[35] Douglas Howland, *Translating the West: Language and Political Reason in Nineteenth-Century Japan* (Honolulu: University of Hawai'i Press, 2002), p. 18. The term on which debate hinged in the Japanese context was *bunmeikaika* (enlightened civilization).

[36] C. A. Bayly, *Recovering Liberties: Indian Thought in the Age of Liberalism and Empire* (Cambridge: Cambridge University Press, 2012), p. 2.

[37] Uday Singh Mehta, *Liberalism and Empire: A Study in Nineteenth-Century British Liberal Thought* (Chicago: The University of Chicago Press, 1999), p. 46.

[38] Ibid., pp. 49–50.

preoccupation of nineteenth-century British liberalism.'[39] A 'commitment to progress' in turn justified colonial power to bring into line those who did not seem to be fulfilling the expectations that entailed.[40]

The claim to bring progress served to legitimize European colonialism in late nineteenth- and twentieth-century Africa. Colonial governments of the late nineteenth and early twentieth centuries drew on a language of progress to argue that societies ought to progress from a disordered past to a peaceful and harmonious future, and that states, in this case colonial states, constituted the chief agent of change. In German East Africa, missionary newspapers such as *Pwani na Bara* had celebrated the spread of 'commerce and Christianity' under the leadership of the German Emperor.[41] When the British took over, they used *Mambo Leo* and other didactic texts to inculcate new conceptions of the relationship between state and subjects, a conception which might be termed liberalism without liberties, founded on an understanding of citizenship based on duties rather than rights.[42]

But the concept of progress was itself embraced and appropriated by many colonial subjects, who sought to explore and define what it might mean in an African context.[43] In this sense, it constituted a shared language between some, though not all, rulers, and some, though not all, subjects. Over time, a particular discourse developed, the overriding features of which were self-help, association and comparative thinking, together forming a language for talking about progress that had a great deal in common with that found in other parts of the colonial world in the mid-twentieth century.

Crucially, the centrality of conceptions of progress persisted through the interwar period, a fact which might at first seem surprising. This was, after all, a period often assumed to have been defined by re-traditionalization, as ideologies of 'indirect rule' focussed on finding 'traditional' rulers and tight government budgets meant little spending on social or economic development.[44] Certainly, the case was emphatically made by some

---

[39] Ibid., p. 77.
[40] Ibid., p. 78.
[41] See, e.g., Martin Ganisya, 'Siku kuu ya kuzaliwa Kaiser Wilhelm II', *Pwani na Bara*, January 1910, p. 1.
[42] S. Rivers-Smith and F. Johnson, *Uraia* (London: Macmillan, 1928).
[43] Rathbone, 'West Africa: Modernity and Modernization', p. 25.
[44] On interwar Tanganyika and indirect rule see Iliffe, *A Modern History of Tanzania*. This paragraph draws on arguments made in Emma Hunter, 'A History of *Maendeleo*: The Concept of 'Development' in Tanganyika's Late Colonial Public Sphere', in Joseph M. Hodge, Gerald Hödl and Martina Kopf (eds.), *Developing Africa: Concepts and*

colonial officials and by some of their African subjects that conserving society as it was should be the priority. But this view was rarely heard in texts such as *Mambo Leo*, and it must be remembered that even Lord Lugard's concepts of indirect rule, as described in *The Dual Mandate for Tropical Africa*, published in 1922, were indelibly linked to a conception of progress.[45] Ruling through 'traditional authorities' was a route to eventual self-government, not an end in itself. Similarly, even the numerous 'ethno-histories' which appeared in *Mambo Leo* in the period and which are often taken as evidence of such re-traditionalization were themselves focussed on comparing the past with the present, and with telling a story of increasing political unity over time, informed by a narrative of progress.[46]

Two points about conceptions of progress should be made here. The first is that they had clear Christian undertones. On a broad scale this is not surprising, given the strong belief in the period, manifested in the language of the League of Nations, that the Western version of civilization was applicable as a universal standard. But the link between Christianity, progress and development projects can also be traced at the local level, as has been shown by studies of other regions, such as interwar India.[47] The second, and related, point is that this was an idea of progress and civilization that was deliberately exclusionary. In a highly divided society like Tanganyika, adopting these ideas for oneself served as a means of differentiating oneself from others, though decreasingly so after 1945.

Though there was broad continuity across the period from 1923 to the mid-1950s, the language used to talk about progress changed. In the interwar period, the term *ustaarabu* or 'civilization' tended to be employed as a shorthand for progress. After 1945 there was something of a discursive shift and while the term *ustaarabu* did not disappear, the term *maendeleo*, progress or development, increasingly came to serve as shorthand for progress, in this sense reflecting a shift in global discourse from 'civilization' to 'development'.[48] We can see this shift in a

Practices in Twentieth-Century Colonialism (Manchester: Manchester University Press, 2014), pp. 87–107.

45 Frederick Lugard, *The Dual Mandate in British Tropical Africa* (London: Frank Cass, 1965), p. 86.

46 On the ethno-histories see Geider, 'The Paper Memory of East Africa: Ethnohistories and Biographies Written in Swahili', pp. 263–268.

47 Benjamin Zachariah, *Developing India: An Intellectual and Social History c. 1930–50* (Oxford: Oxford University Press, 2005), p. 114.

48 I discuss these themes at greater length in Hunter, 'A History of *Maendeleo*: The Concept of 'Development' in Tanganyika's Late Colonial Public Sphere'. See also Bromber, '*Ustaarabu*.' We can see this shift of usage in East Africa more widely, Kenda Mutongi,

text published in 1947. The text, published by the East African Literature Bureau as a contribution to the growing genre of ethno-histories, was both an account by the Kilimanjaro chief Petro Itosi Marealle of the customs and traditions of the Chagga people, and an account of recent political changes and his hopes for the future. The district had recently undergone an administrative reorganization, which had seen Petro Itosi Marealle elevated to the new position of 'Divisional Chief', charged with governing a third of the mountain of Kilimanjaro.

In his book, entitled *Maisha ya Mchagga Hapa Duniani na Ahera*, we see a web of meanings associated with the term *maendeleo*. Marealle used the term in a series of different senses. Some of these uses reflect colonial discourse regarding political steps towards self-rule and the 'social development' of solving society's ills. But there are also traces of the broader sense of progress found in dictionaries and newspapers in the interwar years. In the first place, it was employed in the general sense as meaning change associated with modernity. 'The proper development [*maendeleo*] of a tribe' depended, he argued, on making far-reaching changes. This meant adopting new customs from outside and either abandoning or improving existing bad customs. 'In this way by combining good foreign customs with our own good customs we shall have true *ustaarabu* [civilization] in Africa.'[49] But *maendeleo* was also used in a specific sense which reflected the emphasis in colonial discourse on development projects. Marealle referred to the need to cooperate in *kazi za maendeleo* or 'development work' to solve problems of landlessness, health and education.[50] He also engaged with the idea of political development, much under discussion in the district in the 1940s, writing that 'In the development of governance, Britain has been a famous example for the people of the entire world', and going on to discuss the potential for building democracy at the local level.[51] Yet elsewhere in the text, *maendeleo* also had a sense of human flourishing, as an organic development rather than one planned from above. Thus Marealle expressed his concerns that the erosion of chiefly power would be a great loss for the '*maendeleo mema* of the people.'[52]

Worries of the Heart: Widows, Family, and Community in Kenya (Chicago: University of Chicago Press, 2007), p. 120; Emma Wild-Wood, *Migration and Christian Identity in Congo (DRC)* (Leiden: Brill, 2008).

[49] Petro Itosi Marealle, *Maisha ya Mchagga Hapa Duniani na Ahera*, Dar es Salaam: Mkuki na Nyota, 2002 [1947], p. 99.
[50] Ibid., p. 100.
[51] Ibid., p. 104.
[52] Ibid.

That said, the term *ustaarabu* did not disappear completely, and still served as a means of discussing the future, with the flexibility to accommodate conservative agendas as well as agendas focussed on change, and the differences should not be overstated.[53] Crucially both terms tended to be positive markers, and while the question of what constituted either *ustaarabu* or *maendeleo* might be open for debate and doubt expressed over particular strategies, their status as ideals to be worked towards was not in doubt. Thus when a frequent correspondent and published poet in the pages of the Ukerewe district newspaper *Ekome* found himself in court accused of deception, another correspondent wrote to draw attention to the fact that this wrong-doer had had the cheek to use 'Mr Maendeleo' as his pseudonym.[54]

As mentioned previously, the idea of progress was captured and debated through discussion of self-help. What constituted this nexus of self-help, unity and a place in the world? In the newspapers of this period, it meant that news sent in from local areas, and letters to the editor, were dominated by reports of new associations being formed to achieve 'self-help' through unity. In Tanganyika, as in the interwar Ghanaian press studied by Stephanie Newell, distinctive echoes of Samuel Smiles were frequently to be heard.[55] The foundation of self-help was unity, and a common refrain from the 1920s onwards was that 'unity is strength'.[56] Readers, contributors and editors shared a broad conception that Africa's problem was disunity, and that the answer to that disunity was the building of friendship, cooperation and greater unity. Greater unity through cooperation, particularly through associations, was praised for the economic and social goods it could bring, as well as the role it could play as preparation for self-government.

New associations were at the heart of efforts to build unity and achieve self-help through unity. Social and political historians have long

---

[53] This flowed from its origins, see Katrin Bromber, '*Ustaarabu*'; Emma Hunter, '"Our Common Humanity": Print, Power and the Colonial Press in Interwar Tanganyika and French Cameroun', *Journal of Global History* 7 (2012), 279–301.

[54] Letter from "Mpenda Haki", 'Maendeleo au udanganyifu?', *Ekome*, September 1952, p. 2. Mpenda Haki is a pseudonym which means 'Lover of Justice'.

[55] Stephanie Newell, 'Entering the Territory of Elites: Literary Activity in Colonial Ghana', in Karin Barber (ed.), *Africa's Hidden Histories: Everyday Literacy and Making the Self* (Bloomington: Indiana University Press, 2006), pp. 211–235, p. 214.

[56] On establishing the Tanganyika Territory African Civil Service Association in 1922, the Anglophile colonial official Martin Kayamba said: 'Unity is strength – and unless Africans sooner or later come to realise this their future is dark and gloomy.' John Iliffe, 'The Spokesman: Martin Kayamba', in John Iliffe (ed.), *Modern Tanzanians* (Nairobi: East African Publishing House, 1973), pp. 66–94, p. 74.

understood the importance of the new welfare associations that formed in the 1920s and 1930s, often organized along ethnic lines, as well as religious groupings and dance societies, particularly in urban centres such as Dar es Salaam or Tanga.[57] They provided social security when the state did not, and frequently created the political alliances which would form the basis of later nationalist movements.[58] But they should also be understood as part of an intellectual framework which conceived of social progress as coming from individuals working together, either forming new associations or joining in transnational associations, rather than from the state. In the formation of such associations and the celebration of their formation in print, we see our historical actors embracing a liberal understanding of the path to human flourishing.

It is also important to remember just how geographically widespread enthusiasm for such associational life was in Tanganyika. It was not restricted to the growing urban centres or the rich cash-crop areas, and across the territory very similar language appeared. So, for example, in the relatively poor region of Sumbawanga in western Tanzania, the *Ufipa Production Co-operative Association* was founded in 1945 with the aim of 'raising Ufipa in the progress of the world', while from Singida in central Tanzania Juma Mwekwa reported the foundation of the Singida Muslim Association, through which Muslims in Singida 'tied themselves together like a rope, those without relatives and those with relatives, natives and strangers, all equally'.[59] Some, such as the African Catholic Association founded in September 1950, envisaged an association which would encompass Catholics across the territory, but organizers writing about it in the Catholic newspaper *Kiongozi* employed the same, now familiar phrase: 'Unity is Strength'.[60] The Tanganyikan Scout movement, which in its Tanganyika form originated in Bukoba in the north-west of the country, also spread widely and was understood, like other associations, as a

---

[57] On the history of these associations, see Iliffe, *A Modern History of Tanzania*, esp. pp. 284–286, pp. 389–395. See also Claire Mercer, Ben Page and Martin Evans, *Development and the African Diaspora: Place and the Politics of Home* (London: Zed Books, 2008), p. 108.

[58] Susan Geiger, *TANU Women: Gender and Culture in the Making of Tanganyikan Nationalism, 1955–65* (Oxford: James Currey, 1998), p. 63.

[59] News from the Towns, 'Sumbawanga – maendeleo ya nchi', *Mambo Leo*, September 1945, p. 100; Fundi Juma Mwekwa, 'Chama cha Waislamu Singida', *Mambo Leo*, September 1947, p. 102.

[60] Letter from John Nz Gaspar, 'Umoja ni Nguvu', *Kiongozi*, November 1950, p. 173; see also Andrew K. Tibandebage, '"A.C.A." inaomba msaada', *Kiongozi*, September 1950, p. 142.

space in which new types of solidarity might be developed to build unity and self-help.[61] In the Songea District Newspaper *Mzungumzi Wetu,* an article in praise of Boy Scouts ended with the appeal: 'Friends, let us open associations in the country so that we can cooperate with each other and love one another.'[62]

While association, unity and self-help might form the basis for 'progress', the pursuit of progress demanded comparative thinking. As in other parts of the world, an important aspect of public thinking in this period was of thinking about one's place in the world, and thinking comparatively about what should constitute progress. Thus, for example, a lengthy letter in *Mambo Leo* in 1946 on the way forward for Tanganyika which started with a discussion of how African Americans had built a place for themselves in America through working together, contributing funds and building their own institutions, ended with an expression of hope that educated Tanganyikans and returning servicemen would play a leadership role to enable Africans in Tanganyika to achieve the same ends.[63] In a similar vein, a soldier serving in Ceylon reported an encounter with a local man and concluded that women were treated very differently in that country. His broader conclusion was that progress did not lie simply in speaking English or adopting Western dance styles, but in treating women with respect.[64] Political comparisons were also made. Reports from across the world described the steps which countries were taking towards self-rule and returning soldiers described the excitement about 'Independence' which they had encountered in Asia, though in

---

[61] Timothy Parsons, *Race, Resistance and the Boy Scout Movement in British Colonial Africa* (Athens, OH: Ohio University Press, 2004), p. 126. For a comparative case on scouting in the Anglo-Egyptian Sudan, see Heather Sharkey, *Living with Colonialism* (Berkeley: University of California, 2003), p. 46.

[62] Letter from Mrs Flora H. S. Msumba, 'Sasa naanza kuelewa Boy Scouts ni' *Mzungumzi Wetu,* May 1952, p. 5, TNA 41176. See also 'Unyanja, Chama cha Uskauti', *Mzungumzi Wetu,* June 1952, p. 3; 'Uskauti', *Habari za Upare,* November 1952, p. 7, TNA 41176.

[63] Letter from Peter Mgohakamwali, 'Weusi tunavyoweza kuendelea', *Mambo Leo,* February 1946, p. 13. 'Burma nayo itajitawala', *Mambo Leo,* December 1947, p. 134; Letter from Ex-Serviceman Seleman Juma, 'Nani asiyependa haki yake', *Mambo Leo,* December 1947, p. 134.

[64] Letter from BT. 110 L/Cpl Victor Elliott Mtutuma, 'Kuheshimu mke wako ni sheria tokea zamani', *Mambo Leo,* November 1944, p. 130. On ideas of respectability in *Mambo Leo* in this period, see Maria Suriano, 'Letters to the Editor and Poems: *Mambo Leo* and Readers' Debates on *Dansi, Ustaarabu,* Respectability, and Modernity in Tanganyika, 1940s-1950s', *Africa Today,* 57 (2011), 39–55, and on gender relations in *Mambo Leo,* see Brennan, 'Realizing Civilization through Patrilineal Descent'.

the 1940s not all were convinced that Tanganyika was yet ready to rule itself.[65]

Newspapers encouraged such comparative thinking. Periodicals such as the Catholic *Kiongozi* and the government's *Mambo Leo* encouraged readers to produce historical accounts of local heroes such as Mirambo of Unyamwezi who could serve as an example of virtue.[66] Comparisons also provided a yardstick: one writer in the pages of the Newala newssheet in 1952 exuberantly declared (in English), '[t]herefore there is no misery at Newala nowadays! Pombe [beer] can be obtained and people are very rich. We have got a big Hospital and Houses where sickers [sic] can sleep. We can say that Newala is like Europe.'[67]

Closer to home, exhortations to greater exertion in the pursuit of progress were frequently made through comparisons. M. Madiwa Sefu wrote to *Maendeleo ya Shambalai*, a newssheet published in Lushoto in the Usambara mountains, to call for more pictures in the paper, and for the news to be organized by area, and ended by stressing the need for progress to catch up with the neighbouring Wapare people, who were 'far in front'.[68] Arguing from comparisons was also a way of claiming greater legitimacy for the argument. A 1952 letter in the Songea newssheet *Mzungumzi Wetu* argued in favour of girls' education on the grounds that this was the norm in other countries. Thus 'our elders of Songea should send their daughters to school so that Songea too can be a country among countries'.[69]

We can see in this discussion in the press the continued importance across Tanganyika in the period after 1945 of a liberal narrative of progress that had developed in the interwar period, a narrative based on a language of cooperation and self-help, and on explicit comparison. But an alternative and less optimistic narrative was also articulated in the public sphere, and it is to this that we now turn.

---

[65] Letter from Z. M. s/o Kaseko (Mwenda wazimu bin Shetani), 'Hatujafika Wakati wa Kujitawala Waafrika', *Mambo Leo*, July 1947, p. 73; Letter from Augustino Muller, 'Haujafika wakati wa kujitawala Waafrika', *Mambo* Leo, September 1947, p. 108; Letter from A. M. Mrega Jawewa, 'Elimu huhitaji fedha', *Mambo Leo*, October 1947, p. 119.

[66] See, e.g., 'Waafrika! Someni Habari za Kale!!', *Kiongozi*, June 1951, p. 2.

[67] Letter from George N. D. Fadhil, 'Come to visit Newala', *Uchele*, November 1952, p. 2.

[68] M. Madiwa Sefu, 'Barua za Wasomaji', *Maendeleo ya Shambalai*, June 1952, p. 4.

[69] Letter from Mgeni Gazetini, 'Elimu kwa Wasichana wa Songea', *Mzungumzi Wetu*, April 1952, p. 3. *Mgeni Gazetini* was a pseudonym meaning 'Stranger to the Newspaper', and the correspondent introduced him- or herself as one who had not previously written to *Mzungumzi Wetu*.

PROGRESS AND ITS DISCONTENTS

The other side to the intellectual context of this period was darker and tended more towards a concern with fragility than with triumphalist narratives of progress. For alongside measurements of *maendeleo* was an argument that *maendeleo* was fragile and could go backwards as well as forwards. There were fears that *maendeleo* was having harmful as well as positive effects, and that true *ustaarabu* was being lost.[70] Although the ability to acquire new consumer goods and pay for education was celebrated, such changes also provoked anxieties that inequality was increasing and that solidarity might be forgotten in pursuit of profit. This was understood at the time as a fear of 'individualism'.

The dangers individualism posed to community were captured by the Kenyan nationalist politician Tom Mboya when he wrote in 1963:

When a man earns his own salary and begins to buy a gramophone or a bicycle or a suit of clothes, he ceases to look on certain things as belonging to the community and begins to regard them as personal. This is a main area of conflict with tribalism, where adjustment is most necessary. He asks himself: 'Am I going to become individualistic like the European, or can I own something of my own and still belong to the tribe?'[71]

But what we see in the newspapers is more than the straightforward counterpoint of individual versus community portrayed at the time. Worries about individualism constituted a starting point from which to think about how to construct new forms of community and new bonds of solidarity. Moreover, it was not, as in Mboya's analysis, simply a question of men and their relationship to others, for very often it was the position of women in society and relations between men and women which served as a focal point of anxiety. How much bridewealth should be paid and the question of whether women should inherit became dividing lines between different understandings of what constituted *maendeleo mema* or 'good progress'. Exploring these questions requires that we look in closer detail at areas which might seem to be a long way from more straightforwardly political questions of political community and accountability.

Anxiety about wealth, inequality and gender relations existed at the intersection of political and moral thinking, and the attention devoted to such ostensibly moral questions in the press of the period is arresting. Partly, this was a consequence of what could be published under

[70] Cf. James Howard Smith, *Bewitching Development: Witchcraft and the Reinvention of Development in Neoliberal Kenya* (London: University of Chicago Press, 2008).
[71] Tom Mboya, *Freedom and After* (London: André Deutsch, 1963), p. 69.

a regime of colonial censorship. Yet even with that caveat, the sheer quantity of letters received and the tenor of these letters indicates that they are deserving of attention. In just one month in 1952, the newspaper *Habari za Upare* received no fewer than fifty letters on the subject of bridewealth.[72] The strength of feeling which these questions raised is evident in the language used to discuss them. The rhetoric of freedom and slavery, one of the most powerful rhetorical languages available to East Africans in the twentieth century, occurs frequently.[73] One example of such language can be found in a letter sent to the Kilimanjaro district newspaper in 1953 from a correspondent complaining about his enforced exile in Mombasa.[74] He had, he wrote, spent seven years working away from home so that he could afford to marry. Bridewealth payments in the Chagga district now cost 'more than pearls', forcing young men to leave the district to earn enough to marry. Rather than contributing to the progress of the country, young men like him were, he claimed, driven away, and enslaved to the Europeans on whose wages they depended.[75] Calling on biblical precedents, he wrote: 'When God made Adam and Eve he didn't tell Adam that he was selling Eve to him but told him "this is your helpmeet"'. In contrast, Chagga parents were 'selling their daughters like slaves used to be sold'.

In letters like this, we see processes which elsewhere are conceived of as aspects of progress to be celebrated – moving away to the city to work and cultivating cash crops to bring wealth to a district – redescribed as negative. More specifically, we find three strands at work in this text: an idea that growing inequalities of wealth meant growing risk of excessive dependence on others, gender relations as an index of progress, and the idea that progress was fragile and could easily slide backwards or be undermined. In the next section we move to examine these three strands in more detail.

---

[72] Editor's note, *Habari za Upare*, May 1952, p. 8. On the debates about marriage in Tanganyika in this period, see Margot Lovett, 'On Power and Powerlessness: Marriage and Political Metaphor in Colonial Western Tanzania', *International Journal of African Historical Studies*, 27 (1994), 273–301.

[73] Derek R. Peterson, 'Introduction' in Derek R. Peterson (ed.), *Abolitionism and Imperialism in Britain, Africa and the Atlantic* (Athens, OH: Ohio University Press, 2010), pp. 1–3. This was equally true in West Africa, on which see Christine Whyte, *Whose Slavery? The Language and Politics of Slavery and Abolition in Siera Leone, 1898–1956*. Unpublished PhD thesis, University of Zurich (2013).

[74] Letter from Fernandis S. s/o Lammomba, 'Mahari', *Komkya*, August 1953, p. 3.

[75] Ibid.

WORKING FOR OTHERS

To see the first process in action, we might look at the way in which shifts in economic thought at the high political level were reflected in published writings. After 1945, colonial policy and the policy of international institutions developed a broad consensus in favour of increasing economic growth in East Africa, from across the political spectrum. This was driven by different motivations. For some, like the left of centre British Fabian Colonial Bureau or anticolonial voices on the United Nations Trusteeship Council, it was an essential prerequisite to self-government and eventual independence. In America, for President Truman developing Africa and other parts of the newly constituted 'Third World' was a way of preventing the rise of communism. A consensus in favour of economic development did not, however, preclude divisions emerging when the question was raised of what the motors of such growth should be.

The investment of colonial development funds in Africa was in part intended to achieve this aim of growth, alongside attempts to encourage external private investment.[76] But the colonial office also believed that legal and social norms within African society needed to change. In 1948, an announcement in *Mambo Leo* entitled 'Development Commission' gave details of the process by which Africans might apply for loans.[77] What is striking about the announcement is the emphasis placed on the fact that only *individuals* could apply for loans.[78] The East Africa Royal Commission report of 1955, described by critical commentators as 'Adam Smith in East Africa', best summed up this perspective on economic development, with its vision of individualism and private land ownership.

However, if the Royal Commission Report was unequivocal in its support for moves to greater individualism and market-driven economic activity, the interviews conducted by members of the Commission in East Africa showed deep concern about the prospect of increasing private landownership and the inequalities of wealth which it was feared would result. In short, economic thought was divided between those who celebrated individualism and those who feared its destructive effects.

---

[76] The most comprehensive study of economic development is to be found in Michael Havinden and David Meredith, *Colonialism and Development: Britain and Its Tropical Colonies, 1850–1960* (London: Routledge, 1993). See also Joanna Lewis, *Empire State Building: War and Welfare in Kenya 1925–52* (Oxford: James Currey, 2000).

[77] 'Development Commission', *Mambo Leo*, July 1948, p. 82.

[78] The term used is *mtu mmoja mmoja*.

Underlying these divisions was a deeper set of economic and social arguments, around the themes of dependence and self-sufficiency, often debated in a language of freedom and slavery. Some sought to make that case that mutual dependence was an inevitable by-product of welcome economic change. Newspaper editors often preached the advantages of education, hard work and the careful use of money as the path to upward mobility. They criticized an attitude which equated working for others with slavery, and argued that working for others was virtuous.[79] In 1952 a letter in the district newspaper *Katapala* embarked on a lengthy criticism of what the author saw as the backward-looking habits of the Makonde people of south-eastern Tanganyika and their outdated ideas of what it meant to be civilized. The Makonde, the author wrote, saw themselves as civilized because they refused to work with their hands or to work for others. But what sort of civilization, this correspondent asked, was a life without work, without money to pay for education, without morality?[80] From the other end of the country, the editor of the newspaper *Ekome* published on the Lake Victoria island of Ukerewe put it most clearly. Attacking those who believed that working for others meant losing *uung-wana*, or civilized, non-slave status, he wrote that while this might have been acceptable in the past, these days, people depended on each other, and this mutual dependence was at the heart of modern civilization.[81]

Colonial officials, anxious at the lack of jobs for school leavers, agreed that greater economic interdependence was a positive step. In 1954, reviewing the increasing numbers of middle school leavers in Kilimanjaro for whom there were no jobs, the provincial education officer described the problem. A middle school education – in other words seven years in school – was a general education, which equipped its recipient to be 'an intelligent citizen not only as a Government employee but also by his own enterprise'. Such men, the education officer continued, would else-where become 'waiters, bus conductors, shop assistants, tractor drivers, barbers, market gardeners, insurance agents, agricultural workers and factory hands. They would become strong supporters of the football team

[79] We shall see in later chapters how TANU equated independence with freedom from slavery. See also Steven Feierman, *Peasant Intellectuals: Anthropology and History in Tanzania* (Madison, WI: University of Wisconsin Press, 1990), pp. 213–222, especially p. 214.

[80] Letter from Nyuki bin Manyigu, 'Kabila la Kimakonde Wenyewe Wamakonda wanalir-udisha nyuma', *Katapala*, December 1952, pp. 3–5, TNA 41176.

[81] Utangulizi, 'Ustaarabu Ni Kutumikia', *Ekome na Bukerebe*, September 1952, p. 1, TNA 41176.

of their choice and would hold vociferous but tolerant political views. Many of them would rise to managerial or executive positions.' But no such careers existed in the region. The provincial education officer had no answers to this growing problem, but was certain on one point: 'the Chagga have got to take in much more of one another's washing.'[82]

In this context, enthusiasm for self-help, either on an individual basis or through joining together with others, can be seen as an alternative to a model of interdependence. Founding cooperatives, or returning to work on the land, was understood to be an alternative to working for others. In March 1946, a serviceman wrote in the pages of *Mambo Leo* of how the many soldiers soon to return to their villages would not wish to continue in a life of service, but would hope to set up their own cooperative societies and trading societies.[83] Others called for a return to the land. The language of one correspondent, Simeon Mbaruka Muya, writing from the Church Missionary Society station at Katoke in Bukoba district, is particularly striking in this regard. Although many Africans used new languages of citizenship to make claims on government, for Muya this was 'begging'.[84] He began his letter by stating that some people seemed to think that modern civilization would come from 'demanding things be done by the Government or by labour unions'.[85] He had in mind such things as 'demanding large salaries, demanding our crops be sold at a high price, demanding that large houses be built for government workers; demanding that the number of schools be increased'. But he believed that true civilization would not come from begging for help from others, but from working to increase agricultural production.[86] The alternative to working the fields to increase food production was dependency on Europeans and Asians, raising the spectre of bankruptcy, increasing immorality and prostitution.

Fear of slavery and dependence was one current underlying concern about economic change. Another concern was of changing dynamics within families and communities. The emergence of new forms of wealth, and new understandings about wealth and what it meant to be rich,

---

[82] Provincial Education Officer, 'Future of Ex-Middle School Boys', TNA 5/9/24, f. 130.

[83] Letter, 'Hamu na Haja ya Mwafrika', *Mambo Leo*, March 1946, p. 25. Cf. Hal Brands, 'Wartime Recruiting Practices, Martial Identity and post-World War II Demobilization in Colonial Kenya', *Journal of African History*, 46 (2005), 103–125, pp. 111–115.

[84] Frederick Cooper, *Decolonization and African Society: The Labor Question in French and British Africa* (Cambridge: Cambridge University Press, 1996), p. 468.

[85] Letter from Simeon Mbaruka Muya, 'Ustaarabu wetu utegemee kilimo', *Mambo Leo*, July 1946, p. 74.

[86] Ibid.

raised new questions about individual and community. We are accustomed to think of this period as one characterized by a developing middle class. Indeed, newspaper culture appealed precisely to these new middle classes. Many newspapers carried adverts for the luxuries which were available to those with cash incomes – shoe polish, baby milk and bottled beer. But there was considerable anxiety about wealth too.

In areas experiencing land shortage, like the Kilimanjaro region in north-eastern Tanganyika, there seemed to be a growing tension between those with land and those without. Jealousy, it was said, was holding back development. In 1957, a writer from Rombo in eastern Kilimanjaro alleged that a man had recently been killed by a family member who wanted to inherit his property. The author saw this as a general problem: 'If you have just a little money, or a few cows, or perhaps you have a good job, Wachagga feel jealousy towards you.' This jealousy drove the poor to seek out medicines with which to kill and thus to inherit. In this way, jealousy was holding back progress and would result in the Chagga being left behind.[87]

To be entirely self-sufficient was of course impossible, even if access to land was achieved. But the responsibilities of individuals to their family and to their community provoked dissent, with a constant theme that the rich were spending their money in the wrong way. Those who had made good money through coffee sales were advised by *Bukya na Gandi"*s editor to spend it on buying property rather than taxis or lorries, for the latter could prove expensive to run.[88] When in 1955 the coffee price fell, hitting coffee-producing areas such as Kilimanjaro very badly, the sympathy of the district newspaper *Komkya*'s editor was muted. This should not be such a problem, he wrote. Had coffee farmers done as they had been advised and put their money in the savings bank, they would now have savings to call on. But while the coffee union (the Kilimanjaro Native Co-Operative Union, or KNCU) had 35,000 members, only 1,352 had put their money in the savings bank.[89] Where had the rest of the money gone and why had it not been saved in case the price fell? Many of those who wrote to *Komkya* were very clear as to where the money had gone: it had been spent on beer. A letter published in *Komkya* in 1953 claimed that the Chagga spent their coffee wealth badly.[90] On receiving

---

[87] Letter from Pelaji Lakinboya Kinabo, 'Wivu katika nchi ya Uchagga', *Komkya* 15 February 1957, p. 3.

[88] 'Wasomaji Salaam', *Bukya na Gandi*, 25 December 1952, TNA 41176, p. 4.

[89] Editorial, *Komkya*, 15 May 1955, p. 2.

[90] Letter from Anthony R. Sendau, 'Fedha zinavyotumika Uchaggani', *Komkya*, August 1953, p. 3.

payment they immediately 'went to bars every day from morning until evening. They did no work at home. They gave no money for food. All the money would be wasted at the bar', while at home their wife and children went without.[91]

Yet while some preached careful saving and husbanding of resources, not everyone agreed that money should be saved. Some believed that it was the failure of the rich to spend which was the real block on development. In *Komkya*, a letter from Romani S. Waiso in 1957 attacked those rich people who hid their wealth when they could spend it on luxuries, dressing well, building impressive houses or buying minibuses. Spending their wealth in such ways would bring praise and *maendeleo mema* for themselves and for the whole country.[92] Spending money on education was also generally seen as an unproblematic good, and many letters and news articles sent in from individual villages and districts called for more schools and attacked parents who failed to educate their children. A letter published in *Komkya* in 1955 noted that in Kibosho many parents sent one child to school and the other to herd goats. But the author called on his fellow inhabitants of Kibosho to reconsider this strategy, for 'today's world is different' and 'these days every person should be educated'.[93]

Whether the rich should be spending or saving, the strand of both of these lines of argument was in favour of a wealth being kept within the family, to promote that family and its children. While this might suit liberal understandings of individualism, it was understood that it also meant neglecting responsibilities to others. Just as some of those interviewed by the East Africa Royal Commission expressed their fears that Adam Smith's arrival in East Africa would presage a crisis in social relations, so some correspondents to the 1950s press raised their concerns that new forms of economic thought would encourage the rich to neglect their duties to the poor. A letter to the *Kondoa News* in 1957 reflected this anxiety in more explicit form than was common. Its author noted that many letters appeared calling for an end to corruption and more generally for an end to 'trouble-making', indicative of some of the ways in which those without wealth were seeking to access it. Most stopped at simply saying these were bad habits which should be stopped. But this

---

[91] On Kilimanjaro complaints that money was being wasted on beer were frequent. But elsewhere, the availability of foreign beer was taken as a sign of progress. See 'Furaha ya pombe hapa Songea', *Mzungumzi wetu*, September 1952, TNA 41176.

[92] Letter from Romani S. Waiso, 'Matajiri wanaoficha Utajiri wao Hawaleti Maendeleo Nchini', *Komkya* 15 January 1957, p. 3.

[93] Letter from Eseb Protas, 'Masomo Kibosho', *Komkya*, 15 August 1955, p. 6.

correspondent wanted to go further, and asked what caused the trouble-making. His answer was simple: it occurred when a rich person was asked for help by a poor person, and he failed to give that help. Progress (*maendeleo*), he argued, was achieved by helping each other, not by hoarding.[94]

The idea of encouraging mutual dependence, of the 'self-help' of communities rather than individuals, found echoes elsewhere, particular on the issue of paying for education. Was the failure to have money to pay for education due to a private failing, for which the children of those families would pay the price? Or was education a public good, deserving of the support of the community? A teacher who wrote in 1952 to the district newspaper *Ekome* published on the island of Ukerewe in Lake Victoria under the title 'unity is strength' was in no doubt. Lamenting the fate of those students who could not finish their schooling because they lacked money to pay their school fees, he called on others in Ukerewe to help them. They were wrong to see education as a private good, beneficial to the individual rather than to the community. After all, an educated person would serve their country and their people.[95] An alternative path was suggested in a letter to the Newala district newspaper in southern Tanganyika. Noting that in Newala finding money for school fees was often a struggle, one correspondent called on those with more means to help by setting up an association for those who could not pay the fees. Government and missions donated money in such a way, so should people not also cooperate to help themselves?[96]

Correspondents echoed the fears which had long been raised by missionaries and colonial officials that change was not uniformly positive, particularly if it destroyed the social bonds that helped to bind society together. Some young writers sought to reclaim old ways for a new era. Many complained about the ways in which their contemporaries failed to respect the old, and reminded their peers that 'to show respect is not slavery'.[97] But if new modes of constructing community solidarity needed to be found, and if communities should work together to achieve development, then the question of the boundaries of community became extremely important.

New associations were one way of providing mutual assistance beyond the bounds of the nuclear family. But while they constituted an effort to

---

[94] Letter from D. H. Mohamedi, 'Acha Fitina', *Kondoa News*, October 1957, p. 8.
[95] Letter from Mwalimu F. M. Bakaraza (Mangu) Mwadui, Shinyanga, 'Umoja ni Nguvu', *Ekome*, July 1952, pp. 2–3, TNA 41176.
[96] Letter from Augustino F. Mkuchika, *Uchele*, November 1952, p. 4, TNA 41176.
[97] 'Heshima si Utumwa' *Komkya*, 1 November 1954, p. 3.

remake social bonds, they also imposed boundaries on who could claim mutual aid and who might access resources. In this way, new forms of local citizenship accompanied the growth of a sense of Tanganyikanness. We can see this in an editorial in *Ekome*. In 1952, the editor of *Ekome* called on the farmers of Ukerewe Island in Lake Victoria to work harder and grow more food. It was not enough, he wrote, for them to grow enough food to feed themselves and then stop. The modern world was a more specialized world, in which people were compelled to depend on each other. Fellow Tanganyikans working on plantations or in towns could not grow food to feed themselves, but they were performing an important service for the nation. It was the responsibility of those who remained on the land to grow enough food to feed those who could not feed themselves.[98]

In this editorial, readers of *Ekome* were encouraged to imagine fellow citizens far away from home, but food was an issue closer to home as well. Newcomers to Ukerewe used the pages of *Ekome* to complain about the difficulties they faced in acquiring food at a reasonable price.[99] The same trope was employed to encourage residents of Ukerewe to sign up for work which the Government was offering. If they did not volunteer to do the work, people would have to be brought in from outside who would use up the Native Treasury's resources by demanding higher salaries, and would eat the food produced in Ukerewe. 'Do you want our country's money to be sent to the countries of other tribes? Don't you know that if this money was paid to the people of Ukerewe it would enrich our country?'[100] The question of what constituted progress and modernity in economic terms, and its dangers, was, then, an open one.

GENDER AND MODERNITY

The same was true of gender relations. In 1953, the Kilimanjaro district newspaper *Komkya* devoted considerable space to an interlinked set of issues around marriage, initiation rites and inheritance that predominantly affected the young, both male and female. The first issue of *Komkya* in 1953 made clear that this was not to be a purely male space, though it did try to gender space within the newspaper.[101] The editorial

---

[98] Hamza K. B. Mwapachu, 'Utangulizi', *Ekome ya Bukerebe*, November 1952, p. 1.

[99] Letter from Mwl. Francis L. Kato, 'Shukurani', *Ekome ya Bukerebe*, May 1952, p. 2.

[100] Utangulizi, 'Ustaarabu ni Kutumikia', *Ekome ya Bukerebe*, September 1952, p. 1.

[101] The practice of having a women's page was fairly common. *Habari za Upare* also had a women's page. Beyond Tanganyika, Deborah Kallmann has described the ways in which particular forms of morality were expressed through the women's pages of Northern

announced that there was a woman on the staff, and that a page would be set aside for women in each issue in which they could discuss 'clothes and other female things', while the front page article informed women that 'we also want to get female councillors in our councils from the village to the chiefdom and from the Division to the Chagga Council.'[102] Yet from the first issue onwards, women immediately asserted the right to use this new space for themselves, ensuring that the women's page was more concerned with female inheritance rights than with the latest fashions. At the same time, young men used the letters pages both to support female correspondents and to challenge new concepts of femininity.

The argument in favour of equal inheritance rights was made on the grounds of progress and comparison with other countries. According to a nurse, who gave her name as Mary Shilley, 'in all countries which have progressed inheritance is divided between all children without considering whether this one is male or that one is female.'[103] Another letter the following month agreed, but sought to broaden the issue out beyond inheritance to consider the wider problems caused by the unequal ways in which men and women were treated by their parents. A letter from K. Weraikunda Obadia in 1953 complained that many parents failed to educate their daughters, forgetting that those daughters would be the parents of the next generation, and would fail to do their job effectively if they were not themselves educated, putting the very progress of the country at risk.[104] She called on all readers to share these views with the elders and all those who wanted good progress or *maendeleo mema* in the region.

The argument against high bridewealth could similarly be made on the grounds of comparative thinking. A letter from two nurses began by saying that 'in any country which wants to have civilization and to progress well it is essential that everyone has unity, love and respect'.[105] How then could it be that parents think it acceptable to 'love their male children and

---

Rhodesian newspapers, and the ways in which these constructions were engaged with and challenged. Deborah Kallmann, 'Projected Moralities, Engaged Anxieties: Northern Rhodesia's Reading Publics, 1953–1964', *The International Journal of African Historical Studies*, 32 (1999), 71–117.

[102] '1952 Mwaka wa Kutajika katika Historia ya Wachagga', *Komkya*, March 1953 p. 1. The paper's female member of staff was introduced as Bibi Martha Paul Muro. *Komkya*, March 1953, p. 2.

[103] Mary Shilley, 'Mabibi na Urithi', *Komkya*, July 1953, p. 7.

[104] Letter from K. Weraikunda Obadia, 'Wasichana na Urithi', *Komkya*, August 1953, p. 7.

[105] Letter from Josephine Godwin and Mary Mathew, 'Mahari Uchaggani', *Komkya*, August 1953, p. 7.

sell their female children'? They described the 'shame' they felt when they described Chagga practices away from home. For young men, as we saw earlier, a similar dynamic was at work, a fear of being unable to marry. Brett Shadle has described for the Gusii region of Kenya the impact of growing inequality of wealth on the ability of those young men who were dependent on wage labour to marry, with the average time needed to earn enough money to marry increasing from around six to eighteen months in the 1920s to three to four years in the 1940s and 1950s.[106] As in Gusii, the amounts paid as bridewealth had been steadily increasing and many men were clearly worried that they would fail to marry and so fail to achieve full adulthood. But the arguments they deployed were rather different to those made by women and focussed on the loss to the nation that would result. In this vein, Dunstan M. Kawa, working in neighbouring Mbulu, claimed to have discovered many Chagga men who had failed to earn sufficient bridewealth to marry at home and so instead had married Mbulu women. As a result they were now lost to the *taifa* (nation), all because Chagga parents insisted on 'selling' their daughters.[107]

Like other newspapers, *Komkya* tended to attract young voices, and so in September 1953 the editor called for parents to give their opinions. In an editorial entitled 'Customs and Traditions' he framed the issue in clear generational terms. The editor argued that while bridewealth and female circumcision had doubtless been practised 'by the Chagga tribe since the time of our ancestors', a new generation which had been taught to question everything was now questioning these practices. They were not satisfied with the answers given by their parents, that they were justified by the fact that they had always been followed and that they were part of the cultural practices which defined Chagga identity.[108] What did parents think? Did the failure of the 'previous' generation to write to the newspaper with its thoughts indicate agreement with the ideas of the 'current' generation?

Apparently not. In response letters arrived from older men defending a social system which they believed was still functioning and should continue to function. A letter from J. Tirishia addressed to 'my daughters, and my children, and all who oppose bridewealth' argued in favour of

---

[106] Brett Shadle, '*Girl Cases': Marriage and Colonialism in Gusiiland, Kenya, 1890–1970* (Portsmouth NH: Heinemann, 2006), p. 107.

[107] Dunstan M. Kawa, 'Mahari Uchaggani', *Komkya*, August 1953, p. 3. 'Kwa kusema kweli hawa wenzetu wamekwisha potea. Je! Hili si pengo? Na hili pengo limetokea kwa sababu wasichana kwetu wanauzwa sio kuposwa.'

[108] Editorial, 'Mila na Jadi', *Komkya*, September 1953, p. 2.

bridewealth and against female inheritance and education.[109] The reasons for demanding bridewealth were, he argued, twofold, to strengthen religion and to protect their daughters. If a man had not had to work in order to marry, then when he grew tired of his wife he would simply chase her away in favour of someone younger.[110] Older women intervened in the debate too, arguing that young men had misunderstood the nature of bridewealth. It was not a case of parents selling their daughters; rather bridewealth was a gift offered in thanks to a bride's parents in gratitude for the work they had done in raising her.[111]

While the debates in *Komkya* were framed in relation to local identity and employed a language of local patriotism to express the dangers of either changing the system or of failing to change systems perceived as out of date, they echoed arguments going on throughout Tanganyika. The Catholic newspaper *Kiongozi* asked whether it was right for 'modern Africans' to keep the tradition of bridewealth but reduce the level, or abandon it and find a new system, suited to African needs.[112] Others framed the debate in terms of freedom – a letter to the Ukerewe newspaper *Ekome* entitled 'We should give women freedom' described the habit of marrying women off without their permission as akin to slavery and claimed that 'we cannot progress until we have released women from their shackles'.[113]

MAENDELEO IN REVERSE

In his study of the Zambian copperbelt in the aftermath of the collapse in copper prices, James Ferguson wrote eloquently of the way in which the experience of the copperbelt runs counter to ingrained ideas that progress always continues in one direction. For mineworkers in Kitwe, Ferguson found, '[a]ccess to the "first-class" things of this world – cars, suits, fine

---

[109] Letter from J. Tirishia, 'Mahari, Urithi wa Wasichana na Elimu ya Wasichana', *Komkya*, September 1953, p. 3. An eloquently argued response entitled 'Elimu ya wasichana wa Kichagga sio sumu bali ndio maendeleo ya leo na kesho' appeared the following week from V. K. Mali, sent from the Government Girls' School at Tabora. *Komkya*, October 1953, p. 3.

[110] Letter from J. Tirishia, 'Mahari', *Komkya*, September 1953, p. 31.

[111] Letter from Mrs. K. H. Mambo, 'Kuoana Uchaggani', *Komkya*, April 1955, pp. 3, 6. This letter, which appeared two years later when the debate had been reignited, further argued that the gifts which the parents made to the new couple generally exceeded that given as bridewealth.

[112] Editorial, 'Mahari', *Kiongozi*, April 1953, p. 1.

[113] Letter from Ladislaus Luhuta, 'Tuwape Uhuru Wanawake', *Ekome ya Bukerebe*, June 1952, p. 2. TNA 41167.

clothes, a decent necktie – was not something to look forward to in an anticipated future but something to remember from a prosperous past – a past now "gone, gone never to return again."[114] Ferguson contrasts this sense of loss in the 1980s with the greater optimism of the 1960s. Yet in 1940s and 1950s Tanganyika, *maendeleo* was already well understood to be fragile.

Many letters complained about the risks posed by those who spoke against progress, often targeting an undefined group of elders. In this vein, a letter published in the Ukerewe newspaper *Ekome* in 1952 took aim against those elders who compared the past with the present and claimed that the past was better. Elders claimed that whites had brought illness to the land, by making it impossible for witches to be dealt with effectively. But these elders had, the letter argued, forgotten the bad aspects of the past. 'They forget that their fathers were captured into slavery in the days of the Arabs.' Life was violent, and survival depended on military success. In contrast, the British government had put an end to slavery and calmed the land, allowing everyone to live in peace. This made progress (*maendeleo*) and success possible.[115] In a similar vein, another letter attacked those people who accused others who had made money and sought to build a better house or dress well of seeking to be like Europeans. Those who criticized progress were 'enemies of *ustaarabu* and *maendeleo*' who sought to keep everyone living as they had in the past, and they should be ignored by those with education.[116] In similar vein, a letter from Bernard A. M. Daniel, of St. Andrew's College in Minaki, to the district newspaper *Habari za Upare* in 1952 argued that although the Pare had recently made excellent progress in matters of 'farming, business, education and other elements of modern civilization', jealousy, lack of trust and corruption now endangered this progress. He ended by saying that 'if we do not abandon these bad habits, our *maendeleo* will not come at all quickly.'[117]

Others claimed that it was the youth who were responsible for endangering *maendeleo*. A letter printed in *Komkya* in May 1955

---

[114] James Ferguson, *Expectations of Modernity: Myths and Meanings of life on the Zambian Copperbelt* (Berkeley: University of California Press, 1999), p. 13.

[115] Letter from Bernatus s/o Zephania, 'Mawazo ya Wazee yamewaingia hata Vijana', *Ekome ya Bukerebe*, June 1952, p. 3.

[116] Letter from Nomezi Chrysostome, 'Anataka kuwa kama Mzungu', *Ekome*, August 1952, p. 3.

[117] Letter from Bernard A. M. Daniel, 'Malendeleo na ubovu wa Wapare', *Habari za Upare*, November 1952, pp. 8–9, TNA 41176.

accepted that some young people were decent, but railed against those who spent their time drinking or playing cards, ran off to town when there was farming to be done, and expected their fathers to pay for them to marry wives whom they then fought with and drove away.[118] He called on parents and elders to put a stop to this behaviour, 'which sends us backwards'.[119]

CONCLUSION

By exploring public debate with a particular focus on conceptualizations of *maendeleo*, ranging from debates over wealth to debates over gender relations, we have uncovered a set of reflections on social change and hinted at some of the political questions which these reflections provoked. Although such reflections were taking place across Africa, the nature of the public space created by the press in Tanganyika was also distinctive. As we saw in the first section of the chapter, in contrast to other parts of East Africa where political space was divided by language and the vernacular press was dominated by the often patriarchal concerns of local patriots, the more amorphous public addressed in Swahili allowed for a greater openness. It also meant that shared languages for reflecting on political and social change were developing over the course of the twentieth century. Phrases like 'unity is strength' were shared in two senses. They constituted a political language shared by colonial officials and African contributors to the press, though their practical meaning could be contested and they could often be employed to very different ends. They were also shared in the sense that they were used across the territory, and were not restricted to particular localities, though the presence of shared languages did not mean absolute uniformity, and as we have seen, there was also space for the expression of local patriotism and for discussing locally specific problems.

This chapter has sought to set out the parameters of this public space, but it has also traced the narratives at work within it, and identified both an overarching liberal narrative of progress, defined by self-help, association and global comparison, and its underbelly, a darker story of ambivalence, fear and disagreement about the implications of social change. By tracing this thinking, we can better see the context in which new political thinking developed during this period. The fragility of progress, and

[118] Letter from Honorati S. Martin, 'Tabia za Vijana', *Komkya*, 15 May 1955, p. 3.
[119] Ibid.

indeed the perceived fragility of social relations more widely, inspired a search for new institutions of protection as well as calls to maintain or resurrect old institutions, in ways which could be either innovative or conservative. As we move on in the next chapter to consider political reform agendas which emerged after 1945, we should remember both the optimism of the period and the ambivalence and concern which political and social change provoked.

2

Transnational Languages of Democracy after 1945

In 1942, as politicians and intellectuals across the British Empire recovered from the shock of the fall of Singapore to the Japanese, the West African Students' Union joined activists from around the world in writing to the periodical *Empire*, journal of the British Fabian Colonial Bureau which was part of the left of centre Fabian Society, to insist that, for them, the world had now changed forever. They called on Britain to change its approach to its Empire and institute rapid reform. 'In the interest of Freedom, Justice and true Democracy', they wrote, 'and in view of the lessons of Malaya and Burma, as well as the obvious need of giving the peoples of the Empire something to fight for, the West African Students' Union of Great Britain strongly urges the British Government to grant to the British West African colonies and protectorates *internal self-government now*, with a *definite guarantee of complete self-government within five years of the war*.'[1]

Similar declarations came from East Africa. The editor of the African independent newspaper *Kwetu* wrote in 1941,

If India is to have her HOME RULE as a reward for her sacrifices... will it mean a little more social freedom and direct representation for the native? The African has done his duty ... in a war that only indirectly concerned him, will the victory be the old fable to him or is he going to be allowed a share of it this time – a share which will not make him bitterly regret his many losses and sacrifices? *Kwetu* had only one conclusion to come to: '"The orange that is squeezed too hard yields a

---

[1] No author, 'A Letter from the West African Students' Union,' *Empire*, 5, 1, May 1942, 4. Italics in original.

bitter juice". We must go back to Mr Kenyatta's fine conclusion too: "WE ASK FOR A GOOD DEMOCRATIC GOVERNMENT".[2]

The Second World War, particularly the years between the promulgation of the Atlantic Charter in August 1941 and the ratifying of the Universal Declaration of Human Rights in December 1948, marked a rupture in international political thinking. For the first time, the right to self-government was established as a universal goal, enshrined in the founding documents of the United Nations. The Universal Declaration of Human Rights similarly marked a new departure from previous traditions of political thinking.[3] For the first time, diplomats and philosophers from across the world set out to create a document that would apply to all humankind. At the heart of the new political thinking of what we might term the 'United Nations moment' was the principle that power should lie with the people, often described as a commitment to democracy.

The apparent convergence of political thinking implied by the creation of new international institutions and shared documents with universal ambition in this 1940s moment is remarkable in the history of the twentieth century. However, we should pause to reflect on what this convergence means. For shared political languages did not indicate unanimity of political thinking. Very often, apparent consensus masked important divergences in understanding, and beneath apparently universal and universalizing languages of political reform lay different conceptions of the political subject. When activists and intellectuals across the world wrote in favour of 'democracy', they did so in answer to different problems and in pursuit of very different political ends.

This has implications for the political reform projects which emerged from the 1940s and helps explain why a transnational discourse developed in divergent ways in local settings, both in the late colonial period explored here and in the postcolonial state to which we turn in Chapter 7.[4] Breaking down democracy into three models, David Held draws a distinction between 'direct or participatory democracy', 'liberal or representative democracy', and finally socialist or 'one-party democracy'. This distinction is particularly helpful in thinking about the way the word was used in mid-twentieth-century debates. Anticolonial activists understood

---

[2] Nicholas J. Westcott, *The Impact of the Second World War on Tanganyika, 1939–1949.* Unpublished PhD thesis, University of Cambridge (1982), pp. 304–305.

[3] I am grateful to Annabel Brett for emphasizing this point in discussion.

[4] For a comparative example from West Africa, see Frederick C. Schaffer, *Democracy in Translation: Understanding Politics in an Unfamiliar Culture* (Ithaca, NY and London: Cornell University Press, 1998).

'democracy' to imply the equal participation of all citizens in their own government.[5] Yet British officials were more comfortable with a version of the gradualist path to representative democracy which Britain had itself followed, and which did not imply universal equality, for the right to involvement in the political process could in their eyes properly be limited only to those deemed politically mature.[6]

In this chapter, I start by setting out the emergence of a transnational language of democracy and democratization which dominated global debate and structured colonial political reform projects after 1945. Yet behind apparent consensus lay significant differences of political theory, between on the one hand a conception of the individual as autonomous and rights-bearing, and on the other a conception of the individual embedded in society. To understand these differences demands that we recognise the conservative as well as the radical potential of the postwar moment. I then move to briefly discuss competing colonial reform programmes in Tanganyika in the period after 1945 in light of this.

The focus in this chapter is on transnational arguments more than arguments taking place within Tanganyika. Although colonial officials in Tanganyika claimed that they were engaging in a process of democratization, the term 'democracy' was not widely used in the Swahili public sphere until the 1950s; rather the language was one of 'representation', and this is the focus of Chapter 3. Yet the ideas explored here are important not only because they structured colonial reform projects in postwar Tanganyika, but also for two further reasons. First, as we shall see in Chapters 6 and 7, languages of democracy would become increasingly important in Tanganyika's Swahiliphone public sphere from the late 1950s. Second, they show us that as languages of democracy were universalized after 1945 they also increasingly functioned as sites of contestation. Crucially, the ideas discussed here serve to remind us that the political thought of the mid-twentieth century was characterized by a concern with community and the place of individuals within social relationships as much as it was by projects which understood individual rights as a route to liberation and freedom from oppressive power. This was true at the transnational level, but it would be equally true of

---

[5] This was the sense implied by the black intellectuals chronicled by Penny von Eschen in *Race against Empire: Black Americans and Anticolonialism, 1937–1957* (Ithaca, NY: Cornell University Press, 1997).

[6] David Held, 'Democracy: From City-states to a Cosmopolitan Order?' in David Held (ed.), *Prospects for Democracy, North, South, East, West* (Cambridge: Polity Press, 1993), pp. 13–52.

political argument in decolonization-era Tanzania, as we shall see in the chapters which follow.

THE 'UN MOMENT' AND THE EMERGENCE OF A TRANSNATIONAL LANGUAGE OF DEMOCRACY

The years between 1941 and 1948 served to crystallize a long history of transnational political thinking and activism which demanded equal rights for all, including the right to political participation. In a rich intellectual history of pan-Asian and pan-Islamic thought, Cemil Aydin has shown that in Asia, as late-nineteenth-century imperialism increasingly came to rest on racial exclusion, intellectuals who had once engaged productively with apparently universalist discourses emanating from the West became disillusioned by the West's failure to honour their own universalism.[7] They turned instead towards other visions of world order which provided a mode of claiming an equal place in the world.[8] Pan-Africanism had the potential to serve similar purposes in the Atlantic world. In the 1930s and early 1940s, the development of a transnational print media helped to produce a diasporic identity which linked the shared problems of Africans and African Americans to an imperial economic and political system which systematically denied social and political rights on the basis of race. Again, this constituted a claim to equality within a new international order.[9]

An argument for equality between peoples was echoed in national contexts by the growing power of mass politics and arguments for equality and universal political rights as a foundational principle within nations. In India, by 1946 the Indian National Congress had moved to a position of supporting universal suffrage. C. A. Bayly has argued that this move derived in part from a growing trust of the people and the way in which the principle of equality was heightened by the Second World War, when Congress leaders had argued that if they were to fight against fascism they must be 'acknowledged as a democratic nation themselves.'[10]

The wartime moment had deep roots, yet it nevertheless constituted a watershed. If the principle of equality between peoples and races was

---

[7] Cemil Aydin, *Politics of Anti-Westernism in Asia: Visions of Pan-Islamic and Pan-Asian Thought* (New York: Columbia University Press, 2007).

[8] Aydin, *Politics of Anti-Westernism in Asia*, p. 6.

[9] Von Eschen, *Race against Empire*, p. 22.

[10] C. A. Bayly, *Recovering Liberties: Indian Thought in the Age of Liberalism and Empire* (Cambridge: Cambridge University Press, 2012), p. 309.

acquiring universal status in the 1930s and 1940s, the Second World War played a crucial role in coupling this principle with a language of freedom, self-determination and the 'democratic principle', and reconceptualizing the argument in terms not of equality of peoples but rather on the basis of individual rights.[11] From the declaration of war in September 1939 the British described the war as a war for freedom, an argument reinforced in the eyes of colonial subjects by the Atlantic Charter of 1941 with its famous third clause promising to 'respect the right of all peoples to choose the form of Government under which they will live'.[12]

These declarations were overheard, as it were, in the wider world. Nationalists in Tanganyika had copies of the Atlantic Charter in their personal papers.[13] In the Swahili press in Tanganyika, links were made with Tanganyika's own history of German rule. For the correspondent to *Mambo Leo* E. Hasani Bahsan bin Mwalim, this had been a war for freedom, for 'if the British Empire had not stood firm with her allies, the Nazis would have put people into slavery', as they had done in Tanganyika in the past. Slavery was now gone, and freedom achieved.[14] Another correspondent recounted the way that elders asked for news of the war, and their children responded that 'the war is over, the British have fulfilled their promise to remove slavery from the world'.[15]

The association of war aims with the defence of freedom provided an opening to speak about the lack of freedom within colonial contexts, and a language of freedom, equality and anti-imperialism served to unite activists and intellectuals who had often had little in common in the past. In the African American press, liberals and leftists came together to hold Churchill and Roosevelt to the anti-imperialist interpretation of the Atlantic Charter, warning them that if the racial discrimination was not tackled 'the colored peoples of India, China, Burma, Africa, the West Indies, the United States and other parts of the world will continue to

---

[11] Saul Dubow, *South Africa's Struggle for Human Rights* (Athens, OH: Ohio University Press, 2012), p. 56.

[12] Alfred W. B. Simpson, *Human Rights and the End of Empire: Britain and the Genesis of the European Convention* (Oxford: Oxford University Press, 2001), p. 180. On the making of the Atlantic Charter, and its reception in Africa, see Elizabeth Borgwardt, *A New Deal for the World: America's Vision for Human Rights* (Cambridge, MA: Belknap Press, 2005), p. 29.

[13] Westcott, 'The Impact of the Second World War', p. 304, fn. 105.

[14] Letter from E. Hasan Bahsan bin Mwalim, 'Vita ya Uhuru', *Mambo Leo*, January 1946, p. 2.

[15] Letter from K. I. S. Milimba, 'Minong'ono imekwisha imebaki labda', *Mambo Leo*, March 1946, p. 25.

view sceptically assertions that this is a war for freedom and equality.'[16] In South Africa, the African National Congress took the Atlantic Charter as the basis of a claim to freedom and called for the immediate granting of 'full citizenship rights such as are enjoyed by all Europeans in South Africa'.[17] In Britain too, Labour politicians and others on the left rejected Churchill's efforts to restrict the right of self-determination to those under Nazi rule in Europe and called instead for a new 'Colonial Charter' which would, in the words of the prominent internationalist Julian Huxley, be 'for the colonial peoples what Magna Carta was to medieval England or the Declaration of Independence to the infant United States.'[18]

But homology of language did not indicate consensus. Rather, shared languages of rights, freedom and democracy provided a space for argument.[19] Unexpected alliances emerged and then dissolved almost as quickly as they had appeared. And throughout the second half of the 1940s, competing agendas jostled for dominance. We can see this very clearly if we look at discourses of rights. There were profound differences among those using a language of rights, and these differences crossed national and political divides. Conceptions of personhood and the relationship of an individual to his or her community were at the heart of these arguments. Were the subjects of universal human rights to be understood as free-standing rights-bearing individuals, or were they to be understood as embedded in a community?[20] For this latter group, rights and duties were inseparable.

While the Anglo-American tradition of individual rights is well studied, the second set of ideas has only recently attracted renewed attention, in part as attention has turned to those involved in the drafting of the Universal Declaration of Human Rights who came from a Catholic tradition. As Samuel Moyn shows, concepts of 'personalism' began to develop in interwar Europe as a third way between individualism and

---

[16] Von Eschen, *Race against Empire*, p. 42.

[17] Dubow, *South Africa's Struggle for Human Rights*, p. 57.

[18] No author, "Colonial Charter", Empire, 5, 2, July 1942, p. 1; Julian Huxley, 'Colonies in a Changing World', in Julian Huxley (ed.), *Man in the Modern World* (London: Chatto and Windus, 1947), pp. 235–248, p. 240.

[19] Kenneth Cmiel, 'Human Rights, Freedom of Information and the Origins of Third-World Solidarity', in Mark Philip Bradley and Patrice Petro, eds., *Truth Claims: Representation and Human Rights* (London and New Brunswick, NJ: Rutgers University Press, 2002), pp. 107–130, p. 108.

[20] Samuel Moyn, 'Personalism, Community and the Origins of Human Rights', in Stefan-Ludwig Hoffman (ed.), *Human Rights in the Twentieth Century*, pp. 85–106, pp. 99, 105; Mary Ann Glendon, *A World Made New: Eleanor Roosevelt and the Universal Declaration of Human Rights* (New York: Random House, 2001), p. 75.

communitarian thinking. The Catholic philosopher Jacques Maritain played a crucial role in linking personalism, the natural law tradition and a language of human rights through his book, *Droits de l'homme et la loi naturelle*, published in French in 1942 and in English as *The Rights of Man and Natural Law* in 1944.[21] In it, he made a case for a 'new Democracy', based not on bourgeois-individualism or on the totalitarian model, but rather on a shared 'political task' which, for Maritain, was 'the good human life of the multitude.'[22] The sole reason why, in Maritain's view, 'men assemble within the political community is to *procure the common good of the multitude, in such a manner that each concrete person, not only in a privileged class but throughout the whole mass, may truly reach that measure of independence which is proper to civilized life and which is insured alike by the economic guarantees of work and property, political rights, civil virtues, and the cultivation of the mind.*'[23]

Maritain's thinking emerged from a distinctly European intellectual context, but a similar emphasis on the human person was developed by other Catholic thinkers from around the world. Through the Lebanese philosopher Charles Malik in particular, a language of personhood found its way into the Universal Declaration of Human Rights. As he wrote in 1951, 'The ultimate ground of all our freedom is the Christian doctrine of the inviolability of the human person'.[24] For Malik, personhood was not the same as individualism. As Mary Ann Glendon explains, 'Malik saw man as uniquely valuable in himself, but as constituted in part by and through his relationships with others – his family, his community, his nation, and his God.'[25]

This stress on human relationships echoed the views of many others from Latin America, Asia and beyond. In 1946 Panama proposed an international bill of rights which 'contained a list of specific duties almost as long as the list of rights.'[26] A committee set up by UNESCO in 1947 to seek the views of thinkers from around the world to feed

[21] Moyn, 'Personalism, Community and the Origins of Human Rights', p. 94.
[22] Jacques Maritain, *The Rights of Man and Natural Law* (London: The Centenary Press, 1944), p. 26.
[23] Ibid. p. 27. Italics in original.
[24] Moyn, 'Personalism, Community and the Origins of Human Rights', p. 99.
[25] Mary Ann Glendon, 'Introduction', in Habib C. Malik, *The Challenge of Human Rights: Charles Malik and the Universal Declaration* (Oxford: Charles Malik Foundation, 2000), pp. 1–9, p. 3.
[26] Cmiel, 'Human Rights, Freedom of Information and the Origins of Third-World Solidarity', p. 118.

into the drafting process of the Universal Declaration of Human Rights received seventy responses from Asia, America and Europe. Many respondents from around the world stressed duties and relationships between individuals within societies as much as individual rights.[27] As the Indian nationalist Mohandas Gandhi famously wrote in his contribution, he had learned from his 'illiterate but wise mother' that 'all rights to be deserved and preserved came from duty well done.'[28] The Chinese philosopher Chung-Shu Lo wrote that 'the basic ethical concept of Chinese social political relations is the fulfilment of the duty to one's neighbour, rather than the claiming of rights.'[29] Similarly, the French Jesuit Teilhard de Chardin and the Spanish philosopher Salvador de Madariaga called for a 'focus on "man in society" rather than as an isolated individual'.[30]

Thus although the drafting committee of the UN Universal Declaration of Human Rights included those like Eleanor Roosevelt who drew on a long-standing Anglo-American tradition of individual rights and for whom the focus on duties was an excuse for repression, the voices of those like Charles Malik, Carlos Romulo and René Cassin should be taken seriously.[31] They helped ensure that the document which finally resulted was a compromise, and one which could be used in very different ways in different contexts. In Samuel Moyn's words, it was, 'a profoundly communitarian document – precisely a moral repudiation of dangerous individualism, albeit one equally intended to steer equally clear of communism.'[32]

But they were also espousing a political philosophy which could easily tend towards conservatism, which reminds us that the 1945 moment was characterized by this tendency as well as the reemergence of radical languages of rights. Focussing on individuals as members of society rather than as free-standing rights-bearing individuals left open the possibility that human flourishing might come through the reconstruction of community on a new basis, and could be compatible with arguments for the maintenance of hierarchy and older forms of social inequality.

---

[27] Glendon, *A World Made New*, p. 75.
[28] Mahatma Gandhi, 'Letter to the Director-General of UNESCO', in Jacques Maritain (ed.), *Human Rights: Comments and Interpretations* (London: Allan Wingate, 1949), p. 18.
[29] Glendon, *A World Made New*, p. 75.
[30] Ibid. p. 76.
[31] Cmiel, 'Human Rights, Freedom of Information and the Origins of Third-World Solidarity', p. 118.
[32] Moyn, 'Personalism, Community and the Origins of Human Rights', p. 105.

DEMOCRACY AND THE LIMITS OF UNIVERSALISM

As the end of the Second World War approached, politicians, international statesmen and intellectuals turned their attention to the new world order that was to come. For anticolonial activists, this new moment in world affairs offered the possibility of reshaping power relations in specific local contexts, as well as the hint of an even greater revolution in the global world order. As Mark Mazower has argued, 1945 and the foundation of the United Nations marked a break in the constitution of the world order in that it marked the end of the 'concept of civilization as an ordering principle for international politics' and the first time in which 'the question of rights was detached from the notion of civilization.'[33] Although the UN did not take over supervision of all colonial territories, as some had hoped, the foundation of the Trusteeship Council demonstrated the change which had taken place in comparison to its predecessor, the Permanent Mandates Commission of the League of Nations. In his speech opening the Trusteeship Council in 1947, the Secretary General of the United Nations would explicitly define the mission of the Trusteeship Council as time-limited, noting that '[f]ull success... will automatically put this organ out of existence, since your ultimate goal is to give the Trust Territories full statehood.'[34]

For the African nationalists who petitioned world leaders gathering in San Francisco in 1945, democracy was defined in opposition to colonialism. Democracy meant first and foremost self-government, taking back control from colonial rule which could not, by its nature, be democratic. Colonial rule was the antithesis of rule by the people. As world leaders met to discuss the postwar settlement, the Nigerian nationalist Mbono Ojike argued against British plans for Trusteeship which he saw as an 'equivocation for maintaining the status quo.' 'Africans', he wrote, 'want self-government comparable to that of the Americans... They want democracy, and they want it now... The dates for the achievement of

---

[33] Mark Mazower, 'The end of civilization and the rise of human rights: the mid-twentieth-century disjuncture', in Stefan-Ludwig Hoffmann (ed.), *Human Rights in the Twentieth Century* (Cambridge: Cambridge University Press, 2010), pp. 29–44, p. 30.

[34] United Nations Trusteeship Council [UNTC], First session, 26 March 1947, *Official Records*, p. 5. For the most complete account of Tanganyika's relationship with the Trusteeship Council, see Ullrich Lohrmann, *Voices from Tanganyika: Great Britain, the United Nations and the Decolonisation of a Trust Territory* (Berlin: Lit., 2007). See also Margaret L. Bates, *Tanganyika under British Administration, 1920–1955*, unpublished DPhil thesis, University of Oxford (1957); B. T. G. Chidzero, *Tanganyika and International Trusteeship* (London: Oxford University Press, 1961).

freedom for each colony must be set now – and the farthest date should be 15 years.'[35]

For nationalists, democracy was self-evidently incompatible with colonialism. But for others, this opposition was less clear cut. For the Colonial Office civil servant Hilton Poynton, speaking in front of the Fourth Committee of the General Assembly in 1947, the 'colonial system was a practical illustration of democracy under tuition.'[36] This statement is important both because it demonstrates the extent to which the language of democracy had, by 1947, become an unproblematic 'good', and because it speaks to an alternative mode of thinking about democracy which was embedded in British political thinking and which to some degree crossed party divides.

The expansion of the franchise in Britain in 1918 to include all adult males and some adult women led to a new emphasis on preparing new voters to exercise their rights responsibly. As the historian of interwar Britain Helen McCarthy has argued, this 'theme was evident in many aspects of interwar culture', present 'in the speeches of party leaders, in the sermons of archbishops and Free Church ministers, in the educational broadcasts of the BBC and in the creative output of a new generation of progressive filmmakers, publishers and artists.'[37] Voluntary associations, McCarthy argues, were particularly important 'schools of citizenship' for interwar Britons, and understood to play a crucial role in ensuring that Britain avoided the totalitarian path taken by other states in the same period.[38]

Democracy, in this reading, was a set of practices which would act as a bulwark against totalitarianism. This opposition between democracy and totalitarianism remained a prominent strand of British thinking. And if equipping individuals for democracy required training, this was understood to be doubly true in colonial settings. For Julian Huxley wrote in 1941, developing Britain's colonial empire was a crucial part 'of the job of British democracy outside its own country.'[39] This did not, however,

[35] Cited in Marika Sherwood, '"There Is No New Deal for the Blackman in San Francisco": African Attempts to Influence the Founding Conference of the United Nations, April–July 1945', *International Journal of African Historical Studies*, 29 (1996), 71–94, p. 86.

[36] Simpson, *Human Rights*, p. 294; Mark Mazower, *Governing the World: the History of an Idea* (London: Penguin Books, 2012), p. 251.

[37] Helen McCarthy, 'Associational Voluntarism in Interwar Britain', in Matthew Hilton and James McKay (eds.), *The Ages of Voluntarism: How We Got to the Big Society* (Oxford: Oxford University Press, 2011), pp. 47–68, p. 54.

[38] Ibid., p. 54.

[39] Julian Huxley, *Democracy Marches* (London: Chatto and Windus, 1941), p. 85.

mean 'immediate political democracy with its apparatus of votes and elected representatives', rather it meant 'a steadily increasing measure of self-government.'[40]

The emphasis on gradualism and the argument that democracy required tuition can be found too in the writings of the Fabian Colonial Bureau. After the landslide victory of the Labour Party in Britain in 1945, the Fabian periodical *Empire* recognized in a postelection editorial that Labour's victory had 'aroused the keenest expectations throughout the Empire', and that from 'Colony after Colony come letters and newspaper articles expressing confidence that at last the problems and grievances which have agitated the people for so long will be resolutely tackled.' But the Fabians rejected calls for immediate self-government, arguing that '[n]o declaration of 'freedom' or 'self-determination' is in itself an answer. Political 'freedom' will not solve the problems of finding a fair price in the world markets, of defence, of putting a halt to soil erosion, of good labour conditions.'[41] The answer was, rather, 'advance towards democratic self-government wherever possible'.[42] Reflecting on 'disappointed hopes' a year later, *Empire* accepted that '[t]hese slow, painstaking and often painful steps towards democratic self-government have given the world the impression that the Colonies' advance to 'freedom', under the British method, must take centuries; and in the frustration of the colonial peoples with what seems to be a snail-like progress, the suspicion has grown that Britain has no intention of ever relinquishing control.'[43] But they continued to defend their rejection of 'slogans such as 'freedom for the Colonies' and their support for 'stable constitutional evolution'.[44] This had implications for the British approach to political reform in colonial settings, to which we now turn.

POLITICAL REFORM IN NEW YORK
AND TANGANYIKA

If languages of 'democracy' and commitment to 'democratic principles' were used in different ways by different people engaged with the making

---

[40] Ibid., p. 93.
[41] Editorial, 'The Labour Victory and the Colonies', *Empire*, 8, 3, September–October 1945, 1–2, p. 1.
[42] Ibid., p. 1.
[43] Editorial, 'Advance to democracy', *Empire*, 9, 6, November 1946, 1–2, p. 1. See also 'Disappointed hopes', *Empire*, 9, 1, May–June 1946, 1–2.
[44] Editorial, 'Advance to Democracy', p. 1.

of the new world order, it should not be surprising that there was no uniformity in thinking about how to achieve 'democratization' through political reform, a process which colonial powers, whose actions were now under the scrutiny of the Trusteeship Council, were committed to. How were 'democratic principles' to be achieved, and would their achievement take different forms in different settings?

At the Trusteeship Council, debates over 'democratization' showed up a sharp divide between representatives of the Soviet Union who understood democratization to mean sweeping away existing social structures and the attitudes of British representatives charged with defending British policy in Tanganyika who understood 'democratization' as grafting 'western methods of autonomous government upon native practices'.[45] British representatives at the Trusteeship Council in 1950 confidently defended their approach as being akin to that of a gardener:

It would be easy for the administrative gardener to abandon the patient task of watering, weeding and watching the natural growth of his young political seedlings and to place them all in hot-houses to bring them rapidly to an outward show of maturity. He would no doubt win applause for such a step. But the life of the hot-house plant was short compared to that of the outdoor variety.[46]

But in fact the process of political reform as it was being enacted in British colonial settings suggested that the process was not as simple as this description suggested. In an article published in January 1947 entitled 'African Tribes and Western Democracy', the Fabian socialist Rita Hinden drew attention to a divide which was emerging between two modes of political reform. As Hinden explained:

In every African Colony one crucial problem stares us in the face when it comes to constitutional advance – how to discover the link between the traditional framework of tribal society, which is still so potent a reality in African life, and the Western forms of Parliamentary democracy which, under European influence, are developing in almost all Colonies.[47]

A dual process was taking place – the democratization of Native Councils at the local level on the one hand, and the expansion of central Legislative and Executive Councils at the centre on the other. Where, Hinden asked, 'do these two parallel lines of progress meet – if indeed they should meet

[45] UNTC, Third Session, 30 June 1948, *Official Records*, p. 154.
[46] UNTC, Sixth Session, 1 February 1950, *Official Records*, p. 74.
[47] Rita Hinden, 'African Tribes and Western Democracy', *Empire*, 9, 8, January 1947, 5–6, p. 5.

at all?' The result, Hinden suggested, was the development of a hybrid form, embodied by chiefs acquiring a role on central representative bodies. Hinden recognized the concern which many educated Africans felt about this, but suggested that this was not necessarily to be feared, simply because it did 'not conform to British practice at home.'[48] Something like an electoral college system might, in fact, be the best way for the wider African population, beyond the elites, to achieve political representation. At the same time, Hinden regretted other aspects of the reform process, notably the growth of separate electorates for different communities.

Hinden's article indicates a sense that there might be more than one way of building a democratic system. We are presented, in effect, with a conceptualization of a distinctively African solution to the problem of how to achieve rule by the people, though coupled with an awareness that this runs counter to other processes at work. In suggesting that there might not be one single path to democracy but that it might take different forms in different contexts, Hinden echoed the views of some reformers on the ground in Tanganyika.

BUILDING DEMOCRACY IN LATE COLONIAL TANGANYIKA

After 1945, younger colonial officials, aware of the fast pace of political change across the world and in some cases influenced by wartime service alongside colonial troops in the decolonizing world, pushed for reform which would move Tanganyika away from the interwar system of indirect rule through a hereditary chief and towards a system of local government with a role for educated non-chiefs. Developments across the territory accelerated after 1947 when the Labour Colonial Secretary Arthur Creech Jones set out his plans for movement towards representative government. He contrasted the relatively 'static policy' of indirect rule with the new postwar era, writing:

We are now called to apply a new yard stick to an awakening African society. We use the word development to describe the new process. Development or progress, planned and inter-related change and improvement in all fields, economic, social and political, are the keynotes of our present policy.[49]

---

[48] Ibid., p. 6.
[49] Arthur Creech-Jones, 'The Place of African Local Administration in Colonial Policy', *Journal of African Administration*, 1 (1949), 3–6. p. 4; D. A. Low, *Eclipse of Empire* (Cambridge: Cambridge University Press, 1991), p. 202.

Colonial officials in postwar Tanganyika recalled that they understood their task as lying in the democratization of local government.[50] What this meant in practice was a shift away from the focus on African chiefs which had characterized the political systems of the 1920s and 1930s and a growing emphasis on ensuring African representation in local councils. For the colonial state, increasing African representation was part of the wider state-building efforts of what has been termed the 'second colonial occupation' of the period after 1945.[51] New social services and development projects required revenue, and bringing more African representatives into local government was one way of managing the ever fraught task of increasing taxes and handling the opposition which development schemes often provoked.[52]

But beneath the common language of 'democratization' used by the colonial government after 1945, there was a contrast between a gradualist approach to political change, based on a conception of the political subject as a member of a community, and an alternative conception of political change based on transferring power rapidly to individuals whose claim to authority rested on literacy or wealth. In Tanganyika, one of the most thoughtful agents of colonial reform projects on the ground was the Viennese anthropologist Hans Cory, appointed to the post of Government Anthropologist on 1 January 1945 as movements towards political reform gathered pace.[53] Cory understood democratization to mean moving away from a system of European-imposed chiefs and towards institutions which were more responsive to the will of the people. Unlike those who saw politics as something which needed to be 'introduced' to Tanganyika, he insisted that there was an already existing

[50] Interview with E. G. Rowe, 24 September 1969, RHO Mss.Afr.s.1698, p. 18.

[51] D. A. Low and J. M. Lonsdale, 'Introduction: Towards the New Order 1945–1963', in D. A. Low and Alison Smith (eds.), *History of East Africa*, Vol. 3, (Oxford: Clarendon Press, 1976), pp. 1–63; Tanganyika Territory, *Development of Tanganyika: Report of the Post-war Planning Advisory Committee* (Dar es Salaam: Government Printer, 1944), p. 1.

[52] Rohland Schuknecht, *British Colonial Development Policy after the Second World War: The Case of Sukumaland, Tanganyika* (Berlin: Lit. Verlag, 2010).

[53] University College Dar es Salaam, *The Papers of Hans Cory in the Library of the University College Dar es Salaam*, Dar es Salaam, 1968. Originally from Vienna, Hans Cory moved to Africa before the First World War, settling permanently in 1926. On his role in researching customary law, see Jennifer Widner, *Building the Rule of Law: Francis Nyalali and the Road to Judicial Independence in Africa* (New York and London: W. W. Norton, 2001). On the ways in which his writings about law and custom sparked new literature disagreeing with his analysis, see Thomas Geider, 'Swahilisprachige Ethnographien (ca. 1890-heute): Produktionsbedingungen und Autoreninteressen', in Heike Behrend und Thomas Geider (eds.), *Afrikaner Schreiben Zurück: Texte und Bilder afrikanischer Ethnographien* (Köln: Koeppe, 1998), pp. 41–79.

political life, but that colonial officialdom understood little about it. In a paper written in March 1950, he argued that the reason for slow economic development lay 'in the ignorance and fundamental strangeness which exists between Europeans and Africans, between teachers and pupils. The teacher knows only the lessons but not the pupil; he knows only the school but not the pupils' home life. The pupils are adults, citizens of a community, leaders and protectors of families, subjects of an indigenous authority which shows one face to the teacher and one to the pupil.'[54] Of this home life, the most important aspect was, for Cory, 'the political right of the individual which implies his security within his community. No tribal structure as it has developed in contact with European Colonial Powers has yet taken into consideration such rights.'[55]

Cory's task, carried out most fully in Sukumaland in north-western Tanganyika, was to investigate the local political culture, and then to create institutions which grew organically out of it. In this project, he had something in common with the German missionaries of the earlier twentieth century, who sought to introduce Christianity through local social structures, rather than against them.[56] He was insistent that change should come from within, not through external imposition, writing in 1950 that 'the way of living of one race cannot be definitely designed by another, especially under present circumstances where the element of freedom is the decisive factor.'[57] Moreover, it would inevitably take distinctive local forms. He was arguing, in short, against the notion of a 'one size fits all' model of democratic development, and in favour of locally specific solutions. His Sukumaland colleague Donald Malcolm put it succinctly: 'Democracy has many forms; representative government as practised in Great Britain is one; it may not be audacious to suggest that Sukumaland has another.'[58]

Crucially, Cory did not believe this rejection of universal structures to be a rejection of the principle of democracy. Writing in 1953 at the

---

[54] Hans Cory, 'The Necessity for Co-ordination of Economic and Political Development', TNA 215/647/2, f. 335.

[55] Ibid.

[56] Ernst Jaeschke, *Bruno Gutmann: His Life, His Thoughts and His Work* (Erlangen, Germany: Verlag der Ev.-Luth. Mission, 1985); Klaus Fiedler, *Christianity and African culture: Conservative German Protestant Missionaries in Tanzania, 1900–1940* (Leiden, The Netherlands: Brill, 1996).

[57] Cory, 'The Necessity for Co-ordination of Economic and Political Development', TNA 215/647/2, f. 342, p. 8.

[58] D. W. Malcolm, *Sukumaland: An African People and Their Country* (London: Oxford University Press, 1953), p. 106.

height of the Mau Mau uprising in Kenya, his prescriptions for political peace were simple. He believed that reform was essential, and that crucially reforms must be enacted before they were demanded. Moreover, he wrote, 'a democratic constitution offers a great obstacle to revolutionary agitation; I cannot see why this common truth should not be valid in Africa'.[59] But his reforms nevertheless set him apart from much contemporary thinking about political change. In his 'Proposals for Constitutional Reforms of the Sukuma tribal structure', written in 1950, he outlined his plans for representative government at the parish level, defining the parish as units composing between 200 and 400 taxpayers.[60] His sympathy was with the 'common villager', who was confused by the multitude of reforms around him. 'What should he think', Cory asked, 'when he hears that his chief has flown to Iringa to attend a Territorial Cattle Board? And now on top of all this upheaval, for him the caprices of superior beings, he himself is called upon to appear. Now the commoner is pulled out of his hole and dragged forward from his corner.' Although Cory did not regret this development, he nevertheless believed that work was needed to make political engagement meaningful. 'If there is to be any hope that the representatives of the people play their part, they must be given teaching, security, belief in continuity and finally public spirit.'[61]

Cory's reforms aimed at creating just such a public spirit. Beyond constitutional structures, he also sought to construct new rituals for the performance of public office. He outlined ten rules for the Bagunani, or council representatives, to be read in the Sukuma language at the beginning of each Council meeting, a practice which he was sure would have a psychologically beneficial effect' and in line with practice 'all over the world'.[62] The rules stressed the duties and responsibilities of each councillor: their duty to attend meetings regularly, not for money but for the good of their neighbours and children; their duty to protect the weak and poor; their duty to live an 'upright and dignified life' in their community. They were reminded both of the responsibilities of public office, for a '*mugunani* in council has no relatives and no friends', and that on leaving office they would 'become a commoner again'.

---

[59] Hans Cory, 'Maji Maji and Mau Mau', April 1953, Cory Papers 129, University of Dar es Salaam Library.

[60] Hans Cory, 'Proposals for Constitutional Reforms of the Sukuma Tribal Structure', TNA 41462, f. 3a, p. 1.

[61] Ibid., p. 19.

[62] Ibid., p. 11.

While much of this was relatively uncontroversial, Cory laid himself open to the charge that he was too focussed on continuities within African society, and insufficiently aware of the changes underway. He had no sympathy for the idea of a secret ballot, and proposed that '[t]he only council for which the people themselves are the electors is the parish council. From then onwards councils elect a number of delegates for the council on the next level'.[63] But even more controversially, he denied any particular role to the growing numbers of educated Sukuma in the council system. In sharp terms, he argued that '[t]he educated element can only obtain influence in the community by a display of good behaviour, modesty and public spirit; it cannot claim to be a privileged community within a community, the members of which are entitled to public posts because they possess a school certificate. Nowhere in the world are young school students elected or appointed as delegates on the parish level and there is no reason for considering African scholars to be particularly suited to be so.'[64]

Cory was aware that he risked the charge of being opposed to 'progress', but argued that he was not against progress in general, only the 'unbalanced' progress that the colonial state was helping to create. In his 1950 paper on economic and political development he pointed to the context in which what he termed 'intellectual progress' was taking place: 'We open wide the doors to western Culture without reservation to those Africans who have arrived at a certain standard of learning. It would, in fact, be impossible under the present development of the means of communications, press, wireless, aeroplanes and under the influence of our quickly changing minds to hide or distort any aspect of European life. These Africans hear and learn of the European revolutions, fought for the rights of man, they also – either here or in Europe – come into contact with the European mind which at the moment has a strong trend towards equalization.'[65] The result, he feared, would be that such young men would 'begin to consider their home situation' and 'find nothing upon which they could start to build up their self-governing paradise'. With no public forums within which to develop their demands, they would be 'pressed into political secret societies and onto the top of shaky soap boxes from which they address, without sense of responsibility,

---

[63] Ibid., p. 12.
[64] Cory, 'Proposals for Constitutional Reforms', TNA 41462, f. 3A, p. 3.
[65] Hans Cory, 'The Necessity for Co-ordination of Economic and Political Development', TNA 215/647/2, f. 337–338, pp. 3–4.

the political analphabets – the people.'[66] It was the duty of government to develop healthy political institutions before such radicalization occurred.

Cory's position was fully in line with views from above, and particularly from the Governor, Edward Twining. Reflecting on his experiences in Tanganyika after his departure as governor, he reflected that 'Westminster parliamentary democracy may be right in Westminster, but I am not quite so sure that it is always so suitable for an African territory that it should be slavishly copied.'[67] He reiterated his belief that political change must start from the ground up, because 'the tribal system is their sheet anchor, something they know, something they have evolved, something they have developed, and so is the chiefly office.'[68]

Others disagreed. In the early 1950s, A. C. A. Wright, a research officer recently arrived from Uganda, wrote critically of Cory's system which, he felt, left too much power in the hands of the chiefs who, even if elected, were 'still in practice likely to be put in by the "old gang" of headmen and courtiers, who will influence the electors.'[69] These chiefs, according to Wright, 'have had no reason up to date, such as dismissal for unsatisfactory work, to be anything but indifferent and inefficient.' For Wright, the answer was a new local government bureaucracy, which would attract the best African graduates. Headmen should be 'made elective by the local inhabitants on a five year basis', sent for training and paid a decent salary. The aim was to create a culture whereby headmen and tax clerks became 'appointments dependent solely upon merit and not on clan relationships.'[70]

In his evidence to the East African Royal Commission in 1953, Wright dismissed 'projects of building separate "Nations" out of the British created territories of Kenya, "Uganda" and "Tanganyika" as quite absurd', and instead proposed a federal system of enlarged provinces, crossing the existing boundaries of colonial territories.[71] His argument was for 'a confederacy of related tribes forming the "nation" in the classical sense', around which people could base their loyalty and commitment, and which would be both sufficiently diverse and sufficiently coherent.[72]

[66] Ibid., p. 4.
[67] Edward Twining, 'The Last Nine Years in Tanganyika', *African Affairs*, 58 (1959), 15–24, p. 23.
[68] Ibid., p. 23.
[69] Wright, 'The Transition from 'Native Administration' to Local Government', TNA 41462, p. 1.
[70] Ibid., p. 1.
[71] A. C. A. Wright to Chairman, East African Royal Commission, 30 November 1953, TNA UK, CO 892/10/2, f. 3, p. 2.
[72] Ibid., p. 1.

There was also a more fundamental problem, which returns us to the point made by Rita Hinden. Cory's pyramid schemes were intended to start at the bottom and work up, but the colonial state had no intention of allowing the will of the people to speak at the national level. At the same time as it claimed that it was building democratic structures from the bottom up, it was seeking to ensure a multiracial future, and building new 'multiracial' political institutions from the top down. What happened when the two structures met, in the mid-1950s, was a combination of conflict and paralysis.

Cory was concerned with the specificities of the context in which he worked, and this determined the approach he took. But in critiquing a mode of thinking which saw only individual rights bearers and not individuals as members of communities, Cory was, as we have seen, part of a wider moment in mid-twentieth-century thought. Arguments taking place in a postwar transnational public sphere were echoed in local contexts. Colonial reform projects were shaped by such ideas, and these ideas would in turn be echoed in debates in the Swahili public sphere.

CONCLUSION

For most of its history, the concept of democracy had a relatively clear meaning. This derived, as Quentin Skinner argued in 1973, from 'the fact that, until relatively recently, few wished to commend the state of affairs which the term described.'[73] But over the twentieth century this changed. As it came to seem 'a commendable form of government', this produced both a 'debate about what range of circumstances should be held to count as a case of "rule by the people" (and thus a case of democracy)' and a shift whereby 'the use of the term *democracy*' came to perform 'the speech act of commending what is described.'[74] As we have seen, the Second World War was a turning point in this shift towards general commendation.[75] What this meant was that, increasingly over time, different conceptions came to be at play when the same terms, 'democracy' or 'democratization', were used, particularly

---

[73] Quentin Skinner, 'The Empirical Theorists of Democracy and Their Critics: A Plague on Both Their Houses', *Political Theory*, 1 (1979), 287–306, p. 298.

[74] Skinner, 'The Empirical Theorists of Democracy', p. 299.

[75] John Dunn, *Setting the People Free: The Story of Democracy* (London: Atlantic Books, 2005), p. 156.

when used cross-culturally or in translation, but also within national contexts.[76]

For the political theorist David Runciman, '[t]he hallmark of the modern idea of democracy is its adaptability. It can accommodate forms of politics that are hierarchical as well as inclusive; it can be identified with leaders as well as citizens; it can combine egalitarianism with many different forms of inequality.'[77] As we have seen in this discussion, the apparent triumph of the 'democratic principle' in 1945 concealed the fact that it continued to mean very different things to different people. For some it required urgent radical reform, for others, reform had to be gradual. Some drew on a radical tradition of individual rights; others understood individuals as socially embedded. For some democracy and equality were inseparable; for others equal political rights were consistent with the maintenance of other forms of social and political hierarchy. This was significant for colonial reform projects.

These global debates shaped colonial projects and were echoed in political arguments within Tanganyika, as we shall in the chapters which follow. But while the language of democratization was widely used in the Anglophone literature in relation to Tanganyika, particularly by colonial officials, the language of democracy as such, and the term *demokrasi* in particular, appeared rarely in Tanganyika's Swahili public sphere in the late 1940s and early 1950s. The reason for this absence may in part lie in the British focus on gradual progress towards representative government. It may also be due to the range of very different political projects which the language of democracy could be used to articulate, weakening its political traction. We must therefore look elsewhere for changing conceptions of political society.

---

[76] Michelle L. Browers, *Democracy and Civil Society in Arab Political Thought: Transcultural Possibilities* (Syracuse, NY: Syracuse University Press, 2006); Edmund S. K. Fung, *In Search of Chinese Democracy: Civil Opposition in Nationalist China, 1929–1949* (Cambridge: Cambridge University Press, 2000), p. 14.

[77] David Runciman, *The Confidence Trap: A History of Democracy in Crisis from World War 1 to the Present* (New Haven, CT: Yale University Press, 2013), p. xxiii.

3

Representation, Imperial Citizenship and the Political Subject in Late Colonial Tanganyika

In October 1955, the editor of *Komkya*, the district newspaper published in the town of Moshi on the slopes of Mount Kilimanjaro, used his editorial to address what might appear to be a fairly obscure linguistic point. Many correspondents were, he wrote, misusing a word. That word was *raia*, a term which is usually translated as 'subject' but which was at times used as a translation for 'citizen' and at other times to mean something more like 'the people'.[1] The editor remarked that many letters had been received which employed phrases like 'we *raia* want this' or 'The *raia* don't like this'. But, he argued, only those who had been 'elected or sent' by the people had the right to use the term and to do so in the knowledge 'that he represents people or a particular group of people who elected him or sent him to speak on their behalf.'[2] Moreover, the editor feigned uncertainty as to the meaning attached by these writers to the word *raia*. Did *raia* not simply mean 'a person or people who are under a certain authority'? When writers claimed to speak on behalf of the '*raia* of Kilimanjaro', were they really claiming to speak on behalf of all men, women and children who live on the mountain? Or was there a second meaning, which referred to a group of people rather than all people? If so, this should be explained clearly.[3]

As we have seen, after 1945 the term democratisation acquired a new centrality in English-language discourse about political development in

---

[1] Ludwig Krapf, *A Dictionary of the Swahili language* (London: Truebner and Co., 1882), p. 315; A. C. Madan, *Swahili-English Dictionary* (Oxford: Clarendon Press, 1903), p. 325.
[2] Editorial, 'Raia', *Komkya*, 1 October 1955, p. 2.
[3] Ibid., p. 2.

Tanganyika as the colonial state sought to reform political structures from the bottom up. But in Swahili public discourse, the word *demokrasi* appeared relatively late, and appeared with any frequency only towards the end of the 1950s. Often, both before then and afterwards, there was no attempt to offer a Swahili spelling, and the English spelling of 'democracy' was simply inserted. We must therefore look elsewhere to trace changing political thinking on the ground in Tanganyika. This chapter argues that we should look instead at the ways in which an old word, *raia*, came to be used in new ways, and to the concept of representation.

The concept of representation has often been neglected by political theorists, in part because of its ability to have very different connotations in different contexts and thus to be compatible with both more and less democracy.[4] This ambiguity ostensibly sets it apart from the term 'democracy' which, Brito Vieira and Runciman argue, is far more straightforward in its meaning of 'rule by the people', though as we saw in the previous chapter and will explore more fully in Chapter 7, putting 'rule by the people' into practice is far from straightforward. More specifically, the relative neglect of the notion by those studying twentieth-century Africa lies in the fact that those advocating new forms of representation were often not concerned with equality but were seeking to reinforce old hierarchies or create new ones. As such, a focus on representation of this kind sits awkwardly with a narrative of the twentieth century which associates the post-1945 period with discourses of egalitarianism and democracy.

From the 1920s we can trace the development of new concepts of representation, and we can do so through tracking the changing use of the word *raia* in the 1920s and 1930s to embody new conceptions of political subjecthood. After 1945, these development intersected with transnational arguments and the new prominence given to the aim of building representative government in colonial discourse which we explored in the previous chapter and whereby, as in James Brennan's words, 'unrepresented "natives" in colonial Africa before the Second World War became poorly represented "Africans" …during the 1940s'.[5]

To make these arguments I start by briefly reflecting on the concept of representation. I then explore the ways in which political subjecthood was reconfigured in the political discourse of 1920s and 1930s and the new ways in which the term *raia* was employed in political argument, before

[4] Monica Brito Vieira and David Runciman, *Representation* (Cambridge: Polity Press, 2008), pp. 58–59.
[5] James R. Brennan, *Taifa: making nation and race in urban Tanzania* (Athens, OH: Ohio University Press, 2012), p. 13.

moving on to consider how new conceptions of political subjecthood were put to work in the era of political reform which followed 1945. While this chapter focuses on these debates at a fairly abstract level, in the next chapter I shall illustrate the wider arguments made here with a case study looking at one organization in the Kilimanjaro region which sought to use new concepts of representation in the late 1940s and early 1950s to reconfigure local political authority.

REPRESENTATION AND 'IMPERIAL CITIZENSHIP'

In their study of the concept of representation, Monica Brito Vieira and David Runciman argue that the concept needs to be taken far more seriously than it has been. While many political theorists follow de Tocqueville in understanding 'democracy as the founding principle of modern political life and representation as the appendage', in fact, they argue, the historically 'dominant tradition ... takes representation to be the essential idea and democracy, at best, to be the qualification'.[6] They make a convincing case that 'representation', rather than 'democracy', is the basis of modern politics.

The reason for putting representation at the centre of modern politics is because, as Brito Vieira and Runciman argue, 'it was only when the people could be conceived as being *represented* by their governments that it became possible to say that, where the government rules, it is the people who also rule'.[7] Yet 'representation' can have many different meanings. It is used in ways that have nothing to do with politics or with the relationship between individuals and the state. Even for those using it to describe a political relationship, it opens up as many questions as it answers.

An early, heated and extraordinarily influential debate which hinged on notions of representation took place during the English revolution and particularly in the arguments of the Levellers. In the Putney Debates of 1647, participants disagreed as to whether the right to elect representatives should be a birth right owned by all, or should be restricted to those with sufficient property to constitute 'free men'.[8] How were those in a permanent state of dependence, such as women, servants and beggars, to be represented? If representation was at the heart of debate on the parliamentary side of the conflict, this was equally true of their

[6] Brito Vieira and Runciman, *Representation*, pp. 59–60.
[7] Ibid., p. 5.
[8] Ibid., p. 23.

royalist opponents. Representation, as Quentin Skinner has argued, was central to Hobbes's argument in *Leviathan*, for the state was created at the moment when '[a] Multitude of men are made *One* Person, when they are by one man, or one Person, Represented… For it is the *Unity* of the Representer, not the *Unity* of the Represented, that maketh the Person One.'[9] For Hobbes, this understanding of the state had the function of ending the political conflict which had torn early seventeenth-century states apart, and set up the state as a replacement for earlier modes of absolutist government; in fact it opened up new channels of argument, by raising, in Brito Vieira and Runciman's words, 'the possibility that otherwise unwieldy political units – multitudes of individuals on the scale and of the diversity of the populations of modern states – could still impose their collective identity on the political life of the nation, if only they could find representatives willing to act for them.'[10]

But if representation was the key to popular participation in the modern state, for colonial populations this was explicitly excluded. As Uday Singh Mehta has recently shown, as mentioned in Chapter 1, it was here that one of the great paradoxes of mid-nineteenth-century liberalism lay.[11] For John Stuart Mill, writing in 1861, everyone was potentially capable of choosing their representatives but it was only with education and tutelage that that potential would be realized. Translated to a colonial setting, what this meant was that while some of Britain's colonies, the colonies of white settlement, were able to have representative government, others were not. This latter group must, he argued, 'be governed by the dominant country, or by persons delegated for that purpose by it'. Crucially, a mode of government entirely at odds with the principle of representation was not illegitimate in such a case, according to Mill. Indeed,'[t]his mode of government is as legitimate as any other if it is the one which in the existing state of civilization of the subject people most facilitates their transition to a higher stage of improvement.'[12]

This legitimized a model of empire as tutelage. But it also helped ensure that representation would continue to be a central area of claim-making and argument. In India, nineteenth-century liberals argued for Indian

[9] Ibid., p. 26.

[10] Ibid., p. 30.

[11] Uday Singh Mehta, *Liberalism and Empire: A Study in Nineteenth-Century British Liberal Thought* (Chicago: University of Chicago Press, 1999), pp. 195–196.

[12] J. S. Mill, *Utilitarianism, on Liberty, Considerations on Representative Government* (London: J. M. Dent, 1993), p. 415.

representation in the civil service and as elected members of new bodies.[13] But they also sought to create representation in spaces where this was not explicitly offered.[14] Where imperial thought disqualified Indians within India from the possibility of representation on grounds of race, limiting representation to those who were members of a white imperial family, the politician Dadabhai Naoroji used the same language of familyhood but turned it on his head in his campaigns for a Westminster parliamentary seat in 1886 and 1892. Naoroji was able to construct an alternative narrative, stressing the affective bonds of familyhood which bound India to an imperial family, in so doing constructing a model in which Indians could play a role in an imperial polis.[15] As Sukanya Banerjee argues, his own 'indeterminacy meant that not only was Naoroji himself considered eligible to stand for elections, but also that he could stand in for those not incorporated in the liberal contract of citizenship', notably women and workers who were excluded by the nineteenth-century British franchise.[16]

The flexibility of discourses of imperial citizenship which Banerjee identifies in late Victorian Britain and India was also present in early twentieth-century Africa. For the post-Revolutionary French empire in Africa as elsewhere, the promise of possible eventual elevation from the status of French subject to that of French citizen, with its accompanying legal and political rights, played a crucial role in developing a workable ideological compromise between Republicanism and empire. Yet although the ideology was clear, reality on the ground was always far messier, and the contrasting statuses of *citoyen* and *sujet* were as much a battleground for claim-making and for the defence and extension of rights as they were a settled fact.[17]

In monarchical Britain and its empire, conceptions of citizenship had to coexist with a legal status of 'subject' which was shared by both metropolitan and imperial Britons.[18] Within British constitutional discourse, all were subjects of His Majesty, though the rights and duties which accrued to that status differed within and between the constituent parts of the British Empire, and changed over time as the gradual expansion of the

---

[13] C. A. Bayly, *Recovering Liberties: Indian Thought in the Age of Liberalism and Empire* (Cambridge: Cambridge University Press, 2012), p. 1.

[14] Sukanya Banerjee, *Becoming Imperial Citizens: Indians in the Late-Victorian Empire* (Durham, NC and London: Duke University Press, 2010), p. 3.

[15] Ibid., p. 63.

[16] Ibid., p. 70.

[17] Alice Conklin, *A Mission to Civilize: The Republican Idea of Empire in France and West Africa, 1895–1930* (Stanford, CA: Stanford University Press, 1997).

[18] Banerjee, *Becoming Imperial Citizens: Indians in the Late-Victorian Empire*, p. 5.

franchise saw a shift from a notion of citizenship based on duties to one which combined duties with political rights. Very often, terminology was treated loosely, and with little relation to legal fact or political practice.

If this was true of Anglophone discourse, it was no less true of colonial Swahiliphone discourse in Tanganyika. The same term *raia* was employed in colonial texts before the Second World War to denote both the fact of being simply a subject of His Majesty and a more invested sense of being a political subject, first simply with duties and later with both rights and duties.[19] Just as within Anglophone discourse a language of 'citizenship' could be used in the metropole in the late nineteenth and early twentieth centuries even by and with reference to those yet to be accorded political rights, so the term *raia* could expand to incorporate new additions, as in the quotation with which this chapter began – in spite of attempts to rein it back in. In contrast, where the more specific status of African subject was intended, with the limitations on rights which that status entailed, the term *mwenyeji* or 'native' was used. This flexibility of language offered considerable scope for the remaking of political subjecthood.

REMAKING POLITICAL SUBJECTHOOD
IN INTERWAR TANGANYIKA

We can see the remaking of political subjecthood in practice if we look in more detail at the ways in which political society and the place of the political subject within that society were reconceptualized in inter-war Tanganyika. While the interwar period has long been seen as one in which the British colonial state in Africa lacked both the means and the motivation to do a great deal in Africa and relied on a resurrected chiefly power to govern on its behalf, recent historiography has started to paint a different picture, one in which many of the later developments associated with the post-1945 period had their roots in the 1920s.[20] While the focus of this literature has been on development policies, the same was true in politics. As we saw in Chapter 1, although indirect rule is often portrayed as part of a conservative agenda of resurrecting and sustaining chiefly power at the expense of emergent elites, this agenda coexisted

---

[19] T. R. Batten, *Thoughts on African Citizenship* (Oxford: Oxford University Press, 1944), p. 1.

[20] Helen Tilley, *Africa as a Living Laboratory: Empire, Development and the Problem of Scientific Knowledge* (Chicago: University of Chicago Press, 2011); Helen Tilley and Robert Gordon (eds.), *Ordering Africa: Anthropology, European Imperialism and the Politics of Knowledge* (Manchester: Manchester University Press, 2007).

with an explicitly transformative project, whereby supporting chiefs in the present was a means of working towards self-government in the future.[21] We can see this dimension in the didactic texts produced by the colonial state and the way they described the difference between precolonial political society and the political society they claimed to be in the process of creating.

An important element of this reconceptualization was the promotion of a new concept of political subjecthood, achieved in part through a discursive intervention and the remaking of the term *raia*.[22] The term itself was not new, having long been used on the Swahili coast to indicate subjecthood.[23] In Zanzibar, according to Jonathon Glassman, the status of *raia* or subject was 'the lowest common denominator of civic status, available to all who accepted the sultan's authority', and this language was borrowed by colonial rulers in their own citizenship laws. As a result, 'citizenship was defined, both in law and in common political rhetoric, as the status of being a "subject of His Highness"'.[24]

However, in a series of didactic texts published in the Swahili-language periodical *Mambo Leo* and then in the Swahili-language citizenship primer *Uraia* first published in 1927 and revised and republished in 1935 and 1943, colonial officials redefined the terms of citizen and citizenship away from signifying a relationship with an individual based on the acceptance of authority towards a more dynamic relationship with a state.[25] They did so in the context of making an argument that political society, and living under the authority of a government in a state, was compatible with freedom. The arguments set out in *Mambo Leo* and repeated in *Uraia* reached an expanding, though always relatively small, readership of those literate in Swahili and, increasingly over the interwar period, attending schools. By the 1960s, writers to the Swahili-language Catholic newspaper *Kiongozi* could refer to characters who appeared

---

[21] Frederick Lugard, *The Dual Mandate in British Tropical Africa* (London: Frank Cass, 1965). Cf. Karuna Matena, *Alibis of Empire: Henry Maine and the Ends of Liberal Imperialism* (Princeton, NJ: Princeton University Press, 2010); Mahmood Mamdani, *Citizen and Subject: Contemporary Africa and the Legacy of Late Colonialism* (Princeton, NJ: Princeton University Press, 1996).

[22] This section develops arguments made in Emma Hunter, 'Dutiful Subjects, Patriotic Citizens, and the Concept of "Good Citizenship" in Twentieth-Century Tanzania', *The Historical Journal*, 56, 1 (2013), 257–277.

[23] S. Baldi, *Dictionnaire des emprunts arabes dans les langues de l'Afrique de l'Ouest et en Swahili* (Paris: Karthala, 2008), p. 215.

[24] Jonathon Glassman, *War of Words, War of Stones: Racial Thought and Violence in Colonial Zanzibar* (Bloomington: Indiana University Press, 2011), p. 52, 319fn.

[25] S. Rivers-Smith and F. Johnson, *Uraia* (London: Macmillan, 1943), p. 5.

in the primer *Uraia* with the assumption that they would be familiar to other readers.[26]

The first step made in *Uraia* was an argument for political society. Against those who argued that freedom was possible outside political society, the book's authors argued that the insecurity of living outside the state made true freedom impossible. But the nature of political society was no longer the same as that which had existed before, and this change was symbolized by a shift in meaning in the term *raia*. The book explained that the word *raia* had once referred to 'the person who was under the leader of a tribe or a country and who paid tax to that person' but stated that its meaning had now changed slightly, 'and we use it for a person who is under a particular state, such as a subject [*raia*] of the British state or a subject [*raia*] of the French state'. The nature of the political community in question had therefore changed: rather than being the subject of an individual, the 'leader of a tribe or a country', the *raia* was now the subject of a state.

Moreover, the authors of *Uraia* explained that the content of political subjecthood had also changed. Whereas the status of subjecthood had once been a fairly passive one, conceived in terms of accepting the authority of a ruler, coupled with the status of being the subject of a state was a new concept of 'citizenship', or *uraia*, which they glossed as 'the duties which a subject [*raia*] has to his country'.[27] In adding a 'u' to the word *raia*, they self-consciously created a new abstract noun. In this formulation, citizenship or subjecthood now meant something more active, with an implied moral content.

In essence, there was a deliberate blurring of subjecthood and citizenship, which was reflected in colonial era dictionaries. While A. C. Madan's 1902 English-Swahili dictionary rendered 'citizen' as 'mkaa mji, mtu wa mji, mwenyeji', Frederick Johnson's 1939 dictionary offered 'raia' as a possible translation for citizen, as well as subject.[28]

---

[26] Hunter, 'Dutiful Subjects, Patriotic Citizens, and the Concept of "Good Citizenship" in Twentieth-Century Tanzania', p. 275.

[27] Rivers-Smith and Johnson, *Uraia*, p. 7. Inventing new Swahili words was common practice in the early 1920s as colonial officials across East Africa sought to standardise the language. On the process of standardization of Swahili, see Derek Peterson, 'Language Work and Colonial Politics in Eastern Africa: The Making of Standard Swahili and "School Kikuyu"', in David L. Hoyt and Karen Oslund (eds.), *The Study of Language and the Politics of Community in Global Context* (Lanham, MD: Lexington Books, 2006), pp. 185–214, at pp. 185–186; W. H. Whiteley, *Swahili: The Rise of a National Language* (Aldershot, UK: Gregg Revivals, 1993 [1969]).

[28] A. C. Madan, *English-Swahili Dictionary* (Oxford: Clarendon Press, 1902), p. 56; Frederick Johnson, *A Standard English-Swahili Dictionary* (London: Oxford University Press, 1939), p. 90.

More broadly, we see here an attempt to shift the concept of political subjecthood from indicating a relatively passive and self-evident relationship with a person to indicating a more active relationship with the state, itself a more abstract concept than that of a relationship with a chief. But in practice the two senses continued to overlap, not least because the summit of the British imperial state was represented by a person, that of the monarch, so that the term could indicate a person or body of people both in relation to government and in relation to chiefs.

In this model, Africans were understood to be represented by their chiefs. Yet the breadth of the term *raia*, and the fact that it was used both to denote colonial subjects, such as those living in Tanganyika, and subjects of the metropole, led to a curious ambiguity in *Uraia*'s section on 'Government'. There we find that in Britain, the House of Commons was elected by the people or subjects (*raia*), and one of their number, the colonial secretary, was responsible for colonies such as Tanganyika. The only way of specifying the difference between metropolitan subjects and colonial subjects was by using terms such as the subjects 'over there' or 'other subjects of the King'.[29] When necessary, events in Tanganyika would be discussed in Parliament.[30] Yet the text repeatedly insisted that all were subjects of the British Empire. The interests of Tanganyika were thus represented by a colonial secretary, elected not by Tanganyikans but by other *raia*, like those in Tanganyika and other parts of the British empire, yet also not like them.

The new language of political subjecthood thus both closed opportunities and opened them. Although it did not offer the prospect of political rights, it did construct a semblance of equality of all subjects of King George. Over time, this concept came to provide a space in which to critique local power structures, and in practice, given the importance of chiefs to structures of rule in Tanganyika, these focussed on critiques of chiefship.

CHIEFSHIP AND SUBJECTHOOD

The arguments over chiefship which took place in colonial Tanganyika have often been understood as constituting a form of 'pre-nationalist' politics, evidence of the ways in which indirect rule shaped and restricted Tanganyikan politics in the years before the foundation of Tanganyika's

[29] Rivers-Smith, *Uraia*, pp. 185, 183.
[30] Ibid., p. 185.

first nationalist political party in 1954. Yet these arguments were not simply stunted politics; they were central to the remaking of political languages in the mid-twentieth century and to the development of new conceptions of representation.[31] There was an important shift in the way that chiefship was discussed which we can see if we compare a text from the 1910s with debates in the African independent newspaper *Kwetu* in the 1930s and 1940s.

We begin with the earlier discussion of chiefship, contained in a text which has come to be known as the *Nine Notebooks of Chagga History*, written by Nathaniel Mtui for the Lutheran missionary Bruno Gutmann between around 1913 and 1916 and describing chiefship on the mountain of Kilimanjaro.[32] The text deals most comprehensively with the history of the Chiefdom of Marangu. It describes both the earliest chiefs, who supposedly came from Kamba in Kenya in an undated historical past, and those in power at the time of writing. In particular, the *Notebooks* deal with how chiefs came to power, their conflicts and the ways in which they lost power.

The author of the *Nine Notebooks*, Nathaniel Mtui, was born in 1892 on Kilimanjaro. He began attending mission school in 1902 and then converted to Christianity. Nathaniel, the name which Ndeseiya Mtui took on his baptism, wrote frequently in the Lutheran Swahili newspaper *Pwani na Bara*, and after the First World War when *Pwani na Bara* ceased publication he became a regular correspondent to the new British government's monthly Swahili publication, *Mambo Leo*. He was a mission teacher, but also engaged in research, first on behalf of the German missionaries Johannes Raum and Bruno Gutmann and later on behalf of the British colonial official Charles Dundas, a step which saw him become involved in the British colonial administration, ultimately as a clerk. The outcome of his research was a series of notebooks prepared for Raum, Gutmann and Dundas, nine of which constitute the *Nine Notebooks* discussed here. He was killed in 1927.[33]

Three elements of Mtui's understanding of chiefly power are striking. In the first place, the metaphor of eating and the consequences which

[31] As Steven Feierman has shown in his study of political discourse in the Usambara Mountains, *Peasant Intellectuals: Anthropology and History in Tanzania* (Madison, WI: University of Wisconsin Press, 1990).

[32] This text was never published, but was translated into English in 1958–59 and is preserved on a microfilm available at Leipzig University Library.

[33] John Iliffe, *A Modern History of Tanganyika* (Cambridge: Cambridge University Press, 1979), p. 337. 'Kifo cha Ajabu', *Mambo Leo*, March 1927, p. 602.

ensue when food is not shared form an important theme through the notebooks.[34] Thus of one nineteenth-century Chief, Mtui wrote: 'After the installation Mwinjie began to eat a lot of food and he became very fat because he was also heavily built.... Then Mwinjie started killing innocent people. When he went for a walk & met some people on the way he ordered that they should be killed.'[35] Mtui offers graphic descriptions of the consequences faced by chiefs who overstepped the limits of legitimate power and ate too much. Selengia, Chief of Mamba, also on Kilimanjaro, did not 'collect bullocks from the people and kill them for meat to feed the men', but rather demanded 'heifers' which would add to his own wealth, and fined those who did not deliver them. According to Mtui, he enlisted the power of the German district officer, a certain Mr Freitag, to extort cattle from his subjects. Yet in a note added later, Mtui wrote that Selengia had died on 29th January 1917. The reason for his death was stomach ache, attributed by the people 'to the fact that he had robbed too many things from the people.'

Second, power, in Mtui's account, was cyclical, and held within it the seeds of its own destruction. Again, this is at times explicitly linked to overeating. According to Mtui, when another nineteenth-century chief, Itosi, was installed, people complained that 'Itosi is a glutton of everything and if he becomes a chief he will grab everything from us and leave us poor.' Unfortunately, a chief even more powerful than Itosi (Horombo) insisted, and so Itosi was appointed. But Itosi's fatness came back to haunt him. For he was, apparently, too fat and lazy to attend meetings, and so sent his fitter brother Nderima instead, whose power rose in consequence. The same cyclical aspect was true of extending power over other parts of the country. Moving forward in time, Mtui also tells of the late-nineteenth and early twentieth century chief Marealle, who had first inherited a country with little cattle but gradually built up both his own personal wealth and that of his country, partly through exploiting other parts of Kilimanjaro. Yet there came a point at which the abuses which the rich carried out to exploit the wealth of other areas became so excessive as to result in the loss of his power.

Third, chiefly power depended both on having wealth and on bringing wealth to one's followers, but chiefs needed to ensure that their subjects did not become too independent, in Mtui's account. It was in part

[34] Jean-Francois Bayart, *The State in Africa: The Politics of the Belly* (Cambridge: Polity Press, 2009); Michael Schatzberg, *Political Legitimacy in Middle Africa: Father, Family and Food* (Bloomington: Indiana University Press, 2001).

[35] Mtui, *Nine Notebooks of Chagga History*, p. 25.

a failure to manage the crucial relationship of dependence between chief
and rich subjects which caused Marealle's temporary downfall. Mtui told
how Marealle's subjects became too rich, enslaving the people from a
neighbouring country so that 'a rich man had as many as 30 to 40 maid
servants to work for his wife, & the man had about the same number of
male servants to look after his beasts & other donkey work in the homestead. Mangi Kilamia [Marealle] himself had about 500 slave servants
(from Tsimbii) of both sexes.' But this served to reduce chiefly power, for
'everyone in Marangu was rich and consequently they cared little about
the Mangi [chief].' From the point of view of the poor, rich men could act
as vital intermediaries, helping to remove unjust chiefs. One person, the
brother of a chief, escaped the assassination his brother had planned for
him and was himself installed as chief by the help of a 'rich man'. Rich
men were preferred as headmen, the agents of the chief, as they would
be respected by the chief and thus better able to defend people against
their exactions. Of his own uncle who had succeeded his father as headman Mtui wrote: 'The people of Marangu did not like him much, partly
because he was not as rich as his late brother, partly because he did not
behave as well as Mkindi. In Marangu to be a headman one should have
much riches without which both the Mangi and the other headmen will
always despise you.'[36]

In this text, chiefly power could be held in check both by cyclical
forces which meant that an oppressive chief would lose power, and by
intermediaries such as headmen. But while the *Nine Notebooks* give a
clear account of the ways in which chiefly power could and should be
held in check and highlights the role of intermediaries in doing so, there is
no sense of intermediaries directly transmitting the feelings of a popular
body of opinion – no sense, in other words, of a concept of representation. In contrast, in the public sphere of the 1930s and 1940s, those who
were critical of Kilimanjaro's chiefs could make use of the new language
of political subjecthood to argue that chiefs were behaving unjustly and
were not acting according to the wishes of the people.

In the pages of the African independent newspaper *Kwetu* in the
1930s, we can see the potential offered by the new language of subjecthood, defined in relation both to a chief and to a colonial state. We can

---

[36] Mtui, *Nine Notebooks of Chagga History*, para. 232. Elsewhere he wrote: 'True it is
v. difficult to administer a rich man in Chagga through the headman because the rich will
not obey him and when they are given orders they abuse the headman or beat him, (to
pay a fine of up to 20 head of cattle is just nothing to them.)'

see the term *raia* used both in the older way of referring to the subjects
of a chief and in the newer way of describing a relationship between the
people and the government.³⁷ Thus an article in *Kwetu* in 1940 entitled
'Sacking of a Chief' employed the term *raia* to discuss the difficulties
faced by a chief in trying to maintain the esteem of his subjects.³⁸ Yet a
conceptualization of a relationship between the *raia* and the government,
as envisaged in the didactic primer *Uraia*, was also apparent in the pages
of *Kwetu* and provided a means of bypassing local authorities and going
straight to the centre. In January 1938, an inhabitant of Ilala in Dar es
Salaam appealed on behalf of 'all *raia*' to 'our Father, the Government'
to help to remove the problems that confronted them and other resi-
dents.³⁹ The attribution of the qualities of fatherhood to the government
is not surprising – the paternalism of colonial language has been detected
across Africa, and Michael Schatzberg has described the ways in which a
language of 'fatherhood' became a central part of the political imaginary
in states across Africa after independence.⁴⁰ But continuity of language,
the *raia* appealing to his father, masked a shift in political theory, now
very different from that described by Mtui.

The way in which the language of imperial citizenship could now
be used by dissidents to criticise chiefly power was demonstrated by a
series of Chagga correspondents to *Kwetu* in 1940 who wrote to complain about the Chagga chiefs. One, who signed himself as Msafiri, used
the term *raia* in the older sense of denoting the subjects of a chief. The
Chagga Council was, he reminded his readers, known as the *Baraza ya
Wenyeji* or Native Authority and ought, therefore, to include the *wenyeji*
or natives. Yet it seemed to represent only the chiefs, and 'the things
done by the Council were not in line with the thoughts of the *raia* at
all.'⁴¹ He went on to argue that when servants of the government visited
chiefs in their districts, those with problems were not given the chance
to explain these openly in front of the meeting, and the government
listened only to those on its payroll.⁴² Another correspondent, a certain
M. M. B. Masawe, appealed to the government as 'Father of all *Raia*' in
an appeal to the state to take action against chiefs who were not acting

---

³⁷ In the 1940s it was also used to signify 'civilian' as opposed to soldier.
³⁸ 'Sacking of a Chief', *Kwetu*, 4 August 1940, p. 2.
³⁹ Letter from Salimu bin Ismail and Musa Kinaogo, 'Mji wa Ilala, Dar es Salaam', *Kwetu*,
    14 January 1938, p. 9.
⁴⁰ Schatzberg, *Political Legitimacy in Middle Africa: Father, Family and Food.*
⁴¹ Msafiri, 'Mashaka ya Kilimanjaro, Moshi, 1930–1939', *Kwetu*, 11 June 1940, p. 7.
⁴² Ibid., p. 7.

justly.[43] Yet in the absence of any developed theory of representation on the part of the political state, it was easy to dismiss interventions of this sort as the work of 'agitators'.

REPRESENTATION AFTER 1945

After 1945, arguments over the position of chiefs dovetailed with the colonial state's new concern with developing representative structures which we discussed in Chapter 2. Although the development of new representative structures occurred primarily at local council level, 1945 also saw a new departure at the centre. For the first time, two African representatives were nominated by the governor to serve on the Legislative Council, the body which served to advise the governor but which until 1945 had included only white and Asian representatives. Both new African representatives were chiefs, Chief Abdiel Shangali and Chief Kidaha Makwaia.[44] Although this went some way towards meeting demands heard regularly in the pages of *Kwetu* and in the African Association that there should be African representation in the Council, they were not elected, and indeed the first election of African members of the Legislative Council had to wait until 1958.[45] In the localities, as we saw in Chapter 2, colonial officials worked to develop new local councils which included African representatives, moving away from an interwar model in which the chief was the sole legitimate representative of African opinion.

The new African representatives on the Legislative Council were understood by the colonial state to be representatives of Tanganyika's African community, to sit alongside other representatives who spoke for Tanganyika's European and Asian community. It was indeed in these terms that their arrival in the Legislative Council was greeted by correspondents to *Mambo Leo* as a welcome opportunity to have someone to represent African interests there.[46] In a letter published in June 1946,

[43] Letter from M. M. B. Masawe, 'Mateso ya Wachagga yatakwisha lini?', *Kwetu*, 23 February 1940.

[44] A further two African representatives were appointed in 1948. John Iliffe, 'Breaking the Chain at Its Weakest Link: TANU and the Colonial Office', in Gregory Maddox and James Giblin (eds.), *In Search of a Nation: Histories of Authority and Dissidence in Tanzania* (Oxford: James Currey, 2005), pp. 168–197, p. 169; James Clagett Taylor, *The Political Development of Tanganyika* (London: Oxford University Press, 1963), p. 78.

[45] Iliffe, *A Modern History of Tanganyika*, p. 420; Iliffe, 'Breaking the Chain at Its Weakest Link', p. 183.

[46] The Swahili term used to describe them in the pages of *Mambo Leo* is revealing: they were termed 'mawakili', which can serve as a translation both for lawyer and for representative, e.g., 'Mawakili wa wenyeji tuliowatangaza mwezi uliopita', *Mambo Leo*, February 1946, p. 16.

responding to another letter which had asked why an African worker was paid half as much as a Goan worker for the same work, E. F. Chemponda wrote that this was a question asked by all Africans from time to time and that there was no satisfactory answer, though he expressed the hope that answers would soon be provided by the new African representatives in the Legislative Council such as Chief Abdiel Shangali, who, Chemponda wrote, 'is one of those who represents we who have black skin in the Legislative Council.'[47] At the same time, other associations claimed to speak on behalf of an African political community. The African Association aimed, according to one of its leaders, Ali Ponda, to 'raise the condition of all Africans' and in particular to help those who lacked any other association and intervening with the government.[48]

But the language of representation was interpreted in diverse ways. African representatives in the Legislative Council were understood as having been sent to Dar es Salaam to represent their regions, rather than to represent an imagined community of Tanganyikan Africans. In 1951 a correspondent wrote to the *Tanganyika Standard* to complain that Chief Abdiel Shangali had not been replaced by a representative from the same region when his membership in the Legislative Council expired. If it was true that he had been replaced by someone from the Southern Province 'it is indeed a great loss to Africans in the N.P to have no representative to speak for the Province. I trust that even critics will share my submission that the Africans of the Northern Province do not beat the other Provinces in population, but in general progress in the field of Politics, trade, societies are far ahead. If that is so, it would appear that not a minimum error has been made by depriving the N.P its member but a maximum error.'[49] He was not alone in thinking that the new African members of the Legislative Council had appointed to represent their regions. In the following year the Bukoba independent newspaper *Bukya na Gandi* printed a demand for a representative in the Legislative Council who would represent Bukoba.[50] A note printed below Mawalla's letter dismissed this conception of representation, citing a government

[47] Letter from E. F. Chemponda, *Mambo Leo*, June 1946, p. 61.
[48] Mwalimu Ali Ponda, 'Maendeleo ya Tanganyika', *Mambo Leo*, February 1947, p. 14. This had been the African Association's goal from its earliest days, as shown in Brennan, *Taifa*, p. 68. The point was still being made in 1951; see, e.g., a letter from Stephen Mhando, *Tanganyika Standard*, 21 April 1951, p. 13; 'Tanganyika African Association', *Tanganyika Standard*, 28 April 1951, p. 13.
[49] Letter from G. M. S. Mawalla, *Tanganyika Standard*, 28 April 1951, p. 21.
[50] 'Tunaomba Mjumbe wa Legco Bukoba', *Bukya na Gandi* September 1952, p. 1, TNA 41176.

spokesman saying that 'Members are not appointed as representatives of any particular Province'.[51] But the link here between representation and local development was an important one, as we shall see.

DEBATING CHIEFSHIP IN THE PAGES
OF *MAMBO LEO*

At the same time as new structures of representation were being introduced, there was a new impetus to debates over whether chiefs could represent their people. In 1946 and 1947, the letters' pages of *Mambo Leo* were filled with arguments refuting this claim. One of the most significant, in terms of the number of letters printed, was a debate which began in 1946 and stretched on into 1947. The focus of debate was initially very specific, and constituted an attack on the Wakilindi chiefs of the Usambara mountains.[52] But it quickly broadened out into a wider debate about chiefship and government.

The discussion began with a letter complaining about the lack of education of the Wakilindi chiefs and calling for the educated to play more of a role in local government. There were two elements to the criticism of the Wakilindi chiefs: on the one hand, the argument that they lacked education and on the other an argument that they were outsiders to the area whose rule may have been necessary in the past but was no longer legitimate. Although this argument was on one level a very local argument rooted in long-standing conflicts in the Usambara mountains, they spoke to much larger themes, and correspondents from elsewhere in Tanganyika were quick to join in, beginning with a letter from Signalman Siguu H. K. Salim which complained that the Wakilindi chiefs were blocking progress (*maendeleo*). You could, he complained, 'walk many miles without encountering hospitals or schools.'[53] He raised the prospect of a 'President instead of chiefs' which would allow the country to develop properly. And he called on young people who had left the army and returned home also to make an effort and 'speak up for our country'.

---

[51] Other correspondents echoed the government's stance, e.g., Letter from A. L. Mpewembe, *Tanganyika Standard*, 17 May 1951, p. 14.

[52] For details of the political context to this discussion see Feierman, *Peasant Intellectuals: Anthropology and History in Tanzania*, pp. 140–153.

[53] Letter from H. K. Salim, 'Katika Usambaa uchifu usomewe', *Mambo Leo*, October 1946, p. 110.

The idea that a particular responsibility lay on those leaving the army was echoed in letters which followed.[54] Some of the arguments were quite specific to the Usambara Mountains. Reference was made to the large families of the Wakilindi chiefs and the temptation towards bribery this opened. But this spoke to wider concerns about chiefs governing in their own interests rather than in the interests of the people that were being voiced elsewhere at the same time, echoed in other letters and petitions.[55] And the question of education resonated across Tanganyika. The future nationalist politician Job Lusinde wrote to agree with H. K. Salim, arguing that in the country of Ugogo 'many problems are brought by our rulers lacking sufficient education'. F. S. Gendaeka, who attached the prefix 'teacher' to his name, admitted that he was not himself a Shambaa but he believed that it was necessary to consider chiefs across the whole of Tanganyika, and called for them all to be educated.[56]

Others disagreed, and argued that rule should be determined by descent, not by education. One writer, Mr Mnkande, defended the Wakilindi chiefs on the grounds that in Europe there were still rulers who owed their position to descent, notably the British monarchy. He called for the retention of a system whereby rulers owed their position to descent, but for their sons to be educated and advisers to be appointed.[57] But for J. M. Andrew, this was a mistaken comparison, for in Britain, as in all developed countries, hereditary rulers might be in charge but decisions were made by a 'Council or by associations of educated people'.[58] He also reminded Mnkande that in many countries – Russia, Holland, Spain and Yugoslavia – traditional rulers had been removed completely. The answer was not only rule by the educated, but that all *raia* of the Shambaa region who wanted the best for their country should 'join together' and find a solution. Other correspondents drew lessons from elsewhere in British history, for example, the case of King Charles I who, like current chiefs,

---

[54] Letter from F. Alfred Kiluwa and Ramadhani S. Hoza, 'Ni Haki Chief Aelimike', *Mambo Leo*, December 1946, p. 133.

[55] For example, 'Appeal from Mohamed Husain, Tanga, 13 March 1945, re. Graduated Tax – Pare District', TNA UK, CO 691/186, f. 13.

[56] Letter from Mwalimu F. S. Gendaeka, 'Nahodha aaminiwa kwa kujua', *Mambo Leo*, December 1946, p. 134.

[57] Letter from Dennis Mnkande (Mwendapole), 'Utawala ni jadi si elimu', *Mambo Leo*, February 1947, p. 13.

[58] J. M. Andrew, 'Utawala wa jadi usiofaa si ajabu kukataliwa', *Mambo Leo*, April 1947, p. 37.

had failed to listen to his subjects, though this particular letter seems not to have been published in *Mambo Leo*.[59]

Chiefs were therefore charged with corruption and with failing to bring *maendeleo* to their districts. One correspondent compared the way in which money was spent by the government on good quality schools and hospitals with the ways in which local administrations spent the proportion of taxes left over to them and found the latter distinctly wanting.[60] The letters which criticized existing modes of chiefship in Usambara appealed to the colonial state from their authors' position as subjects of the colonial state, or 'your subjects' (*raia zako*). But they also constituted an appeal for an active citizenry to take on a role in government and in bringing *maendeleo*. In this debate, the term *raia* was being used not just to mean those under the rule of a chief, but also to mean an active citizenry, which could and should act to deliver more just and more effective rule. There is a clear sense of the *raia* as a category denoting a body of people which could unite and use their abilities to achieve progress, led by those with education.

Thus by the 1940s we can see the term *raia* being used in a new way, as indicated in the editorial with which we began. Rather than simply signifying the position of being under the rule of a chief, there was a sense of the *raia* as a political subject. On one level, this meant that the colonial state could be appealed to above the heads of local authorities. But it also meant that associations and individuals could rhetorically constitute a constituency of political subjects and claim to speak on their behalf.

But what this development did not imply was any principle of equality or commitment to the ideals of freedom and democracy which were so important in transnational political discourse at that time, as discussed in the previous chapter. Freedom, in discourses such as that of the Shambaa critics of the Wakilindi, meant freedom from oppression by unjust chiefs. And as in the colonial didactic text *Uraia*, freedom was to be found within a reconstituted political society, not in the absence of political authority and the licence to do as one pleased. Indeed, as Derek Peterson has shown, the new political associations which appeared across Tanganyika in the late 1940s and 1950s not only were often profoundly nonegalitarian, but

---

[59] The letter is preserved in the Tanzania National Archives and cited in Feierman, *Peasant Intellectuals: Anthropology and History in Tanzania*, p. 141.

[60] Letter from Mwalimu A.Wilson Chidali, 'Chifu aliyeelimishwa husaidia nchi', *Mambo Leo*, March 1947, p. 25.

they often also argued against greater personal freedom, particularly for women and younger men.[61]

It is here that we find the answer to something which puzzled Steven Feierman in his study of critics of chiefly power in the Usambara Mountains in the mid-1940s. He saw them as both democratic and anti-democratic: democratic in that they demanded access to power for all, regardless of birth, but antidemocratic in their insistence that government should be in the hands of the educated. Thus 'alongside the democratic demands for a government open to all educated people, irrespective of race or chiefly lineage, could be found anti-democratic strains in the same discourse – calls for control of government only by those who had the proper qualifications.'[62] Yet in eastern Africa in the 1940s, claiming to speak for the people rarely meant an adherence to principles of equality. More often, such claims were based on the construction of new hierarchies. They recognized that some could not speak openly in the face of the chief, but they did not seek to give those people the power to speak; they sought to speak on their behalf.[63] As will be shown in the next chapter by means of a case study of one new political organization, the Chagga Union, the power of new political organizations came from their claim to speak for newly constituted citizenries, in relation both to local chiefs and to the colonial state.

CONCLUSION

When the British colonial state sought to establish a new understanding of political society in the early 1920s, as we saw in the didactic primer *Uraia*, it was assumed that chiefs would represent their subjects. The *raia*, subject or citizen, was both the subject of a colonial state and the subject of a chief. But this same language of political subjecthood or citizenship was appropriated by political actors and employed as a new means of critiquing power, particularly chiefly power, challenging the claim of chiefs to represent those they governed. After 1945 this mode of conceptualizing political subjecthood intersected with new languages of democratization to provide the basis for new concepts of representation. It is here that we find

---

[61] Derek Peterson, *Ethnic Patriotism and the East African Revival: A History of Dissent, 1935–1972* (Cambridge: Cambridge University Press, 2012).

[62] Feierman, *Peasant Intellectuals, Anthropology and History in Tanzania* p. 141.

[63] W. H. Whiteley, 'Political Concepts and Connotations: Observations on the Use of Some Political Terms in Swahili', in Kenneth Kirkwood (ed.), *African Affairs, 1*, St. Antony's Papers, 10 (London: Chatto and Windus, 1961), pp. 7–21, p. 15.

the roots of the 'representation of place and local community' which John Dunn has described as 'the aspect of authentic political representation that has been most successfully (and least coercively) institutionalised in African societies since independence'.[64]

This chapter has argued that the concept of representation was central to political argument in the 1940s and early 1950s in Tanganyika. Those engaged in the public sphere drew on a language of citizenship which had developed over the interwar period and employed it to build new political constituencies and engage with the state. These developments were framed by colonial thinking, expressed through didactic texts, policy shifts and legal structures. But they also had their own logic and were created in dialogue with comparisons from across the world.

Exploring the language of citizenship in colonial Africa might seem anachronistic, and indeed the terms 'citizen' and 'subject' have recently become highly charged in the historiography of twentieth-century Africa, as a consequence of the interventions of the political scientist Mahmood Mamdani. For Mamdani, in his 1996 book *Citizen and Subject*, central to the governance strategies of colonial regimes and decisive in shaping their postcolonial legacies was the denial of citizenship rights to the rural African majority, most of whom were condemned to a life of 'subjecthood'. In the absence of political rights they were compelled to live under the 'decentralized despotism' of a chief.[65] Drawing on a close reading of colonial legislation, he argues that legal distinctions between 'citizens' and 'subjects' shaped the political culture of both colonial and postcolonial Africa.

But this focus on legal status and terminology misses the ways in which there have always been different sorts of subjects, with different sorts of rights, duties and prerogatives negotiated on the ground as much as defined in colonial law and in ways not captured by a 'citizen' and 'subject' dichotomy.[66] The ambiguities of the term *raia* remind us of this space for negotiation. Increasingly, it was used as a basis from which to create new constituencies from below which could claim legitimacy from

[64] John Dunn, 'Politics of representation and good government', in Patrick Chabal (ed.), *Political Domination in Africa: Reflections on the Limits of Power* (Cambridge: Cambridge University Press, 1986), pp. 158–174, p. 167.

[65] Mahmood Mamdani, *Citizen and Subject: Contemporary Africa and the Legacy of Late Colonialism* (Princeton, NJ: Princeton University Press, 1996); Frederick Cooper, 'Review of Citizen and Subject: Contemporary Africa and the Legacy of Late Colonialism by Mahmood Mamdani', *International Labor and Working Class History*, 52 (1997), pp. 156–160.

[66] Lahra Smith, *Making Citizens in Africa: Ethnicity, Gender, and National Identity in Ethiopia* (Cambridge: Cambridge University Press, 2013), p. 22.

a transnational language which valued the voice of 'the people'. But these new constituencies were not egalitarian; instead they often sought to recreate older hierarchies in a new vein.

In the next chapter, I build on this discussion and explore the ways in which a new breed of 'Citizens' Unions' took this agenda forward in the late 1940s and early 1950s, by looking in detail at the history of the Kilimanjaro Chagga Citizens Union. They claimed to speak on behalf of a Chagga citizenry, and by doing so to deliver the combination of *maendeleo* or progress with social harmony, re-creating relationships of trust and dependence which, they felt, were breaking apart.[67]

---

[67] Feierman, *Peasant Intellectuals, Anthropology and History in Tanzania*, p. 195; Peterson, *Ethnic Patriotism and the East African Revival: A History of Dissent, 1935–1972*, p. 128.

4

Patriotic Citizenship and the Case of the Kilimanjaro Chagga Citizens Union

In this chapter, we step outside the Swahiliphone public sphere shared across Tanganyika and move to northeast Tanganyika and the mountain of Kilimanjaro, home of the Chagga, one of Tanganyika's more than 120 ethnic groups. In the late 1940s, this region was rich, thanks to wealth earned through coffee production, and growing richer. But the land on which coffee could be grown was in increasingly short supply, and the gap between rich and poor seemed to be widening. The region's language was Kichagga, but for historical reasons, the local political debate which took place through text, whether in the circulars produced by political parties and copied to the local administration or in the district newspaper *Komkya* which we encountered in Chapter 1, took place in Swahili.[1] This was therefore a smaller and more tightly defined public sphere, but it overlapped and intersected with a wider pan-territorial Swahiliphone public sphere. Our focus is on the arguments of a political association called the Kilimanjaro Chagga Citizens Union. To make the twists and turns of this story easier to follow, I shall refer to this association, which employed different names at different times, including the Kilimanjaro Union, as the Kilimanjaro Chagga Citizens Union (or KCCU) throughout.

Exploring the Kilimanjaro Chagga Citizens Union's arguments means taking seriously the political thinking of a body which has often been styled as backwards-looking or neo-traditionalist, and has generally been explored in the context of political histories of a tumultuous

[1] Chapter 1, p. 58.

local politics.[2] Dominated as it was by older men who sought to restore traditional values, in part through a defence of hereditary chiefship, it is not hard to see why it has been understood in this way. In this respect, it was typical of ethnic associations across East Africa which, in Derek Peterson's words, 'sought to stitch society together in a hierarchical relationship of trust and dependence'.[3]

For Peterson, the projects of these 'ethnic patriots' were very different from those of territorial nationalists. Ethnic patriots across East Africa were not interested in territorial nationalism or wider political projects of self-rule. Rather, they were 'driven by the urgent need to find institutions that could protect civic virtues and define honourable conduct.'[4] This is the domain which John Lonsdale has termed the 'deep politics' of 'moral ethnicity'.[5] Through the cultural work of writing histories, defining territory and disciplining women and the young, these male patriots 'created a community for which to speak'.

But political organizations defined in ethnic terms such as the KCCU and those advocating territorial nationalism had more in common than we might think. In this chapter, I argue that both were engaging with the same intellectual context which we have traced over the preceding three chapters. We have seen that the backdrop to political thinking after 1945 was a vernacular understanding of modernity articulated through arguments over the term *maendeleo*. We have also traced the intersection, after 1945, between a new language of political progress articulated in terms of freedom and democracy, and changing conceptions of citizenship employed to rearticulate relationships between the political subject and the state.

It is at this point of intersection between locally specific arguments over the meaning of citizenship and transnational projects of political reform that we should situate bodies like the Kilimanjaro Chagga Citizens Union. Their political language seemed contradictory, at times apparently egalitarian and at times paternalist and hierarchical. Yet once we put to one side the assumption that freedom and equality will always and in

---

[2] Susan G. Rogers, *Search for Political Focus on Kilimanjaro: A History of Chagga Politics, 1916–1952, with Special Reference to the Cooperative Movement and Indirect Rule.* Unpublished PhD thesis, University of Dar es Salaam (1972).

[3] Derek Peterson, *Ethnic Patriotism and the East African Revival: A History of Dissent, c. 1935–1972* (Cambridge: Cambridge University Press, 2012), pp. 127–128.

[4] Ibid., p. 16.

[5] John Lonsdale, 'KAU's Cultures', *Journal of African Cultural Studies*, 13 (2000), 107–124.

all circumstances be preferable to freedom with and through belonging, as discussed in the Introduction, its appeal becomes more comprehensible. The Citizens Union used the new opportunities brought by political reforms and by new languages of politics rhetorically to create a new political community and claim a role for itself as the legitimate spokespeople for the *raia* in politics. Theirs was a vision of a political community which offered the people a greater voice and freedom from oppression by unjust rulers. It also sought to create structures in which the rich would help the poor and the strong would help the weak. And although its appeal would not last long, it was briefly compelling.

To make this argument, I first set out the distinctive local context which helps make sense of the political arguments which followed, drawing particular attention to inequalities of wealth and land shortage, and then explore the debates which these anxieties provoked in the local district newspaper, *Komkya*. I then set out the political history of the Kilimanjaro Chagga Citizens Union, before moving on to explore the political languages of the Citizens Union at the intersection of local, national and transnational arguments.

LAND AND COFFEE ON KILIMANJARO

The local context on Kilimanjaro was distinctive, and provides a crucial backdrop to the political thinking of the 1940s and 1950s. Long before the 1940s, Moshi was an area well known to the colonial government in Dar es Salaam and the Colonial Office in London as one from which political trouble often emanated. It was one of Tanganyika's richest regions. It was also one of a few areas in Tanganyika which had a high level of European settlement, on a par with parts of Kenya. The quality of the land had attracted white settlers from the beginning of the German era in the 1880s onwards and towards the end of the German period, in 1913, nearly 800 square kilometres of land had been transferred to European ownership, of which around 200 square kilometres were arable land and a further 567 square kilometres were pasture.[6]

Whereas in Kenya white settlers succeeded in preventing African farmers from taking advantage of the potential offered by similar regions for the growing of lucrative cash crops, on Kilimanjaro the British colonial official Charles Dundas encouraged Africans to grow coffee. Coffee proved

---

[6] John Iliffe, *A Modern History of Tanganyika* (Cambridge: Cambridge University Press, 1979), p. 144.

a valuable cash crop and the establishment of cooperative organizations, first the Kilimanjaro Native Planters' Association (KNPA) and then, following allegations of corruption, the Kilimanjaro Native Co-Operative Union (KNCU), ensured that the wealth deriving from coffee found its way into the hands of the African growers rather than middle-men. But the quality of the land also ensured that it was in high demand, particularly so given a rapidly growing population, so conflict over land between Africans and white settlers and between chiefs and their subjects was a regular feature of local political life.

Coffee brought wealth to Kilimanjaro but it also provided something more fundamental. It seemed to offer economic autonomy as an alternative to the dependence of wage labour on European farms. In the early 1930s, KNCU's periodical *Uremi* welcomed the opportunity which coffee offered to an alternative to labour migration to the coast. Thus the first issue of *Uremi* in 1932 began by explaining what cooperation was and emphasized that it meant 'many people sticking together for the profit of each individual person and of the whole nation (*taifa*) and this is indeed what the Society will do.' The aim of the KNCU was, the editor continued, 'to increase the profits of farmers by all means.'[7] A letter from the President of the KNCU, Joseph Maliti, went on to explain the opportunities offered by coffee.[8] First and foremost among these opportunities was that of rescuing those youth whom Maliti believed were increasingly forced into labour migration to the coast. Maliti's answer to this problem was that 'each year we will increase our agriculture in order that we profit from our country and can thus bring back our children who are lost and poor, going to the coast with an emptiness in body and soul.'[9] In the pages of *Uremi*, slavery was equated with labour for Europeans, and freedom with working together through the cooperative union to produce coffee. But producing coffee required access to land, and as a consequence of population growth and the growing wealth of some coffee farmers, land was in increasingly short supply, and land mattered, not only because it was the source of wealth but also because political membership was defined by ownership of one of the plots of land held on a permanent and hereditary basis and known as a homestead plot or *kihamba*.

The competition for land on Kilimanjaro had two aspects. In the first place, there was a tension between those who argued that the land

---

[7] 'Jina letu jipya', *Uremi*, June 1932, p.1, TNA 20984.
[8] Joseph Maliti, 'Letter from the President', *Uremi*, June 1932, p. 3, TNA 20984.
[9] Ibid.

should be farmed by European settlers to increase productivity and those who argued that Tanganyika was an African country and that the land should be farmed by Africans. In the second place, there was an argument between those who thought that those Africans who had already demonstrated their productivity by farming the land well and amassing wealth should acquire more land, and those who believed that every Chagga man had a right to own a piece of land.

Pressure on land in the 1940s and 1950s came from two sources. The first was growing European settlement. Whereas the amount of land in non-African hands in 1939 had been roughly equal to that at the end of the German period, by 1953 it had increased from around two million to around three million acres.[10] The second was demographic. The population of Moshi District increased from 123,443 in 1923 to 230,665 by 1948.[11] By 1949, 3 per cent of people in Moshi District were landless.[12] While this figure might sound relatively trivial, this equated to around 13 per cent of adult males who were landless, a large part of an important constituency. The value of land was also increasing. Paul Maro suggests that the value of an acre of *kihamba* land, the permanent plots of land on which coffee and bananas were grown, rose from five hundred shillings in the 1930s to two thousand shillings for an acre planted with coffee in 1955.[13] The average income per coffee grower also grew substantially, according to Maro's figures, from '70 shillings in 1933, to 750 shillings in 1950, and 1,600 shillings in 1955.'[14] The increasing scarcity of land, coupled with the wealth it could bring, meant an increase in litigation and legal arguments over land.[15]

By the late 1940s the combined result of coffee, European settlement and population growth was increasing inequality of wealth between those who had land and those who did not. This leads us to the second aspect of competition for land, between an argument that those who

---

[10] Notes on a Meeting between the Chairman and Members of the Royal Commission and Sir Edward Twining at the Colonial Office on the 15th of July, 1953, TNA UK, CO 892/3/1, p. 2; East Africa Commission, *East Africa Royal Commission 1953–1955: Report* (London: H.M.S.O., 1955), p. 22.

[11] P. S. Maro, *Population and Land resources in Northern Tanzania: The Dynamics of Change 1920–1970*. Unpublished PhD thesis, University of Minnesota (1974), p. 160.

[12] Ibid., p. 129.

[13] Ibid., p. 178.

[14] Ibid., p. 83.

[15] Sally Falk Moore, 'From Giving and Lending to Selling: Property Transactions Reflecting Historical Changes on Kilimanjaro', in Kristin Mann and Richard Roberts (eds.), *Law in Colonial Africa* (London: James Currey, 1991), pp. 108–145.

already had land should acquire more and an argument that everyone had a right to land. In his investigations into landholding in 1946 for the Arusha-Moshi Lands Commission, established to decide what to do with the land owned by former German settlers, Sir Mark Wilson found that the unequal distribution of land was defended by elites as legitimate because 'it was recognized that the rich man had responsibilities as well as rights: for example, he had the duty, when the tribe went to war, of providing the sinews of war – food and equipment for the warriors and so forth. He also, by custom, expended his wealth freely on the entertainment of visitors and wayfarers and the relief of the sick and needy.'[16] As a result, Wilson reported, 'the slogan favoured by the men of property on Mount Kilimanjaro – and they are not by any means few – is, "To him that hath shall be given...."'[17] More broadly, Wilson identified an 'excessive, and therefore unhealthy, desire to possess themselves of land, and then more land, which they have come in recent years to regard as the only source of wealth and power and all good things.'[18]

However, a sense of the broader importance of possessing a plot of land, beyond questions of mere subsistence, informed the local administration's hostility to the development of a landless class. Writing in 1946, Wilson agreed that the 'Chagga system is based primarily on the acquisition, as of right, of a stated portion of the tribal lands by each young man of the tribe on his coming of age.'[19] In developing this conception of the importance of owning an individual plot of land, administrators drew on information given to them by Chagga informants. A committee of the Chagga Council set up to represent Chagga views to Wilson's Arusha-Moshi Lands Commission stated that 'A Mchagga values his piece of soil inconceivably greatly, and he considers it is the essence of his very living. A plot of land (*kihamba*) holds a peculiarly important position on the body of the Chagga tribal traditions and customs; amongst other things it confers upon its owner the overruling significance of belonging to the tribe.'[20]

---

[16] *Report of the Arusha-Moshi Lands Commission*, pp. 24–25. Mark Wilson noted wryly that these days with the increased availability of consumer goods more Chagga than before were 'willing to take on themselves the burden of wealth'.

[17] Ibid., p. 42.

[18] Ibid., p. 38.

[19] Ibid., p. 24.

[20] 'A Memorandum to the Commissioner Moshi-Arusha Land Commission, by a Committee Appointed by the Chagga Chiefs' Council, Moshi', United Nations Trusteeship Council [UNTC], Fourth Session, January to March 1949, Annexe, *Official Records*, p. 320.

The special qualities of this homestead plot were stressed too by landless or migrant Chagga living away from the mountain. In 1953, a body calling itself the Chagga Association in Mombasa in Kenya wrote to Thomas Marealle in his capacity as paramount chief or *Mangi Mkuu* of the Chagga supporting Petro Njau's memorandum to the East Africa Royal Commission which called for the creation of new plots. They wrote that 'there is no Chagga person today even if he is far from Moshi who would not like to get a homestead plot.'[21] 'Even here in Mombasa', they wrote, 'there are a large number of Wachagga' who for various reasons were without land. They were thus forced 'to live here [Mombasa] to avoid a hard life.'[22] Were new land to be opened up, large numbers of Chagga would, in their opinion, certainly return.

Debates about land distribution therefore had to work between these two conflicting aims, that of a piece of land for all versus consolidation of holdings by a landed class. Chiefs were encouraged by the local administration to adhere to their policy of avoiding the growth of landlessness, so in 1947 the Divisional Chief of Rombo, one of three administrative divisions into which Kilimanjaro was divided following administrative reorganization in 1946, wrote to all chiefs in his Division directly challenging the notion that 'to him that hath shall be given'. He stated that acquiring extra plots of land was a 'way of profiting for oneself and oppressing the citizens (*raia*) of the future who when they are born will lack space for a plot of land.' If this continued there would be no land left. He ordered all chiefs to cease giving plots of land to those already in possession of a plot. The final clause stated explicitly that 'A Mangi can only give plots of land to people who do not have a homestead plot.'[23] What he saw greed was, however, considered by elder men as a means of fulfilling patriarchal responsibilities towards sons, wives and clients.[24] Yet the demands of these elites to hold more land than was needed for a homestead or the establishment of a family brought them into conflict with younger men. The position of women in society became a core battleground, as rich older men could afford to marry additional wives

---

[21] Chagga Association, Mombasa to Mangi Mkuu, 16th October 1953, TNA 5/20/16, Vol. I, f. 75.

[22] Ibid.

[23] Mangi Mwitori of Rombo to all Rombo Chiefs, 'Kutoa vihamba vipya zaidi kwa walio na vihamba', 11th June 1947, TNA 5/687, f. 474.

[24] On the importance attached to acquiring land for children and the lengths which parents would go to achieve this see generally F. S. Lerise, *Politics in Land and Water Management: Study in Kilimanjaro, Tanzania* (Dar es Salaam: Mkuki wa Nyota, 2005).

at the expense of younger men who could not meet escalating expectations of bridewealth.

This local context is important, because in the political debates of the 1940s and 1950s, these very local arguments about land, virtue and wealth intersected with wider arguments about democracy, freedom and citizenship. We can see this intersection if we look at the arguments which took place in the pages of the local newspaper *Komkya* which we first encountered in Chapter 1.

PUBLIC DEBATE IN THE 1950S: KOMKYA, CITIZENSHIP AND LAND

Founded in 1953, *Komkya* was a district newspaper, but one which had a slightly different heritage from that of other district newspapers. Establishing a local newspaper was one of the priorities of the paramount chief of the Chagga, Thomas Marealle, after he took office in January 1952. Marealle intended *Komkya* to serve to develop a new Chagga nationalism, and while it never began publishing in the Chagga language as he had originally hoped and was instead published in Swahili, it was used to print the new Chagga song, report on Chagga Day activities and to bring news of development projects to those Chagga living far away.[25] It provided, as one correspondent to the paper wrote, 'a place for exchanging ideas between ourselves, we Wachagga, to obtain prosperity for ourselves and the progress of our country of Kilimanjaro.'[26]

Komkya was intended to provide written truth to combat the oral rumour which the local colonial administration felt plagued the mountain, and was intended to be 'a "Newspaper" and not a "Views–paper".'[27] Yet the editorials and articles offer glimpses of a particular mid-twentieth-century political imaginary, while the letters pages offer up the traces of a fractious public sphere. Although it is the voices of younger people which are easiest to hear, read carefully their letters offer

---

[25] Mangi Mkuu to D. C., 20th October 1952, TNA 5/10/21/6.

[26] Letter from U.L.M.J. Rengia Senguo, 'Mangi wa nchi awe mkuu wa kiti wa chama cha kugawa ardhi' *Komkya*, 15 September 1955, p. 3. Another correspondent on the same page began his letter 'Nipate nafasi hapo gazetini la Wachagga, nizungumze na Wakubwa hata wadogo' or 'that I should have the opportunity here in the newspaper of the Chagga in order to talk with the big and the small.' Letter from Francis Kimaro, 'Habari za vihamba Uchaggani', *Komkya*, 15 September 1955, p. 3.

[27] 'News Paper for the Wachagga', TNA 5/10/21, f. 10.

a sense of the tensions which prompted them to write, taking advantage of a democratic forum in which all had the right to speak.[28]

Like other district council newspapers, *Komkya* was not political, in the sense that it was not a forum in which anticolonial thinking was expressed. But it was deeply political in another sense. As with *Mambo Leo*, it connected a locality with the wider world. News of young people from the district who had gone to study overseas or achieved educational qualifications helped readers to imagine their place in the world, and to conceive of education and progress in new ways. Reports of development projects helped to give concrete meaning to vague talk of development or *maendeleo*. *Komkya* helped to bring into being a new sort of public. It proceeded as if it was speaking to a known constituency, but in fact there are hints in its pages of the ambiguities of political community in the 1950s. Was it speaking to an imagined ethnic community, a Chagga people? Or to a geographically defined constituency of all those living within the district of Moshi who were therefore ruled, at the local level, by the Chagga Council?

Its pages also contained hints of arguments over the limits of belonging and the nature of local citizenship. Those who wrote to *Komkya* offered a vernacular understanding of citizenship. For them, the citizenship that mattered was Chagga citizenship, and that was defined in terms of land ownership, and specifically, the ownership of the permanent and inheritable plots on which bananas were grown. The point was made very clearly in one letter, published in 1955. 'A homestead plot [*kihamba*] is indeed of great value to any Mchagga'. 'As the part of the country which a person obtains, then builds on' and grows permanent crops, it was 'absolutely essential that we should treasure these things in order that we do not lose our roots.'[29] Yet, the writer continued, land had 'become hard to obtain particularly for those youth who want to start life and follow the customs of a true Mchagga.' Without land a man could not marry, for when he wished to become engaged the first question his intended would ask about was whether they would have a homestead plot on which to live.[30]

[28] John Lonsdale, '"Listen While I Read": Orality, Literacy and Christianity in the Young Kenyatta's Making of the Kikuyu', in Louise de la Gorgendière, Kenneth King and Sarah Vaughan (eds.), *Ethnicity in Africa: Roots, Meanings and Implications* (Edinburgh: Centre of African Studies, 1996), pp. 17–53.

[29] Letter from Petri B. Saika M. Jairo, 'Habari za kihamba Kilimanjaro', *Komkya*, 1 March 1955, p. 3.

[30] Ibid.

Land was therefore understood to be essential, yet it was in ever shorter supply. The reasons for the lack of land seemed to Komkya's correspondents to derive the fact that some had amassed a great deal of land while others had none, and that land was allocated unfairly. Where the issue of land shortage was raised in *Komkya*, attention was drawn to the number of Europeans still occupying land on the mountain, as in a 1959 letter about land shortage in Kibosho claiming that 'half the country has been distributed to Europeans'.[31] The second issue, that of greed and excessive landownership, was the focus of a letter to *Komkya* in July 1955. This unsigned letter began by stating that if a young Chagga man reached the age of eighteen and had no land it was said that he did not have a home. Even if he went away and earned money he often still could not acquire land. Yet there were others who already had one homestead plot and desired more. They would go to the chief and say that they planned to marry a new wife. Given more land for this wife, some would then fail to marry but simply use the new land to feed their animals. Once they had planted a few banana trees and built a house there that land was their property. Chiefs should ensure that those who claimed they needed land for a wife or child actually used them for this purpose.[32] Implicitly, this was an attack on wealthy and influential older men who were in a position to acquire additional land in a way that young men were not.

If unfair allocation of land was the problem, the answer was agreed by *Komkya*'s letter writers to lie in more accountable structures of land allocation, but there was no agreement as to what would constitute accountability. For some, new Land Boards established on a democratic basis were the answer, while for others, an older system should be resurrected whereby land was allocated by chiefs taking due account of the needs of both rich and poor.[33]

Arguments over the position of women also intersected with wider debates. Women who wrote in to *Komkya* made use of a language of progress, and compared their situation with that of women in other countries which had achieved civilization (*ustaarabu*). By the 1950s increasing

---

[31] Letter from M. K. Bruno Leu, 'Taabu ya vihamba Uchaggani', *Komkya*, 1 April 1959, p. 3.
[32] Letter (anon.), 'Vihamba Uchaggani', 1 July 1955, *Komkya*, p. 3.
[33] 'Nchi ya Kibosho itaendelea na mpango wa zamani wa kugawa Ardhi', *Komkya*, 1 August 1955, p. 5; '"Mangi wa Nchi awe Mkuu wa Chama cha Kugawa Ardhi" – Mangi Mwitori, Hai', *Komkya*, 1 September 1955, p. 1. U.L.M.J. Rengia Senguo, 'Mangi wa Nchi awe Mkuu wa Kiti wa Chama cha Kugawa Ardhi', *Komkya*, 15 September 1955, p. 3.

numbers of girls had been to school and were seeking paid employment in Moshi town and beyond, while women were frequently exhorted to stand for election to councils at all levels.[34] Yet away from this shared 'official' discourse ran deeper currents. The position of women provided a second focus for some of the generational tensions explored in the preceding section, while younger men's fears regarding their ability to acquire land and marry were expressed in terms of anxieties over women's sexuality and prostitution.

These arguments focussed on the interconnected nexus of bridewealth, female circumcision and the right of women to inherit land. As we saw in Chapter 1, debates were often framed along generational lines, with young men and women uniting against their fathers. But there were also hints of a conflict along gender lines, and of growing male anxiety about female power. This was the case in the programme of the Chagga Association, the young members of which used letters not only to *Komkya* but direct to the District Office to stress their levels of education and begged that they be allowed gently to explain plans for increased taxation to less-educated fathers on the mountain. For the Chagga Association, the issue of women's behaviour was framed in terms of their wider desire to reduce antisocial behaviour and to enable the Chagga to attain a 'good name'.[35] With regard to prostitution, their proposed solutions were expressed in town-focussed, bureaucratized and medicalized terms. So they attached 'a list of the Chagga prostitutes at present in the Moshi Township with a request to ask the Police to raid them and have them sent back to their homes in the mountain'.[36] Beyond mere information gathering, they offered practical assistance, claiming that they had 'arranged for three members of the Association to guide the Police Constables to the places and houses where these Chagga Prostitutes live and that they were ready at any time to attend your call.'[37] Once arrested, the women in question should be 'sent for Medical Examination: those found suffering from venereal diseases should be maintained for medical treatment in any custody you may consider fit for them until they are quite cured and certified fit for repatriation.'[38]

---

[34] '1952 mwaka wa kutajika katika historia ya Wachagga', *Komkya*, March 1953, p. 1.
[35] Chagga Association, Moshi to District Commissioner, re 'Wachagga Association Moshi', 18 November 1944. TNA 5/25/16, f. 1.
[36] Chagga Association, Moshi to D.C. n.d., c. 1946, TNA 5/25/16, f. 15.
[37] Ibid. Once repatriated, the Mangi should be informed that they 'should not be allowed to visit the Moshi Township without a pass which would be made valid for 12 hours only.'
[38] Chagga Association, Moshi to D.C. n.d., c. 1946, TNA 5/25/16, f. 15.

In complaining about bridewealth, young men not only criticized the elders who demanded excessive sums but also the blamed the women who only wished to marry young men with money or who demanded expensive presents from their boyfriends.[39] Remarking that this was a particular feature of girls who had been to school, Aloisi Ngauyaku finished a 1955 *Komkya* letter by asking rhetorically: 'If rich men marry all the girls, what will we who are not rich do?'[40] The idea that educated young women were making wealth a prime consideration in their choice of a partner meant that fears about prostitution were closely intertwined with fears of increasingly independent women, and these points complicated men's attitudes towards female education.

As elsewhere in the era of decolonization, the theme of *maendeleo*, progress or development, both in material terms relating to wealth and how it could be acquired and in social terms relating to women's rights to education, land and employment, was debated through the lens of intensely local debates and in relation to vernacular conceptions of what it meant to be a Chagga citizen. To be successful, political narratives had to speak simultaneously to global languages of political reform and the locally situated ways in which these questions were debated. The Kilimanjaro Chagga Citizens Union succeeded, very briefly, in seeming to offer a narrative which did both.

THE RISE OF THE KILIMANJARO CHAGGA CITIZENS UNION

In 1949, two men, Joseph Merinyo and Petro Njau, broke away from the Moshi Branch of the territory-wide African Association. The African Association had been founded in Dar es Salaam in 1929, and sought to unite Africans and engage the state under the slogan 'unity is strength'.[41] By 1949 it had expanded across the territory with active branches in a range of provincial centres across the territory. Merinyo and Njau had in mind to establish a new body with themselves at the helm, initially known as the African Association – Moshi Branch, then variously known

---

[39] Letter from Aloisi Ngauyaku, 'Wavulana na wasichana', *Komkya*, 15 September 1955, p. 3; Letter from Joseph L. Masama, 'Mavazi ya wasichana Uchaggani', *Komkya*, 15 November 1955, p. 3.

[40] Letter from Aloisi Ngauyaku, 'Wavulana na wasichana', *Komkya*, 15 September 1955, p. 3.

[41] Iliffe, *A Modern History of Tanganyika*, p. 406.

as the Kilimanjaro Union and the Kilimanjaro Chagga Citizens Union or KCCU.

The term 'Citizens Union' is important. This was a time when similar Citizens Unions were appearing across East Africa, from the Mijikenda Union in Kenya to the Wazaramo Union in Tanzania. Like the African Association, they too sought to build unity, but on an ethnic rather than a pan-African or territorial basis. They were concerned with welfare, but also with political campaigns which included, in the case of the Wazaramo Union in Dar es Salaam, campaigning against Asian traders and fighting to secure the land rights of its members.[42]

East African governments were unsure what to make of these new organizations. On the one hand, they were concerned that they were fronts for the personally ambitious. Writing about the Wazaramo Union in 1948, officials concluded that: '[t]he character of many of the leading members' of the Zaramo Union was 'not good, and the activities of the Union are directed towards their own personal ends to an extent which does not apply in the case of the African Association.' But on the other, officials could see that the new 'tribal societies' had 'potentialities for future political development.'[43]

Historians have been similarly puzzled. Once seen as forces of reaction, standing in the way of nationalist movements, more recently they have attracted attention as crucial factors in the creation of new ethnic identities in late colonial East Africa.[44] But while they did seek to create new ethnic identities, this was not an end in itself. Rather these projects formed part of a larger endeavour which we can place in the context of the issues we have looked at so far in this book. They were creating political subjects under their authority, on whose behalf they would speak, drawing on new concepts of representation.

The two men responsible for the Kilimanjaro Chagga Citizens Union were Joseph Merinyo and Petro Njau. Joseph Merinyo had long been a central figure in the political life of Kilimanjaro. He was born in 1878 and sent to school with the Leipzig missionaries in 1896. As a young man, he travelled to Europe with the German settler Emil Forster and on his return worked as a clerk for Forster and overseer of one of his shops,

---

[42] Brennan, *Taifa*, pp. 68–69; Justin Willis and George Gona, 'The Mijikenda Union, 1945–1980', *Comparative Studies in Society and History*, 55 (2013), 448–473.

[43] East African Political Intelligence Report, November 1948, TNA UK, CO 537/3646, pp. 32–33.

[44] For a helpful summary of the literature, see Willis and Gona, 'Mijikenda Union', pp. 448–452.

then opened his own shop in Moshi in 1911. When the British arrived in 1916, he became a key intermediary, working closely with the colonial official Charles Dundas to promote coffee growing on the mountain. He then became a leading figure in Kilimanjaro's first cooperative organization, the Kilimanjaro Native Planters' Association.

Merinyo's relationship with the district administration, however, became increasingly tense. In 1928 the Provincial Commissioner recorded that, having regard for Merinyo's 'semi-educated and semi-civilized condition', he had been generally tolerant of his activities 'except when he wrote me a scurrilous letter against certain Europeans in which he stated that he regarded it as his duty to champion the rights of the Wachagga.'[45] The District Officer, Captain Hallier, told Merinyo that his claim to represent the Chagga people was incompatible with his position as a civil service clerk and that 'I have no knowledge of an organisation called the "Chagga Community" of which you state you are Secretary, and I shall be glad to be informed who the office bearers are and what the aims and objects are, and whether such organization has the support of the Chagga Chiefs.'[46] In 1929 Merinyo found himself in conflict with the German Lutheran missionaries on Kilimanjaro. Finally in 1931 he was forced out of the Kilimanjaro Native Planters' Association over allegations of corruption. In 1934 he left Moshi to take up a post around seventy miles away at Monduli, in the neighbouring district.[47]

But by 1947 Joseph Merinyo was back in Moshi. Also back in Moshi was Petro Njau, who had been associated with Merinyo's campaign against the Lutheran missionaries in the late 1920s, but had since spent fifteen years away from the mountain, working across Tanzania from Kondoa and Irangi in the centre of the country to Tabora and Kigoma in the far West.[48] Merinyo and Njau both became active in the local African Association, gradually engineering a split in the Association and establishing their own branch of the African Association which then turned

[45] Susan G. Rogers, *Search for Political Focus on Kilimanjaro: A History of Chagga Politics, 1916–1952, with Special Reference to the Cooperative Movement and Indirect Rule'*, p. 345.

[46] Hallier to Merinyo, June 1928, cited in Rogers, *Search for Political Focus on Kilimanjaro: A History of Chagga Politics, 1916–1952, with Special Reference to the Cooperative Movement and Indirect Rule*, p. 347. Rogers was given access to these personal files during her fieldwork in Kilimanjaro.

[47] Rogers, *Search for Political Focus on Kilimanjaro: A History of Chagga Politics, 1916–1952, with Special Reference to the Cooperative Movement and Indirect Rule*, p. 549fn.

[48] Ibid., p. 817fn.

into the Kilimanjaro Chagga Citizens Union. They toured Kilimanjaro hearing complaints about land shortage, abuses of chiefly power, and the recent reorganization of local administration which had radically transformed the role of the chief and the way in which land was allocated. These reforms had been sold as a progressive step, whereby land was allocated by divisional land boards rather than by a chief.

At the same time, the mountain was undergoing major political and administrative reforms. In 1946, Moshi District was divided into three divisions and three superior chiefs, known as 'divisional chiefs' above the existing chiefs. These reforms were hailed by local chiefs as a step towards greater unity. The Chagga chiefs described the reforms as the beginning of a veritable 'democracy in our Chagga land' which would in the future culminate 'in a federated territorial democracy', valuable because: '"Unity is strength".'[49] One of the divisional chiefs appointed, Petro Itosi Marealle (whose ethnography of the Chagga was discussed in Chapter 1), agreed, welcoming the reforms as a step forward in the development of 'modern civilized government', but there was still more to do.[50] For Marealle, restoring harmony in the body politic rested on achieving a suitably blended political system. Marealle found much to praise in the British system, remarking that in matters of government 'England has been a great example for the people of the whole world.' England's system was known as 'democracy', he wrote, using the English word, a system in which the people rule themselves through elected representatives.[51] But although the British had much to teach, masters as they were of 'self-rule', he stated that this system could not simply be imported. Such a system depended for its success entirely on the people who elected their rulers and therefore development in government needed to go alongside development in other areas, particularly of education, universities and agriculture.

But Merinyo and Njau were unhappy about the new system of divisional chiefs and the new system of allocating land. They tapped into a widespread concern about the cost of the administrative reorganization, and the reemergence of long-standing demands for a paramount chief. The idea of a paramount chief for the Chagga had first been mooted in 1934, but had been struck down by the government in Dar es Salaam.[52]

---

[49] Chagga Chiefs to His Excellency the Governor, 26th January 1946, TNA 12844/2, f. 13A.
[50] Marealle, *Maisha ya Mchagga*, p. 127.
[51] Ibid., p. 126.
[52] 'Mangi Mkuu wa Wachagga aliechaguliwa'. *Uremi*, 12th July 1934, p. 1, TNA 20984, f. 45; Rogers, *Search for Political Focus on Kilimanjaro: A History of Chagga Politics,*

By the late 1940s, both the wider context and the specific local context made the idea of a paramount chief once again sound attractive to the people of Kilimanjaro and tolerable to colonial officials. In the first place it appealed to a strand of dissatisfaction with existing chiefs, who were seen as having amassed too much land and coffee wealth, and having failed to stand up for their subjects in arguments over the return of land previously owned by German settlers. But it also made sense in the context of new ideas about locally driven social and economic development. With new potential for raising taxes locally, particularly through taxes on coffee, to fund economic and social development projects, having a clear leader to drive through development projects seemed an attractive proposition.

Merinyo and Njau mobilized public opinion against the divisional chiefs, then when the government agreed to appoint a paramount chief they worked to install their own candidate, supporting the campaign of Thomas Marealle, the nephew of the divisional chief, who was duly elected paramount chief, or *Mangi Mkuu*, of the Chagga in 1951. Their vehicle for doing so was the Chagga Citizens Union.

Once in office, however, Marealle worked hard to distance himself from the Citizens Union which had campaigned so hard for his election. The relationship between Petro Njau and Joseph Merinyo broke down and they stopped working together. The Citizens Union increasingly turned to neo-traditionalism with a sharp disciplinary edge. Yet a close reading of the Citizens Union's political writings from 1949 to the late 1950s shows a striking continuity in their thinking, and strong similarities with other associations across Tanganyika, particularly the Haya Union in Bukoba and associations in the Usambara mountains.[53]

THE POLITICAL LANGUAGE OF THE KCCU

The political language of the Kilimanjaro Union combined transnational idioms with a distinctive construction of history and an innovative use of discourses which had long been current in the region and particularly in the Lutheran church of which Joseph Merinyo and Petro Njau were both members. Their reading of Chagga history led them to construct

---

1916–1952, with Special Reference to the Cooperative Movement and Indirect Rule, pp. 567–573; Ag. Provincial Commissioner to Chief Secretary, 12th October 1934, TNA 13368, f. 194.

[53] Steven Feierman, *Peasant Intellectuals: Anthropology and History in Tanzania* (Madison, WI: University of Wisconsin Press, 1990).

a narrative of a corrupted ancient democracy which could be restored through judicious political reform. In doing so, they imagined a new form of polity which blended older understandings of political membership with newer idioms and contemporary arguments over the meaning and the practice of citizenship.

For the KCCU, the existing structures of rule denied citizens (*raia*) a voice in their own governance. This had to change, but their answer did not lie in giving the people a *direct* voice. Instead, they proposed a new form of citizenship mediated through membership of the Kilimanjaro Union and which devolved to the Union the authority to speak on its members' behalf. Their conception of citizenship institutionalized inequality, linking full political membership to the status of adult land-holding male. Yet it did so in a way which spoke both to the optimistic side of contemporary intellectual life – the developmentalist agenda of *maendeleo* on the one hand and the desire for a new political order which replaced discredited colonial structures on the other – and to the darker side, speaking to contemporary concerns about moral decay coupled with very local concerns about the shortage of land.

The critique of chiefship developed by the KCCU in the late 1940s and early 1950s stemmed from the idea that power had once rested with the people but had been wrested from them by the chiefs. Their understanding of the past drew on historical research conducted earlier in the century by the colonial administrator Charles Dundas and the missionary Bruno Gutmann.[54] Drawing on this research, they offered a distinctive history of the origins of political authority. In the distant past, Chagga people had lived in parishes. Yet conflicts over hunting grounds ensured frequent arguments between parishes. And so the elders of each parish began to define boundaries and to nominate leaders. In choosing leaders, they nominated two for each parish, one to be called headman, and the other to be called *mkudi* or 'customary leader'.[55] This had taken place long ago, before people had begun to keep cattle, but, the Citizens Union claimed, it remained the case that powers should be kept separate and that the people retained the power to appoint and remove headmen and customary leaders as well as the right to allocate land.

Thus, the Union wrote in one of their circulars, 'since ancient times the authority of the people stood above the authority of the chiefs.' The

---

[54] Their historical thinking was set out in a 1950 document called 'A History of the mila ya Wachagga', TNA 5/584, f. 154.
[55] Ibid.

authority of the chief did not include the power to 'install or remove a chief' or a headman or preside over a 'divorce or marriage.' Nor did it include the right to 'give a person land' or move him from his parish.[56] They appealed to the imperial monarchy, and claimed that the king had made a commitment 'to all peoples under his flag' that these laws should be maintained and that the 'customs of the people should continue'. Yet, they argued, an original separation of powers had been corrupted, and the chiefs had taken over powers which should lie with the people.[57]

They attacked the recently imposed divisional chiefs, and called for them to be abolished. Instead, they argued for a nonpolitical head, who should not be called a paramount chief because this would encourage him to think he held the post by hereditary right, a political prime minister and ministers. Separation of powers would be achieved through resurrecting the distinction between headmen who would be the executive power and a post which they termed *Njama* which would be the legislative power. The holders of this post would, they argued, be educated and appointed, in contrast to chiefs.[58] They suggested a few names, all of whom were highly educated.[59]

These reforms, along with abolishing the divisional chiefs, would, they argued, offer the basis of democracy. Yet this democracy would not be an innovation, but rather a restoration of a democracy which had once existed and had been corrupted. In its annual report for 1949 the KCCU wrote that the divisional chiefs were sowing 'hatred, envy and disunity'. They called instead for a 'Paramount Ruler and a Legislature and Executive Councils, with a view of maintaining a full democratic Native Authority' which was a restoration of an earlier principle. They continued, '[s]ince democracy is that Government of the people for the people and by the people. Wachagga had this system of democratic [rule] from very old days and they are right to claim it as one of their Native Custom and Law.'[60]

For the Citizens Union, political reform was a means of restoring a lost world in which power lay with the people. But they did not intend to return power to the people directly, or at least not to all the people. Instead they offered themselves as representative intermediaries, ready

---

[56] 'True Statement Concerning mila ya Wachagga Establishments', TNA 5/584, f. 105.

[57] Ibid.

[58] 'Kilimanjaro Union Moshi Yearly Report 1949', TNA 5/584, f. 101.

[59] Ibid. The names were Thomas Marealle, John Maruma and Thomas Abraham Salema. Their current locations were also given, Maruma in England, Salema at Makerere.

[60] 'Kilimanjaro Union Moshi, Yearly Report, 1949', TNA 5/584, ff. 101–104.

to speak on behalf of those who were currently afraid to speak freely in front of their chiefs. Echoing the language of the seventeenth-century Levellers, their right to speak on their behalf was defended on the grounds that they were 'free-men'.[61] For the Levellers, as discussed in Chapter 3, restricting political representation to those propertied men who could claim the title of 'free-men' was a way of limiting political rights, and a similar hierarchy was implicit in the writings of the KCCU, though often concealed by the use of the ambivalent term *raia*, citizen or subject. There was therefore an implicit hierarchy of rights and it was made increasingly clear in the years after 1951 that true Chagga citizens were older, land-holding, males.

This definition drew on the vernacular understandings of citizenship we explored earlier in the chapter whereby citizenship was defined by ownership of a plot of land, but it also went further in redefining citizenship as mediated through membership of the KCCU. The Union was, they argued, 'the total of all people who are citizens of the country by virtue of working to develop their country for the benefit of all'. They claimed that only those with membership cards could claim special inheritance rights within the country.[62] Membership of the Union therefore conferred citizenship rights and consequently, land rights. Yet membership of the Union carried duties as well as rights.

It was not enough simply to join the Union. Citizenship was conditional and had to be earned. As they wrote in another document, these days 'a cook is not a cook until it is agreed that he knows how to cook', similarly, 'A modern Mchagga is only so when it is agreed that he is a citizen [*mwananchi*] according to the customs of the Chagga, without this he should not be called Mchagga'.[63] Moreover, the same document argued that it was a responsibility of Chagga citizens 'to assist our more unfortunate brethren and prepare our children for posterity.'[64] Evidently such 'unfortunate brethren' were not considered as full members of the KCCU's ideal community.

The recognition of both generational inequality through the need to 'prepare our children' for the future and of inequality within generations,

[61] Rogers, *Search for Political Focus on Kilimanjaro: A History of Chagga Politics, 1916–1952, with Special Reference to the Cooperative Movement and Indirect Rule*, p. 654.

[62] Petro Njau, Kilimanjaro Chagga Citizens Union, Tangazo No. 8 of 1953, 24th November 1953, TNA 5/25/7, f. 189.

[63] 'Mkutano wa mwakani 1953', p. 2, TNA 5/25/7, f. 204.

[64] 'The Constitution of the Kilimanjaro Chagga Citizens' Union', TNA UK, CO 892/10/1.

'our more unfortunate brethren', speaks to a central element of the Chagga Citizens Union's political language: the concern with the duty which those with wealth had to those without. As Steven Feierman shows in his study of the Usambara Citizens Union in the 1950s, opposition to new agricultural legislation derived not from hostility to capitalism per se but from a concern with ensuring the welfare of all. As Feierman wrote, 'According to my observations in the 1960s, prosperous coffee farmers were never criticized for taking up commercial farming. This was accepted as admirable. They were criticized only if they did not use the profits to help meet the needs of less fortunate relatives.'[65] In a similar vein, the KCCU sought to reestablish older hierarchies whereby the rich were both able and willing to fulfil their duties towards poorer kinsmen, and to provide for their children.

Although it was the demands for political reform which captured attention, the KCCU was also, like the Haya and other similar unions, concerned with a perceived breakdown of the moral order.[66] Echoing the arguments made in *Uremi* in the 1930s, Petro Njau in 1957 blamed Chagga for wasting their labour power on Europeans who were willing to pay for it, but he also attacked the stupidity of self-interested pursuit of wealth which brought riches to some while forgetting the poverty of others.[67] He lamented that the modern Chagga man did not real-ise the loss caused by selling his labour power, or the greater loss, that of personal moral decline, which he suffered as a result. Working for Europeans was an error which, Njau wrote, led a person to 'drink much beer, smoke more cigarettes, go to the cinema, encourage prostitution and buy cars'.[68]

Rather than realizing that unity was the best path to wealth, they were competing against each other and depending on working for Europeans which was in itself debasing. There had been a breakdown of trust, so that one could see 'people of one family in one village on the mountain unable to trust each other. That is, the child does not trust the father and the mother does not trust the child, similarly even the rich person does not trust the poor person and the poor person does not trust the rich person.' All this was the result of 'robbery and jealousy', the removal of

---

[65] Feierman, *Peasant Intellectuals: Anthropology and History in Tanzania*, p. 195.
[66] See Peterson, *Ethnic Patriotism and the East African Revival: A History of Dissent, c. 1935–1972*.
[67] 'A Memorandum on the Proposed Demonstration Farm, Hillcrest Estate', 5 August 1957, TNA 5/25/7, f. 299.
[68] Ibid.

which were as urgent as the fight against the plague.[69] Their enthusiasm for capitalism was tempered by a sense of the mistrust which it brought.

The Union's founding document echoed the sense of moral decay found in church councils and the polemics of church periodicals in the interwar period.[70] What was new was offering a framework of social, political and moral regeneration which went beyond confessional boundaries, and indeed beyond religious ones. Moreover, the Union's explanation for the root of moral decay was different from that of the Lutherans. It did not lie in greed, whether of a desire for clothes or money. The ambition to create wealth was considered a good one. The problem was the way in which people were making money and the mistrust which this brought.

The answer Njau offered was discipline under the leadership of the Union. In the first meeting, held in January 1949, he spoke of moral decline among the Chagga and a lack of trust in the Government. He offered the Union's services as moral policeman, stating that if anyone was found to be guilty of theft or dishonesty, they should immediately be accused before the Union. And if the person was not a member of the Union, they should be dealt with by the structures of local government. If that did not work, then the Union should inform the government immediately.[71] In this way, the Union was setting itself up as a disciplinary organization which would restore order, much in the way that the Lutheran Missionary Bruno Gutmann's system of church discipline in the 1920s and 1930s had been intended to restore order and harmony among the Lutheran community.[72] Njau insisted that the way to restore trust and unity was to accept the leadership of the Union. In the same vein, he called for the reinstitution of a 'traditional oath'.[73]

If discipline and trust could be restored through the Union, then this would be the basis of true civilization (*ustaarabu*) and 'a new life' for a new Chagga people. Echoing earlier debates about the nature of civilization among missionaries and in the pages of *Mambo Leo*, Njau offered his own definition of this key concept, writing that this civilization was

[69] 'Kilimanjaro Chagga Union amezaliwa Moshi', TNA 5/584, ff. 30–38, p. 1. The theme of unity as an essential prelude to wealth creation was central to the Union's thinking throughout the period. See also TNA 5/25/7, f. 204, p. 3 and f. 234, p. 2.

[70] See the Lutheran periodical *Ufalme wa Mungu*, e.g., Letter from Ruben Moshi, *Ufalme wa Mungu*, January 1930, p. 9.

[71] 'Mkutano wa Halimashauri wa Kilimanjaro Branch, Tanganyika African Association, Moshi tarekh 20th January 1949', TNA 5/583, f. 825.

[72] J. C. Winter, *Bruno Gutmann, 1876–1966: A German Approach to Social Anthropology* (Oxford: Oxford University Press, 1979), pp. 209–211.

[73] 'Kilimanjaro Chagga Union amezaliwa Moshi', TNA 5/584, f. 31.

not about adornments for the body while 'leaving body and soul in the mud'; rather it was about 'purifying body and mind' through hard work and cooperation.[74]

One element of the new disciplinary order which the Chagga Citizens Union had in mind was to resurrect the institution of clanship and the position of clan elders. They described the problems which had increased since the authority of the clan elders had been lost, citing in particular 'the price of bridewealth, lack of manners and respect, dishonesty in relation to property'. Solving these problems should not be left to the Native Authority or the government but lay in male and female clan elders reasserting their authority too.[75]

But while resurrecting old institutions was one element of their agenda, they also thought creatively about new institutions which could be developed. A petition delivered to the East Africa Royal Commission addressed the problem of unemployed or underemployed youth, those with neither salaried jobs nor a future on the land. It lamented the position of those youths who left school after Standard IV unable to 'make efficient farmers because even their knowledge of soil and its uses is so scanty'. Not only was this lack of knowledge detrimental to the task of bringing development, but these youth were also tending to leave the mountain and 'drift into the towns to swell the numbers of spivs.'[76] The Union clearly saw these people as a problem, rather than as a support base. Their solution was a technical school catering to those leaving after four years of primary education, and described this school as 'Rika and Ngasi', terms which referred respectively to the age-grade system and an initiation ritual.[77] They envisaged the 'formation and institution of an inter-racial cooperative farm with a village school attached for the Three R's and simple understanding of the arts.' This, they claimed, was

---

[74] p. 1 of document missing from file, but title likely to be 'Minutes of Meeting, Kilimanjaro Union, 28 April 1949', TNA 5/584, f. 14, p. 10.

[75] 'Mkutano maalumu wa wanachama', 2 February 1956, TNA 5/25/7, f. 266; Kilimanjaro Chagga Citizens Union Pamphlet No. 4 of 1954, 'Urithi wa Wenyeji wa Nchi ni Mila, Iliyotokana na Wakale Wao', 26 July 1954, p. 5, TNA 5/25/7, f. 221.

[76] 'A Full Report on Recent Tour of the Mountain by President, Kilimanjaro Chagga Citizens Union', p. 7. TNA UK, CO 892/10/1. The report was attached to the Kilimanjaro Chagga Citizens Union Memorandum, which they sent to the East Africa Royal Commission care of the Colonial Office on 28th June 1953.

[77] See Rogers, *Search for Political Focus on Kilimanjaro: A History of Chagga Politics, 1916–1952, with Special Reference to the Cooperative Movement and Indirect Rule*, pp. 85–86. She emphasizes that chiefly control over these occasions was an important factor in establishing chiefs' authority and allowing them to operate successful war machines; thus the claim by the KCCU to take responsibility for such things is significant.

'the missing link in the true development of Uchagga Citizenship.'[78] Citizenship, as has already been suggested, required training, it was not a right.

The KCCU's political vision then, like that of the Haya Union in Bukoba, resurrected and institutionalized the authority of male patriarchs. It balanced the conservatism of a search to restore older bonds of community with a promise of a better future, speaking to developmentalist discourses. The reassertion of a particular form of social power, under the leadership of the KCCU, would be the basis of future wealth for the district. Yet it also spoke to the mood of political reform after 1945.

POLITICAL REFORM AND THE KCCU

The KCCU's memorandum to the East African Royal Commission in 1953 called on the Commission to 'work out a scheme whereby Citizens in Tanganyika are enabled to unite together to exchange views under a *Tanganyika Citizens Union* scheme so as to see how their fellows are fairing [sic] in the different districts and how they are tackling their common problems.'[79] In 1956, shortly after the establishment of the United Tanganyika Party (UTP) which the governor Twining hoped would provide a conservative opposition to TANU, Njau announced that 'I'm happy to confirm our aim of uniting the unity of Wachagga in a union has been the foundation of building friendship and peace in the country, although it is not easy for the neighbouring tribes to do this.' The intention of this friendship-building was 'finally to reach the aim of leading the whole of Tanganyika to be a Union of all the Tribes of Tanganyika.'[80] The KCCU claimed that they could teach a new model of good citizenship based on trust, unity and cooperation. They claimed that this could serve as the foundation for a new model of Tanganyikan citizenship, through a gradual process of exporting the model.

But thinking about citizenship also entailed thinking about the rights and responsibilities of non-Africans. In many parts of Tanzania, opposition to the political and economic dominance of Europeans and Asians was a central motive in political activism. In Mwanza, it was hostility

---

[78] 'A Full Report on Recent Tour of the Mountain by President, Kilimanjaro Chagga Citizens Union', p. 7. TNA UK, CO 892/10/1.

[79] Kilimanjaro Chagga Citizens Union, 'Memorandum', to East Africa Royal Commission, 28 June 1953, p. 10. TNA UK, CO 892/10/1, f. 29.

[80] Kumbukumbu ya Mkutano wa Executive Committee ya Kilimanjaro Chagga Citizens Union, 5 May 1956, TNA 5/25/7, f. 270, p. 2.

towards Asian business practices and perceived exploitation of Africans which encouraged the setting up of the successful Victoria Federation of Co-operative Unions, while S. A. Kandoro's accounts of African Association meetings in the region carry a millenarian tone which included a generalized anti-Europeanism.[81] In contrast, despite Njau's general opposition to multiracialism, he attempted to consider ways in which non-Africans could be integrated into the political system. At a KCCU meeting in 1956, Njau claimed that the demand by Europeans and Asians to cooperate in developing the country was 'undoubtedly the best way to bring prosperity in the country between Europeans, Asians and native Africans.'[82] The message was emphatically inclusive, and a similar tone appeared when in July 1956 Njau announced that the Kilimanjaro Union would henceforth be known as the Tanganyika Citizens Union. He explained that the expansion of the work of its work had necessitated this change of name. Their objects included the cultivation and development of 'a civic sense of pride in our country and responsibilities of Citizenship within the territory', the extension and advancement of 'a healthy public opinion' and the maintenance and strengthening of 'contacts with the outside world with a view to exchanging ideas for the mutual benefit of all free men', but also an increased concern with relations between the races.[83]

What was innovative about Njau's thinking regarding the politics of multiracialism was his suggestion that including Europeans and Asians did not mean accepting non-African domination. He presented a subtle set of arguments which rested on the idea that there were different levels of citizenship. In the minutes of an Annual General Meeting held in September 1956 the question was raised, 'Who is a *mwenyeji* (native) and who is not a *mwenyeji*?' As we have seen, the term *mwenyeji* (pl. *wenyeji*) was used by the colonial administration to signify 'Africans' or 'natives' in contrast to European or Asian settlers, but in the 1940s, as the term 'African' came to replace the term 'native' in colonial discourse, the term *mwenyeji* was increasingly used within African political discourse to play an important role as an affirmative category, which gave rights to some while excluding others. James Brennan describes the 'powerful first-comer overtones' of the Swahili term *mwenyeji*, connotations not present in the

---

[81] S. A. Kandoro, *Mwito wa uhuru* (Dar es Salaam: Thakers, 1961), p. 39.

[82] Kumbukumbu ya mkutano wa executive committee ya Kilimanjaro Chagga Citizens Union, 5 May 1956, TNA 5/25/7, f. 270, p. 4.

[83] Tanganyika Citizens Union to Editor, *Tanganyika Sunday News*, 14 June 1956, TNA 5/25/7, f. 274. The letter was printed in the *Sunday News* of 1 July 1956, p. 3.

English term.[84] In Dar es Salaam, the term was a weapon which not only could be directed against Europeans and Asians but was also used by long-standing Swahili families in Dar es Salaam to defend their rights above those of more recent immigrants, and we see the development of a similar language of claim-making in rural areas. Here it linked an idea of 'the people' to a claim to rights of citizenship in the region.

The record of the 1956 meeting began by stating that there were some *wenyeji* who were failing to inherit land and that this would continue as all the land would soon have been 'swallowed'. The mistake the Chagga had made had been to believe that the land could reproduce itself in the way that people did.[85] There would therefore increasingly be people without land. They went on to say that Europeans and Asians did not have traditional plots of land but rather derived their claim to political membership from farms and rental plots. This could also apply to the children who lacked permanent plots but instead relied on a weaker tenure of land-holding.

This left open the possibility that Europeans and Asians too might, over time, become a certain type of native (*mwenyeji*). Ideas for their incorporation seem to have been modelled on ideas surrounding the incorporation of strangers. Clans had long accepted so-called 'strangers' from elsewhere and given them certain rights over land in return for their provision of labour and other services. Later, chiefs had adopted the same strategy to increase the number of men under arms, then in the colonial period to ensure that all land claimed by the chiefdom appeared to be lived in and to increase the number of inhabitants which could be claimed, a larger number having beneficial consequences for chiefly remuneration, both official and less-official.[86] Thus when the meeting went on to talk about the need to build trust between the races, emphasizing the role which the Tanganyika Citizens Union could play in this task, they discussed how a stranger (*mgeni*) could become a *mwenyeji* (native). The minutes recorded that: '[m]any people do not like to hear a person being called a foreigner, not realising that a person cannot become a *mwenyeji* without

[84] James R. Brennan, 'Realizing Civilization through Patrilineal Descent: African intellectuals and the making of an African Racial Nationalism in Tanzania, 1920–50', *Social Identities*, 12 (2006), 405–423, p. 410

[85] 'Mkutano Mkuu wa Mwakani wa Kilimanjaro Chagga Citizens Union, Uliokutanika kwenye jengo la Head-Quarters la Union, Tarehe 25th September, 1956', p. 2., TNA 5/25/7, f. 285.

[86] Griffith, 'Chagga Land Tenure Report', p. 81 and M. Howard and A. V. Millard, *Hunger and Shame: Poverty and Child Malnutrition on Mount Kilimanjaro* (New York: Routledge, 1997), p. 51.

starting with "foreignness" (*ugeni*).'[87] Therefore there were various types of foreignness, just as there were various types of *wenyeji*. According to Chagga custom, Njau claimed, there were two stages in becoming a *mwenyeji*, the first of which could be completed after five years and the second after thirty years. It was up to clan leaders to manage this incorporation.

The possibility that such ideas could be applied more generally proposed a radical reworking of the discussions around multiracialism which were going on in Tanganyika at that time. It offered a territorial definition of citizenship and a citizenship which could be earned over time, providing an answer to what Njau thought was wrong with movements like TANU which the KCCU had, in 1954, denounced as a 'racial group'.[88]

Moreover, if the new structures imagined were decidedly local, Njau's idea was not that Kilimanjaro and its people should cut themselves off from the rest of Tanganyika, but that these local foundations were needed to build a nation. When the KCCU had broken away from the territorial African Association in 1949 they had justified it by saying that the Association was best formed as an agglomeration of 'tribal branches'. For him, not only was the Tanganyika African Association simply one 'large branch within Africa', but it was also important to recognize that 'Tanganyika itself also has its groups within it'. But whereas for later nationalists, recognition of difference seemed to threaten unity, for Njau it was the foundation of unity, through building 'peace, hope and love'.[89] In a similar vein, in a memorandum to the Committee on Constitutional Development which visited Moshi in 1950, Njau's organization compared their task to that of missionary work, stating that 'Kilimanjaro Union is a Mission of the Natives of Tanganyika'.[90] Their task was to teach other ethnicities to do as the people of Kilimanjaro had done, that is, to 'love each other, to trust each other and to unite' in order to build civilization (*ustaarabu*).[91]

---

[87] 'Mkutano Mkuu wa Mwakani wa Kilimanjaro Chagga Citizens Union, Uliokutanika kwenye jengo la Head-Quarters la Union, Tarehe 25th September, 1956', p. 7, TNA 5/25/7, f. 285.

[88] Iliffe, *A Modern History of Tanganyika*, p. 515.

[89] Kilimanjaro Branch African Association, 'Mkutano wa watu wote kufungulia office ya Umoja wa Kilimanjaro', 7 November 1948, TNA 5/583, f. 820.

[90] Government of Tanganyika, *Report of the Committee on Constitutional Development, 1951* (Dar es Salaam: Government Printer, 1951), p. 27.

[91] Kilimanjaro Union, Moshi, Memorandum, TNA 5/39/12, f. 9. The same analogies appeared in a 1955 circular: Kilimanjaro Union Free-Men's, Circular No. 2 of 1955, 27th September, 1955, p. 1, TNA 5/25/7, f. 255.

The narrative presented by Njau and the Kilimanjaro Chagga Citizens Union was briefly compelling, but using transnational idioms also opened up the potential for those same idioms to be used against them. The Union was charged with misusing the term 'democracy' to describe the original political formation in the region. The argument that an original democracy had existed which had then been corrupted was challenged on the grounds that it had not existed historically. In his response to the Union's challenge in 1949, the divisional chief Petro Itosi Marealle argued that there had been no system of democracy in the 'Chagga tribe' of the past 'since their Chiefs were esteemed as gods'. Yet in contrast, he understood the new administrative reforms to have begun the process of bringing democratic government to the mountain. 'Democracy', he argued, was 'now in practice in the country.'[92] The Provincial Commissioner also believed that democracy existed on Kilimanjaro, stating that 'that the Regional and Chagga Councils are fully democratic bodies to which the majority of Councillors are elected by the people to be the mouthpieces and the eyes and ears of the people'.[93]

Just as the Union's use of the term democracy was challenged, so too was their use of the term 'free-men'. The charge was made that they were misusing this term, and employing it to claim rights to which they were not entitled and as a way of avoiding their obligations. At a meeting in September 1949, Kilimanjaro's chiefs informed the Provincial Commissioner that 'the K.U. was engaged in undermining the authority of the Native Authority and by the use of the words "free men", and their speeches and writings in connection with these words, had led the people to disobey the orders of constituted authority'.[94] At a meeting held by the divisional chiefs in October, attended by various headmen, elders and councillors, the same point was made. It was claimed that the effect of the word 'free-men' was that members of the Union refused to do communal work for the good of the country.[95] One elder named Michael from the chiefdom of Kirua Vunjo said 'on the mountain when there is any government work to do the members of the Kilimanjaro Union refuse and show contempt for the native authority saying that they are 'Free men' because

---

[92] Mangi Mwitori, Vunjo to D. C. Moshi, 'Re Kilimanjaro Union Annual Report 1949', TNA 5/584, f. 150.

[93] T. M. Revington to Liuham Martin, the Kilimanjaro Office, 4 April 1950, TNA 5/584, f. 173.

[94] 'Notes on a Meeting held with … Chiefs at Hai Headquarters on.. 20 September, 1949', TNA 5/584, f. 84.

[95] Mangi Mwitori, Hai, to Provincial Commissioner, 'Extraordinary Meeting held at Chagga Council 17 October 1949', 19 October 1949, TNA 5/584, ff. 76–80.

they are members of the Kilimanjaro Union.'[96] Another said that 'parties which are led in this way are dangerous and can bring difficulties like in the time of coffee', referring to the coffee riots of 1937, provoked when the government insisted that coffee growers sell their crop through the cooperative, despite the low prices offered.[97]

The Union was also criticized for its attempt to redefine citizenship, and equate it with membership of the KCCU. The claim that full citizenship was to be confined to those who carried membership cards became the focus of a new party established to oppose the KCCU, labelling it a 'subversive organisation' and objecting to 'the statement made by the [Kilimanjaro Union] that only those people with membership cards ... would be considered true Wachagga; anyone without a membership card being classified as an outcast.'[98] Interestingly, this party, the Chagga Congress, argued that 'the cards in themselves were harmless, but alarm was felt concerning the fact that a photograph of the member was required for each card'.[99] The District Commissioner welcomed the new party, 'since it may tend to restore a sense of proportion in the local outlook towards such associations, which has been liable to confuse the functions of party and state and led to claims to identify membership of an association with the rights of citizenship'.[100]

The KCCU combined a distinctive reading of Kilimanjaro's history and tropes which had long had currency both in Swahili newspapers like *Mambo Leo* and in the local Lutheran and cooperative press with an innovative use of new transnational idioms which had gained currency after 1945. Their ability to respond to deeply felt concerns at the heart of Kilimanjaro's public Swahiliphone debate combined with the use of transnational idioms helped the KCCU gain a hearing, but also opened it up to alternative constructions of history and alternative readings of Kilimanjaro's past and visions of its future.

[96] Ibid.
[97] Kimari, 'Mzee wa Baraza'. Cited in Mangi Mwitori, Hai, to Provincial Commissioner, 'Extraordinary Meeting held at Chagga Council 17th October 1949', 19 October 1949, TNA 5/584, ff. 76–80. For a full narrative account of the coffee riots, see Rogers, *Search for Political Focus on Kilimanjaro: A History of Chagga Politics, 1916–1952, with Special Reference to the Cooperative Movement and Indirect Rule*, pp. 776, 776fn, 711. See also Charlotte Leubuscher, 'Marketing Schemes for Native-Grown Produce in African Territories', *Africa* 12 (1939), 163–188; Provincial Commissioner to Chief Secretary, 8th March 1938, TNA UK, CO 691/168/2, ff. 14–15.
[98] Minutes of the Meeting of the Chagga Congress which met in the Welfare Centre on Saturday 30th January, 1954 at 11am', TNA 12844/4, f. 538, p. 2.
[99] Ibid., p. 2.
[100] District Commissioner to Provincial Commissioner, 24 March 1954, TNA 12844/4, f. 545A, p. 1.

CONCLUSION

This chapter has argued that from its foundation in 1949 the KCCU used the new opportunities brought by political reform and new languages of politics rhetorically to create a new political community. This was a vision of a political community which offered the people a greater voice and freedom from oppression by unjust rulers. But it was not a vision of political, social or economic equality. Rather they promised *maendeleo* on the basis of reconfigured social relations, so that the rich would help the poor, and the strong would help the weak. Parents would once again be able to provide land for their children, and patrons could deliver for their clients. This conservative vision was briefly attractive to a wide constituency, but, as we shall see in Chapter 6, it could not sustain political support.

As we shall see, the difference between the KCCU and other ethnically based Citizens Unions on the one hand and nationalist organizations like TANU on the other, was less that the first group were formed on ethnic lines and the latter on 'national' lines, and more that they provided different sorts of answers to the same set of questions about social change and political authority and where it should lie. This microhistory of a political movement in one locality has also suggested wider themes. First, we have seen that while arguments about political reform were increasingly framed in terms of arguments about democracy and citizenship, they did not simply reproduce these languages, but rather keywords and concepts were reworked and deployed in different ways. Second, we can see here in condensed form some of the key themes which defined the politics of the late 1940s and early 1950s. Membership, and possession of a membership card to prove belonging, was important not just for political societies but for other associations. It was, for example, claimed that the popularity of a local youth club grew when membership cards were introduced. A membership card was understood to bestow particular rights and the capacity for claim making on its bearer.

But this case study also shows the importance of realizing freedom through membership and the tensions which this invoked. The KCCU was briefly able to do this, at the time of the election of the paramount chief in 1951, but thereafter it became increasingly apparent that the exclusionary and hierarchical nature of the political community they imagined was incompatible with the idea of freedom articulated in the locality. In the next chapter we shall look at this idea of freedom in more detail.

5

Freedom in Translation

What did 'freedom' mean for mid-twentieth-century Tanzanians? In a letter written to a former colonial official shortly after independence in 1961, Gicha Mbee, a resident of Mbugwe in north-east Tanzania, tried to explain. In his letter, Mbee recounted events in north-eastern Tanganyika as independence approached. 'As the day of freedom approached, many were assailed by doubts. But when the day arrived all doubts were thrown aside and there was only rejoicing. I must say that everyone believed in Freedom'.[1] But there was a problem, for as Mbee continued, 'everyone understands Freedom to mean that we shall rule ourselves – this has been thoroughly explained – but the elders and the youths interpret self-rule in different ways, and this has caused misunderstanding and quarrelling'.[2]

Mbee set up a clear contrast between an understanding of 'freedom' as a return to life without the political society constructed under colonial rule and an alternative understanding of freedom which he termed 'modern', in which freedom was found within political society and entailed the duty of hard work to build that political society. According to Mbee, the elders imagined that self-rule meant a return to life before colonial rule. Officials from the new Tanganyika African National Union (TANU) government would call meetings and explain what 'Freedom' meant, but the elders said that nothing had changed. Why had precolonial officials not been restored, why were taxes still demanded, and why could they not hunt game without a licence? 'We younger men', Mbee continued, 'tried

---

[1] Gicha Mbee, 'Letter from Mbugwe, Tanganyika', *Africa*, 35 (1965), 198–208, p. 199.
[2] Ibid., p. 199.

to explain the meaning of Freedom under modern conditions, but the elders would not listen to us.'[3]

This chapter tracks the Swahili term *uhuru* ('freedom') as a 'word in motion' in twentieth-century Tanzania. To say that freedom came before independence is to turn mid-twentieth-century nationalist discourse on its head, yet this formulation contains an important truth. Across the world, postcolonial states turned 'freedom' into 'independence', which is to say that they reworked terms which had once carried an infinite array of mutually incompatible yet extraordinarily powerful meanings associated with a conception of 'freedom', and translated them simply as 'independence'. In doing so they sought to close down the challenge which languages of freedom posed to their authority. Yet this post hoc imposition of singularity masks the range of languages at freedom at play in colonial contexts in the mid-twentieth century, and it draws attention away from the local contexts in which freedom was defined.

Recent studies of South Asia and Indonesia, discussed in the text that follows, serve as comparative reminders of the variety of vocabularies of freedom which existed in colonial settings in the twentieth century. In this chapter we start by looking at the richness of languages of freedom in the mid-twentieth century. Across the colonial world, new languages of freedom were developed in dialogue both with older understandings of freedom and with newer articulations of liberty and freedom. As a result, languages of freedom were both global and locally specific, and could be employed to multiple ends in local contexts. We then move on to explore the term *uhuru* in Tanzanian discourse and track it as it became increasingly important over the course of the 1950s. While the term had powerful connotations of what might be termed negative freedom, as a way of articulating freedom from colonial authority or indeed freedom from all authority, this conception coexisted with an older idea of freedom through belonging. Briefly in the late 1950s, and crucially for their success, nationalists appeared to be able to offer both freedom from authority and freedom through belonging, through linking it with the concept of *maendeleo*, progress or development, the history of which was discussed in Chapter 1.

MERDEKA, FREEDOM, UHURU

After the Second World War, the language of 'freedom' flourished across the colonial world. This was a global process, but to acquire meaning in

[3] Ibid., p. 199.

local contexts, transnational languages of freedom had to engage with local ideas, both older resonances and competing understandings of freedom in the present.

The use of vernacular languages ensured that languages of freedom had local inflections. Thus, for example in Japan, users of the compound *jiyū*, used to mean 'freedom' or 'liberty', had to navigate a tension between a conception of liberty in the sense of freedom of the press or freedom of religion and a negative sense of freedom as 'selfishness'.[4] In Indonesia, the term *merdeka*, meaning a legal status of 'free' as opposed to 'slave', akin to the Arabic term *hurr*, had roots in the Sanskrit term *maharddika* which had a sense of wisdom, eminence and wealth. The word *merdeka* seems to have arrived in Indonesian languages in contact with Malay-speaking areas by around 1600.[5] In Javanese texts in the nineteenth century, this sense coexisted with an older idea of 'being pensioned or liberated from government service' so, for example, the '*pardikan desa* ('freed villages') of Java were given a charter freeing them from any tax or service to the king.'[6] When English writers began to produce Malay dictionaries, in dialogue with Malay thinkers such as Munshi Abudllah bin Abdul Kadir, they employed *merdeka* as the equivalent of the English term 'free'.[7] As a result, it became the site at which arguments over the meaning of true liberty were debated.

The multilayered dimensions of *merdeka* ensured that tensions persisted between freedom from authority and the fear from those who sought to create authority that complete freedom would lead to a loss of control. Conservative politicians such as Ki Hadjar Dewantoro defined *merdeka* as 'not the absence of authority', but rather 'knowing how to control oneself'.[8] Similar tensions persisted as the term was increasingly appropriated by nationalists to mean national independence. In Indonesia in the autumn of 1945, the term *merdeka* became, in Anthony Reid's words, 'a talisman, the key word of an aroused people', echoing on

[4] Douglas Howland, *Translating the West: Language and Political Reason in Nineteenth-Century Japan* (Honolulu: University of Hawai'i Press, 2002), p. 96.
[5] There was an older Sanscrit term, *maharddika*, present in Indonesian languages before 1600 which had a sense of wisdom, eminence and wealth. Anthony Reid, 'Merdeka: The Concept of Freedom in Indonesia', in David Kelly and Anthony Reid (eds.), *Asian Freedoms: The Idea of Freedom in East and Southeast Asia* (Cambridge: Cambridge University Press, 1998), pp. 141–160, p. 143.
[6] Reid, ibid., pp. 142–143.
[7] Ibid., p. 151.
[8] Ibid., p. 154.

the streets of Jakarta and across Java and Sumatra.[9] As the writer K'tut Tantri explained: 'Merdeka, in the language of Indonesia, means freedom. Nothing more.'[10]

For the postcolonial state in Indonesia, *merdeka* was used to mean simply independence, but in the 1940s it had been much more than that. *Merdeka* had the power to capture imaginations because it could articulate so many different ideas. It was powerful precisely because it did not simply mean political freedom. The same expansive yet potent term carried ideas of political freedom, social revolution, and, on the individual level, something 'far more immediate and personal'.[11] In South Asia too, postcolonial narratives of the 'transfer of power' have eclipsed the richness of thinking about freedom in the 1940s, a time when there was not one but many 'vocabularies of freedom'. As Yasmin Khan writes, 'The words "Pakistan", "*swaraj*" and "Partition" have acquired concrete meanings in the intervening sixty years. In contrast, "freedom" was not clearly defined in 1947.'[12] On his tour of North India in 1946, the retired official Malcolm Darling found that *azadi*, freedom, was 'the word which comes up sooner or later at every meeting'.[13] Yet its meaning was expansive. As Darling explained, 'When the word *azadi* – freedom – was mentioned there was no dissentient voice. All wanted it and when I asked what they would do with it when they got it, a Sikh replied, "Now we are slaves. When we are free we shall serve ourselves and do as we like. Then we shall gladly pay more taxes".'[14] Politicians manipulated this very ambiguity. In a speech in 1946, Jawaharlal Nehru said that a free India would mean that 'everybody would be provided with sufficient food, education and all the facilities including a house to live', whereas, in contrast, Pakistan would mean 'slavery forever'.[15] In Zambian political discourse, described by David Gordon, the Bemba language had two terms, one for 'freedom' which was *butungwa*, which meant the 'cutting off and castration of old kinship ties', while the term for 'independence' was *tekele*, which had a sense of 'taking control of oneself'.[16]

[9] Ibid., p. 155.
[10] Ibid., p. 141.
[11] Ibid., p. 156.
[12] Yasmin Khan, *The Great Partition: The Making of India and Pakistan* (New Haven, CT: Yale University Press, 2007), p. 5.
[13] Ibid., p. 12.
[14] Ibid.
[15] Ibid., p. 33.
[16] David M. Gordon, *Invisible Agents: Spirits in a Central African History* (Athens, OH: Ohio University Press, 2012), p. 116.

But the expansiveness of late colonial languages of freedom faded quickly after independence as postcolonial states took possession of these languages of freedom and purposively sought to subordinate freedom to political independence. In Indonesian official texts, *merdeka* was used to mean 'national independence'. In East Africa, the term *uhuru* was, increasingly from 1955, similarly fixed to the specific context of political independence, a shift recognized by the East African Swahili Committee in their annual meeting in 1961 when they minuted their regret that 'Tanganyika had chosen to use 'uhuru' to mean both 'freedom' and 'independence'.'[17] In making this move, postcolonial elites established control over the meaning of freedom, and closed down the multiple meanings which had once circulated.[18]

In a transnational context, if 'freedom' in its various expressions could be a powerful political slogan precisely because it could articulate such a wide array of competing political projects, it also prompted explicit debates about its meaning which were inflected by the Cold War context of the 1950s. When twenty-nine newly independent African and Asian nations met at Bandung in April 1955, it was no longer clear that national self-determination would ensure individual freedoms. Speeches by delegates from Iran, Iraq and the Philippines, among others, expressed concern about the risk which communism posed to individual freedoms, and by a more general risk posed by the temptation of one-party rule and authoritarianism. As the representative from the Philippines, Carlos Romulo asked:

Is the struggle for national independence the struggle to substitute a local oligarchy for the foreign oligarchy? Or is it just the beginning of the conquest of real freedom by the people of the land? Is there political freedom where only one political party may rule? Is there political freedom where dissent from the policy of the government means imprisonment or worse? It strikes me that autocratic rule, control of the press, and the police state are exactly the worst features of some colonialist systems against which we have fought all our lives and against which so many of us are still fighting. Is this really the model of freedom we seek? Or is it the free interplay of contending parties, the open competition of ideas and political views in the market place, the freedom of a man to speak up as he chooses, be he right or wrong?[19]

---

[17] 'Minutes of the Twenty-fifth Annual General Meeting of the East African Swahili Committee held in University Hall, Makerere University College, Kampala, Uganda on Tuesday 14th and Wednesday 15th November, 1961', *Swahili: Journal of the East African Swahili Committee*, 33 (1962/3), p. 142.

[18] Harri Englund, *Prisoners of Freedom: Human Rights and the African Poor* (Berkeley: University of California Press, 2006), p. 3.

[19] Roland Burke, *Decolonization and the Evolution of Human Rights* (Philadelphia: University of Pennsylvania Press, 2010), p. 30.

In response to attacks on the risks communism posed to individual freedoms, the Chinese premier Zhou Enlai added a new section to his speech, claiming that religious freedom was respected in communist China and that his government would 'respect all those who have religious belief'.[20]

In the colonial and emerging postcolonial world of the 1940s and 1950s, languages of freedom thus served as rallying cries which could bring people out onto the streets and compel them to action. But 'freedom' was not straightforward; its meaning was debated and discussed. Moreover, while it might be a transnational language on the move, it took on distinctive inflections depending on the language used and the political context. We move now to see how it was interpreted and employed in 1950s Tanganyika.

LANGUAGES OF FREEDOM IN TANZANIA

The Swahili term *uhuru* derives from the Arabic root *hurr*, with its association with the legal status of not being enslaved. For the missionaries who arrived on the Swahili coast in the late nineteenth century, it was a natural choice to convey the meaning of emancipation. In his 1882 *Dictionary of the Suahili Language*, the CMS missionary Ludwig Krapf defines freedom as the *opposite* of slavery. For Krapf, *hurru* signifies 'free, not in a state of slavery', while *uhurru* is rendered as 'freedom', in the sense of a person being 'given his freedom from slavery'.[21]

Yet as Jonathon Glassman has shown, there is a contrast between missionary understandings of freedom as emancipation, and the understanding of freedom current on the coast at that time. When missionaries celebrated the arrival of escaping slaves at their mission stations, they understood them to be freeing bondage in pursuit of individual liberty. Yet this explanation tells us more about missionary ambitions than about slave motivation. For the missionaries, 'the free individual was placed at the centre of the "natural" social order', but for the slaves themselves, to seek independence would have 'entailed a completed rejection of the ideological structures with which slaves had lived all their lives'.[22] Slaves did

---

[20] Burke, ibid., p. 32; Anna Lowenhaupt Tsing, 'Adat/Indigenous: Indigeneity in Motion', in Carol Gluck and Anna Lowenhaupt Tsing (eds.), *Words in Motion: Toward a Global Lexicon* (Durham, NC: Duke University Press, 2009), pp. 40–64, p. 51.

[21] Ludwig Krapf, *A Dictionary of the Suahili Language* (London: Truebner and Co., 1882), pp. 104, 396.

[22] Jonathon Glassman, *Feasts and Riot: Revelry, Rebellion, and Popular Consciousness on the Swahili Coast, 1856–1888* (London: James Currey, 1995), p. 107.

not seek out missionaries 'in search of "freedom," but in search of sustenance and protection, just as they might seek refuge with other powerful patrons.'[23] The missionaries themselves were perceived by others on the coast as behaving very much like other patrons, and indeed some of those formers slaves who lived on mission stations were known quite simply as 'slaves of the Christians'.[24]

Freedom, then, was not a birthright, but was 'rather a condition that was bestowed on a slave, by the master or by some other powerful patron.'[25] This understanding was not unique to the Swahili coast, but had much in common with other African and Indian Ocean understandings of slavery. Whereas slaves in the Atlantic world have been understood, in Claude Meillassoux's words, as 'a social class oppressed and exploited by the slave-owning class', this formulation does not represent the experience of slavery in the Indian Ocean world or the societies of which slavery was a part.[26] This was an uncertain world, in which reciprocal obligations between superiors and inferiors were crucial to the functioning of society. As Gwyn Campbell writes, 'In such contexts, concepts of 'slave' and 'free' are of limited analytical utility. For most of the Indian Ocean World population, security, food and shelter rather than an abstract concept of liberty, were the primary aims.'[27] In times of famine or dearth, one might voluntarily enter slavery, or pawn one's children in the hope of redeeming them when times were better. Slavery, like other forms of dependence and unfree labour, offered protection, while personal autonomy and independence were to be feared rather than celebrated by the vulnerable.

This reading of slavery in the Indian Ocean world forces us to revisit the assumption that 'slavery' is always the antonym of 'freedom'. This was a world in which everyone, slave and free, was part of 'a social hierarchy of dependence', with obligations owed on both sides.[28] Legal status was often less important than other factors in determining status, and slaves could and did seek to ameliorate their position over time, though status could be lost as well as gained.

---

[23] Ibid., pp. 107–108.
[24] Ibid., p. 108.
[25] Ibid., p. 113.
[26] Gwyn Campbell, 'Introduction' in Gwyn Campbell (ed.), *The Structure of Slavery in Indian Ocean Africa and Asia* (London: Frank Cass, 2004), pp. vii–xxxii, p. xx.
[27] Ibid., pp. xxiv–xxv.
[28] Ibid., pp. xxvi–xxvii.

We thus begin to see the extent to which Krapf's rendering of the term *uhuru* was shaped by the abolitionist discourse of his time.[29] This line of thinking was taken further by later Swahili dictionaries. Frederick Johnson's 1939 dictionary, published by the Inter-Territorial Language Committee for the East African Dependencies, continued to define *uhuru* as 'freedom from slavery, liberty, emancipation'. Yet it also linked the root *hurr* to a new idea, offering the noun *huria* as 'freedom, i.e. in the sense of being able to do what one wishes.'[30]

Their definitions fitted into a wider Christian discourse in which freedom was equated with the struggle against the slave trade in Africa. These twin themes were at the heart of one of the most popular volumes published by the East African Literature Bureau, James Mbotela's *The Freeing of the Slaves [Uhuru wa Watumwa]*, which appeared in 1934.[31] Across East Africa, as Derek Peterson has argued, a language of freedom from slavery was employed in political debate, particularly when political entrepreneurs sought to gain the ear of the colonial state.[32] In Bunyoro in Uganda, complaints against the oppression suffered under Ganda rule was framed in terms of a claim that Bunyorans were enslaved and an appeal to the 'British Government that every country subject to the English Flag should enjoy freedom and that slavery should be done away with.'[33]

This binary between freedom and slavery remained an important component of understandings of *uhuru* into the 1950s. This sense of freedom brought to mind very localized hierarchies of dependence, as much as the external processes of enslavement by Arab or European slave traders which Mbotela described. As Steven Feierman has shown, when Shambaa peasants in north-eastern Tanganyika heard Julius Nyerere talk about *uhuru*, 'they also knew *uhuru* in their observed experience as the release from *utung'wa*, "slavery" or "pawnship," which in their thinking presupposed an entire system of descent-group rights in persons.' In this way, '*uhuru* resonated with overtones of individual responsibility,

[29] Glassman, *Feasts and Riot: Revelry, Rebellion, and Popular Consciousness on the Swahili Coast, 1856–1888*, p. 113.

[30] Frederick Johnson, *A Standard Swahili-English Dictionary* (London: Oxford University Press, 1939), p. 138.

[31] James Mbotela, *Uhuru wa Watumwa* (London: Sheldon Press, 1934), pp. 79–80. For publication figures see *East African Literature Bureau Annual Report 1955–56*, p. 11.

[32] Derek Peterson (ed.), *Abolitionism and Imperialism in Britain, Africa, and the Atlantic* (Athens, OH: Ohio University Press, 2010), p. 1.

[33] Ibid., p. 1.

of young men and women standing on their own, independent of their fathers.'[34]

But by the 1950s the term was also overlaid with newer meanings in ways which intersected both with new universalisms and with the binaries of the Cold War context described earlier. As we saw in Chapter 2, *uhuru* had been employed by the colonial government to describe the 1939 to 1945 war as a 'war for freedom'.[35] And as the war ended, Africans employed the same language of freedom to make claims on the government. One writer in the Usambara mountains, for example, wrote that 'Now is the time for the British to fulfil their promise that when the war ended the world would be made new and all men would gain freedom'.[36]

Second, the term was used to describe personal freedoms, such as freedom of religion, or the freedom to join political parties, which had been enshrined as universals by the 1948 Universal Declaration of Human Rights, the first article of which declared that 'all human beings are born free and equal in dignity and rights'. This language of individual freedoms could be, and was, employed in political contexts, but it was also far broader than that, and could be used by the colonial state and those who sought to work within colonial state structures, as well as by those opposing the colonial state.

Speeches referred to the freedom, or otherwise, to hold meetings.[37] In the Catholic newspaper *Kiongozi*, *uhuru* was frequently discussed in terms of the freedom to practise religion and to choose their own partners. In January 1954 a teacher named F. Marenge wrote to bring news of a new law passed in North Mara 'to give women the freedom' to choose a husband for themselves, without the involvement of their parents, 'in the way that is done by Christians all over the world'.[38] A series of articles in *Kiongozi* on the subject of freedom for women insisted that women be granted the freedom to practise their religion, a practice often denied to them, according to *Kiongozi*'s then editor Father von Oostrom.[39]

In the government periodical *Mambo Leo*, women used the letters' pages to challenge patriarchal attempts to limit their freedom of mobility.

---

[34] Steven Feierman, *Peasant Intellectuals: Anthropology and History in Tanzania* (Madison, WI: University of Wisconsin Press, 1990), p. 213.

[35] John Iliffe, *A Modern History of Tanganyika* (Cambridge: Cambridge University Press, 1979), p. 378.

[36] Ibid., pp. 378–379.

[37] KCCU Circular No. 5 of 1954, 'Chama cha Wanawake Uchagga: The Kilimanjaro Chagga Citizens Union', TNA 5/25/7, f. 225, p. 2.

[38] Letter from Mwl. F. Marenge, 'Hali mpya ya ndoa 1954', *Kiongozi*, January 1954, p. 8.

[39] Father van Oostrum, 'Uhuru wa Wanawake', *Kiongozi*, December 1952, p. 1.

In 1956, writing under pseudonyms, three women from the Lake Province wrote to *Mambo Leo* complaining that although freedom was enjoyed by men, women were still in a state of slavery.[40] The response of male correspondents was fierce, accusing the women of seeking only the freedom to prostitute themselves, of seeking to reject their husbands and taking as their inspiration Haya women who were often associated with prostitution.[41] Others claimed that male power over women came from God. In response, *Mambo Leo*'s editor sought to mediate, rejecting these claims and saying that 'every person has been created with a complete right to freedom on earth, not only men. But this freedom has limits.'[42]

Third, new transnational discourses of anti-communism intersected with colonial conceptions of freedom. In the government newspaper *Mambo Leo* and in the Catholic newspaper *Kiongozi*, the concept of freedom was tied to an international discourse of anti-communism. In 1950 a series of articles on *Communism and Christianity* in the pages of *Kiongozi* set out a world view which contrasted the freedom promised by communism with the state of slavery it delivered.[43] Those living in Eastern Europe were described as the 'slaves' of the Communists, and Africans were called on to unite against communism to preserve their freedom, particularly the freedom of religion. The regular series *Habari za Dunia*, or world news, continued this theme. In a divided world, readers were encouraged to look to America for protection, even after independence, for 'it is clear that without the help of America we cannot hope to protect our freedom'.[44] America was not, as the column *Habari za Dunia* insisted in 1953, content for the world to be divided between those countries with freedom and those without, but would help all to fight against communism.[45]

Just as a language of individual freedoms could serve to defend colonial rule as much as to attack it, the same was true of freedom defined in opposition to communism. In 1951, the editorial column, which had in

---

[40] Letter from Mimi Mawazo bt. Kilasiku, Mimi Shida bt. Hayasemeki, Mimi Hasikilizwi bt. Kuumia, 'Uhuru ni wa Wanaume tu: Wanawake Hawana Uhuru kwa nini?', *Mambo Leo*, March 1956, p. 10. Derek Peterson, *Ethnic Patriotism and the East African Revival* (Cambridge: Cambridge University Press, 2012), pp. 152–177.

[41] Letter from Mohamedi Omari, *Mambo Leo*, April 1956, p. 4.

[42] Editorial, *Mambo Leo*, April 1956, p. 5.

[43] See, e.g., Father van Oostrum, 'Ukommunisti na Ukristu', *Kiongozi*, February 1950, pp. 20–22.

[44] 'Habari za Dunia', *Kiongozi*, September 1951, p. 3.

[45] 'Habari za Dunia', *Kiongozi*, April 1953, p. 3.

the preceding years been missing from *Mambo Leo*, was reintroduced as a means, in the words of the Public Relations Officer G. K. Whitlamsmith, of 'putting across to a large number of readers Government's views on various questions of the day'. The first editorial was to be on the subject of 'Freedom, contrasting conditions in free countries with those under Communist rule'.[46] The three part series of editorials which followed, entitled 'The Blessings of Freedom', contrasted the personal freedoms enjoyed in Tanganyika with the absence of freedom under communist rule.[47] In this context, the term 'fighting for freedom', which later came to be used to refer to the struggle for independence, was first used for the fight against communism. An article entitled 'Fighting for Freedom' described the decision of the Ethiopian emperor to send troops to North Korea to fight for freedom.[48]

We can also see the term 'freedom' being used to link up with transnational discourses, both by African and by European political actors. When in 1951 one hundred socialist MPs in Britain published a statement in support of the principle that all human beings were born free and equal, the Tanganyika European Council denied this very possibility, but had to engage in the same terms.[49] Other political organizations in Tanganyika saw the power of using languages of freedom to engage with the colonial state and with the United Nations, drawing both on the idea that the Second World War had been a war for freedom, and the language of the foundation of the United Nations and of the Universal Declaration of Human Rights. When twenty-two Africans from Shinyanga in north-western Tanganyika met the 1948 Visiting Mission of United Nations Trusteeship Council, they complained that many Africans had lost their lives in the Second World War but that after the war they continued to lack any freedom, including the freedom to speak about their problems.[50]

---

[46] Letter from G. K. Whitlamsmith, 13 April 1951, TNA 71/217, f. 660.

[47] Editorial, 'Neema ya uhuru nchini', *Mambo Leo*, May 1951, p. 50; Editorial, 'Neema ya uhuru nchini', *Mambo Leo*, June 1951, p. 62; Editorial, 'Neema ya uhuru nchini', July 1951, p. 74.

[48] 'Kupigania Uhuru', *Mambo Leo*, June 1951, p. 62.

[49] Frank Hinds, 'Colonial Policy and Western Leadership', April 1951, TNA UK, CO 691/217, f. 6.

[50] E. B. M. Barongo, *Mkiki Mkiki wa Siasa Tanganyika* (Dar es Salaam: East African Literature Bureau, 1966), p. 38. Ullrich Lohrmann, *Voices from Tanganyika: Great Britain, the United Nations and the Decolonization of a Trust Territory, 1946–1961* (Berlin: Lit. Verlag, 2007), p. 216.

Increasingly, as the 1950s progressed, *uhuru* was linked to a conception of freedom from colonial rule. In Dar es Salaam, Mombasa and, particularly, in Zanzibar, listeners tuned into Radio Cairo's Swahili-language broadcasts including, from 1957, the station 'Voice of Free Africa' or *Sauti ya Uhuru wa Africa*.[51] Broadcasters appealed to the spirit of the Bandung conference of 1955, and celebrated a struggle for freedom waged against the forces of imperialism. Africans, Indians and Arabs were described 'as brothers, as shown by the Bandung Conference', and Africans were called upon to 'work together with the Arabs and Indians, to fight those white pigs side by side until freedom is attained.'[52] Here, as in nationalist movements elsewhere in the colonial world, freedom was tied to political independence.

This was the context in which TANU, Tanganyika's first political movement to explicitly set out to argue for self-rule and ultimately independence, emerged in July 1954. TANU appropriated a language of freedom from slavery and attached it to the pursuit of self-government. In a 1956 speech, its leader Julius Nyerere argued that slavery was in part an attitude of mind, for in Tanganyika 'the population not only tolerate foreign control but are, in fact, afraid of self-government.' This put them in a position of self-enslavement, for '[h]e who fails to realise that to be governed is intolerable places himself in the position of a slave.'[53]

The rich nexus of ideas of freedom could be used in different ways, both to defend colonial rule and to attack it. Using a language of 'freedom' was powerful both because it served as a way of rejecting increasing demands being made by the colonial state, and because it was a way of linking up with transnational organizations. There is much that looks familiar in the way that *uhuru* was employed in 1950s Tanganyika. Yet there was also, as we shall see, more that was distinctive, and we should not see it as simply a replica of transnational languages of freedom. For in the mid-twentieth century, as in the earlier Swahili discourse which Jonathon Glassman identified on the pre-conquest coast, *uhuru* was a mode of incorporation into new relations of belonging as much as it was a mode of rejecting those relations.

[51] James R. Brennan, 'Radio Cairo and the Decolonization of East Africa, 1953–64', in Christopher J. Lee (ed.), *Making a World after Empire: The Bandung Moment and Its Political Afterlives* (Athens, OH: Ohio University Press, 2010), pp. 173–195, p. 177.

[52] Ibid., pp. 181–182.

[53] Extract from *Tanganyika Sunday News*, 11 December 1955, 'We must not expect everything from Government – Nyerere', TNA UK, CO 822/859, f. 44.

FREEDOM AND BELONGING IN TANGANYIKA
IN THE 'TIME OF POLITICS': *UHURU* AND TANU

In 1950s Tanganyika, there was a growing association between *uhuru* as 'freedom' and *uhuru* as 'political independence'.[54] For some writers, the distinction was preserved by employing *Uhuru* with a capital 'U' for the sense of political independence and an uncapitalized *uhuru* for the sense of freedom, but others were willing to embrace the ambiguity.[55] The term served as a powerful political slogan. Describing a period of civil disobedience in the Lake Province, the staunchly antinationalist provincial commissioner Stanley Walden referred to the power attached to 'that magic word "*uhuru*"'.[56] At public meetings, TANU speakers would shout *Uhuru!* And the crowd would respond with the same cry of *Uhuru!* Commenting on a TANU meeting held in October 1958, the governor's private secretary, Brian Eccles, wrote that: 'It was my impression that the first shout of 'uhuru' always came from within the enclosure: it was then incumbent on anyone who heard it to reply with another shout of 'uhuru'. For, as my servant who was at the meeting said, "if you did not reply they would think you were UTP or something". A cry of 'uhuru' over the loudspeaker therefore got a reply from nearly everyone present.'[57]

This description offers a glimpse of the slogan *uhuru* in practice, but it also offers something more, and is indicative of something much larger. In pointing out that the call 'freedom' was as much a declaration of allegiance as a demand for the absence of authority, Eccles hints at an important truth. For to shout *uhuru* was to make a declaration of belonging, and specifically of belonging to TANU.

As we have seen, in the unstable world of nineteenth-century Africa, freedom demanded security, and security came through membership, not through autonomy.[58] For the anthropologists Harri Englund and Francis Nyamnjoh, this crucial point, that 'in a historical context of widespread mobility, labour-intensive livelihoods, slave raiding and animosities fuelled

---

[54] G. Andrew Maguire, *Toward 'Uhuru' in Tanzania: The Politics of Participation* (Cambridge: Cambridge University Press, 1969), fn. p. xxix.

[55] For an example of distinguishing between *uhuru* and *Uhuru*, see Barongo, *Mkiki Mkiki wa Siasa*, pp. 35, 37.

[56] Cited in Maguire, *Toward 'Uhuru in Tanzania: The Politics of Participation'*, p. 240.

[57] Report by Brian Eccles on TANU meeting, 21 October 1958, TNA UK, CO 822/1362. The UTP was the United Tanganyika Party, formed in opposition to TANU.

[58] Igor Kopytoff and Suzanne Miers, 'African 'Slavery' as an Institution of Marginality' in Suzanne Miers and Igor Kopytoff (eds.), *Slavery in Africa: Historical and Anthropological Perspectives* (Madison, WI: University of Wisconsin Press, 1977), pp. 3–85, p. 17.

by early colonial encroachments, 'freedom' was 'belonging' rather than 'autonomy", should hold important lessons for us when seeking to understand later periods too.[59] We should not be as quick to assume that freedom comes from autonomy as the liberal tradition assumes.

This point was well understood by the colonial state in Tanganyika. The colonial state in interwar Tanganyika appropriated an abolitionist discourse of freedom, but also claimed to have brought freedom through security. We can see this in the didactic text *Uraia* which we encountered in Chapter 3. An imagined dialogue between an elderly spokesman for the past and a spokesman for the present and future served to illustrate why freedom from government was in reality no freedom at all. While the old man, Mzee Siku bin Kale, recalled a time when one could wander freely, hunt anywhere and where no taxes were demanded, his younger friend reminded him of the other restrictions on freedom at that time. Yes, in theory one might be able to wander freely, but what sort of freedom was there if wild animals and dangerous vagabonds posed a constant threat? Yes, there might have been no taxes, but without taxes there were also no schools or dispensaries.[60] *Uraia* thus contrasted a precolonial state in which insecurity meant that freedom was more apparent than real, with a colonial condition of freedom from slavery and from insecurity. It was in colonial Tanganyika, not precolonial Tanganyika, that the 'blessings of freedom' could be enjoyed.[61]

The concept of freedom *through* government rather than freedom *from* government is important. There was a tension in colonial discourse, in that *uhuru* was both freedom from slavery, and freedom through belonging. As the call of *uhuru* was increasingly heard across the Territory, the colonial Government's response was to reiterate the argument for political society made in citizenship primers like *Uraia*. They sought to make the case that freedom came from security, and that the existence of government was the key to security. Starting in July 1956, a series of articles appeared in *Mambo Leo* called 'Why we need Government in the country'.[62] In August 1956 an editorial was published in *Mambo Leo* in both Swahili and English entitled 'Uhuru' and 'Freedom' which made the same point even more explicitly. The editorial began by drawing attention to the new political mood in Tanganyika: '[i]n these days of growing

---

[59] Harri Englund and Francis Nyamnjoh (eds.), *Rights and the Politics of Recognition in Africa* (London: Zed Books, 2004), p. 17.

[60] Stanley Rivers Smith and Frederick Johnson, *Uraia* (London: Macmillan, 1928).

[61] Ibid., p. 25.

[62] 'Kwa nini tuna haja ya serikali nchini', *Mambo Leo*, July 1956, p. 5.

political consciousness we are told that Tanganyika is "struggling for freedom". We are told that to be ruled by another people is a reproach, that immigration should be drastically reduced and that the inhabitants of this country must have restored to them their former freedom.'[63] But, the editorial continued, it was important to 'understand clearly what this precious word freedom really means'. For 'freedom' came in two varieties: '[f]irstly, freedom of the individual; freedom from fear of being killed or robbed, freedom from hunger and disease, freedom of religion and of speech, which might be described as the basic freedoms of mankind and secondly, freedom of whole nations to rule their own countries and decide their own fate, which may be called political freedom'. *Mambo Leo* denied that the first sort of freedom had existed before colonial rule when 'famine, fear and disease stalked the land' and there 'were few parts of the country where a man could walk for 20 miles without fear of his life'. The argument continued, echoing earlier didactic texts, that colonial rule had worked to make individual freedom possible, and the second freedom, that of a nation to rule itself, would follow in time.

TANU, however, sought to negotiate a similar process. What TANU proposed, in the second half of the 1950s, was not freedom through autonomy but freedom through belonging, and this was as true of popular nationalist discourse employed in the countryside as it was of the leadership's pronouncements, though the two narratives were not identical. To make this argument is to diverge from an emerging literature which sees in TANU's late 1950s politics the origins of postcolonial authoritarianism. But it is also to draw attention to a tension in TANU's discourse, a tension which was also present in the discourse of the colonial state. Both TANU and the colonial state based their claim to legitimacy in part on a claim to have brought freedom from slavery. For TANU, this was freedom from the slavery of being ruled by an outside power, and for the colonial state it lay in the claim to have driven the slave trade and the legal status of slavery from the land. Yet at the same time, both sought to reject an argument that claimed that true freedom consisted in the absence of authority. Rather, they argued, freedom came through membership of political society with the acceptance of authority and law which that entailed.

As historians have increasingly turned their attention to the postcolonial state, the spotlight has fallen on the nationalist parties of late colonial and early postcolonial Africa. Once seen as the source of liberation, a

---

[63] Editorial, "'Uhuru' and 'Freedom'", *Mambo Leo*, August 1956, p. 2.

newer literature has instead uncovered the degree of continuity between late colonial and early postcolonial authoritarian styles of government.[64] Already in the late 1950s, nationalist parties were basing their claim to authority on a claim that they could maintain order. In late colonial Dar es Salaam, James Brennan has argued, TANU asserted that it would combat *fujo* or disorder with *maendeleo* or progress.[65] In the Lake Province, a crucial turning point came when it was TANU leadership, not the colonial state, which was able to restore order after a breakdown of authority.[66]

This has fed into a wider argument about continuity between the late colonial and the early postcolonial state. Andreas Eckert has charted shifts in local government and the cooperative movement before and after independence, and argued that '[d]espite a rhetoric that stressed popular participation, decentralization, and democratization, both the British colonial Administration and subsequently the Government of independent Tanzania largely pursued a policy of centralization and bureaucratic authoritarianism.'[67] Such continuities, he suggests, were not simply 'institutional legacies', as Leander Schneider has argued, but were constituted in more subtle ways, for example, in terms of a 'deeply paternalistic imagination that constructed the state, with its philosopher president at the helm, as the only authority competent to make judgements about the lives of a "backward" population'.[68] But while strategies of governmentality do suggest continuity, the basis on which authority was constructed had changed.

Certainly, TANU's leadership sought to disown those TANU activists in the countryside who were preaching freedom from all authority. In the TANU newssheet *Sauti ya TANU*, following the forced closure of TANU branches in Pangani and Handeni in 1957, Julius Nyerere railed against the 'anti-TANU' activity of the colonial government which sought to

---

[64] Andrew Burton and Michael Jennings, 'Introduction: The Emperor's New Clothes? Continuities in Governance in Late Colonial and Early Postcolonial East Africa,' *International Journal of African Historical Studies* 40 (2007), 1–25.

[65] James Brennan, 'Youth, the TANU Youth League and Managed Vigilantism in Dar es Salaam, Tanzania, 1925–73', *Africa*, 76 (2006), 221–246. See also James Brennan, *Taifa: Making Nation and Race in Urban Tanzania* (Athens, OH: Ohio University Press, 2012), pp. 164, 250.

[66] Maguire, *Toward 'Uhuru' in Tanzania: The Politics of Participation'*, pp. 252–253.

[67] Andreas Eckert, '"Useful Instruments of Participation?" Local Government and Co-operatives in Tanzania, 1940s to 1970s,' *International Journal of African Historical Studies* 40 (2007), 97–118, p. 97.

[68] Leander Schneider, 'Colonial Legacies and Postcolonial Authoritarianism in Tanzania,' *African Studies Review* 49 (2006), 93–118, p. 107.

persuade the 'world that TANU has one policy for the U.N., the Colonial Office, Government House, public gathering at Mnazi Mmoja and other places but has a very different policy in the remote corners in the villages where the local Headman tells the D.C. that TANU preaches sedition daily.' And if the world was not persuaded, the colonial state would 'couple it with the conviction of one or two irresponsible [people] who, according to the infallible local Headmen, have been telling the people that they will receive "benefits" if they support TANU; that there will be "no taxation, no game and forest licences"; that there will be "freedom from the jurisdiction of the Native Authority etc. etc."'[69] This was, Nyerere argued, all part of a campaign against TANU, and rested on the claims of 'illiterate headmen'.

TANU leaders explicitly rejected the argument that politics itself meant the rejection of authority and the wider negative associations which the concept of politics had acquired. Colonial officials advocated keeping 'politics out of local government'.[70] In 1958, the TANU leader G. H. Pacha used the pages of the Catholic newspaper *Kiongozi* which was by then openly supporting TANU to argue against this idea. In an article entitled 'What Is Politics?' Pacha listed a series of responses that were commonly heard when people were asked what was meant by the term *siasa* or politics. One of those answers was to say that politics meant creating 'fujo' or disorder by not obeying the government's laws and by not paying tax.[71] This was not, Pacha insisted, the true definition of politics.

Just as other nationalist leaders had done before, TANU's leadership presented itself to the colonial state as the only organization with the ability to contain those who were rejecting authority, both in the towns and in the countryside, papering over the ways in which its own language of *uhuru* both drew on political arguments already happening at the local level and in turn provided a vocabulary with which local TANU activists could inspire and mobilize the population. But this does not mean that TANU was simply using a language of *uhuru* when it was useful but then seeking to impose its own authority on those who went out to claim *uhuru* as freedom from authority. Rather, TANU was, at both local and national level, developing a narrative in which it offered freedom *through* membership.

[69] 'Government's War against TANU', *Sauti ya TANU*, No. 8, 20 April 1957, p. 2.
[70] Letter from district commissioner, Masasi to provincial commissioner, Southern Province, 5 November 1958, TNA L5/30, f. 51, p. 1; Address to Masasi District Council, 30 October 1958, TNA L5/30, f. 50F, p. 2.
[71] G. H. Pacha, 'Siasa ni nini?', *Kiongozi*, 16 June 1958, p. 4.

From this perspective, a speech which Nyerere made in Bukoba in 1959 is revealing. In it he argued that TANU would no longer go out seeking new members. The movement had been encouraging Tanganyikans to join for four years, and for Nyerere, this was enough: addressing those who had not yet joined, he said 'you are not the slaves of some person so that I should have to keep coming back to tell you to claim that which is yours.'[72] It was up to them to join TANU and claim their freedom. Freedom, then, came through joining TANU.

In this respect, a letter to the nationalist newspaper *Mwafrika* from a TANU organizer in 1958 is typical. TANU's publicity secretary, R. Kaminyoge Mwanjisi, had visited the district of Kilwa in southern Tanganyika, a region which was frequently marked out as having been neglected during the colonial period. After stating that lack of water was a serious problem in Kilwa and that women often had to spend entire days waiting their turn at the well, Mwanjisi informed readers that this was a problem for the citizens of Tanganyika, and so would only be properly solved by their own government. 'The task of getting water in Tanganyika is not the task of the British Government, they are not hurt by it. It teaches us that when we get our Government it will take steps to put the problems of the citizens first.... The freedom which we demand is not simply that of escaping the shame of being ruled'. For TANU, Manjisi explained, freedom meant working 'so that all will have water.' He continued: 'The people will say to their government: "we have paid our taxes, you must remove our problems"'.[73] Freedom, then, would mean accountability, government resting on the consent of the governed, demonstrated by elections and the payment of tax, and in return demands could be made for the essential services which were everyone's right in the modern world.

TANU was engaged in gathering people under its authority, and setting itself up as an intermediary with the colonial state. We can see this process in District files from across Tanganyika in the late 1950s and in intelligence reports which reached the Colonial Office. In Bukoba, the District Commissioner's regular letters to local TANU officials refusing to deal with third parties had little effect in stemming the tide of communications which he received. The TANU Chairman's response was to write that 'I have now 7,462 members who hold Membership Cards and

---

[72] 'Kujitawala ni karibu sana', *Buhaya Co-operative News*, 1 January 1959, p. 1.
[73] Letter from R. Kaminyoge Mwanjisi, 'Shida ya Maji Kilwa', *Mwafrika*, 19 December 1959, p. 3.

some more thousands waiting to have M/cards any times we get some from Dar-es-Salaam' and that at times 'these people are submitting their complaints to us that we may present their views before the local government.'[74] We can see clear similarities with the role which the Kilimanjaro Chagga Citizens Union (KCCU) and other associations discussed in Chapter 4 saw themselves as performing. Just as the KCCU had argued that ordinary people could not speak freely in front of those with authority, so TANU argued that the people could communicate through TANU. In another letter to the District Commissioner, the chairman stressed his aim was not to interfere in the system of local government, but a consequence of the fact that 'sometimes while rounding the District on my TANU business I may hear what people are saying or grumbling of, and sometimes the people themselves may approach me on some matters of importance asking me to bring same before the Local Government. I or we find it undesirable to keep silent. We are writing to our Government not to criticize but with bona fide hoping to give some help to our Local Administration towards further advancement of our country.'[75]

In November 1956 E. A. Kisenge, TANU's Provincial Secretary in Tanga Province, issued a notice which laid out this aspect of TANU's role very clearly. It stated that citizens (*raia*) faced many difficulties of which the district office, the native authority, the Liwali or the elected council were unaware, or if they were aware of them, they failed to remove them to the satisfaction of the people. It went on to argue that a TANU Council could state these difficulties openly to the native authority and the government, so that they were listened to, and would do whatever it could to solve them. TANU claimed that it would ensure that the government or the native authority would address those problems which TANU brought to its attention.[76]

At Handeni, at the height of opposition to soil cultivation rules in 1956, it was reported that the Swahili version of the Universal Declaration of Human Rights had become 'widely known in this District as "the laws of TANU" and was used as the basis for opposition to the cultivation rules.'[77] Local officials argued that this represented a dangerous claim to authority by

---

[74] Letter from H. Rugenyibura, TANU chairman, to provincial commissioner, 2 February 1957, TNA 71/A6/16, f. 186.
[75] Letter from H. Rugenyibura, TANU Chairman, to district commissioner, Biharamulo, 21 May 1957, TNA 71/A6/16, f. 219.
[76] E. A. Kisenge, 'Tangazo', 17 November 1956, TNA 476/A6/4, f. 35.
[77] A. J. Grattan-Bellew, 'TANU, Tanga Province', attachment to Twining to Gorrell-Barnes, 3 April 1957, TNA UK, CO 822/1361, f. 37, p. 2.

TANU, and that in circulating 'the laws of TANU', the local TANU branch was accused of trying to 'give the impression that TANU was a superior authority.'[78] It was further reported that the chairman of the sub-branch had written insisting that a man appear at the TANU office with the threat of arrest were he not to do so. He was later convicted of usurping judicial powers and by the time of his conviction had apparently left TANU, but this incident was indicative of wider processes occurring across the country, in which the blurring of political party and polity seemed to be taking place.[79] But that, of course, was the crucial point – TANU was not using the Universal Declaration simply as a means of rejecting colonial authority, but rather as a means of constructing an alternative authority.

In this context, rumours spread of the power offered by possession of a TANU membership card. An American official travelling across the country in 1958 was told of a group of Barabaig from northern Tanganyika who had joined TANU 'in the mistaken belief that possession of the green membership card and utilization of the TANU slogan "Uhuru" (freedom) gave special license for stealing cattle from neighboring tribes.' When they were duly arrested, they 'displayed their membership cards and were sharply disabused of its advantages.' This marked the end of their association with TANU.[80] Although TANU's central leadership were dismissive of such local rumours, they helped to encourage them by insisting on the acquisition of a membership card. As TANU's vice-president John Rupia said in a speech in 1957, reported in the TANU newssheet *Sauti ya TANU*, 'let every African support our organisation. Those in possession of membership cards should see that they pay their monthly subscriptions regularly, and those who merely support us without having membership cards is not enough. To support TANU is to be in possession of membership card. To-day the Governor may refuse to see us, but when you are all joining the Union and demonstrably united behind TANU the Governor will invite TANU. It has been like that everywhere. It is not going to be different in Tanganyika.'[81]

At the same time, TANU was claiming the moral high ground from which to define the meaning and practice of good citizenship, and was doing so both in national interventions, as in the pages of *Sauti ya TANU*,

---

[78] Ibid., p. 2.

[79] Ibid.

[80] Dar es Salaam to State Department, 'Report of Travel through Tanga, Northern and Central Provinces of Tanganyika', 5 December 1958, p. 4, Central Decimal Files, 1955–59, National Archives II, College Park, Maryland.

[81] No author, no title, *Sauti ya TANU*, No. 3, 16 March 1957, p. 2.

and at the local level. Accused of disrespect towards Governor Edward Twining in the spring of 1957, Nyerere countered that 'it is not part of respect for authority to let those in authority say or do what they like without criticism. Respect for authority is undoubtedly the duty of every citizen, but applauding the mistakes of those in authority is the duty only of slaves.'[82] Here, the traditional binary of 'freedom' and 'slavery' was reworked, so as to contrast the 'duty of the citizen' with that of the slave. Crucially, the status of 'citizen' has meaning only within the context of political society.

In January 1959 the local TANU branch in Tanga Province in central Tanganyika published an announcement addressed to all TANU members in the Province. In it, they outlined the sort of person who would be required in a free country. 'Free people', the announcement stated, are 'good citizens'.[83] The announcement continued: 'Every good citizen must fulfil his or her responsibilities. And the responsibility of a good citizen is to pay his tax himself without being forced', for tax was essential if the government 'is to be able to fulfil our demands, for example, to build schools, hospitals, roads, bridges and other things which will enable the citizens of the country to live in peace and happiness.' But paying taxes on time was not the only responsibility of the good citizen. A good citizen must also obey the laws of the country, 'if the country was to progress and not go backwards'. Finally, an appeal to those members of TANU who drank alcohol called on them to moderate their consumption, for alcohol caused drunkenness, and drunkenness brought laziness and discord. As such, drunkenness was 'an enemy of freedom!'

This announcement is worth quoting at length, to reflect on the way in which it seeks discursively to unite authority and freedom by arguing that political subjecthood is compatible with liberty. The language of *uraia mwema* or good citizenship is the same as that employed in colonial-era citizenship texts such as *Uraia* which we explored in Chapter 3, though here it is associated with 'freedom' in a way that it is not in those texts. Rather, for TANU good citizenship was a response to the concern which we saw in Chapter 1 that progress was fragile and could go backwards as well as forwards. If it was possible for the country to go backwards as well as forwards, good citizenship was one way of ensuring that progress did not go into retreat. The argument about taxation is also important, and reflects attempts to make subjection to taxation appear as a

---

[82] No author, no title, *Sauti ya TANU*, Date illegible but Spring 1957, p. 3.
[83] TANU, 'Tangazo', 12 January 1959, TNA 476/A6/4, f. 126.

willing subjection. But finally, the concern with drunkenness is important. Freedom was not a licence to behave in whichever way one desired, such licentious behaviour was an enemy of freedom.

This moralizing language was of course shaped by the fact that all TANU's official announcements were read in the District Office. The same was true of applications for public meetings and reports made to the District Office of meetings which had been held, both of which were similarly loyal in tone. One typical report from Kipumbwi branch in Tanga Province in 1958 set out the themes for a public meeting as having included an injunction to pay taxes or else face exclusion from TANU, a similarly strong injunction against the drinking of the local drink of tembo which, TANU argued, led to disorder and disrespect for government, and an injunction to obey the orders of central government.[84]

But even where the discussion at meetings served to provoke a report from police officers alleging breach of the peace, similar themes can be detected. At a public meeting in Pangani in January 1960 attended by around nine hundred people, the illegitimacy of the colonial Government was apparently described by TANU orators in the following terms: 'Their government is just like that of a male goat... The foreigners entered this country and ... made themselves masters to the Native. They are helpless to those who are in pecuniary difficulties. Their usual answer when they are approached about such difficulties is that "The Govt. has no money".' The unidentified speaker continued to say: 'We want our self Govt. which will be helpful and impartial.'[85]

More broadly, TANU promised that it alone could bring *maendeleo*, and we can see this in particular in arguments it made against the new ethnically or locally based political associations which sprang up across the country in 1959 and 1960. New associations, such as the UDU, the Undali Democratic Union, claimed that they were not political parties but associations which sought *maendeleo*, progress or development.[86] They were not interested in tribalism, they simply aimed to provide a voice for their people so that the government could be made aware of their problems. History had shown that this worked. The Masasi African Democratic Union (MADU) argued that it was needed because those regions which had enjoyed the most progress were those, like Moshi,

---

[84] Mkutano wa Chama cha TANU Kipumbwi, 20 January 1959, TNA 476/A6/4, f. 128a.
[85] 'Meeting Report', TNA 476/A6/4, f. 178, p. 2.
[86] Letter from R. S. Mackinnon Mogha, 'Hakipingi TANU', *Mwafrika*, 24 December 1960, p. 2.

Bukoba or Mwanza, which had local associations of this type. Yet in the pages of *Mwafrika,* TANU supporters argued back, and maintained that the existence of multiple parties would lead to division along ethnic, racial or religious lines, to the detriment of the nation's development.[87]

TANU's own press releases, reported in *Mwafrika,* rejected MADU's analysis and claimed that it was not local political parties that had enabled them to progress, but local cooperative societies, stating in October 1960 that 'TANU wants freedom for this country and for the whole of Africa', rather than 'for the district of Masasi alone like MADU.'[88] TANU, in this reading, was the only legitimate voice and the only political vehicle which Tanganyikans needed.

TANU, then, would create new political relationships in which those with power would respond to those without, and deliver the *maendeleo* demanded. In a sense, this was a version of Nkrumah's famous dictum to 'seek ye first the political kingdom', but it was rooted in the deep arguments of Tanganyika's public sphere.

CONCLUSION

As we have seen in this chapter, the term 'freedom' was powerful in Tanganyika, as it was powerful across the decolonizing world, because it was broad enough to carry meaning both at the high political level and at the very personal level. But it was also a sphere of contestation, which derived both from its multiple and contested meanings in a global traffic of ideas, and in part from the two different ways in which the concept was embedded in East Africa: on the one hand, the antonym of freedom and slavery, and on the other, the idea of freedom through belonging.

In the mid-twentieth century, an older idea that *uhuru* was acquired through relationships persisted at the same time as the concept of *uhuru* was overlaid with new ideas of 'freedom' as a birthright. In the 1950s, TANU nationalists did not simply demand *uhuru*; rather they navigated a complex world in which freedom held very different, and contradictory, meanings. The discursive struggle over what freedom meant was not just an important context for politics, it was an important *part* of politics. We will see in the next chapter how some of these conceptual debates played out in a local context.

---

[87] Letter from Leo Philip Ibihya, 'Matatizo na Madaraka', *Mwafrika,* 2 April 1960, p. 2.
[88] 'Jihadharini na Chama Kipya – TANU', *Mwafrika,* 29 October 1960, p. 8.

6

Languages of Democracy on Kilimanjaro and the Fall of Marealle

When nationalists and nationalist parties wrote their histories, they had a tendency to neglect their ancestors. Earlier political activists went unmentioned, or were reduced to a role of forerunners who had either not yet perceived the urgent necessity of independence or had not been brave enough to demand it.[1] In particular, the work of political organizations organized on an ethnic basis was deemed of little importance in an era of nation-building. Early accounts of African nationalism similarly stressed the rupture constituted by the formation of parties which went beyond arguing within the colonial structure in favour of increased rights for Africans, and instead argued that self-rule and independence were not only moral imperatives, but they were also necessary prerequisites for meaningful change.[2]

In describing his own path to power in the Gold Coast, Kwame Nkrumah put himself at the centre of the story. In his autobiography, published in 1957, he described the anticolonial struggle as something which had begun in the first days of colonial rule and continued throughout the colonial period. But, he said, the fact that political movements were dominated by elites – what he called 'the merchant and lawyer class of the country' – meant they were 'doomed to failure'. And so he broke away and formed the Convention People's Party (CPP) to campaign for immediate self-government. Nkrumah continued: 'I saw that the whole solution to this problem lay in political freedom for our people ... It is

---

[1] For a comparative case study from Kenya, see Marshall Clough, 'Review: Kaggia and Kenya's Independence Struggle', *Africa Today*, 24 (1977), 89–93.
[2] See, e.g., Thomas Hodgkin, *Nationalism in Colonial Africa* (London: Muller, 1956).

far better to be free to govern, or misgovern yourself than to be governed by anybody else.' He then described how this became a mass-movement:

The formation of the CPP coincided with a political reawakening among the workers and young people of the country. Ex-servicemen who had taken part in the 1939 world war returned to the Gold Coast dissatisfied with their position after having been given the chance of comparing their lot with that of other peoples, and they were prepared to take any line which would better their conditions.[3]

Everyone, then, was united behind the demand for self-government.

Nkrumah's autobiography was published at the precise moment of independence. From that vantage point, it was an easy task to write history backwards and show how all came together under his leadership in pursuit of the same goals. Many of the first studies of nationalist movements in Africa took a similar perspective. They focussed on the top-down creation and development of mass movements, and the ways in which they mobilized core constituencies, such as the youth and war veterans. They considered the organizational structure – the fact that Nkrumah modelled the CPP's organization on that of the Congress party in India, while in Tanganyika, Nyerere modelled the Tanganyika African National Union (TANU) on the CPP in Ghana.

After a generation in which the history of 1950s nationalism was neglected, historians of Africa have recently questioned this top-down approach. Borrowing from the subaltern studies school of Indian history, they have argued for a 'bottom-up' alternative. In her study of the nationalist movement in Guinea, Elizabeth Schmidt argues that the driving force of the Guinean Rassemblement Démocratique Africain (RDA) was not Sékou Touré but rather the grassroots activists who pushed Touré to break decisively with France in 1958.[4] Yet although this work has done much to revitalize the study of African nationalism, it remains firmly within a nationalist framework of enquiry, and gives little sense of the relationship between nationalist movements and their supporters and those engaged in other intellectual and political projects.

As a result such approaches do little to help us understand why this apparent mass show of support unravelled so rapidly after independence. In partial response, other work questions whether there were any nationalists at all. For example, war veterans, often thought to have been

---

[3] Kwame Nkrumah, *The Autobiography of Kwame Nkrumah* (Edinburgh: Thomas Nelson and Sons, 1957), p. ix.

[4] Elizabeth Schmidt, *Mobilizing the Masses: Gender, Ethnicity, and Class in the Nationalist Movement in Guinea, 1939–1958* (Athens, OH: Ohio University Press, 2005), p. 6.

the shock troops of African nationalism, were in fact far more ambivalent in their attitudes, as Gregory Mann shows in his book *Native Sons.*[5] War veterans in Mali had bonds of loyalty to the French state, and were indeed dependent on the continuation of that relationship for the payment of their pensions, and were therefore frequently reluctant to involve themselves in nationalist political organization.

Others, such as Jean Allman writing about the Asante, have instead focussed on unpacking the alternative imaginaries of the nation which were at play in the 1950s. Where Kwame Nkrumah proposed a centralized nation-state in which Asante cocoa wealth would drive development projects for the benefit of all Gold Coast people, Asante political entrepreneurs responded with an alternative vision of an Asante nation within a looser, more federal structure.[6] In the same way historians of Katanga have begun to take seriously the ways in which the Katanga secession was a serious nationalist project, rather than simply the by-product of capitalist and Cold War interests.[7]

However, we might go further in stepping outside nationalist frameworks of analysis. Arguments about politics and debates over the location of legitimate rule did not arrive in Africa with the mass nationalist parties of the 1950s: they had always been there, though the nature of those debates changed over time. The new nationalist organizations of the 1950s had to work in existing intellectual and political contexts, and seek to construct a narrative which would serve to persuade listeners that they offered the most compelling vision of the future.[8] But such narratives were fragile and were never all-encompassing. By switching our perspective and focussing not on the nationalist movement but on the ongoing political arguments in local contexts with which their projects interacted, we can better understand when and why nationalist arguments were powerful, and understand their fragility and their limits. In this chapter, we look at how this happened in one case, taking as our

---

[5] Gregory Mann, *Native Sons: West African Veterans and France in the Twentieth Century* (Durham, NC: Duke University Press, 2006).

[6] Jean Allman, 'The Youngmen and the Porcupine: Class, Nationalism and Asante's Struggle for Self-Determination', 1954–57, *Journal of African History*, 31 (1990), 263–279.

[7] Miles Larmer, 'Local Conflicts in a Transnational War: The Katangese Gendarmes and the Shaba wars of 1977–78', *Cold War History*, 13 (2013), 89–108. See also Catherine Porter's forthcoming University of Cambridge PhD thesis, entitled *Nationalism, Authority and Political Identity in the Secession of Katanga, 1908–1963*.

[8] As Steven Feierman has shown in the Usambara mountains. Steven Feierman, *Peasant Intellectuals: Anthropology and History in Tanzania* (Madison, WI: University of Wisconsin Press, 1990).

focus the deposition in 1960 of Thomas Marealle, paramount chief, or Mangi Mkuu, of the Chagga.[9]

In Chapter 4, we set Marealle's rise to power in the context of the campaign led by the Kilimanjaro Chagga Citizens Union. But there is another context in which we might place this story, that of the struggle between federalism and a central state which characterized the process of mid-twentieth-century decolonization in many parts of the world. In South Asia, arguments over partition and the creation of Pakistan were in part arguments about whether the pursuit of a strong centre and the benefits which such a structure might bring in terms of economic development and security outweighed the risks which centralization posed to the political rights of minority religious communities.[10] Similar arguments were replayed in Africa a decade later. In Kenya, KANU's pursuit of a strong centre was countered by the federalist arguments of its rival KADU, an ideology which came to be known as *majimboism*.[11] In the Congo, the approach of independence saw the country divided between the centralizing nationalism of Patrice Lumumba and Joseph Kasavubu's alternative vision of one Congo made up of many different peoples. Independence for the Congo on 30 June 1960 was swiftly followed by the secession of the mineral-rich province of Katanga under the leadership of Moise Tshombe, a long-standing support of a federal Congo.

In Kenya, as in the Congo, arguments in favour of federalism were tainted by their association with the political projects of European settlers, anxious to secure their position after independence.[12] But the argument between centralism and federalism was a serious one, which in Kenya as elsewhere has continued to dominate political debate since independence. It also provides an important context for the political dynamics of 1950s Tanzania, particularly in areas such as Kilimanjaro where cash crop wealth and strong local leadership drove ambitious development programmes. Here *maendeleo* seemed more likely to come from the locality than from the centre.

---

[9] The two terms are used more or less interchangeably in the sources.

[10] Ayesha Jalal, *The Sole Spokesman: Jinnah, the Muslim League, and the demand for Pakistan* (Cambridge: Cambridge University Press, 1985); Yasmin Khan, *The Great Partition: The Making of India and Pakistan* (Newhaven: Yale University Press, 2007).

[11] David Anderson, '"Yours in Struggle for Majimbo". Nationalism and the Party Politics of Decolonization in Kenya, 1955–1964', *Journal of Contemporary History*, 40 (2005), 547–564.

[12] Anderson, '"Yours in Struggle for Majimbo": Nationalism and the Party of Decolonization in Kenya, 1955–1964', p. 564.

Yet by 1957, new languages of politics were gaining a hearing on Kilimanjaro as they were across Africa. Languages of democracy and freedom were becoming a more important part of political discourse. Across Africa, Kwame Nkrumah's insistence that the political kingdom must come first, and that economic development would follow, focussed minds on the pursuit of independence as a prerequisite to material progress. It also linked the pursuit of independence with a message that it would be the central state which would deliver progress. Nationalist parties styled themselves as modern and modernizing.[13] This was reflected in their dress and comportment as much as in their institutional structures. A public role for women was one part of this self-styling, in Tanzania as elsewhere.[14] But nationalist parties had to do more than simply style themselves in such a way as to look as though they were best equipped to deliver progress; they had to persuade potential supporters of their message. Projecting themselves as 'modern' and others as backward or mired in the past took ideological work. This was particularly so when, as in this case, they were faced with an opponent who had once been one of their number.

This chapter shows how a local political party, the Chagga Democratic Party (CDP), which was dominated by leading TANU figures, used new languages of democracy to mobilize support against Thomas Marealle and the institution of the paramount chiefship. It argues that the CDP succeeded not only because it offered *maendeleo*, but also because it was able to combine two distinct but overlapping political languages, languages of membership and belonging on the one hand, and languages of rights and democracy on the other.

THOMAS MAREALLE

Thomas Marealle was the grandson of a powerful chief in the era of German colonization and son of a rather less successful chief, deposed for drunkenness in 1933.[15] A schoolboy at the government school at Tabora at the time of his father's deposition, Marealle's response was to write to

---

[13] Felicitas Becker, *Becoming Muslim in Mainland Tanzania, 1890–2000* (Oxford: Oxford University Press, 2008), pp. 215–220.

[14] Susan Geiger, *TANU Women: Gender and Culture in the Making of Tanganyikan Nationalism, 1955–1965* (Oxford: James Currey, 1997), p. 11; Fowler, Dar H. C. to Bottomley, CRO, 'Visit of the Rt. Hon. Barbara Castle M. P. to Tanzania', 6 May 1965, TNA UK, DO 214/128.

[15] Andreas Eckert, '"I do not wish to be a tale-teller": Afrikanische Eliten in British-Tanganyika. Das Beispiel Thomas Marealle', in Andreas Eckert and Gesine Krueger (eds.), *Lesarten eines globalen Prozesses: Quellen und Interpretationen zur geschichte der europaischen Expansion* (Hamburg: Lit, 1998), pp. 172–186.

the government claiming the chiefship for himself.[16] In an early display of the comparative constitutional thinking which he would frequently employ, he cited the example of a British prince succeeding his father as king. His claim was unsuccessful, the position of chief of Marangu having already been filled by his uncle, Petro Itosi Marealle. But the officer charged with replying to his letter was told by the chief secretary to tread gently and encourage his ambitions in the hope that 'he may become a valuable member of his tribe in the future'.[17]

As Marealle rose in the ranks of the colonial bureaucracy, there was no division between his desire to see Kilimanjaro prosper and to see the Territory as a whole progress. In the early 1940s he contributed reports and, on at least one occasion, a poem to Erica Fiah's African independent newspaper *Kwetu*. In the course of discussions in the paper in the early 1940s as to who should fill Kilimanjaro's 'big-seat', Fiah suggested Marealle as the man for the job. Marealle himself suggested Abdiel Shangali but agreed that some figurehead was needed and that Moshi should not be ruled by 'petty chiefs'.[18] In 1947 he wrote to his friend the former district officer Vickers-Haviland that 'Kilimanjaro is calling – it has been for a long time, but I have turned a deaf ear to those calls for 12 years now'. He told his friend of his frustrations with government service, but his intention to continue to 'serve my people everywhere still from some other angle'.[19] When in 1951 he allowed his name to go forward as a candidate for paramount chief, he was still balancing both a local and a national constituency. When the Chagga Association was formed in Dar es Salaam in 1951, he agreed to act as its patron but was at the same time a leading member of the Tanganyika African Association and the Tanganyika African Government Servants Association, using his role in the African Association to speak out against alienation of land to Europeans and discrimination in hotels, that is, speaking a classic language of anticolonial nationalism.[20]

---

[16] Thomas Mlanga Marealle to Chief Secretary, 'Claims for the Country of Marangu Formerly Ruled by My Father – Mangi Mlanga Marealle' 28 December 1933, TNA 13368, ff. 146–153.

[17] Acting chief secretary to provincial commissioner, TNA 13368, f. 157.

[18] Susan G. Rogers, *Search for Political Focus on Kilimanjaro: A History of Chagga Politics, 1916–1952, with Special Reference to the Cooperative Movement and Indirect Rule*. Unpublished PhD thesis, University of Dar es Salaam (1972), pp. 865–866. The relevant issues are Nov–Dec 1941 and April 1943.

[19] Marealle to Vickers-Haviland, 28th April 1947, RHO Mss.Afr.s.1598, f. 142.

[20] 'East African Political Intelligence Summary, June 1951', p. 4. TNA UK, CO 537/7227; 'Notes of a Meeting between Mr A. B. Cohen, C. M. G., O. B. E., and Members of

His election as paramount chief that year forced him, to a certain extent, to choose between territorial politics and local politics, and he duly resigned from government service and returned to Kilimanjaro. As Susan Geiger found when she conducted interviews on Kilimanjaro in the early 1960s, expectations of what he could achieve were enormous. Her informants told her that 'Marealle would abolish the divisional chiefs, do away with the coffee tax, and lead the Chagga to greatness under an independent sovereign. He would restore respect to the clans and clan leaders and abolish corruption in the administration. He would speak authoritatively to government, and they would be forced to listen. Chagga *vihamba* would be safe forever, and more land provided for all.'[21]

Although Marealle had initially been reluctant to stand for election and was always slightly dubious about the party which had campaigned for his election, the Kilimanjaro Chagga Citizens Union (KCCU), he was swept up in the wave of enthusiasm. The local administration, once opposed to such a post, came eventually to hope that it would help restore legitimacy to local government and allow continued and successful development.

THE PARAMOUNT CHIEF IN OFFICE

Following his election in 1952, Marealle devoted himself to creating a new polity, membership of which was based partly on ethnicity – a Chagga nationalism – and partly on residence on the mountain. As the district commissioner explained in a 'Letter to all Chagga' in 1951, the new office of paramount chief delivered 'One Chief for the whole nation [*taifa*]'.[22] Marealle sought to deliver the social services and material development which were demanded, but to do so in a way which took account of the deeper-rooted fears and anxieties on the mountain which we explored in Chapter 4, that economic progress was harming social relations.

In devising the ceremonial pageantry of his rule, he tried to bridge local patriotism based on territorial residency and ethnic patriotism

---

the Committee of the Dar es Salaam African Association in Dar es Salaam on 28th May, 1951', pp. 1–3. TNA UK, CO 822/644, f. 1, Rogers, *Search for Political Focus on Kilimanjaro: A History of Chagga Politics, 1916–1952, with Special Reference to the Cooperative Movement and Indirect Rule*, p. 868.

[21] Rogers, *Search for Political Focus on Kilimanjaro: A History of Chagga Politics, 1916–1952, with Special Reference to the Cooperative Movement and Indirect Rule*, p. 891 fn.

[22] J. F. Millard, D.C., 'Barua kwa Wachagga Wote', TNA 12844/3, f. 355.

based on imagined ties of descent, with annual Chagga Day celebrations, held for the first time in 1952, providing a focus. The aim of Chagga Day was, in Marealle's words, to commemorate the day 'the Chagga tribe miraculously came together in a unity which has surprised many people' and they were allowed to 'elect one ruler for the whole tribe.'[23] The district commissioner, H. F. Elliott, was enthusiastic, praising in a report the Chagga Day's potential to 'promote the growth of a healthy local patriotism rather than an arid nationalism.'[24] In their public speeches at Chagga Day and other festive occasions, district officials echoed Marealle's language of local patriotism and of a divided body made whole.[25]

This was an inclusive patriotism. The Mangi Mkuu's words at the first Chagga Day sought to define a role for non-Chagga within it when he said 'Chagga day is here and all our friends and they are all welcome. Perhaps "friends" is not the right word, for I have always regarded the Chagga people as a family and the Asians and Europeans in our midst as members of the extended kinship – so we are one big family and that family is fully represented here tonight.'[26] More broadly, the focus on inclusivity included holding prayers in both Christian and Muslim places of worship at the start of Chagga Day.[27] Patriarchal metaphors reinforced the idea of a Chagga body with Marealle at its head. At a party held to mark Marealle's departure for London to attend Queen Elizabeth II's coronation the district commissioner said: 'Now when the father travels he normally leaves the mother at home to look after the children. Well I agree to be the mother and no doubt you will agree to be the children.'[28] Together they would look after the home until the father returned.

As we saw in Chapter 4, Marealle helped to initiate the establishment of a local newspaper, *Komkya*, which became the focus for his nation-building efforts. A new national song was written. Marealle showed a great interest in Chagga history and commissioned a new history of the Chagga people.[29] But Marealle was not only a figurehead, charged with symbolizing the unity of the Chagga people, for as chair of

---

[23] 'Chagga Day Speech at the Sundowner – 10th November 1952 – by the Mangi Mkuu of the Wachagga, Marealle II,' TNA 12844/3; Mangi Mkuu to Colonel Hay, Government House, Dar es Salaam, 24th November 1952, 12844/3, f. 459.

[24] Moshi District Annual Report 1953, TNA 5/38/10/2, no f.

[25] 'Mwili wa Uchagga ni Mzima', *Komkya*, December 1953, p. 1.

[26] 'Chagga Day Speech at the Sundowner', TNA 12844/3, f. 4.

[27] 'Chagga Day 1954', *Komkya*, 1 November 1954, p. 7.

[28] 'Mangi Mkuu wa Wachagga ameagwa na Kilimanjaro Chagga Citizens Union', *Komkya*, April 1953, p. 4.

[29] Kathleen Stahl, *History of the Chagga People of Kilimanjaro* (The Hague: Mouton, 1964).

the Chagga Council, the local district council, Marealle was also at the heart of debates about how revenue was to be obtained and how it should be spent. In what the district commissioner had previously described in 1948 as 'these days of development talk', this was a heavy responsibility.

Raising revenue as a means of funding development was a constant challenge, and public occasions provided valuable opportunities for the paramount chief and district officials to encourage the prompt payment of tax and to support the paramount chief and the Chagga Council in their efforts.[30] Reports for the early 1950s suggested that the appointment of the Mangi Mkuu was indeed having beneficial tax-raising effects. The 1953 Annual Report for Moshi District identified the 'very fair degree of success achieved by the Mangi Mkuu and the Native Authority generally in reconciling the Wachagga people to the Coffee Cess and clearly demonstrating to them its basic contribution to their material progress' as the 'outstanding feature of the year as a whole'.[31] Marealle also used his position to seek more scholarships to enable the young to study abroad.

At the national level, Marealle seemed to offer chiefship in modern form.[32] The governor, Edward Twining, hoped he would provide the focus of a local patriotism which in his view offered the greatest potential for stopping the growth of African nationalism. Marealle played a leading role in the Chiefs' Convention, seen by the government as the possible basis for an 'upper house' which would provide a counterweight to African nationalists. In 1957, Marealle spoke at the Trusteeship Council in New York, alongside the TANU leader Julius Nyerere. Referring to Marealle's success in New York, a Foreign Office brief suggested that 'Marealle may well have a great future as the leader of moderate conservative nationalism drawing its strength from the chiefs and the peasants.'[33] Sir Andrew Cohen contrasted Thomas Marealle and Julius Nyerere and concluded of Nyerere that '[a]s a man I thought him definitely less attractive than Marealle or than some of the political minded Africans in Uganda.'[34]

Marealle's political project was one of developmentalist nation-building. But although he sought progress (*maendeleo*), he was sensitive to

---

[30] 'Mwili wa Uchagga ni Mzima', *Komkya*, December 1953, p. 1.
[31] Moshi District Annual Report 1953, TNA 5/38/10/2, no f., p. 1.
[32] John Tawney, 'Election in Tanganyika', *Corona*, May 1952, pp. 181–183.
[33] Brief for secretary of state's meeting with members of the Labour Party on Tanganyika, TNA UK, CO 822/1319.
[34] Personal and confidential letter, Sir A. Cohen to Sir. E. Twining, 28 June 1957, TNA UK, CO 822/1361, f. 107.

the arguments of those on the mountain who thought that economic development risked increasing inequalities of wealth and breaking the web of social obligations between patrons and clients, fathers and son, which were at the heart of social and political life. He was attracted to the idea, popularized by the KCCU, that the clan was the foundation of Chagga social life, and sought to reassert its importance as a social, economic and political body.[35] And although Marealle had himself been elected to his office, he moved to make the position of paramount chief hereditary.

This shift towards a more assertive conservativism took place against the backdrop of wider changes which followed Marealle's election. On the one hand, while Marealle sought to balance a Chagga nationalism defined in ethnic terms with a broader and more open form of local citizenship, the KCCU sought to establish itself as the gatekeeper of a new Chagga body politic. Their attempt to impose their authority over Marealle and define the boundaries of citizenship began immediately after Marealle's election, as they sought to control the collection of contributions for the celebrations to mark his installation.[36] Their use of familial metaphors at the farewell party for Marealle's departure for England to attend the Queen's coronation in 1952 is telling. Where the District Commissioner had presented Marealle as a father, Petro Njau in his address attempted both to support the Mangi Mkuu's power by using patriarchal terms, and to seek to maintain an advisory role for himself. He described the Mangi Mkuu first as a child of the Chagga people. He was a Chagga child with a Chagga mother and father, and so in going on this journey it was as if 'all we Wachagga have gone. Although he has gone on behalf of all the Africans of Tanganyika'.[37] Yet while he was their child, he was also their 'father', and when travelling abroad he should wear the clothes in which he had been installed as Mangi Mkuu.[38]

As we saw in Chapter 4, the KCCU claimed that land rights and Chagga citizenship should be limited to those in possession of a Union membership card. The District Commissioner attacked the Union on this point, arguing that they suffered from 'complete ignorance of what democracy

---

[35] Interview with Thomas Marealle, January 2006, Moshi; 'Ngyufyari 36 za nchi ya Machame zilimkaribisha Mangi Mkuu na Mkamangi', *Komkya*, 1 January 1957, p. 9; 'Vishari viendeshwe kufuata mila na desturi tu', *Komkya*, 15 February 1957, p. 4.

[36] A number of councillors stated that the Kilimanjaro Union was telling people not to give contributions to headmen or chiefs but to them. Mkutano No 1/52 wa Hai Division, Uliohudhuriwa na Halmashauri wa Hai Division, 11th January 1952, TNA 5/23/25, p. 4.

[37] 'Mangi Mkuu wa Wachagga ameagwa na Kilimanjaro Chagga Citizens Union', *Komkya*, April 1953, p. 4.

[38] Ibid.

and freedom really mean' and that the Union 'should also understand clearly that *all* Chagga have rights whether members of your 'Union' or not.'[39] The Citizens Union's attempt to link Chagga citizenship to Union membership prompted a quick response from a new political organization, the Chagga Congress, which rejected the KCCU's claim 'that only those people with membership cards for the [Union] would be considered true Wachagga; anyone without a membership card being classified as an outcast.'[40] It included many members of the old and now defunct African Association in Moshi, and one of the former leaders of the Union, Joseph Merinyo.[41]

The primary concern of the Chagga Congress was to remove the KCCU, and other 'subversive organisations', from the Chagga Council and attack the idea that only members of the Union were full Chagga citizens. But their approach also demonstrated other differences from the Union, notably in their enthusiasm to accept women as members. As they recorded in their minutes, '[i]t was agreed that women should be allowed to join the Society and that the method of choosing women members should be studied' and they offered a lower membership fee to women.[42]

In response, the KCCU created a new women's organization, legitimated in terms of an appeal to customs and traditions. In a document explaining the establishment of the 'Chagga Women's Association', its leader Mrs Abdi Mankya noted that although it was the case that tradition dictated that women should not hold meetings, nevertheless 'custom permitted women to meet inside the markets in order to conduct business.' This freedom which women had to meet in the markets 'enabled the women of all lands to join together and care for one another with more confidence than was available to men in the lands of Kilimanjaro.'[43] When the men did come together to establish their association to bring together all Chagga, they did not examine these already existing modes of working together. Mrs Mankya therefore called for cooperation between men and women, and offered the services of her association in the specific task of stamping out female drunkenness among the Chagga.[44]

[39] District Commissioner to Secretary, Chagga Citizens Union, October 1951, TNA 5/23/20 vol 1, f. 104. Emphasis in original.
[40] 'Minutes of the meeting of the Chagga Congress which met in the Welfare Centre on Saturday 30th January 1954', p. 2. TNA 12844/4, f. 538.
[41] Mangi Mkuu of the Wachagga to D. C., 8th January 1954.
[42] 'Minutes of the meeting of the Chagga Congress which met in the Welfare Centre on Saturday 30th January 1954', f. 538.
[43] KCCU Circular No. 5 of 1954, 'Chama cha Wanawake Uchagga: The Kilimanjaro Chagga Citizens Union', TNA 5/25/7, f. 225, p. 2.
[44] Ibid., p. 3.

At the same time as the KCCU appeared to go against the times in excluding women, Thomas Marealle's increasing insistence on deference from the young inspired generational revolt. In 1955 he insisted that Chagga students at Makerere apologize after they had been critical of him in an article in the Makerere magazine, and that they do so in a mode deemed to be in accordance with Chagga customs and traditions.[45] For the students involved, this was a humiliation, and it encouraged opposition to Marealle.

Marealle's support of the clan structure also brought him into conflict with the Lutheran Church. Although the Lutheran establishment did not oppose moves to increase the role of the clan in social life, they reminded Christians that they should not allow clan meetings to interfere with Sunday worship, that in these meetings they should do nothing which opposed Christian belief such as sacrificing to the spirits, oathing or slaughtering animals in places of non-Christian spiritual significance; clan meetings should not simply be places of eating and drinking but clans should care for the poor and for widows and orphans. Christians should not tolerate the oppression of members of that clan or other clans but act justly. In an article in the Lutheran periodical *Umoja*, the Lutheran pastor Stefano Moshi argued that God must be at the heart of any process of nation-building if it was to prosper.[46]

A divide was opening up between those who saw a resurrection of paternal authority and hierarchical institutions within which social superiors acted as patrons towards their social inferiors as the basis for reconstructing society to face the future, on the one hand, and those advocating equality between men and women and the rights of the young to speak out in disagreement with their elders on the other. The former was represented by the KCCU and, despite his attempts in the early days to keep it at arm's length, by Marealle, while the latter was represented first by the Chagga Congress, then by a group of opponents in the Chagga Council, and then from November 1958 by a new organization, the CDP, whose leaders were also members of TANU. This latter group tapped into the growing power in Tanzania as elsewhere in Africa of languages of

[45] 'Wanafunzi Wachagga wa Makerere wamejita', *Komkya*, February 1955, p. 1; Kathleen Stahl, 'The Chagga', in P. Gulliver (ed.), *Tradition and Transition: Studies of the Tribal Element in the Modern Era* (Berkeley: University of California Press, 1969), pp. 209–222, p. 218.

[46] Stefano R. Moshi, 'Maoni ya Kanisa Juu ya Mikutano ya Vishari (Jamaa)', *Umoja*, February 1956, p. 3.

democracy, anti-imperialism and a demand for strong central government to drive development.

OPPOSITION IN THE CHAGGA COUNCIL

In 1958 Solomon Eliufoo, a TANU member who had recently returned from the United States, was elected to the Chagga Council. Eliufoo had first played a role in Kilimanjaro politics through his role in the Lutheran Church. He had been a member of the original Constitutional Committee which had been set up in 1951 to debate the creation of a paramount chief. At that time he argued for the introduction of a secret ballot on the grounds that 'an open election could not be conducted fairly.'[47] Awarded a scholarship to study in the United States between 1953 and 1956, on his return to Kilimanjaro in 1957 he took up a post as Assistant Education Officer at the Teachers' Training College in Marangu and increased his involvement in both local and national politics.[48] During his absence, the nationalist party TANU had been founded under the leadership of Julius Nyerere, and on his return in 1957 Eliufoo joined the TANU branch in Machame, the most active TANU branch on Kilimanjaro. In 1958 he became a member of the Chagga Council and was also elected to the Legislative Council in Dar es Salaam, representing TANU.[49]

The elections which brought Eliufoo to the Chagga Council marked a dramatic change in the membership of the Council. Since Marealle's inauguration in January 1952, the Council had been dominated by members of the KCCU, and this remained the case following new elections in 1954. Marealle thus benefited from essentially having his own party within the Council. But the 1958 elections removed all KCCU representatives from the Council, replacing them with a younger contingent less willing to give Marealle unconditional support.

In March 1958 they established an Unofficial Members Organization of the Chagga Council, on the model of the opposition body in the Legislative Council in Dar es Salaam. Their aim, agreed at their inaugural meeting, was to unite together to 'fulfil the responsibilities they had

---

[47] Minutes of the Third Meeting of a Conference Held at the District Office on March 12th. Subject – Constitution, p. 4. TNA 5/23/20, vol 1, f. 50.
[48] Emma Hunter, 'Solomon Eliufoo', in Emmanuel K. Akyeampong and Henry Louis Gates, Jr (eds.), *Dictionary of African Biography*, 6 vols. (Oxford: Oxford University Press, 2012), Vol. II, pp. 291–292.
[49] Stahl, 'The Chagga', p. 219.

been given by the citizens [*raia*].'⁵⁰ Under the chairmanship of Solomon Eliufoo, alongside K. E. L. Mushi acting as secretary and J. G. Mallya as assistant secretary, they agreed on a number of points to be raised at the next Chagga Council meeting, all of which suggested dissatisfaction with the current state of affairs. Key points of complaint included the question of leases in Chaggaland, the ownership of *Komkya*, non-Chagga employed by the Chagga Council and the position of women in the district. Though they did not enlarge on the last point, Eliufoo and others linked to TANU were much better at delineating a role for women within politics than their predecessors in the region had been.

More broadly, the related issues of the paramount chief's accountability to the Chagga Council and the relationship among Marealle, the Chagga Council and the Chagga people was central to their critique. They charged Marealle with misrepresenting Council decisions in public meetings on Kilimanjaro. They proposed that 'discussions held by the Mangi Mkuu on the mountain should be agreed by the Chagga Council', and that after each Chagga Council meeting it should be the responsibility of each chief to call a meeting of all citizens to explain to them matters which had been discussed in the Chagga Council. Again as a means of improving communication, 'Area Councils should keep minutes of all their meetings, and each Area Councillor should be given a copy.'⁵¹ They also attacked the KCCU, as 'those who wear *migorori*' or blankets, the uniform associated with Njau's party.

In return, Petro Njau sought to defend the position of the paramount chief. On 17 March 1958 he wrote to Marealle asking for clarification of his constitutional position according to the 1951 Constitution. He asked for confirmation that the demands of the KCCU had been met, namely that the paramount chief should be 'independent', should have 'executive and legal power', should 'not be regarded as Government Servant' and that his function was to 'be "Head of the Tribe" and "Symbol" of its recently effected unity and as such to coralise [sic] those feelings of loyalty and devotion which are frustrated', as well as to develop policies 'for the progress of the Tribe'.⁵²

Growing criticism of the paramount chief led to the establishment of a new Constitutional Committee. In theory the task of the committee was

---

⁵⁰ 'Chama cha Wajumbe wa Chagga Council Wasio Watumishi wa Utawala', 27 March 1958, TNA 5/23/20, f. 132.

⁵¹ Ibid.

⁵² President, KCCU to Mangi Mkuu, 17th March 1958, TNA 5/23/20, f. 124. Emphasis in original.

to review Marealle's workload and propose reforms, but at its second meeting on 23 May 1958 Solomon Eliufoo, on behalf of the Unofficial Members Organisation, called on the Mangi Mkuu to stop attending meetings of the Constitutional Committee.[53] Although this call was unsuccessful, it showed that their reforming aims were far wider than a simple desire to reduce Marealle's duties.

CONSTITUTIONAL ARGUMENTS

Marealle's fall from power has conventionally been seen as one of the broader effects of the rise of African nationalism. An associated trope was that of the corrupt monarch. Like Louis XVI in the last days of the *ancien régime*, the Mangi Mkuu had become corrupted by greed and pride, relying too much on advisers who wanted to drag society back to a clan age and who lacked the education and understanding needed to face up to modernity.[54]

Yet looking at these debates in more detail, what is striking is not the unanimity in opposition to the Mangi Mkuu, but the ways in which different traditions of constitutional thinking were blended to produce innovative solutions which seemed to address the need for improved accountability. In addressing fundamental questions of political organization, not limited simply to the question of whether a paramount chief was compatible with democracy, the solutions that were offered mixed together ideas conventionally seen as 'traditional' and those seen as 'modern'.[55] Again, this reinforces the need to reinstate a sense of the fluidity of options and uncertainty of the period.

The new Constitutional Committee was composed of various local luminaries, such as chiefs and prominent members of the local Council, and was chaired by the district commissioner. The district commissioner intended it to be concerned with reviewing the paramount chief's workload and the question of whether or not the position should be hereditary. These issues had been left unclear in the 1951 constitutional reforms that established the office of paramount chief, though in the

[53] Minutes of the third meeting of a conference held at the District Office on March 12th. Subject – constitution. TNA 5/23/20, volume 1, f. 50, p. 4.
[54] Michael Von Clemm, *People of the White Mountain: The Interdependence of Political and Economic Activity amongst the Chagga with Special Reference to Recent Changes.* Unpublished PhD thesis, University of Oxford (1962), p. 110 and pp. 236–238.
[55] A similar debate took place when the question of a paramount chief for Bukoba was discussed in 1956. See *Sunday News*, esp. September to December 1956.

intervening period attempts at clarification had been made on a number of occasions, such as at the Chagga Day celebrations in 1955 when the District Commissioner stated that 'The Mangi Mkuu has been elected in order to rule for his whole life'.[56] The question of inheritance had been raised in 1957 when Marealle was about to depart for an extended visit to America. Discussing who should replace him during his absence, the Chagga Council reflected on the broader question of inheritance. In the words of *Komkya's* report of the meeting, 'The meeting was reminded that the Mangi Mkuu of the Chagga had been elected according to customs and traditions in order that he should be a traditional ruler of the Chagga.'[57] According to these Chagga customs and traditions, it was essential that he be succeeded by his son. Despite this confident assertion, no solution was reached and it was agreed that the Chagga Council would return to the matter in future meetings. As for his workload, on his return from America in the autumn of 1957 Marealle was pushed towards abandoning his position on Tanganyika's Legislative Council. The headline 'The Mangi Mkuu should not be a Legco Representative' introduced an account of a Chagga Council meeting which had agreed that the Mangi Mkuu should refuse a position on the national Legislative Council on the grounds of having too much to do in his own country of Kilimanjaro.[58]

But if the district commissioner expected the Committee to focus on the paramount chief's workload as well as matters relating to land allocation and the judiciary, others on the committee quickly moved to take control of its agenda. They argued 'that it would be advisable to investigate the existing constitution to consider whether there are elements which could be changed.' Others said that they would like democratic government (*Utawala wa Democracy*).[59] For them, the purpose of the Committee was to change the system of government, and in their terms, establish democracy.[60]

---

[56] 'Mangi Mkuu Amechaguliwa Atawale kwa maisha yake yote', *Komkya*, 15 November 1955, p. 1.

[57] 'Kurithiwa kwa Mangi Mkuu wa Wachagga', *Komkya*, 1 April 1957, p. 5.

[58] 'Mangi Mkuu asiwe Mjumbe wa Legco – Maoni ya Chagga Council', *Komkya*, 1 October 1957, p. 7.

[59] Minutes of Meeting 1st May 1958, TNA 5/23/20, f. 191.

[60] In part, this reflects the broader national political context as Tanganyika moved towards territory-wide national elections in 1958–59, refocussing discussion on matters of electoral practice. John Iliffe, *A Modern History of Tanganyika* (Cambridge: Cambridge University Press, 1979), pp. 555–557.

It was in this context that an advertisement was placed in the district newspaper *Komkya* on 1 June 1958, shortly after the first meeting of the Constitutional Committee on 1 May 1958. The advertisement sought suggestions for constitutional change. Given the sharp political divides present at the time, it might be expected that responses would have split fairly clearly along party lines, with a majority rehearsing the arguments against the Mangi Mkuu and a minority defending his position as the spokesman of 'the Chagga tribe'. However, the reality was more complex. Although the sharp divide between supporters of TANU and supporters of the paramount chief lie behind the debates, the submissions show an interest in engaging with and reforming the institutions of local government so as to ensure accountability, effective leadership and moral probity. This was a time when discussion at the national level was preoccupied with the elections which would sweep TANU to power and with TANU's demands for self-government with universal suffrage as soon as possible without too much thought as to the specifics of local government. In contrast, these local discussions demonstrate a serious engagement with the relationship between locality and centre and the representation of citizens.

The advert evidently struck a chord, for it drew a large number of responses, preserved in the Tanzania National Archives in Dar es Salaam. Some of these were orchestrated by particular groups – the similarities in tone and language are striking. Others came in from Chagga readers of *Komkya* working in other parts of the territory, and their content and style are more diverse. But in spite of these differences, what is interesting about the responses is the evidence they provide of thoughtful attempts by those interested in local politics in the 1950s to consider how best to achieve accountable governance. Rewriting constitutions was not something which could be done according to a template, but required careful reflection. What we see here, in the responses to the adverts in *Komkya*, are respondents thinking creatively about political authority and how it should operate.

Where political scientists tend to assume a set of fixed attributes associated with 'modern' democratic politics, and a contrasting set of fixed attributes associated with 'traditional' politics, in these responses there was a sense both that some local 'traditions' could be built on, and some discarded, but also that new ideas could be sought from outside and combined with older ideas, or ideas which could be made to appear older. Most significantly, not all those opposed to Marealle agreed with each other about what sort of power structures should be established locally.

Three concerns in particular seem to have animated those who responded to the call for submissions. The first, and most important, was the issue of whether the paramount chief had been, or ought to have been, elected for life, or whether he should face regular elections. Related to this was the option of replacing him with a president of Kilimanjaro, who would serve a defined term. This issue lay at the heart of many of the responses. Although the paramount chief himself used the ambiguity in the constitutional arrangements which had brought him to power to claim that he could rule for life, most of those who responded to the announcement argued that regular elections were essential to ensure legitimate authority.

We can see this most clearly in the submissions made by the secretary of the Chagga Council Unofficial Members Organisation, K. E. L. Mushi. Mushi was opposed to Marealle, and in his response to the *Komkya* advert in July 1958, he proclaimed that they had 'arrived at a cross roads.'[61] The task ahead was to 'increase democracy, prepare for self-government, and avoid being laughed at by the world.' But this did not mean ignoring the past; it meant building on it creatively.

Mushi argued that this was a time of rapid social change and institutions and people must be able to change too. Moreover, men were imperfect; they designed institutions today which might not suit tomorrow. Third, the present Mangi Mkuu had been elected by popular vote and the people should be able to change their vote 'when his popularity wanes.' The institution of a paramount chief had, he argued, been borrowed from outside the country, and thus the institution should in its Tanganyikan form follow the same pattern as in its 'original' formation. It was he wrote, 'against all natural laws and political philosophy to be under the sway of an unpopular head, as the trends of affairs indicate.'

Most of the respondents, including Mushi, made points about systems of government in general, rather than referring specifically to Marealle himself. Like Mushi, they argued in general terms that corruption was inevitable should a leader not face regular re-election. Various arguments were produced to make this case. One correspondent, Israel Lema, argued that because a paramount chief's fundamental duty was to ensure the development of the country, it was important for him to be regularly replaced because he would cease actively to pursue such development after a certain amount of time, and with no elections to fear.[62]

---

[61] K. E. L. Mushi, 'Tunaweza kujitajirika zaidi', TNA 5/23/20, f. 181.

[62] Israel W. Lema to District Commissioner re 'Memoranda Juu ya Mpango wa Utawala wa Ki-Chagga', 11th July 1958, TNA 5/23/20, f. 163.

Others disagreed with Mushi's enthusiasm for respecting the ways in which these institutions were used elsewhere. Defending the office of paramount chief as an office for life, Philip Shirima wrote that a regularly elected president would signify a humiliating 'instability, change of mind and unbalanced determination' and just because regularly elected presidents were popular in some states did not mean that the institution should be copied blindly.

In any case, if the dominant tone was in favour of elections, this did not mean opposition to having a strong local government with an accountable head. This is worth emphasizing, given the dominant feeling at the time across Africa and the wider postcolonial world that strong central governments were essential to bring development. Thus although Mushi believed that a crossroads had been reached and that the way forward was a path to democracy and self-government, he did not believe this meant the end of chiefship. He was in favour of maintaining the most local and 'traditional' institutions of political power, the individual local chiefs. They were, he wrote, the 'authentic and the real traditional rulers of the Wachagga' and their positions 'should be left to go unmolested.'[63]

So what we see is a blend of an enthusiasm for universal suffrage and regular elections with a belief that older institutions should be adapted to fit the modern age. But there was considerable disagreement from correspondents over which chiefs counted as 'traditional' and thus should be saved. There was also considerable disagreement, even from those who agreed that the paramount chief should go, over the question of whether his replacement needed to be from a chiefly clan or not. Some insisted that he did not. Thus a 'Chagga citizen', as he described himself, using the English term 'citizen', working far away in Singida, wrote in to say that the post of paramount chief 'should be filled by a president who will be any competent citizen, not a chief.' Turning familiar arguments about African politics on their head, he went on to say: 'In African minds presidents are more trustworthy than chiefs.'[64] Others insisted that the paramount chief's replacement should be either an existing chief or from a ruling clan.

This was a search for a blended political system, but crucially, one in which it was possible to institute change. As the veteran political activist

---

[63] K. E. L. Mushi, 'Memorandum: The Chagga Constitution', 8th July 1958, TNA 5/23/20, f. 162.

[64] 'Chagga Citizen' to District Commissioner, re 'Memoranda on Chagga Council Constitution', TNA 5/23/20, f. 168.

Joseph Merinyo wrote in his submission, 'If a chief makes a mistake, he should be removed without removing chiefship. If a headman makes a mistake he should be removed without removing the office of headman.'[65] People can be bad, but it should be possible to get rid of them without provoking a constitutional crisis, as seemed to have happened in this case.

A second theme was the search for a way to institute morality. We see this in the repeated attempts to define what sort of person should be allowed to stand for office. A chief should be a person of 'good reputation'. This correspondent went on to specify what this meant. He should be someone over thirty, but not yet an elder, 'who is married and lives happily with his wife, a person who does not drink excessively, nor is a thief nor engaged in prostitution'. Another correspondent explicitly attacked the morality of the current paramount chief, claiming Marealle was spreading immorality in the country. 'Every evening he takes himself off to get drunk with someone's daughter or wife', he wrote. The paramount chief, he claimed, adored corruption (*rushwa*) and 'his house was full of goats'. This was a comment on his immorality. The rich who could afford to bring a goat had access to the chief, but, this anonymous writer continued, 'for a poor person to see him is impossible'.[66]

The emphasis on the personal morality of leaders was clearly to some degree due to rumours which were circulating about the immorality of the paramount chief. In July 1959, reporting on rumours which had filtered down to Dar es Salaam and which may well have been circulating in the region for some time, the American consul, William Duggan, explained that Marealle's chiefship had been criticized for its 'domineering' tone and for its extravagant operations.' He had, Duggan reported, tried and failed to divorce his wife who was now living apart after he had 'injured her very seriously in a recent family quarrel'.[67] He had also, the

---

[65] J. Merinyo to D.C., 'Tangazo Maalum kwa Wachagga la Tarehe 1st June 1958', TNA 5/23/20, f. 149.

[66] This comment provides a stark contrast with the observations made by Michael von Clemm during fieldwork conducted between 1960 and 1962. He noted that concern with wealth and status went alongside egalitarianism, writing that 'The wealthy Chagga businessman or teacher or *Mangi* (especially the *Mangi*) can be approached by any one in public places, and at the same time he is careful to greet all and sundry among passers-by.' Von Clemm, *People of the White Mountain: The Interdependence of Political and Economic Activity amongst the Chagga with Special Reference to Recent Changes*, p. 21.

[67] Dar es Salaam to Washington, 'Visit with Chagga Paramount Chief Thomas Marealle', 9 September 1959, 778.00/9–959, Box 3697, Central Files 1955–1959, National Archives II, College Park, Maryland.

consul wrote, 'developed a widespread reputation for his flirtatiousness and affection toward European (and American) women.'[68]

But more generally, the responses seem to have focussed on how to ensure that political authority went to those of good character, and demonstrated recognition that this could not simply be a question of which family they belonged to. Lists of criteria were often provided in these submissions, of which some concentrated on the general, calling for those who were recognized as good citizens, and who had ability, wisdom, knowledge and education should stand for elections. Others were more specific, composing lists of factors – the appropriate age, gender and level of education, as well as general 'good reputation' were all identified.

What of democracy in these submissions? The original aim of the Constitutional Committee had been, after all, to establish democratic rule. The term 'democracy' itself is reasonably common in the English submissions. Thus one of those who wrote in described himself as 'one of the Chaggas who admire democratic development in Kilimanjaro', while Philip Shirima wrote in defence of the paramount chief: 'Are our democratic rights deprived of us by having a Mangi Mkuu? If anybody thinks they are, he is worse than a conspirator. The Mangi Mkuu should be our sole centre of honour and an emblem of our tribal dignity.'

However, in the other submissions, the term is rarely used, in part because it remained unclear what the Swahili term should be. Joseph Merinyo, who wrote in Swahili, used the term, and associated its meaning with the removal of imperialism. He wrote: 'Many people would like there to be a vote every three years, especially these days. The people should be asked. The people are desperately waiting for the elections which will remove imperialism and bring democracy to Uchaggani.'[69] Both the term he uses for imperialism, 'imperlism', and the term he uses for democracy, 'udemokrasi', look odd in the text.

Where the term 'democracy' appeared in these letters, it tended to be associated with a wider set of 'modern' political attributes. In other words, rather than being a governmental system, it was a way of being 'modern'. It was also associated with nationalism and support for ending colonial rule. Those who defended the paramount chief and his right to

---

[68] Dar es Salaam to Washington, 'Political Turmoil in Chaggaland', Confidential, 22 July 1959, 778.00/7-2259, Box 3697, Central Files 1955–1959, National Archives II, College Park, Maryland.

[69] J. Merinyo to D. C., 'Tangazo Maalum kwa Wachagga la Tarehe 1st June 1958', TNA 5/23/20, f. 149.

remain in office had to deal explicitly with this question, and emphasize that they were not advocating tyranny.

But if few were arguing explicitly over what democracy should mean, all the correspondents were dealing in creative ways with the question of how to hold power to account. There was a general sense that a crisis of authority had emerged, that the paramount chief had gained too much power and that new institutions or new strategies were needed to ensure this did not happen again. On one level, what this shows is an attempt to rethink accountable governance.[70] But there is another layer to this. If the responses show that it was not self-evident that the paramount chief was outdated and that a local president must be installed to take his place, the question then of why the anti-paramount chief lobby proved the most convincing must be asked, and with this we return to the power of new languages of politics, the CDP and the rise of TANU.

THE DEPOSITION OF THOMAS MAREALLE

As the Constitutional Committee continued to argue over Marealle's future, the Unofficial Members Organisation turned itself into a political party. The CDP was established in November 1958. Initially it was hoped that it could remain separate from the Unofficial Members Organisation but that proved impossible and Solomon Eliufoo took a leading role.[71] The party's aims were very much the same as those of the Unofficial Members, namely to establish 'a democratic government within Chaggaland, especially by giving every adult citizen a vote capable of changing the leadership of the government', giving 'citizens an opportunity to participate in political matters connected with Chaggaland' and '[t]o criticise or to praise, in a constructive manner, the local Government.'[72] A further aim was to bring Chagga politics into dialogue with wider territorial politics, by making 'the Chagga people aware of the present progress of Tanganyika, and thus enable them to participate in this progress.'

This concern with the wider context was unsurprising given that many of the CDP's leaders were also members of TANU although they worked hard to keep the two organizations separate, at least rhetorically. At their

---

[70] Tim Kelsall, 'Rituals of Verification: Indigenous and Imported Accountability in Northern Tanzania', *Africa*, 73 (2003), 174–201.

[71] Commissioner of Police to Ministerial Secretary, 'Chagga Affairs: Moshi District', 5 November 1958, TNA UK, FCO 141/17864, f. 1.

[72] Commissioner of Police to Ministerial Secretary, 'Chagga Affairs, Moshi District: Chagga Democratic Party', TNA UK, FCO 141/17864, 8 November 1958, f. 3.

first public meeting, perhaps a third of those attending did so in the belief that they were attending a TANU meeting, and one of the first speakers, Onesmo Lema, had to explain that he was there not in his capacity as a TANU Chairman but as a committee member of the CDP.[73] Yet his decision to begin his speech by repeating the word 'Uhuru' three times, as in TANU public meetings, can only have added to the confusion.[74]

At the same meeting, Solomon Eliufoo repeated the familiar charges against Marealle's moral character heard in the arguments of the constitutional committee. Marealle was accused of bribing subordinates with drink and meat and bringing the Chagga into disrepute. Having a paramount chief was itself a regressive step, Eliufoo argued, and had been seen as such by the UN Visiting Mission which came to Moshi in 1954. Eliufoo insisted on the principle of election, telling his audience that 'in Egypt the people had risen up and thrown out their King because he had been given to bribery. They had elected their own President, who was loved by all the people and who was leading the country well.' In England too the principle of elections was accepted, for 'the Queen was only a constitutional monarch' and 'government policy was formulated by the Prime Minister who was elected by the people.'[75]

In May 1959, the CDP sent a petition calling on Marealle to resign. The basis of their authority to do so was, they claimed, their position as the elected representatives of the Chagga people, with the responsibility of acting as the voices of those people. In the petition, they again reiterated the importance of elections.[76] Marealle was not a customary ruler of the Chagga; he had been elected with the support of the KCCU. Now that he lacked the confidence of the Chagga people he should go and be replaced by somebody elected to serve for a limited period.

Marealle sought to respond to the moral critiques. In a speech March 1959 he told the people of Rombo that he himself had 'given up drinking and smoking as an example'.[77] At the same time he engaged in a major public relations offensive. Visiting Moshi in September 1959, the American consul found him 'more affable toward the reporting officer than he has ever been before' and willing to speak 'most enthusiastically

[73] 'Chagga Democratic Party: (C. D. P.): Moshi District: Public Meeting held 4 April, 1959', TNA UK, FCO 141/17864, f. 7A, p. 1.

[74] Ibid., p. 3.

[75] Ibid., p. 3.

[76] Chagga Democratic Party to Minister for Local Government and Administration, 20 May 1959, TNA UK, FCO 141/17864, f. 13.

[77] Cited in *Umoja*, April 1959, p. 3.

of the TANU leader, Mr Nyerere'. He also showed the American diplomat transcripts of talks to be delivered on Nigerian radio 'as an illustration of the growing relationships between African leaders on both sides of the continent.'[78]

As the pressure on Marealle mounted, the KCCU sought to mobilize support for Marealle in the first half of 1959 but found it hard to gain a hearing with Petro Njau at the helm. In June 1959 a new party, the Chagga Progressive Party, emerged, possibly at Marealle's instigation, to make the case for the continuation of the paramount chiefship, but it too failed to build popular support.[79] In the long run, however, he could not rehabilitate his reputation or win back popular support. Continued pressure from the CDP led the local administration to call a referendum to be held, which duly took place on 4 February 1960.[80] Forty-four per cent of those eligible to vote voted, and of those voters, 22,000 voted for a president, and only 5,000 voted for a continuation of the paramount chief.

Marealle was angry and bitter at his loss of office. In a letter to the American Consul, William Duggan, following the abolition of his post and its replacement with the post of 'President of the Chagga', he listed the contradictory promises of the CDP which included abolition of taxes on coffee and cattle, guaranteed higher prices for coffee, the building of a secondary school and independent primary and middle schools to provide for all children of school age, a new chance of education for those who had only had the opportunity to complete four years of schooling, higher salaries for all school teachers, no increase in the local rate, stimulus for local trading and an increase in bursaries for studies overseas.[81] Marealle was contemptuous of their promise to combine tax cuts and increased social services. He was equally scathing about their claim that they had a greater claim to democratic legitimacy. How, he asked, could they claim that he was undemocratic when he had himself been elected? Finally, at the bottom of the letter under his signature, Marealle asked: 'What is DEMOCRACY??'

---

[78] Dar es Salaam to Washington, 'Visit with Chagga Paramount Chief Thomas Marealle', 9 September 1959, 77.00/9–959, Box 3697, Central Files 1955–1959, National Archives II, College Park, Maryland.

[79] A. R. Denny, 'A note on Chagga Tribal Politics prior to referendum in Jan. 1960', TNA UK, FCO 141/17864, 4 January 1960, p. 3, f. 55A.

[80] Ibid., p. 2.

[81] Personal letter, Thomas Marealle to William Duggan, 27 February 1960, RG 84, UD 3266, Box 6, File 350, National Archives II, College Park, Maryland.

RIGHTS, DEMOCRACY AND TANU

Why, then, had the arguments made against Marealle proved to be more convincing? At first glance, this looks like an example of TANU inserting itself into local debates on the winning side, as they did across Tanzania.[82] A new generation of younger people who felt excluded from the old-style politics of their elders and from the public sphere offered by the newspaper *Komkya*, and who were resentful of the high-handedness of the paramount chief, turned to the CDP and to TANU in the hope of bringing change.

But we can also read this story as being about the successful co-option and deployment of two languages of politics. In the first place, the CDP and TANU co-opted an older and still powerful language of politics which the KCCU had used so successfully in the early 1950s, as we saw in Chapter 4. This was a language of membership and belonging or of citizenship. But they also effectively co-opted and deployed newer languages of politics, of rights and democracy.

Amidst the allegations about Marealle which had built up by the late 1950s, that he was a despotic ruler who suffered from moral failings, were more important charges. It was said that he had failed to offer convincing solutions to land shortage and associated tensions between sons with no land and fathers who failed in their duty to provide. It was also said that taxes were rising but services were not meeting expectations.

Marealle fought back with a pamphlet demonstrating the huge increases in spending on education, health and infrastructure since the creation of the position of paramount chief in 1952. Entitled 'True Picture of Developments in the Chagga Local Government from 1952 to 1958', it showed that spending on those three areas had increased from 440,055 shillings in 1952 to 1,910,555 in 1958.[83] A similar argument took place in *Mwafrika*, where one of Marealle's opponents asked rhetorically whether any development (*maendeleo*) was taking place in Moshi. Three weeks later the Chagga Council's information officer responded with a list of the Council's successes.[84] But attempts by Marealle and his officers to defend their record were unsuccessful.

---

[82] Feierman, *Peasant Intellectuals: Anthropology and History in Tanzania*, p. 212.

[83] Dar es Salaam to State Department, 'Visit with Chagga Paramount Chief Thomas Marealle', 9 September 1959, RG 84, UD 3266, Box 6, File 350, National Archives II, College Park, Maryland.

[84] Letter from L. N. Ninatubu for Information Officer, Chagga Council, 'Moshi kuna maendeleo?', *Mwafrika*, 28 March 1959, p. 2.

One reason was that just as Marealle and the Kilimanjaro Chagga Citizens Union had once offered themselves up as new patrons who would deliver change for those willing to join it and accept their authority, this was what TANU was now doing. In return for membership, it would deliver material and social progress, but it would do so on the basis of recognizing the equality of men and women, young and old, in contrast to the unequal and hierarchical membership proposed by the Kilimanjaro Chagga Citizens Union.

There was a clear contrast between TANU's openness and the association of Marealle and the KCCU with secrecy and exclusiveness. All were welcome at TANU meetings, whether they were members or not.[85] The familiar slogans 'Unity Is Strength' (*umoja ni nguvu*) and 'Division Is Weakness' (*utengano ni udhaifu*) were again deployed, but the path to unity was now through membership of TANU. TANU offered freedom, appealing to potential members with the words: 'You who love freedom yet have not joined TANU, this is your chance to join so that we obtain our freedom more quickly.'[86]

Moreover TANU also offered progress and development. A language of progress was at the heart of every public pronouncement, even down to the agendas for meetings, which spoke of 'Progress of TANU today in the Territory' or the 'Progress of TANU in Northern Province'.[87] But material progress or development was now tied to the ability of TANU in the locality to intercede at the national level, and so win resources for the locality. This was the answer to the paradox which puzzled Marealle, as to how the CDP could promise both lower taxes and more social services.

On Kilimanjaro as elsewhere, TANU also offered practical solutions to serious gaps in provision. In many parts of Tanzania, particularly the wealthier areas like Kilimanjaro, demand for education had long outstripped available supply. It was a constant theme of Chagga petitions to the Trusteeship Council and to the government in Dar es Salaam. Education was seen as the route to prosperity and a place in the world. The Colonial Office saw its role as balancing the demand for more education from those which already had high levels of provision with the need to avoid alienating those areas where educational facilities were lacking.[88] TANU promised

---

[85] Tanu Branch Moshi to all members of TANU in Vunjo and Rombo, Uchagga, 3 June 1957, TNA 5/25/9, f. 326.

[86] Ibid.

[87] See various requests for permission to hold meetings and the permits to hold such meetings in TNA 5/25/9, including ff. 383, 491, 518.

[88] David R. Morrison, *Education and Politics in Africa: The Tanzanian Case* (London: C. Hurst, 1976), pp. 55–56.

education, using it as a central part of political rhetoric at meetings and taking action at the most local level. On a tour of the Northern Province in February 1958, the failure of the colonial government to provide education was the focus of Nyerere's speeches. The Tanganyika government had failed to educate Africans, now in independent Ghana the whole population was being educated and this could be done in Tanganyika too.[89]

At the local level, TANU's independent schools movement offered parents an immediate solution to a perceived lack of school places. An intelligence summary from April 1957 reported on the popularity of these movements, particularly in Bukoba and the Northern Province, Tanganyika's two richest and best provided-for provinces in educational terms.[90] In 1957, TANU's Provincial Secretary in Northern Province wrote to the paramount chief stating that because of the lack of sufficient schools in Chaggaland, he would like some land anywhere the area to build a school.[91] Marealle was ostensibly encouraging, offering him and his association support in their 'big and worth-while venture', but the process of finding and allocating land stretched out over a year and beyond.[92] In the meantime, TANU meetings in the district frequently focussed on secondary and higher education as a problem which needed to be addressed and promised that they would be the source of a solution.[93]

On one level, then, TANU and the CDP had adopted an older but still effective language of politics. Membership of TANU meant accession to a new form of citizenship, in which the duties of membership with access to goods which only TANU could offer. But they had also tapped into something newer. The CDP's campaign took place against the backdrop of debates among Chagga students at Makerere which focussed on the meaning of democratic government. In April 1959, when many Chagga Makerere students were back at home, copies of the fifth volume of the Makerere College Chagga Society Magazine circulated widely in Moshi.[94]

---

[89] Grattan-Bellew to Mathieson, 20 February 1958, TNA UK, CO 822/1362, f. 190.
[90] Extract from Tanganyika Intelligence Summary for April 1957, TNA UK, CO 822/1361, f. 70.
[91] Letter from M. K. Simon to Thomas Marealle, April 1957, TNA 5/25/9, f. 314A.
[92] Correspondence on the matter continued until at least April 1958, see TNA 5/25/9, f. 443.
[93] Requests for meetings on 3 March 1958 and 1 April 1958 included 'education' among the items to be discussed. TNA 5/25/9, f. 403, f. 432. Nor was higher education forgotten: a meeting at Majengo football ground on 18 May 1958 planned to 'preach about the new TANU College in Tanganyika', with the same topic on the list for discussion at meetings on 1 April, 27 April, 6,7 and 8 July, 13 July and 22 July. TNA 5/25/9, ff. 432, 477, 518, 519, 520, 529.
[94] Commissioner of Police to Ministerial Secretary, 'Makerere College Chagga Society', TNA UK, FCO 141/17864, 25 April 1959, f. 10.

The articles contributed to this magazine demonstrate the power of new languages of politics in the spring of 1959.

The magazine began with an editorial lamenting the length of time which constitutional reform was taking in Moshi at a time when political progress in the rest of the territory was moving ahead quickly. This slow pace was particularly aggravating given that, in the editor's view, 'the democratic principle of election will be established', and this would happen 'both in Kilimanjaro and in Tanganyika at large'. To hold out against elections was simply 'delaying the inevitable'.[95]

Elsewhere in the magazine, Chagga students lamented the political apathy they identified among their fellow Chagga youth, who thought that politics was the business of chiefs and elders, failing to understand that government existed by virtue of the people and for the people.[96] E. Alemyo agreed, arguing in an article called 'The Government is us' that while in theory people might agree that government was of the people, in reality they often behaved as though government was in the hands of the chiefs or officials of the central government.[97] Now though the people were coming to see that government was their 'natural right'. God had not, he reminded his readers, created some to rule and others to be ruled, all were equal in front of God. Government was therefore not something placed above the people, but was an association which had been formed voluntarily, and which was controlled by those who had created it who retained control over the taxes they paid and the labour they contributed. This was an appeal too for active citizenship, not to live in fear as in the past, for to do so 'is to sell our natural rights' and indeed to entire into 'voluntary slavery'. This also meant that citizens must have the ability, through elections, to rid themselves of their rulers when it became necessary to do so, as it certainly would, for it was human nature that all rulers would eventually think more of their own interests than that of the people they were elected to serve. For this group of Chagga students, the CDP offered the possibility of change and they urged their fellow students and readers to seize this opportunity and make their own future.[98]

---

[95] Editorial, 'Local Government and Territorial Politics', *Makerere College Chagga Society Magazine*, 1, 5, p. 4, TNA UK, FCO 141/17864, f. 10A.

[96] D. F. P. Ringo, 'Nani alaumiwe: Mtawala au Mtawaliwa?' *Makerere College Chagga Society Magazine*, 1, 5, TNA UK, FCO 141/17864, f. 10A, pp. 11–13.

[97] E. Alemyo, 'Serikali ni Sisi', *Makerere College Chagga Society Magazine*, TNA UK, FCO 141/17864, f. 10A, pp. 14–16.

[98] Ringo, 'Nani alaumiwe', p. 13.

Local debates on Kilimanjaro echoed a wider shift across Tanzania's public sphere. New languages of democracy and rights were now much more important than they had been previously and were very hard to repel. Yet there was a tension between these two arguments. The underlying argument that government comes from the people and that the people must be able to replace that government when it ceased serving their needs was a conception of government that went beyond party, and which understood government to be separate from party. But TANU's argument that defined citizenship and access to the goods of citizenship in terms of membership of TANU was not entirely compatible with that argument, as we shall see in more detail as we move into the postcolonial period in Chapter 7.

CONCLUSION

The nationalist party TANU emerged into very specific intellectual and political contexts, and to win support in particular localities had to engage with local debates. In the area around Kilimanjaro, TANU and its local ally, the CDP, brought novelty. They successfully employed newly powerful languages of rights and democracy against Thomas Marealle and the KCCU, succeeding in persuading their members and voters that they represented the future and could bring progress in a way which Marealle and Njau could not. TANU also proved adept at negotiating the multiple languages of freedom we identified in Chapter 5. For the young who resented their elders' authority, freedom meant throwing off that authority and embracing a new, more egalitarian form of citizenship.

But there were also strong continuities from the era of the KCCU. Just as the KCCU had sought to create a new type of political community under its leadership in which justice could be attained and progress achieved, with the Union serving as an intermediary with power, so did TANU. Like the KCCU, TANU also offered freedom through membership, presenting itself as a patron which could provide for those who joined it, where it differed was in the egalitarian basis of this membership and in situating the locality within a national body politic. But what would happen to this new form of political subjecthood defined in terms of membership of TANU when TANU itself became the state? In the next chapter, we move into the postcolonial period to see how these challenges were dealt with after independence.

7

'One-Party Democracy'

Citizenship and Political Society in the Postcolonial State

In the late 1950s, a language of democracy had a degree of traction in Tanzania's public sphere which it had not had even a decade earlier. Yet by 1965, Tanzania had followed many of its neighbours in Africa and the wider postcolonial world towards a single-party system. This shift rested on an argument that democracy could develop in different ways in different contexts, which in turn drew on arguments that opposition was not a natural feature of all political societies and that developmental imperatives justified restrictions on political liberties.

Across Africa, the early 1960s saw late colonial experiments with multipartyism rapidly abandoned and the single-party state become the norm. For nationalist parties, this step was justified as a reflection of the national consensus in favour of developmentalist nationalism. More recently, postnationalist historians have offered a different analysis, contextualizing the move to one-party states in terms of a defensive reaction prompted by the weaknesses of postcolonial states, unable to meet the high expectations placed upon them.[1] This reading presents single-partyism as a political solution to a political problem, and part of a shift towards authoritarianism and a closing down of political space.[2]

---

[1] Giacomo Macola, '"It means as if we are excluded from the good freedom": Thwarted Expectations of Independence in the Luapula Province of Zambia, 1964–1967', *Journal of African History*, 47 (2006), 43–56.

[2] James Brennan, 'The Short History of Political Opposition and Multi-party Democracy in Tanganyika, 1958–1964', in Gregory Maddox and James Giblin (eds.), *In Search of a Nation: Histories of Authority and Dissidence in Tanzania* (Oxford: James Currey, 2005), pp. 250–276.

That political history is important. But there is also an intellectual history to be told, which builds on the arguments made already in this book. As we saw in Chapter 2, as languages of democracy expanded after 1945, new questions were prompted about the extent to which 'democracy' was one political system which could be transplanted across the world, or whether it could take on different forms in different contexts. An argument about the meaning of democracy took place in decolonizing Tanzania, in dialogue both with global ideas and with local political realities. If one-party democracy gained widespread acceptance after 1965, this was not simply because of the rhetorical power of Julius Nyerere or the authoritarian actions of the postcolonial state, though both were important. Crucially, it was accepted because it had been *authorized* through public debate over the preceding years.[3]

To make this argument, I start by tracing the emerging tension in early postcolonial Tanzania between a definition of citizenship which was open and one which said that being a good citizen meant being a member of the Tanganyika African National Union (TANU). This had implications for the ways in which politics and political engagement was conceptualized. Although opposition was imaginable under the first conception, it was hard to square with the second conception. The solution was a theory of one-party democracy. Yet this was not simply presented to Tanzanians, fully formed; rather it was the outcome of a long-running debate of whether democracy was a universal or should take on distinctive forms in local contexts.

CREATING POLITICAL SOCIETY

Colonial states had appropriated political society for themselves. As we have seen in the case of Tanganyika, they contrasted a pre-political past defined by insecurity with security within states which they had created. This rhetorical move posed a challenge for postcolonial states, which had to reappropriate the state for themselves and show why political society could be a good thing, not simply associated with colonialism. This entailed thinking deeply about the nature of political society and what it meant to be a member of political society and a postcolonial citizen.

Just as the colonial state had worked to argue that freedom came through membership of political society, rather than through throwing off the shackles of government, so did the nationalist government

---

[3] I am grateful to one of the anonymous readers for helping me to articulate this point.

in the postcolonial state of Tanzania. Yet, as we shall see, they had to manoeuvre between two competing understandings of political society and its conditions of membership.

The first understanding was the official one, in which political membership was open to all those who held the legal status of Tanganyikan, and from 1964 Tanzanian, citizenship. This was based on a conception of citizenship which was not tied to race, despite attempts when it was debated in the National Assembly in 1961 to make it so.[4] Anyone born in Tanganyika Territory after 8 December 1961 who was not 'a child of a foreign diplomat or of an alien enemy' would acquire citizenship by birth. For those already living in the Territory, qualification for citizenship was purely on the basis of residency and descent.[5] Thus Tanganyikan citizenship was acquired by all British protected persons and citizens of the United Kingdom provided one of their parents was born in Tanganyika, while others could apply for registration. The 76,536 Asians in Tanganyika and 20,598 Europeans resident in Tanganyika at independence could therefore choose whether or not to seek Tanganyikan citizenship, up to a cut-off date of December 1963.[6] In theory, there was a clear path towards Tanganyikan citizenship. In practice, as May Joseph has argued, 'the transition from minority status to Tanganyikan citizen was more fraught and embattled than was apparent on the surface'.[7]

Yet what is crucial for our purposes is that there was, in the early 1960s, a language of citizenship which was not tied to membership of TANU. It simply entailed being under the authority of a government of Tanganyika. It was also a conception of citizenship based on universal rights and freedoms, not defined in racial terms. We can see both elements of this definition at work in a question and answer session in a meeting of Lindi District Council in 1963. The question was posed: 'In the time of the foreign government, we were called subjects [raia], now that we have our own government, who are the subjects [raia]?' The answer was given

---

[4] Godfrey Mwakikagile, *Life in Tanganyika in the Fifties: My Reflections and Narratives from the White Settler Community and Others* (Grand Rapids, MI: Continental Press, 2006), p. 52; Ronald Aminzade, 'The Politics of Race and Nation: Citizenship and Africanization in Tanganyika', *Political Power and Social Theory*, 14 (2000), 53–90, p. 68.

[5] Tanganyika National Assembly, *Tanganyika Citizenship* (Dar es Salaam: Government Printer, 1961), p. 2.

[6] John Iliffe, *A Modern History of Tanganyika* (Cambridge: Cambridge University Press, 1979), p. 567.

[7] May Joseph, *Nomadic Identities: The Performance of Citizenship* (Minneapolis: University of Minnesota Press, 1999), p. 80.

that 'A person is the *raia* of the Government which is in place. We are all *raia* of the Government in office.'[8]

Already in the late 1950s, the TANU leadership had sought to co-opt the colonial state's language of universal citizenship for itself. Attacking proposals to limit the franchise for Tanganyika's first Legislative Council elections, *Sauti ya TANU* argued, in English, that:

> Citizens have rights and duties. We in Tanganyika have had our rights and duties. We have never had the right to vote, and therefore all Tanganyika citizens have been equal in this respect – and that is as it should be. But now our Government proposes to introduce a system of voting which will divide our citizens into citizens with the right and citizens without the right to vote. The criterion of deserving? Income, education and office. Will the voteless masses, the second rate citizenship, continue to shoulder their responsibilities of citizenship? Or will Government devise a means of exempting them from shouldering those responsibilities? One of the functions of our Legislature is to discuss the raising and expenditure of Government revenue. Since we are deliberately depriving the masses of the right to have a say in the election of our Legislatures shall we continue to tax these irresponsible, second rate masses? Have the masses any right to say "No Taxation without Representation", or is this the right only of the rich, the educated and the office-holders?[9]

When TANU took office, it sought to assume the mantle of a sovereignty whereby all must respect the government in office, regardless of their own political affiliation. In a speech to the Pare Council in October 1960, the TANU Legislative Council Member Elias Kisenge told his audience that although they might not all be members of TANU, they must all respect the elected government, as was the case in all democratic countries.[10]

TANU, then, was offering equal citizenship to all eligible inhabitants of Tanganyika. In theory citizenship was not defined in racial terms, nor were the rights of citizenship restricted. But citizenship involved both rights and duties, and one of those duties was that of participating in political society, and using political rights wisely. An editorial in the Chagga Council newspaper *Kusare* in February 1965 reported a government minister saying that local councils should no longer be places where only the rich could be heard, as in colonial times. The responsibility of rooting out corruption and nepotism did not lie with political representatives alone. Individual voters also had a responsibility to fight against corruption,

---

[8] Minutes of Lindi District Council, June 1963, TNA 252/L5/3/II, f. 53, p. 16.

[9] 'The New Election Proposals', *Sauti ya TANU*, No. 7, Special Number, 16 April 1957, p. 3.

[10] 'Hotuba ya Mheshimiwa E. A. Kisenge M. L. C. katika baraza kuu la Upare, Tarehe 20/10/1960', TNA 562/A2/14, f. 280 Appendix D. On Elias Kisenge's career see Iliffe, *A Modern History of Tanganyika*, p. 558.

a duty which they performed when they went to the ballot box. They should, the minister said, ensure that they 'elect representatives without stains on their character, who will represent the views of the people without bringing their private affairs into the Councils.'[11]

The arguments put forward by the students of the Makerere College Chagga Society, which we saw in Chapter 6, that self-rule meant an engaged citizenry defined in contrast to a political system in which ruling was left to chiefs or elders, was echoed in the wider public sphere and was part of an argument which said that a new political system demanded a new political culture. In 1959, the nationalist newspaper *Mwafrika* began regularly printing quotations from Gandhi and from the Athenian democrat Pericles calling on readers to engage as active citizens and secure their freedom.[12]

In a similar vein, when he replaced Thomas Marealle as the new Chagga president in 1961, Solomon Eliufoo used the pages of the local newspaper to educate readers about the 'Some secrets of democratic life'. Eliufoo's argument against Maeralle and the paramount chiefship had been an argument about democracy. Now that a new system had been achieved, he sought to use his columns in the newspaper to create a new culture of politics associated with this system. His advice for creating a successful democratic system included self-conduct in meetings, wisdom in choosing leaders and general *uungwana*, or civilized behaviour.[13] Defining democratic behaviour also gave Eliufoo the chance to define what behaviour was not democratic. In September 1961, he published a letter he had received which he considered to be damaging to democracy to demonstrate the problems associated with such letters. Noting that a number of letters had been received, all lamenting the course which politics had taken since the abolition of the post of Mangi Mkuu, he stated that if secret machinations of this sort continued to be said and written, then the people of Kilimanjaro should 'start raising your hat to say goodbye to Democracy.'[14]

This 'official' reading of political society was one in which opposition could be possible, but it had to be respectable opposition, conducted openly. This was tied to a new discourse in the public sphere which sought

[11] Editorial, 'Mabaraza', *Kusare*, 27 February 1965, p. 2.
[12] For example, *Mwafrika*, 31 July 1959, p. 2; *Mwafrika* 12 August 1959, p. 2.
[13] The President, 'Siri fulani za uhai wa democracy', *Kusare*, 8 July 1961, p. 4; The President, 'Siri fulani za uhai wa democracy', *Kusare*, 9 September 1961, p. 4; The President, 'Siri fulani za uhai wa democracy', *Kusare*, 30 September 1961, p. 4.
[14] The President, 'Siri fulani za uhai wa democrasi', *Kusare*, 30 September 1961, p. 4.

to remake politics as virtuous, disconnecting the concept of politics or *siasa* from an association with intrigue.[15] In the pages of *Vijana*, or *Youth*, a Lutheran newspaper, in 1960 the pastor K. E. Amos commented that many people thought politics was a new invention, that it was in some way associated with modernity (*mambo ya kisasa*). But, he went on, politics and political understanding had always been important, and 'when we say a person is a politician that is not to say that that person should be despised', rather it means that the person 'understands how the country should be run'.[16] Although it was true that in the past some people entered politics for their own private reasons and their own advancement, this was not the essence of political life. Amos's major purpose in these two articles was to reclaim the art of politics from its association with troublemakers and agitators, and reinstate it as a godly pursuit.[17] He also stressed that politics was now associated with obedience rather than opposition, as the recently elected government had been elected by the people themselves.[18]

TANU sought to co-opt virtuous politics for itself. Yet others were less willing to accept that TANU representatives necessarily had a monopoly on virtuous politics. In the nationalist newspaper *Mwafrika* shortly before independence, the columnist who wrote under the pseudonym Msema Kweli or 'Speaker of Truth' reported that a rumour had spread that some representatives wanted to enter the Legislative Council for money, not for the good of the country.[19] The answer, as he saw it, was for those representatives to set an example by agreeing to reduce their salaries, keeping only enough for them to live and to enable them to visit their constituencies and fulfil their duties. The point about keeping enough money to visit their constituencies was important, for, he wrote, the failure of some legislators to visit their constituencies had been noted by their constituents. He ended by saying that these were some of the complaints which he offered 'without fear', in the belief that his advice

---

[15] W. H. Whiteley, 'Political Concepts and Connotations: Observations on the Use of Some Political Terms in Swahili', in Kenneth Kirkwood (ed.), *African Affairs, 1*, St. Antony's Papers, 10 (London: Chatto and Windus, 1961), pp. 7–21. This association was similarly present elsewhere where Swahili was spoken, e.g., in Kenya. In Wolof, the term *politig* came to mean to 'lie or deceive'. Frederick C. Schaffer, *Democracy in Translation: Understanding Politics in an Unfamiliar Culture* (London: Cornell University Press, 1998), p. 23.

[16] Mchungaji K. E. Amos, 'Siasa na ukristo', *Vijana*, September 1960, p. 4.

[17] Ibid., p. 4.

[18] Mchungaji K. E. Amos, 'Siasa na ukristo', *Vijana*, October 1960, p. 3.

[19] Msema Kweli, 'Serikali ya kujitolea', *Mwafrika*, 25 June 1960, p. 5.

would be followed. Msema Kweli kept up this theme over the months which followed, and particularly after Tanganyika's move to responsible government in October 1960. He reminded the new ministers that they would be expected to keep in close contact with their constituents, for their task of representation did not stop at the doors of Legislative Council, it was required 'every day and at all times'.[20]

On the one hand, then, we see the development of a language of universal citizenship, in which rights and duties, including the duty to pay tax, were owed by all by virtue of their membership of the state. Yet this sat alongside attempts by TANU to monopolize political space and discourses about political membership at the local level which increasingly focussed not on membership of the state but on membership of TANU, and it is to this latter definition of membership that we now turn.

IS A MWANA-TANU A CITIZEN?

In April 1957, the nationalist news-sheet *Sauti ya TANU* asked the question, in an English-language article: 'Is a Mwana-TANU a Citizen?' The question was prompted by the recent closure, by the colonial state, of TANU branches in Korogwe. It was said that the unrest which led to closure was prompted by a boundary dispute involving TANU members. But, the newssheet asked: 'What ... had the dispute to do with TANU at all? Or may not members of TANU, just like other citizens, and as citizens, be involved in disputes of any kind?' *Sauti ya TANU* wanted to know whether the colonial state was seriously suggesting that a person ceases 'to be a citizen on becoming a member of TANU?'[21]

This was a rhetorical question, yet a revealing one. For already in 1957, and increasingly after independence, an alternative understanding of political society was developing, one defined in terms of commitment to TANU. This is rather harder to chart than the emergence of new legal conceptions of citizenship at independence. Yet in their recent study of registration as a process in global history, Simon Szreter and Keith Breckenridge remind us that it is not only states which register people.[22] In colonial Tanganyika, people inscribed themselves into associations of the sort we saw in Chapter 1. Religious organizations performed a similar role of incorporation. So too did political organizations, organizations

[20] Msema Kweli, 'Mawaziri wajumbe wa lejiko na madaraka', 10 September 1958, p. 5.
[21] 'Is a Mwana-Tanu a Citizen?', *Sauti ya TANU*, 27 April 1957, p. 1.
[22] Keith Breckenridge and Simon Szreter, *Registration and Recognition: Documenting the Person in World History* (Oxford: Oxford University Press, 2012), p. 16.

such as the Citizens Unions we looked at in Chapter 4, and such as TANU. In this way, buying a TANU membership card and becoming a member of TANU was an act of registration and incorporation.

As we saw in Chapter 5, TANU membership cards were understood to have power, and TANU's party structures offered services which were not otherwise provided. To some extent these services were material, such as the schools which TANU began to establish in the late 1950s. But TANU also offered an alternative to older structures of mediation and dispute resolution. A speech by the Area Commissioner H. A. Mwakangale on the opening of a new TANU office in Old Moshi in 1964 is revealing in this regard. He expected it to take on a role at the centre of village life 'like the old sacrificial tree of olden times where the elders went to sacrifice in order that their problems would be heard and solved by the ancestors.' In the same way, the TANU office would be a place where 'the people [*wananchi*] can solve their problems by joining TANU', as well as find a hearing for their complaints.[23]

For some, joining TANU and paying dues in return for membership was a voluntary act. Others faced greater compulsion. The TANU Youth League carried, in James Brennan's words, the 'party leadership hopes for a volunteer-led programme of nation building'.[24] They styled themselves as 'volunteers' but they also demanded 'voluntary' efforts from others to help build the nation. Youth Leaguers were frequently accused of rounding up reluctant citizens and insisting they appear for communal work.[25] They made high demands on the population, which went beyond simply paying taxes and obeying the law.

Lying behind the growing role of TANU and the power of the TANU Youth League was an emerging conception of citizenship which went beyond simple political membership of the state and which was established discursively as much as through legal structures. A new figure, the *mwananchi*, or 'child of the country', symbolized this 'patriotic citizenship'. The figure of the *mwananchi* was a moral construction as much as

23 Editorial, 'Kujengwa kwa ofisi za TANU vijijini ni dalili ya maendeleo', *Kusare*, 23 May 1964, p. 2.

24 James Brennan, 'Youth, the TANU Youth League and Managed Vigilantism in Dar es Salaam, Tanzania, 1925–1973', *Africa*, 76 (2006), 221–246; Priya Lal, 'Militants, Mothers, and the National Family: *Ujamaa*, Gender, and Rural Development in Postcolonial Tanzania', *Journal of African History*, 51 (2010), 1–20, pp. 4–6; Andrew Ivaska, *Cultured States: Youth, Gender, and Modern Style in 1960s Dar es Salaam* (Durham, NC: Duke University Press, 2011), p. 60.

25 Brennan, 'Youth, the TANU Youth League and Managed Vigilantism in Dar es Salaam, Tanzania, 1925–1973', p. 236.

a political one. As Andrew Ivaska has shown, the ideal citizen was rural rather than urban, rejecting the 'decadent, unproductive and emasculating' city in favour of hard work and nation-building in the countryside. In the context of postcolonial racial politics, the figure of the *mwananchi* also relied on racial distinctions. While citizenship laws used the term *raia*, and TANU in its public pronouncements tried hard to adhere to a policy of multiracialism, the status of being a true *mwananchi*, or son of the soil, was increasingly understood, as James Brennan has shown, to be limited to those of African descent.[26] The way in which the term *mwananchi* was used in public political discourse made clear that this involved a particular form of commitment to the political community and that the term implied the duty of actively building the nation.[27]

More generally, the way in which nationalist histories rewrote the history of the twentieth century to put the birth of TANU and TANU's leadership of the struggle for freedom at its heart made it hard to create discursive political space to be a loyal postcolonial citizen who was not an active member of TANU. While this new historical narrative was put forward in texts written by TANU members and graced with forewords by Julius Nyerere, texts such as Edward Barongo's *Mkiki mkiki wa siasa* published in 1966 and S. A. Kandoro's *Mwito wa uhuru*, published in 1961, it was also regularly reiterated in the press on key anniversaries and was reproduced by school children when they wrote histories of TANU.[28]

Increasingly, this emphasis on TANU's leadership in the struggle against colonialism had a more menacing air. A letter from the area commissioner of North Mara to all divisional executive officers in August 1963 complained that TANU clerks had been prevented from collecting

[26] James Brennan, *Nation, Race and Urbanization in Dar es Salaam, Tanzania, 1916–1976*. Unpublished PhD thesis, Northwestern University (2002), p. 340.
[27] C. M. Scotton, 'Some Swahili Political Words', *Journal of Modern African Studies*, 3 (1965), 527–541, p. 530; A. Crozon, 'Maneno wa siasa, les mots du politique en Tanzanie', *Politique Africaine*, 64 (1996), 18–30, p. 24. In contrast, Gérard Philippson glosses the term as used in Julius Nyerere's writings more straightforwardly as simply meaning 'citizen of the country'. G. Phillipson, 'Etude de quelques concepts politiques swahili dans les oeuvres de J. K. Nyerere', *Cahiers d'Etudes Africaines*, 10 (1970), 530–545, p. 537. 'Asiyelipa kodi atakiona', *Ngurumo*, 1 January 1965, p. 3. I discuss these themes at greater length in Emma Hunter, 'Dutiful Subjects, Patriotic Citizens and the Concept of 'Good Citizenship' in Twentieth-Century Tanzania', *The Historical Journal*, 56 (2013), 257–277.
[28] E. B. M. Barongo, *Mkiki mkiki wa siasa Tanganyika* (Dar es Salaam: East African Literature Bureau, 1966), S. A. Kandoro, *Mwito wa uhuru* (Dar es Salaam: Thakers, 1961); Mahamedi Ali, 'Historia ya TANU', No date, received 18 November 1965, TNA 476/A6/4/2, f. 113.

TANU dues in places where people were gathered to pay tax and insisted that they be allowed to collect TANU dues wherever they wished. The letter ended with a demand that local officials respect TANU and recognize that 'without TANU even today we would be under the burden of colonialism.'[29] A similar tone was struck in a letter from TANU's Divisional Secretary in North Mara in January 1964 to local headmen complaining that they had been undermining TANU's authority. He reminded them that it was TANU which had 'delivered Tanganyika from the hands of the colonialists' and that it was their 'duty and that of every citizen here in Tanganyika' to respect their leaders as 'heroes' who had fought for Tanganyika's freedom.[30]

That same month, January 1964, marked a key turning point in Tanzania's postcolonial political history.[31] Revolution in Zanzibar and army mutinies across East Africa led Nyerere to leave Dar es Salaam and for a moment it looked as though control might pass to his foreign minister, Oscar Kambona. More than two hundred trade unionists were arrested in the aftermath of the crisis, including Christopher Kasanga Tumbo, who had recently resigned his post as high commissioner in London and returned to Tanzania in the hope of leading an opposition party.[32] An intolerance of dissent which had already been present among Tanzania's ruling elite became more pronounced. It was perhaps symbolic of the times that, in March 1964, St Francis School chose to stage Nyerere's own translation of Julius Caesar, Shakespeare's classic account of political treachery and its consequences.[33]

By the summer of 1964, growing complaints that TANU was setting itself up as an alternative authority to the state in certain areas, and that core rights of citizenship were being denied to those who were not members of TANU were aired in the Catholic newspaper *Kiongozi*.[34] A local TANU Area Chairman, Amina Maufi, had announced that 'anyone

---

[29] Letter from area commissioner, North Mara to all divisional executive officers, 22 August 1963, TNA 544/A6/30/411.

[30] Letter from J. W. Hembura, divisional secretary, to all wanangwa (Headmen) of Kiseru and Girango Division, 13 January 1964, 'Uhusiano kati ya viongozi wa TANU na wanangwa', TNA 544/A6/30, f. 450.

[31] Timothy Parsons, *The 1964 Army Mutinies and the Making of Modern East Africa* (Westport, CT: Praeger, 2003); Brennan, 'The Short History of Political Opposition and Multi-party Democracy in Tanganyika, 1958–1964', p. 267.

[32] Brennan, 'The Short History of Political Opposition and Multi-party Democracy in Tanganyika, 1958–1964', p. 266.

[33] 'Shule itacheza 'Julius Caesar', *Mwafrika*, 16 March 1964, p. 3.

[34] Brennan, 'The Short History of Political Opposition and Multi-party Democracy in Tanganyika, 1958–1964', p. 268.

without a TANU card will be unable to sell anything in the market', prompting a series of letters which made similar claims about the denial of services to those without TANU cards.[35] One writer from Nzega reported that groups of TANU Youth Leaguers were refusing permission to conduct business to those who lacked a membership card.[36] Worse, they were refusing access to medicines to those without a card. This went against the teaching of 'our Government which wants to fight against the three enemies of sickness, poverty and ignorance.' A correspondent from Kahama accused his local council of failing to announce government plans to the people, and told his fellow readers that if 'you shouldn't bother going to the *baraza* if you don't have a TANU card.'[37]

These allegations of abuse of powers at the local level were not separate from wider efforts of state building; they were often closely tied to them, particularly that of tax collection. After independence, new local and national governments sought to tie virtuous citizenship to the prompt payment of tax. Cartoons in the Chagga Council newspaper *Kusare* showed a tax defaulter in rags, hiding pathetically behind his hut from the tax collector, while his friends who paid their tax on time were depicted in smart clothes returning from a bar where they had gone to drink imported beer.[38] Attempts to shame taxpayers into compliance were made by TANU leaders in their speeches as well. In a speech at Bagamoyo in March 1965, the area commissioner, S. A. Kandoro, reminded his listeners that 'tax is the life force of Government', and essential if government were to function. He went on to say that for adults to be chased for tax in front of their children was shameful and called on those present to pay their tax promptly.[39]

Elsewhere, we see the 'Questions and Answers' sections of newspapers become a space in which to argue for the universality of taxation. In 1964 one youth asked why he was expected to pay tax, given that he had no wife and no land and was entirely dependent on his father. He was

[35] 'Watu walilia machozi waliposikia hotuba ya Mtemi Humbi', *Kiongozi*, 1 April 1964, p. 14. On Amina Maufi's later career see Pius Msekwa, *Towards Party Supremacy* (Kampala: East African Literature Bureau, 1977), p. 60.

[36] Letter from Methusela s/o Nuwa, 'Waumiao si wa Buhoro peke yao', *Kiongozi*, 18 July 1964, p. 7.

[37] Letter from Julius Madabala Mdeka, 'Waumiao si wa Buhoro peke yao' *Kiongozi*, 1 August 1964, p. 9.

[38] Cartoon, *Kusare*, 31 March 1962, p. 4; Cartoon, *Kusare*, 7 April 1962, p. 3.

[39] 'Kodi ni roho ya Serikali', *Ngurumo*, 24 March 1965, p. 3. See Henry Bienen, *Tanzania: Party Transformation and Economic Development* (Princeton, NJ: Princeton University Press, 1967), p. 187.

told that taxation had nothing to do with marriage or landownership. Tax was paid 'so that it can be used by the country for example to dig roads which are used by every person whether he has a wife or does not have a wife, whether he owns land or does not own land', as well as to build hospitals, schools and much else besides.[40] Yet the questions did not go away. The following month another reader asked whether he would still have to pay tax if he were to 'refuse all help which comes from the Government' and rely on himself? The editor responded that to refuse all help from the government was impossible. What if he was attacked by hooligans and lost consciousness? The police and hospital staff would have to do their work without him realizing it. 'Therefore', he concluded, 'tax is essential for every citizen.'[41]

Alongside arguments about the legitimacy or otherwise of taxation came mutterings from below about the ways in which tax was collected. Even before independence, news came to the ears of the nationalist newspaper *Mwafrika* that local councils were using aggressive tactics against tax defaulters. An editorial reported in 1960 that councils were 'seizing people who do not pay tax, tying a rope around their neck and putting them in jail', jails in which they were crammed into small rooms. The editor of *Mwafrika* expressed his disappointment that this was happening 'at this time when we have our own government', for 'neck and ankle ropes are signs of slavery.' The editorial reminded readers that many had joined TANU to protest against such actions by the colonial governments, and called on the TANU government to find better ways of collecting tax.[42]

As party and state drew closer together with the announcement that civil servants could now join TANU, *Kiongozi*'s editor in 1964 expressed the fear that civil servants would be compelled to join in view of the reports he was receiving from readers of compulsion.[43] He wrote: 'we have received several letters from readers in various parts of this country complaining about the actions taken against them by some TANU leaders. These people claim that they are forced to be TANU members, that is to have a party card, in order that they can live the normal life of a citizen, for example, without a card they are not permitted to send their crops to market and to sell them, others are prevented from receiving medicine in hospitals unless they have a party card.'[44] This, the editorial reminded its

[40] Question from K. Bureta, 'Maswali na Majibu', *Kusare*, 13 June 64, p. 4.
[41] Question from E. N. Kilawe, 'Maswali na Majibu', *Kusare*, 25 July 1964, p. 4.
[42] Editorial, 'Ukamatiaji wa kodi', *Mwafrika*, 3 December 1960, p. 2.
[43] Editorial, 'Tamko lenye faraja', *Kiongozi*, 1 August 1964, p. 8.
[44] Ibid., p. 8.

readers and the government, went against the rights of individuals to be free to choose whether to join or not join a political party or any other association, and indeed the rights of the sick to be treated.

In return, TANU's party newspaper *Uhuru* charged that *Kiongozi* was opposing TANU. *Kiongozi* fought back and in an editorial in its 15 August 1964 edition denied that its intention was opposition: it was simply calling attention to problems at the local level. It called on TANU as the government to 'listen to the cries of all its children', and ensure that those leaders of TANU who were going against TANU and government regulations orders be warned that they should correct their ways.[45] At the same time, *Kiongozi* continued to print the letters it received. Writing from Sikonge District in Tabora, E. R. Pandisha complained that people attempting to sell their crops were being compelled to join TANU by force. TANU Youth Leaguers were accused of demanding money and giving a membership card in return. In a reference to Christopher Kasanga Tumbo, the trade unionist who had sought to form an opposition party and was imprisoned after the Mutiny, Youth Leaguers were reported as saying to anyone who objected that 'we will send you where we sent Kasanga Tumbo'.[46]

In September, an editorial in the TANU party newspaper *Uhuru* charged *Kiongozi* with setting itself up as a second parliament. Such a move was unnecessary, *Uhuru* argued, for TANU could provide the channels of communication necessary to draw attention to abuses of power at the local level. But *Kiongozi* defended its right to speak on behalf of a political community that was wider than TANU. An editorial declared that '*Uhuru* is Tanu's newspaper. *Kiongozi* is the people's newspaper [*gazeti la wananchi*].'[47] Although *Kiongozi* rejected the idea that it was acting as a counter site of power, it did defend its right to speak truth to power on behalf of the people.

Conceptions of patriotic citizenship were thus closely tied to loyalty to TANU. A letter sent by the TANU regional secretary in Tanga Region to the region's workers' committees in 1966 is revealing in this regard. After urging all members of TANU to pay their dues promptly he continued: '[a]nd those who are not TANU members are requested to buy

---

[45] Editorial, '"Uhuru" imepotosha maneno hatukupinga Tanu au Serikali', *Kiongozi*, 15 August 1964, p. 6.

[46] Letter from E. R. Pandisha, 'Hiyari yashinda utumwa', *Kiongozi*, 15 August 1964, p. 7; On Tumbo see Brennan, 'The Short History of Political Opposition and Multi-party Democracy in Tanganyika, 1958–1964', p. 261.

[47] Editorial, 'Kwa manufaa ya nchi', *Kiongozi*, 1 September 1964, p. 6.

a TANU card as soon as possible so that they too can become TANU members. For if a person calls himself a Tanzanian but is not a member of TANU then his Tanzanianness [*utanzania*] is deficient'.[48] A similar theme appeared in the divisional secretary of North Mara's letter to local headmen in 1964. News had reached the divisional secretary that headmen were telling people that they did not need to join TANU because 'everyone is a Mwanatanu even if they have no card or do not pay their dues'.[49] This was not the case.

The growing tension between a definition of citizenship which was open, and one which said that being a good citizen meant being a TANU citizen, had implications for the ways in which political engagement was conceptualized. Although opposition was imaginable under the first conception, it was hard to square with the second conception. This blurring of party and state gathered pace after January 1964, but it had been implicit in TANU, as in other late colonial political organizations, from the beginning.

ONE-PARTY DEMOCRACY

What these arguments reveal are the dilemmas of finding space for accountability without disloyalty and the search for a conception of democracy which made this possible. The system of one-party democracy which gradually evolved after independence and was realized in the first elections under the new system in 1965 constituted a partial answer to the tension between universal citizenship and TANU citizenship. It did so by putting at its centre a system whereby the two candidates who would stand for election in each constituency would be members of TANU and be selected to stand by TANU.[50] But this system did not come from nowhere. Rather, it emerged out of debates over the meaning and practice of democracy conducted in Tanzania's public sphere after 1958, and particularly after January 1963.

---

[48] Letter from H. S. Urari for TANU Regional Secretary to all Chairmen, workers committee, Tanga Region, 2 February 1966, TNA 476/A6/4/2, f. 134, pp. 1–2.

[49] Letter from J. W. Hembura, divisional secretary, to all wanangwa (Headmen) of Kiseru and Girango Division, 13 January 1964, 'Uhusiano kati ya viongozi wa TANU na Wanangwa', TNA 544/A6/30, f. 450.

[50] Belle Harris, 'The Electoral System', in Lionel Cliffe (ed.), *One Party Democracy: The 1965 Tanzania General Elections* (Nairobi: East African Publishing House, 1967), pp. 21–52, pp. 22–24.

As James Brennan has argued, the period around decolonization saw a defence of political pluralism in Tanzania's public sphere.[51] This was part of a wider argument about what constituted democracy, and whether it required more than one party. As we saw in Chapter 6, and in contrast with earlier periods, the term *demokrasi* had, by the late 1950s, become a powerful one, with the potential to serve to critique TANU as well as to garner support for the party. Those who supported a single-party system therefore had to do more than make a case for it in developmental terms; they had to appropriate the concept of democracy for themselves.

In the late 1950s TANU, together with its local allies, did precisely this, appropriating the language of democracy and arguing that democracy was a universal good which TANU could offer in a way that the colonial state never could. The colonial government claimed that its system of multiracial elections, in which each voter would vote for one European, one Asian and one African candidate, was 'democratic'. In response, correspondents to the nationalist newspaper *Mwafrika* stated simply that 'a democratic government is a government which is ruled by the majority and since in Tanganyika Africans are the majority it is clear that government will be in their hands.'[52] He pointed out that Africans and Asians lived in Britain too, yet there was no proposal for a multi-racial government in Britain. Should the British government therefore be considered undemocratic?

Yet if a discourse of democracy and the charge of lack of democracy constituted a language which could be employed between the colonial state and those opposing it, the pages of *Mwafrika* also reflected wider debates as to the translatability of the system. The *Mwafrika* columnist Msema Kweli addressed this question in November 1958. In a column which asked: 'Will democracy thrive in Africa?' Msema Kweli argued for a return to first principles, and asked what constituted democracy. Abraham Lincoln, Msema Kweli continued, argued that democracy was government 'of the people, for the people and by the people', but Msema Kweli stated instead his preference for Harold Laski's definition, of democracy as a system in which each citizen (*raia*) could reach his or her potential.[53] Msema Kweli glossed this as a space in which each citizen could work as much as he could, was given the opportunity to educate his children, had a voice in the government which ruled him,

---

[51] Brennan, 'The Short History of Political Opposition and Multi-party Democracy in Tanganyika, 1958–1964', p. 252.
[52] Letter from A. M. Kayamba, 'Mabaraza ya mseto kusini', *Mwafrika*, 1 July 1958, p. 2.
[53] Msema Kweli, 'Demokrasi itasitawi Afrika?' *Mwafrika*, 22 November 1958, p. 5.

and a government which acted in the interests of its citizens. But he did not believe any country in the world had complete democracy, any more than there was any country which had a pure communist system. Msema Kweli stressed that democracy adopted a different form in different contexts, and that while it might well be true that the British style of democracy would not prosper in Africa, other forms might.

Attention focussed in particular on the question of whether it was necessary to have more than one party. We have seen that already in the late 1950s the argument in favour of one large party was being made in Tanganyika's public sphere. For Leo Phillip Ibihya of Newala, writing in April 1960, multiple parties risked introducing division along ethnic or religious lines in ways which ran counter to the goal of achieving *maendeleo*. He questioned the extent to which those who founded alternative parties were concerned with the public good, suggesting their real interest was in enriching themselves.[54]

Arguments over whether democracy required more than one party continued after independence in Tanzania's public sphere. They were prompted by steps taken at the high political level as TANU took first to lay out its plans for a one-party system and then to call for public submissions to a commission to work out how this system would work. But arguments also occurred in response to particular points of controversy as individuals left TANU to form an opposition party or rejoined TANU.[55]

Two particular issues were recurring themes in debate. The first was TANU's insistence that religion and politics must be kept separate and that political parties must not be formed along religious lines. Second, TANU's insistence that it was 'the people' as opposed to 'the chiefs' who were the true foundation of political authority led to the removal of chiefs from power and their replacement by TANU appointees in 1962. In Gabriel Ruhumbika's 1969 novel, *Village in Uhuru*, this principle was placed at the heart of TANU's political project as it was understood at the local level. When two TANU ministers arrived in the fictional district of Wantu in July 1962 it was 'above all' to explain 'democracy, and the important Bill their Government had passed in conformity with its resolution and promise to democratise their society, the Chiefs' Bill'. The ministers explained that: 'their nation was a democratic nation. A nation

---

[54] Letter from Leo Phillip Ibihya, 'Matatizo na madaraka', *Mwafrika*, 2 April 1960, p. 2.
[55] 'Halmashauri maalum ya rais: raia wanaombwa kupeleka kumbukumbu', *Kiongozi*, 15 March 1964, pp. 1, 12.

in which all people are equal.' What the people understood by this was that:'[i]n *uhuru* all people were equal. Their mtemi [chief] had become an ordinary person like themselves.'[56] But in the pages of the Swahili press, arguments in favour of a role for chiefs in politics continued to be heard, particularly in November and December 1963 when a new party called for the return of chiefship.[57] Yet these specific issues of religion and politics on the one hand, and the position of chiefs on the other, also sparked more abstract discussion.

After independence in December 1961, the argument against having more than one party, made in the name of prioritizing development, was heard with increasing frequency. For the TANU party newspaper *Uhuru*, it was fruitless to waste time debating democracy when economic development was the priority. 'What is the meaning of democracy?' *Uhuru*'s editorial asked. Its answer was whichever type of government the people wanted, and if, as in Tanganyika, the people wanted one party to rule, that was democracy. Ultimately, the priority was providing the economic and social fruits of independence. What was the point, *Uhuru* asked, of 'fighting over democracy [*dimokrasi*] when people out there are dying of hunger?'[58]

Nyerere's own position, described in the pamphlet 'Democracy and the Party System', echoed this. He argued that a two-party system was inappropriate, and indeed harmful to democracy, in a situation where most of the people were united behind one national movement.[59] Nyerere argued that while the principle of democracy was a universal, the system which enabled the people to rule themselves could take on different forms in different circumstances. In his retelling of African history, chiefly power was not incompatible with democratic principles, for village life was structured by the expectation that people would 'talk until they agree'.[60]

For some, this was a fundamental misreading of African history. The journal *Spearhead*, founded in 1961 as a forum for pan-African discussion, began its first issue with a contribution from Julius Nyerere which argued for distinctive African conceptions of democracy. In response, the politician Christopher Kasanga Tumbo argued strongly against the

[56] Gabriel Ruhumbika, *Village in Uhuru* (London: Longman Group, 1969), pp. 93–94.
[57] 'Chama kipya kinadai uchifu urudi', *Mwafrika*, 5 November 1963, p. 1.
[58] Editorial, *Uhuru*, 30 December 1961, p. 2.
[59] Julius Nyerere, 'Democracy and the Party System' in Julius Nyerere (ed.), *Freedom and Unity* (London: Oxford University Press, 1966), pp. 195–203, p. 196.
[60] Nyerere, 'Democracy and the Party System', p. 195.

idea that there was anything which could be termed 'traditional African democracy' to which Tanganyika should return.[61]

Another line of argument departed from the specifics of the Tanganyikan case and returned to universal questions about human nature and political life. Jackson Saileni, who had taken over the leadership of the African National Congress or ANC following Zuberi Mtemvu's return to the TANU fold, rejected the argument that the people were united and that multiple parties were therefore unnecessary. Not only was division an essential part of being human, true political accountability demanded an open politics and the possibility of opposition.[62] He cited Thomas Jefferson's famous dictum on the natural division of men into two parties, and glossed it with a note to say that this part of the human condition was as true of Africans as of all the other peoples of the world.[63] Citing the political theorist Harold Laski, Saileni wrote of the inevitability that those with power would be corrupted by it and would in time come to act in their own interests rather than in the interests of those they had been elected to serve.[64] Based on his experience, Saileni had little confidence that the one-party system which Nyerere proposed would ensure that bad leaders could be replaced.[65]

This line of argument was echoed by others who were not themselves actively involved in opposition politics but who also rejected the possibility that one-party government could ever be democratic. Just government required not only the ability to criticize but also the ability to choose an alternative which required a choice of parties.[66] Others rejected the claim that the divisions which necessitated opposition parties in Europe and America were simply not present in Tanzania. For one writer, Tanzania's religious pluralism was evidence in itself that TANU could not represent everybody. If God could not unite all men behind one religion, how could a political party hope to do so?[67] Division was human nature. Others saw the fact that legislation was needed to prevent the formation of new parties as evidence of the hollowness of claims that there was a natural unity of all Tanzanians.[68] If there was only one party this must be because

---

[61] Letter from C. S. Kasanga Tumbo, *Spearhead*, 1 (December 1961), p. 24.
[62] Brennan, 'The Short History of Political Opposition and Multi-party Democracy in Tanganyika, 1958–1964', p. 264.
[63] J. H. Saileni, 'Demokrasi laghai ya Tanganyika' ['Tanganyika's pseudo-democracy'], TNA 540/PP/5, p. 1.
[64] Ibid., p. 1.
[65] Ibid., p. 3.
[66] Letter from Juma Sadallah, 'Upinzani', *Mwafrika*, 11 December 1963, p. 3.
[67] Letter from Damas L. Magome, 'Chama kimoja', 6 February 1963, *Mwafrika*, p. 2.
[68] Letter from J. S. Maliza, 'Shirikisho la siasa', 28 June 1963, *Mwafrika*, p. 3.

it had been imposed by force.[69] The developmentalist argument was also turned against those who supported one-party systems. In this reading, TANU's defence of the one-party system was a cynical attempt by those who had benefited from Africanization to keep the fruits of independence for themselves.[70]

Yet for others, the core feature of democracy was rule by the people, and provided that basic condition was in place, the precise form taken by the political system could vary. This was the interpretation offered by the Speaker of Tanganyika's Parliament Adam Sapi in a speech given to receive a present of a Speaker's Chair from Great Britain. Sir Richard Thompson, representing the British Parliament, seemed to support this interpretation, saying 'You Tanganyikans will choose the democracy which you want', and that what was important was that both Britain and Tanganyika believed that 'Government comes from the people.'[71]

Elsewhere in the pages of *Mwafrika* and the Catholic newspaper *Kiongozi*, arguments were more nuanced. For some, it was the ability of the people of a country to criticize their leaders which constituted democracy. Provided that leaders could be criticized and bad leaders removed, two parties were not necessary. But if that was not possible, then new parties should be allowed to form. One writer from the Lake Province criticized local leaders and argued that either TANU should ensure that bad leaders were not allowed to stay in power, or it should allow a second party.[72]

In its editorial of 20 January 1964, *Mwafrika* argued that a one-party system was possible, but it must provide 'true democracy'. Specifically, it must 'permit citizens to elect the representatives they want and to be able to express their opinions without fear.' What this meant was that 'the citizens should have the final say.'[73] It was possible, then, to have open debate and just government within one party. Increasingly, this was coupled with a sense that criticism was illegitimate. *Mwafrika*'s 20 January editorial coincided with the army mutinies which shook governments across East Africa and showed Tanganyikans how easily the government could lose control. For some correspondents writing to *Kiongozi*, opposition was self-evidently unnecessary. Tanzania had a president, and for as long as he was alive no other candidates were required.[74] For others,

[69] Letter from Damas Magome, 'Chama kimoja', *Mwafrika*, 26 February 1963, p. 4.
[70] Letter from Saled Saleh, 'Upinzani katika siasa nchini', *Mwafrika*, 10 January 1964, p. 3.
[71] 'Serikali itoke kwa raia – Mjumbe', *Mwafrika*, 13 February 1963, p. 1.
[72] Letter from Elias B. Timothy, 'Heshima', 14 October 1963, p. 3.
[73] Editorial, 'Siasa ya chama kimoja', *Mwafrika*, 20 January 1964, p. 2.
[74] Letter from Julius Chakunyenga, 'Chama cha uchochezi', *Kiongozi*, 15 February 1964, p. 7.

criticism was unjustified, even shameful, in a postcolonial state in which 'the Government belongs to everyone and TANU belongs to everyone including you yourself'.[75] Other correspondents echoed TANU's argument that the only freedom which mattered was that of political independence. This had been delivered, and there was no need to chase after other, secondary, freedoms.[76]

In news articles and in the speeches of TANU officials, opposition was coded as negative, and its absence celebrated. In this respect, an article in *Kiongozi* about a recent election in Kwimba in Mwanza Region in north-west Tanzania was typical. A story entitled 'In Kwimba there is no opposition', reported that in recent district council elections the thirty-six candidates who were put forward by TANU were all 'elected without opposition'. For the area commissioner Stanley Kaseko this was a sign of progress in a place which had been known as a hotbed of opposition.[77] The corollary of the absence of opposition was more success in achieving *maendeleo*, progress or development.

The argument that it was possible to have the things that mattered most – the ability to criticize and to hold bad leaders to account – within a one-party system was a powerful one, and it was this principle which was embodied in the new system of one-party elections.

THE 1965 ELECTIONS

The new one-party system allowed for the idea that such criticism was at the heart of definitions of politics, or, as a newspaper editorial wrote in 1962, that the definition of politics was 'criticising or correcting the Government'.[78] MPs could not simply assume they would win, but had to stand against a fellow member of TANU. This opened up a space for voters who were not members of TANU to remind MPs of their duty to provide a channel of communication between the locality and the centre, between voters and government. Fieldwork conducted at the time suggests that the first elections held under the new system, the elections of 1965, were indeed perceived in this way.

---

[75] Letter from I. R. M. Kobakusha, 'Mwaisaka katoboa', *Kiongozi*, 1 March 1964, p. 7.
[76] Letter from A. Muhammed, 'Vyama vipya', *Mwafrika*, 11 December 1963, p. 3.
[77] On Stanley Kaseko's career see James Finucane, *Rural Development and Bureaucracy in Tanzania: The case of Mwanza Region* (Uppsala: Scandinavian Institute of African Studies, 1974), p. 109.
[78] Question from Joshua L. Mallya, 'Maswali na majibu', *Kusare*, 16 June 1962, p. 1.

In Dodoma Region, a woman on her way to an election meeting told researchers that her aim in going was to complain about the local co-operative society. 'We take our castor and maize to sell and they give us very little money. Most of it "stays there" with them, the co-operatives. Look, you must tell them this, so that they should stop doing it. Our husbands are troubled by taxes, and when we go to sell products to help them they take that money also. What will our husbands give for tax? We cannot agree to this, we could even be moved to fight. You go and tell them this.'[79]

Reports of election meetings show that there was space for some limited dialogue between candidates and voters. This is not to say that it was an equal relationship. Editorials and speeches sought to educate voters: to remind them to respect their leaders and to use their votes wisely. But candidates also emphasized that voters needed to be respected, and at times their campaigning spoke to voters' expectations of what the candidates should offer. We see this in a focus on personal conduct and character. In the 1965 election in Kilimanjaro Region, Solomon Eliufoo, who had taken the place of the paramount chief after Marealle was forced out, before himself leaving Kilimanjaro to take up the post of education minister, argued that the most important thing for a young country was that the people elect a person 'who would not waver, even when faced with difficulties', a person who 'will not be shaken by a tempest'. But in response, his opponent portrayed him as a person of poor character, who had neglected his constituents in favour of his responsibilities in Dar es Salaam. Aikaeli Mbowe said in a speech to a public meeting that when Eliufoo was offered ministerial power he 'left for Dar es Salaam without bidding farewell to the Chagga'.[80]

A good candidate was one who was open and conducted public affairs in public, while in contrast a frequent complaint against opponents was that they were indulging in 'secret' politicking. In Korogwe, one of the candidates, Samuel Kihiyo, commented that his opponent engaged in

[79] Peter Rigby, 'Ugogo: Local Government Changes and the National Elections', in Lionel Cliffe (ed.), *One Party Democracy: The 1965 Tanzania General Elections* (Nairobi: East African Publishing House, 1967), pp. 77–104, p. 95.

[80] Mwandishi wetu, Moshi, 'Maneno: "Nichague mimi" yaendelea', *Uhuru*, 11 September 1965, p. 2. The complaint that they were neglected by MPs who had left for Dar es Salaam was a constant theme in the early 1960s and cost a number of MPs their seats in the 1965 election. An early example of this complaint can be found in the minutes of the Lindi District Council from September 1962, when Lindi's MPs were accused of failing to 'visit this district and holding meetings and seeing the citizens [raia] of this place.' Minutes of Lindi District Council, September 1962, TNA 252/L5/29/3, f. 33, p. 4.

secret discrimination, behind the back of TANU. His opponent denied this. How could he be a tribalist when he himself was married to three different women, all belonging to different tribes than his own? Against the charge that he had discriminated against the people of Lushoto he reminded listeners of his actions on behalf of the people of Lushoto. When there was hunger in Lushoto in 1945, he had written a letter to Dar es Salaam to accuse the district commissioner of a failure to act. Then in 1948 he had written to the district commissioner in Lushoto to argue that the Washambaa were being discriminated against in terms of access to education.[81]

This history of intervening on behalf of his constituents would most likely have done him some credit, as it spoke to one of the central duties of a constituency MP: raising the electorate's concerns at the centre. Ministers who had failed to visit their constituencies regularly were voted out in a number of constituencies in 1965, and those who survived were more assiduous about visiting their constituencies in the future. Though ministers then, as now, also suffered from another argument which they could do little about, namely that they had had their turn and now someone else should have theirs. Thus, for example, in Rungwe where the minister Jeremiah Kasambala was defeated, a common Nyakyusa saying shortly before the election was apparently 'he has had enough... it is time for a change'.[82]

CONCLUSION

As we have seen over the course of this book, political subjecthood was in flux in mid-twentieth-century Tanzania. Tensions emerged between conceptions of political subjecthood defined by the state and alternative forms of membership offered by churches or Islamic brotherhoods or tarikas, or by political organizations such as the Kilimanjaro Chagga Citizens Union. TANU was part of this wider problematic.[83] TANU's insistence that only those who held membership cards could enjoy the advantages of membership echoed the claims of the Kilimanjaro Chagga Citizens Union (KCCU) at a local level a decade earlier.

---

[81] No author, 'Kilio na Kihiyo Watoana Jasho', *Uhuru*, 11 September 1965, p. 2.

[82] Bismarck Mwansasu and Norman N. Miller, 'Rungwe: defeat of a minister', in Lionel Cliffe (ed.), *One Party Democracy: the 1965 Tanzania General Elections* (Nairobi: East African Publishing House, 1967), pp. 128–154, p. 153.

[83] Felicitas Becker, *Becoming Muslim in Mainland Tanzania, 1890–2000* (Oxford: Oxford University Press, 2008), p. 210.

But at the same time, the rise of TANU with its claim to incorporate all Tanzanians into its structures and the blurred lines between the party and the state after independence threw this old tension into sharp relief and provoked struggles over what political membership should mean – defined from above in one way, in which all are citizens, and from below in another – linking political membership to party membership and the act of being a patriotic citizen. One-party democracy was an attempt to resolve this tension and provide a mediating structure, channel of communication and voice in political life which was broader than TANU. Yet TANU was not strong enough to impose such a system autocratically.

The system that was inaugurated in the 1965 elections was the outcome of a long public argument over the question of what a universal concept of democracy, or rule by the people, might mean in Tanzania. In the pages of the Swahili press, the word 'democracy' was, on one level, employed as a universal term with a generally accepted meaning. When Mennen Williams spoke of his hopes for democracy in Africa or when Lyndon B. Johnson was cited in the pages of *Mwafrika* praising Uganda's democratic credentials in October 1964, nobody felt the need to explain what they meant.[84]

Yet on another level, definitions of democracy were open to debate. For some, democracy meant removal of chiefs and new egalitarian conceptions of society, for others democracy could be compatible with chiefship. For some democracy had to include many parties, for others a one-party system was possible provided there were alternative means of holding those with power to account. As Sir Richard Thompson had said on presenting the gift of a Speakers' Chair to the Tanzanian parliament, the essential point was that government must come from the people; beyond that, it could take on different forms in different contexts.

The move to one-party democracy took place in a context in which the space for debate which had opened up in the late 1950s was narrowing, and the formal suppression of opposition parties further contributed to this process. But public reflection continued to take place in the restricted place of the 1960s, in part through the increasingly powerful language of *ujamaa*, literally familyhood but often used to mean African socialism, and it is this language to which we turn now to explore.

---

[84] 'Ana matumaini ya demokrasi Afrika', *Mwafrika*, 18 March 1963, p. 4; 'Uganda yasifiwa kwa demokrasi', *Mwafrika*, 15 October 1964, p. 6.

8

Ujamaa and the Arusha Declaration

Ujamaa was a powerful word in early postcolonial Tanzania. This was particularly so after the Arusha Declaration of February 1967, in which Julius Nyerere declared that *ujamaa*, literally 'familyhood' but more often translated as 'African socialism', would henceforth define Tanzania's course. This decisive turn in his political thinking from leading a national party of *all* Tanzanians to defining the Tanganyika African National Union (TANU) as a party committed to a specific set of objectives has dominated narratives of Tanzania's post-independence history.

For a long time, the Arusha Declaration was understood first and foremost as a development strategy. In this reading, it marked a decisive shift in policy which set Tanzania firmly on the road to socialism.[1] At first, scholarly interest was largely sympathetic. Indeed, in 1967 Ali Mazrui coined a new term, 'Tanzaphilia', to describe the enthusiasm among Western observers for Nyerere and his project of postcolonial state-building. But by the late 1970s, Tanzaphilia had been replaced by something more like Tanzaphobia. The Arusha Declaration had not delivered economic development or social equality, and the price paid by ordinary citizens in terms of forced villagization was deemed to have

---

[1] Andrew Coulson, *Tanzania: A Political Economy* (Oxford, Oxford University Press, 1982), p. 176; Göran Hydén, *Beyond Ujamaa in Tanzania: Underdevelopment and an Uncaptured Peasantry* (London: Heinemann, 1980). On African socialism see William H. Friedland and Carl G. Rosberg (eds.), *African Socialism* (London: Oxford University Press, 1964); Fenner Brockway, *African Socialism: A Background Book* (London: Bodley Head, 1963); George Bennett, 'African Socialism', *International Journal*, 20 (1964–5), 97–101; Pieter Boele van Hensbroek, *Political Discourses in African Thought: 1860 to the Present* (Westport, CT: Praeger, 1999), pp. 112–119.

been too high for the rewards reaped in terms of nation-building and the relative lack of ethnic conflict.[2]

More recently, however, new political and cultural histories of postcolonial Tanzania have revisited *ujamaa* not as practical politics but as discourse, focussing on the ways in which it provided a language for talking about the divisions in Tanzanian society within a discourse of nation-building. First and foremost, as James Brennan has shown, it provided a way of talking about race without explicitly mentioning it. The TANU booklet 'Lessons on the Arusha Declaration and TANU's policy on *Ujamaa* and Self-Reliance', published in 1967, used white characters to represent a variety of exploiters, including a local employer dressed smartly in a white shirt, pinstripe trousers and shiny shoes giving orders to three workers, and a foreign capitalist holding a sword behind his back while offering money with the other hand.[3] But within Tanzania, it was Asians who were more frequently a target of accusations of immoral economic behaviour. In the nationalist press, it was those labelled by the shorthand 'Patel' who were accused of bad business practices and criticized for behaving in exploitative ways which were contrary to the spirit of *ujamaa*.[4]

By constructing an ideal citizen who was rural rather than urban, *ujamaa* ideology also, as Andrew Ivaska has argued, provided a way of talking about, and critiquing, the dissolute morals and cosmopolitan culture of the town and its accompanying vices of prostitution, drunkenness and youthful disrespect of elders. For Ivaska, '[i]n an era in which civic duty was increasingly being constructed around a healthy, productive rural ideal – epitomized by scenes disseminated widely in the press of young and old, men and women, even politicians, labouring in ujamaa villages – constructions of the city as decadent, unproductive, and emasculating constituted an important foil for TANU's ujamaa ideology.'[5]

---

[2] Dean E. McHenry, *Limited Choices: The Political Struggle for Socialism in Tanzania* (London, Lynne Riener, 1994), pp. 2–3. Severine R. Rugumamu, *Lethal Aid: The Illusion of Socialism and Self-reliance in Tanzania* (Trenton, NJ: Africa World Press, 1997), pp. 267–268. For James Scott and others, it was of interest not as initiating developmental innovation but as a typical example of the high-modernist utopianism which characterised the twentieth century. James C. Scott, *Seeing Like a State: How Certain Schemes to Improve the Human Condition Have Failed* (New Haven, CT: Yale University Press, 1998), p. 234.

[3] TANU, *Mafunzo ya azimio la Arusha na siasa ya TANU juu ya ujamaa na kujitegemea* (no publisher: Dar es Salaam, no date, 1969?), pp. 6, 14.

[4] James R. Brennan, 'Blood Enemies: Exploitation and Urban Citizenship in the Nationalist Political Thought of Tanzania, 1958–1975', *Journal of African History*, 47 (2006), 389–413, p. 404.

[5] Andrew Ivaska, *Cultured States: Youth, Gender, and Modern Style in 1960s Dar es Salaam* (Durham, NC: Duke University Press, 2011), p. 17.

In contrast, this chapter situates the language of *ujamaa* within the longer term intellectual history of Tanzania's public sphere which we have explored over the course of this book. The anxieties about divisions between rich and poor, what constituted *maendeleo* or progress and who benefited from it, and what it meant to be a citizen, were still present in the 1960s, as they had been in the 1940s and 1950s, echoing arguments taking place across the postcolonial world. While those who reflected on these problems could and did turn to languages of development and international socialism, these languages risked bringing out into the open divisions that risked destroying society. The language of *ujamaa* was different, not because it was an appeal to tradition or somehow more authentically African, but because it provided a means of talking about the social and reflecting on what made a good society in ways that were not necessarily tied either to TANU or to Nyerere, though they could be. Indeed it was the very breadth and openness of the language of *ujamaa*, the polysemic character which it had in common with other words discussed in this book, rather than its character as ideology, which gave it purchase in a public sphere in which debate was, in the 1960s, increasingly restricted.

To make this argument, I start by setting out some of the areas on which writers in the public sphere focussed when reflecting on society and social relations in the 1960s. I then consider the power and limits of transnational languages of development, socialism and communism, before showing the way in which, in the early 1960s, a language of *ujamaa* was increasingly used in the public sphere, attractive because it could be used both by radicals who sought dramatic and revolutionary change and conservatives who wished to restore broken social relations. It was in this context that the Arusha Declaration of 1967 which put *ujamaa na kujitegemea* at the centre of public discourse was so powerful.

THE TENSIONS OF AN UNEQUAL WORLD

As we saw in Chapter 1, in the public sphere of the 1940s and 1950s, complaints about inequality of wealth were frequent, as writers worried about the impact of growing individualism on social relations and sought to construct new associations in part to deal with such problems. Nationalist politicians had promised that independence would address these concerns, but had done so in large part by turning the focus on non-Africans, both Europeans and Asians. In Dar es Salaam, the language of *unyonyaji*, which carried both a general sense of 'exploitation' and darker resonances of 'blood sucking', provided a way of critiquing those urban citizens who exploited others, often with a racial inflection in which the blood of Africans was sucked by South Asian businessmen who had come to Tanzania poor but had become rich on the blood of Africans.[6] But it was not only non-Africans who were guilty of *unyonyaji*. An editorial in January 1965 in *Ngurumo*, a newspaper which spoke directly to the urban working class of Dar es Salaam, targeted the so-called 'African capitalists'. The editor reminded readers that where it had once been assumed that those who engaged in exploitation (*unyonyaji*) were non-Africans, it was becoming increasingly apparent that Africans could be equally guilty of exploiting their fellow citizens.[7]

Arguments over inequality and exploitation were thus ever present and conducted in terms which, as with the use of the term *unyonyaji* to describe exploitation, conjured up a very intimate sense of what exploitation meant. At the core of these arguments were fundamental questions about society. What did it mean if some were becoming rich and others were left behind? Who should pay taxes and were the burdens of taxation equally shared? As citizens of the new postcolonial state were enjoined to engage in unpaid work to build new schools, roads and clinics, were some being called upon to do more to build the nation than others? What was the relationship between land and citizenship? At the heart of all these issues was a question of citizenship and what it meant to be a citizen in the postcolonial state.

Arguments over taxation were a key area in which relations between rich and poor were negotiated. Colonial regimes had always placed the duty of paying taxes at the heart of their lists of the qualities of a good citizen, and had worked hard without great success to make taxation legitimate. Growing demand for social services led the colonial government to seek out ways of increasing taxation revenues. In particular, they hoped to tap into rising cash-crop prices by introducing graduated rates of tax, but after an attempt to introduce a graduated rate in the Pare Mountains led to protest and eventual repeal, the colonial administration was nervous about further attempts to introduce graduated rates of taxation.[8]

---

[6] Brennan, 'Blood enemies: Exploitation and Urban Citizenship in the Nationalist Political Thought of Tanzania, 1958–1975', p. 393.

[7] Editorial, 'Mabeberu waafrika', *Ngurumo*, 11 January 1965, p. 2. See Brennan, ibid., pp. 408–413 on the use of class rhetoric as a means by which the poor constructed a claim to urban citizenship.

[8] Isaria N. Kimambo, *Penetration and Protest in Tanzania: The Impact of the World Economy on the Pare, 1860–1960* (London: James Currey, 1991), pp. 91–117.

The only politically acceptable ways of raising additional revenues were to impose local produce cesses or increase the local rate, yet both were enormously politically sensitive. In richer areas, raising the local rate and imposing produce cesses to pay for increased education and other social services was at least an option. Elsewhere in the Territory, it was not. In the south of the country the major theme of local council minutes in the period immediately before and after independence was the shortage of tax revenues. At one point the frustrated district commissioner of Tunduru, Edward Younie, told his local council that the hospital had no drugs, and that no more could be ordered until taxes were paid.[9]

Independence brought the expectation that taxes would be reduced or abolished. In August 1961 a letter appeared in the Chagga Council newspaper *Komkya* expressing surprise at the rumour that no tax would be paid the following year, and asking how schools and hospitals would continue if this were true. The editor responded by stating clearly that tax would not be abolished and reminding readers of the TANU slogan 'Freedom and Work' (*Uhuru na Kazi*).[10] In fact, not only was tax not about to be abolished, a new system was to be put in place which would make local taxation more progressive. In poorer areas to the south, the theme of local council minutes immediately after independence was the same as before independence: how to increase revenue? The minutes of Kilwa District Council's meeting in November 1962 reveal the difficulties of raising tax rates and cutting services. After working through a list of possible taxes and charges that could be increased and concluding that there simply was not enough wealth in the District to allow for any increase, they were left with the hope that redoing the tax registers and bringing more people into the tax system might help increase the Council's income.[11]

At the same time, taxation brought into the open tensions between rich and poor which might otherwise be kept hidden. On Kilimanjaro, the approach of self-government in Dar es Salaam and the advent of a new president, Solomon Eliufoo, offered new opportunities for the poor to appeal for change. A letter written in June 1960 to the local newspaper claimed that poverty was spreading in Chaggaland and that soon '75% of us will be begging like poor people'. The writer called on the Chagga Council to do more to investigate conditions and provide solutions. The

---

[9] Minutes of Tunduru Council, 5 October 1959, TNA 252/L5/32/II, f. 107, p. 1.
[10] Fanel J. Ndemasi, 'Kodi ya mwaka', 26 August 1961, *Kusare*, p. 3.
[11] Minutes of Kilwa District Council, November 1962, TNA 252/L5/1/3, f. 40, pp. 1–3.

president of the Chagga, Solomon Eliufoo, presented himself as the friend of the poor, and it was from this perspective that he defended the coffee cess. He argued that it was a just tax precisely because it was highly sensitive to ability to pay. Those who had more coffee would pay more, and that was right and just. Abolishing it would mean raising the local tax rate by three shillings per person which would hurt the poor. An associated advantage of the coffee cess over the local rate was that all those who grew coffee were compelled to pay, whereas many elders had apparently been excused from paying the local rate.[12] Despite the clear decision of the Chagga Council that the tax should continue, Eliufoo was repeatedly asked to justify it. On a visit to Kilema in February 1961, he again reminded his listeners that it offered the best way of raising revenue without hurting the poor.[13]

In 1964 the area commissioner complained that of Kilimanjaro's 400,000 inhabitants, only 72,000 were registered taxpayers. He called for the cases of those elders who did not pay because they were deemed to lack wealth or suffer from some disability to be looked at again. Seeking to answer the complaint that headmen had behaved unjustly in deciding who should pay tax, he claimed that deciding who should pay was a role for the Village Development Committees as part of their broader development efforts.[14] Village Development Committees were praised for their role in ruthlessly hunting down tax defaulters without fearing witchcraft on the part of nonpayers.[15] The tax collecting effort also focussed on other ways in which potential tax money was being spent. In Marangu in 1965, the answer offered to the area's relatively poor record on tax collection was a campaign against drunkenness, and it was decided that alcohol should be sold only on Saturdays and Sundays.[16]

But moves to include more people in the tax system and to make the local rate more progressive brought accusations that this would hurt the poor. It was claimed that the headmen who would be charged with

---

[12] 'Chagga Council yaonelea ushuru wa kahawa wapaswa kuendelea', 15 November 1960, *Komkya*, p. 1.

[13] 'Ushuru wa Kahawa ni Akiba ya Wachagga', 15 February 1961, *Komkya*, p. 1.

[14] 'Haki ukweli na uwazi vitimizwe – Mwakangale', *Kusare*, 18 April 1964, p. 1.

[15] Letter from Riziki B. Mangumba, 'V. D. C. na Constebo kazi zao kuimarisha na kujenga taifa', *Kusare*, 30 January 1965, p. 3. On the tax system generally, see Eugene Lee, *Local Taxation in Tanzania* (Dar es Salaam: Institute of Public Administration, 1965).

[16] 'Wamarangu Waamua Kuhimiza Mpango wa Miaka Mitano', *Kusare*, 23 January 1965, p. 4. On postcolonial strictures against drunkenness more generally, see Justin Willis, *Potent Brews: A Social History of Alcohol in East Africa, 1850–1999* (Oxford: James Currey, 2002).

assessing the level of contributions would act unjustly and that sixty shillings was too much for a poor person to pay.[17] How, letter-writers wrote to the local newspaper *Kusare* to ask, could an individual find the minimum payment of sixty shillings? One correspondent complained that he did not even earn one shilling per year, though this lament provoked *Kusare's* editor to say that if that were true he surely could not have paid for the pen and paper to write the letter.

The issue was in part a concern about headmen, but it brought up broader issues about the relationships between poor and rich. Who should be expected to work for whom? In 1963 the divisional executive officer in Hai reminded his listeners that a person who did not pay tax was like a thief.[18] Continuing, he said, 'If you don't have money to pay tax don't worry, go to your neighbour and work then after two weeks you will have money to pay tax rather than roaming around without work when your fellow is looking for a worker to harvest coffee or to farm and you are ashamed to work for your neighbour.'[19] Yet such advice foregrounded class tensions which political leaders would have preferred to keep hidden, and worked against TANU's claims to be the friend of the poor.

The response of letter-writers in the local Swahili newspaper was, in return, to compare the new TANU government unfavourably with its predecessor. In April 1962 the Chairman of the Chagga Council used an announcement in *Kusare* to attempt to silence rumours that 'tax will be reduced, that tax will continue to be collected without a fine after 31 May' and that 'the independent government of Tanganyika is unable to be strict like the British government'.[20] The response of at least one correspondent was to claim that the colonial government had in the past allowed tax to be paid until August, and implicitly that TANU should do the same.[21]

There were similar tensions over the labour demanded by TANU to help build the nation. TANU officials attacked those who were reluctant

---

[17] See in particular: Letter from Joseph Mamchony, 'Kodi na ushuru vichunguliwe mwaka ujao', *Kusare*, 18 November 1961, p. 3; Letter from D. E. Nathar, 'Ushuru wa Uchagga 1962', *Kusare*, 18 November 1961, p. 3; Letter from Phillipp M. K. Kisanga, 'Kodi ya mapato', *Kusare*, 23 June 1962, p. 3.

[18] 'Maendeleo yanaanza kijijini – Division Executive Officer Central Hai', *Kusare*, 12 October 1963, p. 1.

[19] Ibid., p. 1.

[20] Announcement 'Mwisho wa kodi', *Kusare*, 14 April 1962, p. 3.

[21] Letter from Alex Mathey Matemelala, 'Muda wa kulipa kodi uongezewe', *Kusare*, 12 May 1962, p. 3.

to engage in nation-building work blaming colonial mentalities which had taught people to think 'they were better perhaps because they were of the same clan as the Chief, or a relative of the headman, while others thought themselves to be rich.' They would therefore send others to perform their duties for them. Today, though, richness was defined not by wealth but by willingness to participate in building the nation, and on this measure the 'rich' were failing.[22]

But there were other more specific race and class cleavages. Criticism of nonparticipation tended to be targeted at Europeans and Asians, on the one hand, and salaried Africans on the other. Voluntary nation-building work was a particularly effective marker of virtuous citizenship, the performance of which privileged those without resources over those with. As one letter criticizing those who failed to participate began, this work done by the citizens 'helps the country to push forward towards *ustaarabu* [civilization], because people develop their country through cooperation although they are paid nothing.'[23] In contrast, those who did not participate were failing to develop their country which suggested disloyalty. One letter expressed surprise at those 'white people who do not want to join with us so that we can build our new Republic.'[24]

The racial dimension attached to discussions of communal work participation was clearly important. Yet more broadly, reluctance to participate was seen by critics as determined more by wealth or class than race, for failure to turn out for voluntary work was also a feature of those with salaried jobs, which increased the resentment of those seeking work. Local officials frequently insisted that those who could not perform voluntary work on Mondays, which was the day communal labour for the chief had been performed and which was now given over to new nation-building work, because they were engaged in salaried work, must contribute financially instead, the precise sum varying according to the local area. Yet the frequent reminders by the editor of *Kusare* that everyone contributed one way or another do not seem to have quelled the perception that voluntary work was something for the young and poor.[25]

Alongside taxation and communal work, the relationship between land and citizenship remained a key area of contention, as it had been earlier. Attempts to introduce a market in land had been a central aim of

[22] 'V. D. C. Mamba Kokirie yafanya maendeleo', *Kusare*, 28 December 1963, p. 5.
[23] Letter from Mathew R. Mchaki, 'Kazi za jumia Uchaggani', *Komkya*, 15 June 1960, p. 3.
[24] Letter from E. Uchai, 'Mataifa yote tujenge taifa', *Kusare*, 4 April 1964, p. 3.
[25] Letter from Alex Mathey Matembelela, 'Kazi za utawala za jumatatu', *Kusare*, 13 October 1962, p. 3.

the East Africa Royal Commission of the 1950s which was discussed in Chapter 1. For the Commission, a move to individual land holding and markets in land was an essential part of a universal process of the transition from 'traditional' to 'modern' society. This was swiftly rejected by representatives of the African Association, the precursor to TANU, who met the Commission in 1953. The African Association spokesmen were troubled by the Commission's vision of economic man in Africa, and sought to articulate a moral economy that would allow for the achievement of 'progress' in a way which did not create mass landlessness. They hinted at the idea that access to land was important in a sense alien to the economic liberalism of the Commission's members, particularly the South African economist S. Herbert Frankel. One of the Lake Province representatives, Mr Hamza Mwapachu, explained that while land ought to be something that could be bought and sold, he believed that for Africans land provided the 'only security, all his liberty and his rights of citizenship.' The chairman, Sir Frederick Seaford, asked if this was a question of social security, suggesting that were more social security in place, there would not be such a need to have land to which to return. Mwapachu again sought to clarify, 'The point I want to make is, if he loses the land, he feels he loses his right to be a citizen of this country.' The issue for Mwapachu was ensuring 'that the rights of citizenship will be secure politically rather than on the holding of land.'[26] The African Association understood that economic relationships were also social and political relationships, and feared the consequences of the form of economic life which the EARC were proposing. In areas of land shortage, the 1960s saw continued pressure on land and it was increasingly hard for the young and poor to access the land which would enable them to become full citizens.

Running through all of these issues was a sense that security was mediated by those with power, and within that a critique of officials who used their access to power for their own ends. Corruption was a frequent theme in the pages of the Swahili press which began before independence. Following an article by the writer Msema Kweli on the subject of corruption in the pages of *Mwafrika* in 1960, correspondents rushed to agree. Abdallah K. Misango maintained that everyone knew how bad the problem was and how difficult it could be to get anything done. He called on the new government to start work immediately to put an end to this problem. In urban areas, there was often a racial undercurrent

---

[26] Meeting with African Representatives of the Lake Province, TNA UK, CO 892/14/3, f. 10.

to complaints about corruption, but elsewhere correspondents emphasized that Africans were as guilty of the practice as non-Africans.

Government speeches responded to these currents. In June 1960, Solomon Eliufoo, Minister of Health, spoke out to attack corruption in the Ministry of Health.[27] In the same month, Nyerere gave a speech saying that the people expected promises to be kept, and that they expected independence to bring an end to corruption.[28] An editorial in the *Buhaya Co-operative News* in the same year expressed similar sentiments. Lamenting that in many offices nothing was done until extra money was paid, the editorial compared this practice to demanding a second level of taxation, and argued that the money wasted on corrupt payments was holding back progress (*maendeleo*).[29] Criticism of corruption was often tied to a critique of nepotism and tribalism. In November 1959, the editor of the *Buhaya Co-operative News* attacked a local TANU representative who was supposed to be speak for a large region but who delivered speeches referring only to his home area.[30] TANU countered with appeals to the people to respect their leaders. But this criticism of profligate officials spoke directly to the larger theme of growing inequality of wealth and the relationship between rich and poor, and the strain this placed on concepts of citizenship.

TRANSNATIONAL LANGUAGES OF POLITICS AND THEIR LIMITS

If arguments over inequality and exploitation could take on multiple forms, the political languages employed to discuss their potential solution also varied. Some borrowed explicitly from a transnational language of socialism. The TANU newspaper *Uhuru*, which began publication at independence, immediately sought to put pressure on the new TANU government to address poverty and inequality. A week after independence, a lengthy article called for all to be able to eat their fill in independent Tanganyika. This was a principle of equality: 'if we laugh we should all laugh, if we cry we should all cry.' In case any ambiguity remained, the article emphasized: 'I say all – all those who are citizens [*raia*] of this country of Tanganyika.'[31] This was, the author continued, a policy

---

[27] 'Waziri ashambulia magendo katika idara yake', *Mwafrika*, 4 June 1960, p. 1.
[28] Mwandishi wetu, Mwanza, 'Nyerere: "Wananchi wanangoja ahadi zetu"', *Mwafrika*, 11 June 1960, p. 1.
[29] Editorial, 'Rushwa', *Buhaya Co-operative News*, June 1960, p. 3.
[30] Editorial, 'Ukabila', *Buhaya Co-operative News*, November 1959, p. 3.
[31] 'Wewe ule na mimi nile', *Uhuru*, 16 December 1961, p. 3.

known overseas as 'Kisoshalista' or 'socialism'. The author called on his readers not to be frightened by the word 'socialism', for 'socialism has been present in Africa since the creation of the world', even before foreigners discovered the word, and this socialism was evident whenever the person with the bigger farm called on his neighbours to help him farm it. The article outlined concrete policies required to achieve socialist ends, including government leadership of the economy and nationalization of land, but also focussed on the moral aspects of socialism. Socialism was, he argued, a policy aimed at removing 'human greed'. It was also, he claimed, a politics of 'justice', one present in the soul of 'anyone who has ever been oppressed'.[32]

But the problem with radical languages of socialism was that they brought divisions into the open. In the first place, as we have seen repeatedly over the course of this book, equality was not popular with everybody. In the second place, transnational socialism at times seemed to verge too close to communism. This was objectionable to some because of the atheism of communism and the repression of religious believers in communist states. The lack of any space for religion in communism seems to have been one element in AMNUT's opposition to TANU.[33] It was also a strong theme in the Catholic newspaper *Kiongozi* in which editorial writers and correspondents argued that communism amounted to a new form of slavery and frequently reported on the trials of Christians in China and the Soviet Union.[34] In response, *Uhuru* charged *Kiongozi* with naively believing anti-communist propaganda, and also brought out a familiar weapon which we have often seen used to shut down debate in Tanzania's public sphere, namely accusing *Kiongozi* of engaging in the dangerous practice of mixing religion and politics.[35] Christianity and Islam themselves could and did offer vocabularies for talking about social division.[36] But strictures against introducing religion into the public sphere remained as important in postcolonial Tanzania as they had been in the colonial period.

Whereas writers in the pages of *Uhuru* understood socialism to be fundamentally concerned with equality and ending oppression and

---

[32] Ibid., p. 3.
[33] David Westerlund, *Ujamaa na dini: A Study of Some Aspects of Society and Religion in Tanzania, 1963–1977* (Stockholm: Almquist and Wiksell International, 1980), p. 95.
[34] Emmanuel Rweramila, 'Tutapinga ukomunisti mpaka dakika ya mwisho', *Kiongozi*, 1 June 1965, p. 2.
[35] Editorial, *Uhuru*, 7 April 1965, pp. 3–4.
[36] Felicitas Becker, *Becoming Muslim in Mainland Tanzania, 1890–2000* (Oxford: Oxford University Press, 2008), p. 210.

exploitation, elsewhere we see 'socialism' defined in different terms, as concerned more with the question of how people might live together. There were strong echoes here of the Fabian socialism which influenced some postwar colonial officials as well as the many Tanganyikan politicians from Julius Nyerere to chiefs like Thomas Marealle who participated in the networks created by the Fabian Colonial Bureau.[37] To see this language of socialism, we might turn to the *Buhaya Co-operative News*, a local newspaper published in Swahili and Kihaya which concerned itself both with specific information pertaining to the Bukoba Native Co-operative Union (BNCU) and with wider local and national news. In 1959, a short series of articles sought to explain why a cooperative was different from a private company, and why it had much in common with a '*chama cha maendeleo*', or 'development association'. In the second article, focussing on the ways in which the BNCU was similar to a *chama cha maendeleo*, the secretary and treasurer of the BNCU, G. Ishengomba, wrote that the origins of the cooperative movement lay in the work of people who cared about the ways in which people live. To describe those responsible for the origins of the cooperative movement, he used the term 'socialists', and put the emphasis on their interest in society, rather than in equality or national-level economic policies such as nationalization.[38]

UJAMAA IN CONTEXT

There were many transnational languages which Tanzanians could draw on, but the attraction of the language of *ujamaa* in the early 1960s was that it could be used both by those who wanted fast and radical steps towards a socialist society, and those who wanted government to concern itself more generally with the strains placed on society by growing inequality. The term *ujamaa* itself was not new in the 1960s, nor was it invented by Nyerere. We can see it employed in earlier texts, such as Petro Itosi Marealle's 1946 text *Maisha ya Mchagga Hapa Duniani na Ahera*, in which it is used to mean something like a harmonious society.[39] In his book, Marealle critiqued European missionaries and colonial

---

[37] Christopher Jeppesen, *Making a Career in the British Empire, c. 1900–1960.* Unpublished PhD thesis, University of Cambridge (2013), pp. 179–186.

[38] G. Ishengomba, 'Chama cha ushirika ni chama cha maendeleo pia', *Buhaya Co-operative News*, August 1959, p. 4.

[39] P.I. Marealle, *Maisha ya Mchagga hapa duniani na ahera* (Dar es Salaam: Mkuki na Nyota Publishers, 2002 [1947]), p. 121.

governments who sought to bring *ustaarabu* but who failed to investigate the existing customs of society and to differentiate between those customs which were good and those which were bad. In particular, they failed to understand Chagga *ujamaa*.[40] Indeed, because their own version of *ustaarabu* existed without this basic structure, their teachings were to some extent incompatible with it. For Marealle, *ujamaa* began in the household, then achieved further realization in the clan, and culminated in the person of the chief. All Chagga worked together in a spirit of *ujamaa* and all reaped the rewards. Thus there was no one who failed to enjoy the blessings of this society.[41] Marealle attributed the problems which Chagga society faced in the late 1940s to incompatibility between the two types of *ustaarabu*, the European and the Chagga. The urgent task confronting Chagga lay in finding a way of uniting the good elements of both.[42] A crucial element of building proper *ustaarabu*, then, would lie in finding a place for *ujamaa* within it, though cooperatives, willingness to pay more tax for education, and better governance.

In Nyerere's own writing, particularly in his 1962 pamphlet, 'Ujamaa – The Basis of African Socialism', we see a combination of orthodox democratic socialist thought and a wider concern with the state of society.[43] In it he laid out his argument for the rediscovery of an 'African socialism' which was, he claimed 'rooted in our own past – in the traditional society which produced us'.[44] In his writing about African socialism, Nyerere stated that capitalist values were becoming too rapidly entrenched, and he wanted to set things back in the right direction. We see this theme both in the 1962 'Ujamaa' article, and in the 1967 pamphlets which accompanied the Arusha Declaration. In 1962, Nyerere complained about the 'antisocial' effects of capitalism as wealth was increasingly accumulated by individuals.[45] Returning to the critiques of untrammelled capitalism of the 1940s and 1950s, and the fear of landlessness that might result, we can see that while Nyerere disagreed with the institutionalized inequality between citizens which conservatives such as Petro Njau took for granted, arguing instead for a 'society in which all members have

---

[40] Ibid., p. 121.

[41] Ibid., p. 121.

[42] Ibid., p. 122.

[43] Julius Nyerere, 'Ujamaa – The Basis of African Socialism' in Julius Nyerere, *Freedom and Unity: A Selection from Writings and Speeches, 1952-65* (London: Oxford University Press, 1967), pp. 162–171.

[44] Ibid., p. 170.

[45] Ibid., p. 164.

equal rights and equal opportunities', and disagreed with Njau's focus on shared responsibilities within an imagined ethnic community, he shared the broader aim of reordering relations between rich and poor so that they would no longer be founded on exploitation.[46]

In the pages of *Uhuru*, the language of *ujamaa* served to discuss core questions of inequality. A letter published in 1965 was entitled: 'What sort of *ujamaa* is this?' and asked how *ujamaa* was possible when one person earned 150 shillings and someone else earned 3,000 shillings. The author called for salaries to be modelled on the Chinese system of equality, in order to build the nation.[47] For others, the term *ujamaa* was used either with the more general meaning of 'the social' or 'society', or to comment on the ills of society and their potential cure. An article in the Catholic newspaper *Kiongozi* in 1964 about local government in Germany used the term to refer to the social services carried out by German local government bodies.[48] Elsewhere in *Kiongozi* it was used to describe associations much like those discussed in Chapter 1, associations concerned with bringing *maendeleo* and helping the poor. Thus an article on 1 March 1964 described a new 'Shirika la Ujamaa' in Tabora, the Ujamaa Building Co-operative Society Ltd., whose aim was to 'remove the enemy of poverty'.[49]

An article which appeared in *Kiongozi* in 1965, on the subject of what it meant to be a good citizen referred to the need to give meaning to the term *ujamaa*, which, according to the author, came from working towards unity, or *umoja*. Tanzania was a country made up of various races, ethnicities and religions, and it was important to treat other Tanzanians as friends.[50] Elsewhere, it was the cooperative aspect of *ujamaa*, the idea of helping each other, which was emphasized, again echoing the language of the associations of earlier times. An editorial in the Chagga Council newspaper in March 1964 entitled 'Helping each other is our custom' argued that there was nothing strange about a spirit of mutual help, for this had existed 'since the time of our ancestors'. But 'colonial slavery made many of us begin to forget the importance of helping each other.' Linking

---

[46] Julius Nyerere, 'Socialism and Rural Development', in Julius Nyerere (ed.), *Freedom and Socialism: A Selection from Writings and Speeches, 1965–1967* (London: Oxford University Press, 1968), pp. 337–366, p. 340. See also Michael Jennings, *Surrogates of the State: NGOs, Development and Ujamaa in Tanzania* (Bloomfield, CT: Kumarian Press, 2008), p. 45.

[47] Letter from Mwamba M. Simbani, 'Huu ni ujamaa gani', *Uhuru*, 8 March 1965, p. 2.

[48] 'Serikali za mitaa Ujerumani', *Kiongozi*, 1 January 1964, p. 2.

[49] 'Shirika la ujamaa mjini Tabora', *Kiongozi*, March 1964, p. 3.

[50] 'Sisi viumbe vya ajabu: taamuli fupi za mmoja wenu', *Kiongozi*, 1 March 1965, p. 6.

postcolonial freedom with the freedom of earlier times, the editorial continued, 'Now that we are free people as in the times of our ancestors, we must bring back our spirit of helping one another so that we can progress in a way fitting to those who live in an *ujamaa* community.'[51]

Ujamaa was thus a language which could be used both to discuss radical projects concerned with equality and to discuss projects which worked to maintain hierarchical relationships but reconstitute them on a new basis. It also left space for religion, while not explicitly talking about religion. This context helps explain why the Arusha Declaration of 1967, which put the language of *ujamaa na kujitegemea* at the centre of political discourse served so powerfully to open up new discursive terrain.

THE ARUSHA DECLARATION

The Arusha Declaration, published on 5 February 1967 after consultation with TANU's National Executive Committee but based on ideas formulated by Nyerere, marked a bold shift. It announced that where TANU had once been open to all who wished to fight for Tanzania's self-government and independence, it would henceforth be a party only for those committed to building a society based on the principles of *ujamaa*. Immediately afterwards, a series of nationalizations were announced, along with 'Education for Self-Reliance', a new educational system which aimed to educate all Tanzanians rather than focussing attention on an academic few, and a plan for rural resettlement and villagization. A Leadership Code made clear that those who held political office must be fully committed to TANU's objectives, and must give up any private or business interests which contradicted those objectives and placed them in the class of 'exploiters'.[52]

Where other postcolonial leaders succumbed to internal criticisms and external pressures, Nyerere and TANU were able to construct a new narrative, which developed themes current in political discourse since 1945. For Nyerere and TANU, the language of *ujamaa na kujitegemea*, socialism and self-reliance, was a means of dominating political space. Yet it also provided an effective language for discussing social relations, for achieving *maendeleo* without destroying society and as such functioned as a discursive resource which went far beyond Nyerere and TANU. Like the word *uhuru*, it was a polysemic word which helped to open up new

---

[51] Editorial, 'Kusaidiana ni jadi yetu', *Kusare*, 7 March 1964, p. 2.
[52] Coulson, *Tanzania: A Political Economy*, pp. 177–179.

discursive terrain, even in the much more restricted public sphere of the later 1960s where public debate and opposition was not possible in the way it had been a decade earlier.[53]

The Arusha Declaration saw TANU respond to arguments taking place in the public sphere and offer a compelling answer in response. The rhetoric of *ujamaa na kujitegemea* and the concrete proposals of the Arusha Declaration held forth a vision of a new society, combining *maendeleo* with newly strengthened social relations. It proposed new ties of dependence, a new contract between party, state and people, but it did so in a language of autonomy, both individual and national, through the resurrection of the principle of self-help which we traced in the first chapter. This would be a society built on the self-reliance and self-help of individuals and communities in relation to the state, and of the state in relation to the international community. Against the charge that corruption, a growing gap between rich and poor, the failure of some to contribute to building the nation and failures of the young to access land and jobs were sending *maendeleo* or progress backwards, the Arusha Declaration responded with the answer that as long as the ideals of African socialism or *ujamaa* were followed, then *maendeleo* would be assured. But though human flourishing could be attained through TANU, it now required ideological commitment, accepting to live according to TANU's principles with the limitations on freedom as autonomy which that entailed. For young men who lacked access to land, the Arusha Declaration offered a way of claiming land. For those who were critical of TANU politicians who seemed to be engaged in corruption, the charge that they were not complying with the leadership code of the Arusha Declaration could be laid against them.

On a political level, the Arusha Declaration constituted a decisive attempt by Nyerere to recapture the initiative. It served as a way of tackling directly criticisms of local officials deemed to behave unjustly or corruptly which also confronting critics within the party, men such as the veteran nationalist and leading minister Oscar Kambona who would soon leave Tanzania and go into exile. It firmly consolidated Nyerere's position within Tanzania. As Andrew Coulson wrote in 1982, '[e]verywhere Nyerere was the hero, and the villains were the politicians and civil

---

[53] Gregory Maddox and James Giblin, 'Introduction' in Gregory Maddox and James Giblin (eds.), *In Search of a Nation: Histories of Authority and Dissidence in Tanzania* (Oxford: James Currey, 2005), pp. 1–12; James Giblin, *A History of the Excluded: Making Family a Refuge from State in Twentieth-Century Tanzania* (Oxford: James Currey, 2004).

servants who had been growing fat at the expense of the masses.'[54] For the American Embassy in Dar es Salaam, it meant that '[w]hichever way things go in Tanzania, it is certain that Nyerere will be making the decisions.'[55] For TANU officials, it showed that TANU would remain in control. The area commissioner of Musoma, O. S. Madawa, said in a public meeting that 'TANU has not died and nor is there any expectation of death: it will continue to lead this country forever in order that it reaches its goal of self-reliance.'[56]

The Arusha Declaration served as a means of re-legitimizing TANU through re-establishing its claim to authority, no longer simply as the party which brought freedom from colonialism but as the party which would combat corruption and ensure justice for all. But the reason it worked as a rhetorical move was because of the context in which it was proposed. Nyerere's *ujamaa* socialism was a progressive discourse anchored in the mid-twentieth century search for a palatable modernity. But while it emerged in dialogue with global arguments about capitalism, international power dynamics and the nature of modernity, it also constituted a response to long-running debates within Tanzania about progress and its discontents. It was in this vein that it was appropriated and came to acquire a renewed importance in mainland Tanzania's increasingly restricted public sphere.

UJAMAA IN THE PUBLIC SPHERE

The relative openness of mainland Tanzania's public sphere in the years around independence did not last. As we saw in Chapter 7, in the tense environment of 1964 the Catholic newspaper *Kiongozi*'s attempts to speak truth to power was challenged by the louder voice of TANU's newspaper *Uhuru*. There were now fewer local and national newspapers to provide alternative voices. *Mambo Leo* was sold and merged with a Kenyan periodical in 1963 while *Mwafrika* ceased publication in 1965. The district newspapers disappeared too. Some, like *Habari za Upare*, were gone by 1963, others, like the Chagga Council newspaper *Kusare*, the post-independence successor to *Komkya*, disappeared in the context of further tightening of the public sphere which followed the

---

[54] Coulson, *Tanzania: A Political Economy*, p. 183.

[55] U.S. Embassy Dar es Salaam to Department of State, 'This week in Tanzania, August 18–24', 25 August 1967, p. 3, Central Foreign Policy Files, 1967–1969, National Archives II, College Park, Maryland.

[56] 'Tanu haijafa na haitakufa milele', *Ngurumo*, 5 August 1967, p. 3.

Arusha Declaration and the departure of Nyerere's rival Oscar Kambona to exile.[57] New government legislation also played a role. The private newspaper *Ulimwengu*, which was edited by Oscar Kambona's brother and acted as Kambona's mouthpiece following his departure from Tanzania, was closed down following an issue published in December 1967 to which the government took objection. Whether the government had the power to do this was unclear, but they acted swiftly to ensure they would have such powers in the future, introducing the Newspaper Ordinance (Amendment) Bill in 1968 giving the president the power to close newspapers.[58] Yet even in this restricted public sphere, the letters' pages remained popular.[59]

In this context, the language of *ujamaa* provided a common vocabulary for discussing injustice and critiquing immoral behaviour, among officials and fellow citizens. Local officials who behaved unjustly could be charged with acting contrary to the spirit of *ujamaa*.[60] More generally, *ujamaa* vocabulary was employed to criticize behaviour deemed to be detrimental to society and to positive social relations. Negative actions deemed to be destructive of community were held to be contrary to the spirit of *ujamaa*. A writer working in Arusha complained in the letters' pages of *Kusare* of the difficulties he faced in finding a house to rent because many landlords would not rent to unmarried men. He asked rhetorically, 'My friends, is this civilization? Is this *ujamaa*?'[61] Bus companies which overcharged or which failed to deliver passengers to their destination were similarly charged with acting in a manner contrary to the spirit of *ujamaa*.[62] Police who abused passengers on buses were asked if this behaviour was that which was expected if they were to fulfil the Arusha Declaration. One correspondent complained about thieves and

---

[57] Martin Sturmer, *The Media History of Tanzania* (Ndanda: Ndanda Mission Press, 1998), pp. 88, 90, 91, 92.

[58] Graham Mytton, *Mass Communication in Africa* (London: Edward Arnold, 1983), p. 104.

[59] James C. Condon, 'Nation Building and Image Building in the Tanzanian Press', *Journal of Modern African Studies*, 5 (1967), 335–354.

[60] 'Kinyume cha ujamaa', *Ngurumo*, 21 October 1967, p. 2. This section builds on and develops arguments first made in Emma Hunter, 'Revisiting Ujamaa: Political Legitimacy and the Construction of Community in Post-Colonial Tanzania', *Journal of Eastern African Studies*, 2 (2008), 471–485.

[61] Letter from H. H. E. Richard, 'Ubaguzi wa nyumba za kupanga kaloleni Arusha', *Kusare*, 8 April 1967, p. 3.

[62] Letter from Felix K. Lyaro, 'Wenye magari ya abiria Moshi to Arusha wapinga siasa ya Ujamaa', *Kusare*, 8 April 1967, p. 3; Letter from G.K. Robert Makange, 'Abiria wanate-seika "Uru"', *Kusare*, 29 April 1967, p. 3.

distillers of illegal alcohol in Kilema. Which declaration were they fulfilling, the author asked, 'that of Arusha or that of the Boers?'[63]

It also provided a language with which to reflect publically on social
relationships, particularly those between men and women and between
young and old. Young men in Dar es Salaam used the language of *ujamaa* to express their frustration with women who moved to town and
succeeded in gaining access to jobs and employment.[64] In Moshi, an
older discourse which sought to remove women from towns was reartic-
ulated in the language of *ujamaa*. Women who depended on relationships with men were labelled 'ticks' or 'exploiters' and enjoined to rely
on themselves.[65]

The power of the language of *ujamaa* came from its ability to articulate abstract concepts in a way that was meaningful. The problem of
exploitation was not an abstract one, as it could sometimes appear in
the discourse of international socialism. Exploitation was, as one TANU
branch wrote in its fortnightly newssheet in June 1968, a practice which
destroyed society, it brought 'misery and misunderstanding'. The solution
was the Arusha Declaration, which would encourage 'us to make each
other happy, to love one another, and to work together in an *ujamaa* fashion with joy and peace'.[66]

For both political leaders and for TANU members, the Arusha
Declaration made it very clear, as Andrew Ivaska and others have argued,
that virtuous citizenship came from behaving in a way fitting to the principles of *ujamaa*. But it also provided a common language between rich
and poor, rulers and ruled. This element can be seen in the example of
an unpublished TANU history which appears to have been written by
the nationalist activist and TANU member Lameck Bogohe in around
1967 or shortly afterwards, the text with which this book began. In a
section entitled *Ujamaa na Kujitegemea* [Socialism and Self-reliance],
Bogohe proclaims the virtue of farming. He defines himself as a farmer, a
role given to him by God, and describes the farmer as being at the root of

---

[63] Letter from Silvester Robert Limo, 'Wezi wamechacha mlimani Kilema', *Kusare*, 24 June
1967, p. 3.

[64] Andrew Ivaska, 'Anti-mini Militants Meet Modern Misses: Urban Style, Gender and the
Politics of 'National Culture' in 1960s Dar es Salaam', *Gender and History*, 14 (2002),
584–607, pp. 589–590.

[65] Letter from Engeni Sirili Tilya, 'Heko majizi kukamatwa mjini', *Kusare*, 15 April
1967, p. 3.

[66] A. K. Ugama, 'Azimio la Arusha lazuia kunyonyana', *TANU Yajenga Nchi*, 23, 15 June
1968, TNA BM/11/01, f. 83.

the economic, political and social life of society. As such, the farmer alone deserves the title 'Mheshimiwa', or 'Honourable'.[67]

Bogohe then went on to make a broader argument as to the loyalty of his ethnic group, the Sukuma. The Mwanza region, home of the Sukuma, was developing a reputation for being politically troublesome and independent-minded. Not only had they refused to reelect the finance minister, Paul Bomani, in 1965, they noisily resented the apparent benefit which their cotton, as Tanzania's highest value export crop, brought to the rest of Tanzania. In return, parliamentarians in Dar es Salaam criticized their tenacious attachment to the Sukuma language, suggesting that if they were to participate fully in the nation's development they should learn Swahili.[68] Yet Bogohe here claimed that if any ethnic group were likely to be in sympathy with *ujamaa* philosophy, it was the Sukuma, for *ujamaa*, familyhood or African socialism, had always been a fundamental element of the life of the Sukuma people. He described the various Sukuma practices which he believed demonstrated that an *ujamaa* style of living had long existed in the region, from cooperation in house-building to harvesting and the delivery of justice. For Bogohe, the language of *ujamaa* provided a common language in which to express loyalty.

For others, a language of *ujamaa na kujitegemea* was a way of making claims from below. It was used in this way by those who felt that they were unable to access the goods which others enjoyed in postcolonial Tanzania. Young people wrote to the Kilimanjaro newspaper *Kusare* expressing their enthusiasm for the principle of self-reliance. 'We understand', one correspondent wrote, 'that we should rely on ourselves (we should not be ticks). But if you have no work how can you rely on yourself?'[69] For another correspondent, the question was how could the poor who lacked land rely on themselves in the way the rich could do?[70]

But the existence of common languages shared between rulers and ruled, those with power and those without, did not mean that employing those languages was necessarily successful. The young who lacked access to land used the language of *ujamaa* to make claims to land, but the same language was also used against them. Those who were reluctant to move were called 'ticks' and 'exploiters' who 'do not want policies of *ujamaa*

---

[67] Lameck Bogohe, 'Ujamaa na kujitegemea', p. 5, *Historia ya TANU*, CCM Archives, Acc 5/686.

[68] On the apparently lower rates of fluency in Swahili among the Sukuma, see *Majadiliano ya bunge*, 10th Meeting, 24–27 October 1967, p. 297.

[69] Letter from James Mungai, 'Darasa la 7 na 8', *Kusare*, 1 July 1967, p. 3.

[70] Letter from Oleti L. Massawe, 'Darasa la 7 na 8', *Kusare*, 15 July 1967, p. 3.

and self-reliance, and who continue to exploit elders of 45–70 years old'.[71] They rejected the equation of moving away to farm elsewhere with older traditions of labour migrancy and instead argued that virtuous citizenship now entailed moving away to take up land where it was available, those who failed to do so were 'ticks who do not rely on themselves'[72]

CONCLUSION

This book began with an analysis of arguments over *maendeleo* and modernity in Tanzania's public sphere in the period after 1945. It ends with a new language in which to conduct these old arguments, that of *ujamaa na kujitegemea*. For TANU, the Arusha Declaration was a means of regaining the initiative and recapturing the imagination of a critical population.[73] But that does not itself explain its appeal or its longevity and power in public debate, both at the time and in the years which followed.

To explain this demands that we detach the language of *ujamaa* from TANU and the politics of *ujamaa* and instead consider its place within the intellectual context of late colonial and early postcolonial Tanzania. By tracing the language of *ujamaa* through the public sphere of the 1960s, we have seen that throughout the 1960s, but particularly after 1967, the language of *ujamaa* was compelling not because it was a means of resurrecting 'traditional' African values for a modern age, but because it provided a new vocabulary for debating the very real challenges facing society in the era of decolonization, with the potential to help construct a distinctive form of modernity which balanced progress with the maintenance and recreation of social bonds. And this long outlasted its failure as a development strategy.

---

[71] Letter from Peter L. M. Mirakuo Mmasi, 'Uvivu wapigwa ziii!', *Kusare*, 22nd April 1967, p. 3.

[72] Letter from P. L. M. Mirakuo Mmasi, 'Maendeleo makubwa ugenini Kabuku', *Kusare*, 25 March 1967.

[73] Marie-Aude Fouéré, 'Tanzanie: La nation à l'épreuve du postsocialisme', *Politique Africaine*, 121 (2011), 69–85, Felicitas Becker, 'Remembering Nyerere: Political Rhetoric and Dissent in Contemporary Tanzania', *African Affairs* 112 (2013), 238–261.

Conclusion

Between 1945 and 1965, a world of empires became a world of nation-states. From one perspective, these new states looked very similar to each other. It is therefore not surprising that, for a long time, a diffusionist model dominated the historical understanding of nationalism, and of the state structures and forms of citizenship that followed independence. But although one part of the story of the twentieth century was the rise to dominance of Western models of organizing state and society, the counterweight to that story was one of intense regional and local engagement with global political discourses. This was true in Africa, as elsewhere.

This book began with the intellectual context of the period between 1945 and the early 1950s. First, we considered the ways in which vernacular conceptions of modernity were debated in Tanzania's Swahiliphone public sphere through a study of ideas about *maendeleo*, progress or development. A close reading of the letters' pages showed a demand for *maendeleo* coupled with a concern that it could go backwards as well as forwards, and a desire to ensure that *maendeleo* did not entail the breaking up of social relations. We then looked at the twin concepts of democracy and representation, before showing how these themes came together in a case study of a local political movement on Kilimanjaro in the late 1940s. We then moved into the era of nationalism, from the founding of Tanganyika African National Union (TANU) in 1954 to independence in 1961. We tracked freedom as a 'word-in-motion', showing that its power derived from its combination of the universal and the locally specific. Freedom was understood in terms of refiguring social bonds as well as seeking to escape them. The next chapter placed TANU's rise in the context of locally specific arguments in a locality, and showed how the rhetorical power of TANU and its local allies came from its ability to tap into a twin set of political languages which responded both to the deep politics of the locality and to wider global shifts. In the final part of the book we explored the first decade after independence. Building on the arguments made earlier in the book, the final chapters offered new readings of two major changes of the early years of the postcolonial state in Tanzania: first the shift to one-party democracy, and second the power of the language of *ujamaa*.

As this book has shown, some of the key political concepts of the mid-twentieth-century – development, freedom, citizenship – were both more and less global than they might appear. Although the concept of freedom was at the heart of political argument in Tanganyika as elsewhere in the colonial world, observers misunderstood what was happening when they thought that *uhuru* was understood simply as the rejection of authority. Rather, freedom was realized as much through the reworking of social and political relationships as in the rejection of them, as we have seen through a close reading of the political language of the Kilimanjaro Chagga Citizens Union (KCCU) and TANU.

The meaning and duties of citizenship were negotiated within these parameters. Arguments over the meaning and practice of democracy were similarly framed in relationship to concepts of freedom and citizenship. The most common definition of democracy that circulated in print was that of having rulers whom the people had elected themselves. That left considerable scope for flexibility in the type of political system chosen, provided elections formed part of it, and could be compatible both with radically egalitarian political projects and projects concerned with recreating and maintaining hierarchy.

Understanding the local depth of these global concepts allows us to understand the challenges faced by political leaders as they sought first to mobilise constituencies of support and then to create legitimate authority. By taking seriously the history of key political concepts and the ways in which they were refashioned over time through a close reading of changing political languages, we can better understand the options available and the political changes that took place in the era of decolonization.

IMPLICATIONS

Despite its relatively close focus, this study has broader implications. First among these is its contribution to the rewriting of the history of mid-twentieth-century nationalism and decolonization. Across Africa, the 1960s saw leaders who had once seemed to carry all before them grow increasingly unpopular, before either being pushed unceremoniously from power, as in the case of Kwame Nkrumah of Ghana, or closing down alternative parties and amassing powers around themselves that made them extremely hard to unseat, as in the case of Kenyatta in Kenya. This once seemed to present a problem. Nationalist parties had won a rhetorical battle to present their rise to power as natural, the only politically thinkable option. For the first generation of historians of Africa, colonial regimes seemed inherently illegitimate whereas in contrast, based as they seemed to be on the self-declared will of the people, the postcolonial regimes which succeeded them were by their very nature legitimate. Histories of nationalism recorded the inexorable rise of nationalist movements until finally they could demonstrate to colonial rulers that they did indeed represent 'the people', at which point power could safely be transferred. Their failure was therefore difficult to understand.

But if we understand political parties as emerging from a crowded and dynamic public sphere, where there were multiple and conflicting political struggles and competing ideas about the meaning of core political concepts, we can better understand the fragility of the constituencies of support they constructed. They had to develop compelling political narratives but these were situational, working at one moment but then breaking down the next. But that fragility and situationality does not mean that they were not powerful while they lasted. And indeed, studying the moments when compelling political narratives were constructed and new political identities were briefly brought into being offers us insights into the paths not taken and the futures which might have been.[1]

It also helps to contribute to a new rethinking of the history of decolonization in comparative perspective. An older literature of decolonization was divided between metropolitan perspectives and decision making within individual empires on the one hand, and an area studies perspective and a focus on nationalist agency on the other. But decolonization was a transnational event which is best understood by historians, as it was by the historical actors involved, in comparative terms.[2] Western forms of

---

[1] Mrinalini Sinha, *Specters of Mother India: The Global Restructuring of an Empire* (London and Durham, NC: Duke University Press, 2006), p. 251.

[2] Examples of a comparative approach from the imperial perspective are Bob Moore, Martin Thomas and L. J. Butler, *Crises of Empire: Decolonization and Europe's Imperial States, 1918–1975* (London: Hodder/Arnold, 2008), Martin Shipway, *Decolonization*

political order were not simply imposed on non-Western societies; rather, emerging elites and decolonizing societies thought carefully about what independence could and should mean, how political subjecthood should be reconstituted and what forms of political organization they should construct. By exploring these universal questions in a specific context, this book opens up the potential for more comparative analysis, bringing Africa into dialogue with other decolonizing societies.

The second way in which this book helps us to understand wider debates relates to the comparative history of democracy in Africa and in the postcolonial world more broadly. Since the 'second wave' of democratizations in Africa which led to the downfall of single-party regimes and the establishment of multiparty elections, a vast literature has emerged which seeks to understand the theory and practice of democracy in Africa.[3] On the one hand, quantitative studies using questionnaires, such as the Afrobarometer project, seek to investigate the attitudes of Africans across the continent to different systems of government. On the other, qualitative studies have explored the range of meanings attached to the term democracy. In this regard, Mikael Karlström's study of the ways in which democracy is imagined in Buganda stands out.[4] But the focus of this literature tends to be on the present and the very recent past, and, with rare exceptions, has little to say about the 'first wave' of democratization across Africa.[5] By going back to that era and tracing the ways in which democracy was defined and discussed in public fora, we can better understand the range of possibilities which were open at that time.

This leads us to the third point. New global and transnational histories have demonstrated the extent to which the twentieth century world was a connected world. We can now see far more clearly than was once possible the ways in which ideas were exchanged across seas and oceans, as well as across land borders. Tracking the mobile people of the twentieth century allow us to see the transnational lives which often drove forward intellectual and political change. But there are risks with this literature of re-marginalizing the people who were less connected, and of

and Its Impact: A Comparative Approach to the End of the Colonial Empires (Oxford: Blackwell, 2008).

3 For a helpful review of this literature, see Abdul Raufu Mustapha and Lindsay Whitfield, 'African Democratisation: The Journey So Far' in Abdul Raufu Mustapha and Lindsay Whitfield, *Turning Points in African Democracy* (Oxford: James Currey, 2009), pp. 1–12.

4 Mikael Karlström, 'Imagining Democracy: Political Culture and Democratisation in Buganda', *Africa*, 66(4), 1996, 485–505.

5 Though see Göran Hydén, Michael Leslie and Folu F. Ogundimu, *Media and democracy in Africa* (Uppsala: Nordic Africa Institute, 2003).

neglecting the deep histories of the places they lived. Some of the individuals whose voices we have heard in this book had travelled, particularly during wartime when service in the King's African Rifles (K.A.R.) took many East Africans across the Indian Ocean. Others travelled within East and Central Africa, leaving homes in Nyasaland or Uganda to come to Tanganyika.[6] But many more did not, and the majority of voices we have heard in this book are those of people who were literate but not members of a continent- or ocean-crossing elite. They tended to write in Swahili, rather than in English. It is important that we do not neglect their voices, some of which have been heard in the Swahili language newspapers and archival records explored here, and their contributions.

For, as we have seen throughout this book, apparent uniformity at the level of words and concepts can hide the multiple and contested meanings developed in local contexts. Appreciation of these meanings and their political implications depends on combining an area studies literature which has provided a deep historical understanding of individual areas with the newer insights of global and transnational history. It is only by doing so that we shall better understand the ambiguities of independence.

---

[6] For examples of movement from Nyasaland to Tanganyika, see Kanyama Chiume, *Autobiography of Kanyama Chiume* (London: Panaf, 1982); Megan Vaughan, 'Mr Mdala Writes to the Governor: Negotiating Colonial Rule in Nyasaland', *History Workshop Journal*, 60, 2005, 171–188. Erica Fiah, whose newspaper *Kwetu* has been discussed at various points, was originally from Uganda. Nicholas Westcott, 'An East African Radical: The Life of Erica Fiah', *Journal of African History*, 22 (1981), 85–101.

References

Archives

Chama Cha Mapinduzi Archives, Dodoma, Tanzania
East Africana Collection, Library of the University of Dar es Salaam, Tanzania
Lutheran Church Northern Diocese Archives, Moshi, Tanzania
Leipzig University Library, Leipzig, Germany
Rhodes House, Bodleian Library, Oxford, U.K.
Tanzania National Archives, Dar es Salaam, Tanzania
United Kingdom National Archives, Kew, U.K.
United States National Archives, College Park, Maryland, U.S.A.

Newspapers and Periodicals

Empire, London
Buhaya Co-operative News, Bukoba
Mambo Leo, Dar es Salaam
Kiongozi, Tabora
Komkya, Moshi
Kusare, Moshi
Kwetu, Dar es Salaam
Mwafrika, Dar es Salaam
Ngurumo, Dar es Salaam
Spearhead, Dar es Salaam
Tanganyika Standard, Dar es Salaam
Uhuru, Dar es Salaam
Umoja, Moshi

Published/Secondary Sources

Allman, Jean. 'The Youngmen and the Porcupine: Class, Nationalism and Asante's Struggle for Self-determination, 1954-57'. *Journal of African History*, 31 (1990), 263–279.

'Phantoms of the Archive: Kwame Nkrumah, a Nazi Pilot named Hanna, and the Contingencies of Postcolonial History Writing'. *American Historical Review*, 118 (2013), 104–129.

Aminzade, Ronald. 'The Politics of Race and Nation: Citizenship and Africanization in Tanganyika'. *Political Power and Social Theory*, 14 (2000), 53–90.

Race, Nation, and Citizenship in Post-colonial Africa: The Case of Tanzania. Cambridge: Cambridge University Press, 2013.

Anderson, Benedict. *Imagined Communities: Reflections on the Origin and Spread of Nationalism*. London: Verso, 1991.

Spectre of Comparison: Nationalism, South East Asia and the World, London: Verso, 1998.

Anderson, David. '"Yours in Struggle for Majimbo". Nationalism and the Party Politics of Decolonization in Kenya, 1955–1964'. *Journal of Contemporary History*, 40 (2005), 547–564.

Aydin, Cemil. *Politics of Anti-Westernism in Asia: Visions of Pan-Islamic and Pan-Asian Thought*. New York: Columbia University Press, 2007.

Baldi, S. *Dictionnaire des emprunts arabes dans les langues de l'Afrique de l'Ouest et en Swahili*. Paris: Karthala, 2008.

Ball, Terence. 'Conceptual History and the History of Political Thought'. In Iain Hampsher-Monk, Karin Tilmans and Frank van Vree (eds.), *History of Concepts: Comparative Perspectives*. Amsterdam: Amsterdam University Press, 1998, pp. 75–86.

Banerjee, Sukanya. *Becoming Imperial Citizens: Indians in the Late-Victorian Empire*. London and Durham, NC: Duke University Press, 2010.

Barber, Karin. 'Translation, Publics, and the Vernacular Press in 1920s Lagos'. In Toyin Falola (ed.), *Christianity and Social Change in Africa: Essays in Honour of J. D. Y. Peel*. Durham, NC: Carolina Academic Press, 2005, pp. 187–208.

Africa's Hidden Histories: Everyday Literacy and Making the Self. Bloomington: Indiana University Press, 2006.

Barongo, E. B. M. *Mkiki Mkiki wa Siasa Tanganyika*. Dar es Salaam: East African Literature Bureau, 1966.

Batten, T. R. *Thoughts on African Citizenship*. Oxford: Oxford University Press, 1944.

Bayart, Jean-Francois. *The State in Africa: The Politics of the Belly*. Cambridge, U.K.: Polity Press, 2009.

Bayly, C. A. *Recovering Liberties: Indian Thought in the Age of Liberalism and Empire*. Cambridge: Cambridge University Press, 2012.

Becker, Felicitas. *Becoming Muslim in Mainland Tanzania, 1890–2000*. Oxford: Oxford University Press, 2008.

'Remembering Nyerere: Political Rhetoric and Dissent in Contemporary Tanzania'. *African Affairs*, 112 (2013), 238–261.

Bennett, George. 'African Socialism'. *International Journal*, 20.1 (1964–5), 97–101.

Berman, Bruce. 'The Ordeal of Modernity in an Age of Terror'. *African Studies Review*, 49 (2006), 1–14.

Berry, Sara. 'Hegemony on a Shoestring: Indirect Rule and Access to Agricultural Land'. *Africa*, 62 (1992), 327–355.

Bienen, Henry. *Tanzania: Party Transformation and Economic Development.* Princeton, NJ: Princeton University Press, 1967.

Bjerk, Paul. 'Sovereignty and Socialism in Tanzania: The Historiography of an African State'. *History in Africa*, 37 (2010), 275–319.

Borgwardt, Elizabeth. *A New Deal for the World: America's Vision for Human Rights.* Cambridge, MA: Belknap Press of Harvard University Press, 2005.

Bose, Sugata. *A Hundred Horizons: The Indian Ocean in the Age of Global Empire.* London and Cambridge, MA: Harvard University Press, 2006.

Brands, Hal. 'Wartime Recruiting Practices, Martial Identity and Post-World War II Demobilization in Colonial Kenya'. *Journal of African History*, 46 (2005), 103–125.

Breckenridge, Keith and Simon Szreter. *Registration and Recognition: Documenting the Person in World History.* Oxford: Oxford University Press, 2012.

Brennan, James R. 'The Short History of Political Opposition and Multi-party Democracy in Tanganyika, 1958–1964'. In G. Maddox and J. Giblin (eds.), *In Search of a Nation.* Oxford: Oxford University Press, 2005, pp. 250–276.

'Blood Enemies: Exploitation and Urban Citizenship in the Nationalist Political Thought of Tanzania, 1958–75'. *Journal of African History*, 47 (2006a), 389–413.

'Realizing Civilization through Patrilineal Descent: African Intellectuals and the Making of an African Racial Nationalism in Tanzania, 1920–50'. *Social Identities*, 12 (2006b), 405–423.

'Youth, the TANU Youth League and Managed Vigilantism in Dar es Salaam, Tanzania, 1925–73'. *Africa*, 76 (2006c), 221–246.

'Radio Cairo and the Decolonization of East Africa, 1953–64'. In Christopher J. Lee (ed.), *Making a World after Empire: The Bandung Moment and Its Political Afterlives.* Athens, OH: Ohio University Press, 2010, pp. 173–195.

'Politics and Business in the Indian Newspapers of Colonial Tanganyika'. *Africa*, 81 (2011), 42–67.

Taifa: Making Nation and Race in Urban Tanzania. Athens, OH: Ohio University Press, 2012.

Brito Vieira, Monica and David Runciman. *Representation.* Cambridge, U.K.: Polity Press, 2008.

Brockway, Fenner. *African Socialism: A Background Book.* London: Bodley Head, 1963.

Bromber, Katrin. '*Ustaarabu*: A Conceptual Change in Tanganyika Newspaper Discourse in the 1920s'. In R. Loimeier and R. Seesemann (eds.), *The Global Worlds of the Swahili.* Berlin: Lit Verlag, 2006, pp. 67–81.

Browers, Michelle L. *Democracy and Civil Society in Arab Political Thought: Transcultural Possibilities.* Syracuse: Syracuse University Press, 2006.

Burke, Roland. *Decolonization and the Evolution of Human Rights.* Philadelphia: University of Pennsylvania Press, 2010.

Burton, Andrew. '"The Eye of Authority": Native Taxation, Colonial Governance and Resistance in Inter-war Tanganyika'. *Journal of Eastern African Studies*, 1 (2008), 74–94.

Burton, Andrew and Michael Jennings. 'The Emperor's New Clothes? Continuities in Governance in Late Colonial and Early Postcolonial East Africa'. *International Journal of African Historical Studies*, 40 (2007), 1–25.

Callahan, Michael D. *Mandates and Empire: The League of Nations and Africa, 1914–1931*. Brighton: Sussex Academic Press, 1999.

A Sacred Trust: The League of Nations and Africa, 1929–1946. Brighton: Sussex Academic Press, 2004.

Campbell, Gwyn. 'Introduction' in Gwyn Campbell (ed.), *The Structure of Slavery in Indian Ocean Africa and Asia*. London: Frank Cass, 2004.

Chabal, Patrick (ed.). *Political Domination in Africa: Reflections on the Limits of Power*. Cambridge: Cambridge University Press, 1986.

Chandavarkar, Rajnarayan. 'Imperialism and the European Empires', in Julian Jackson (ed.), *Europe, 1900–1945*. Oxford: Oxford University Press, 2002, pp. 138–172.

Chatterjee, Nandini. *The Making of Indian Secularism: Empire, Law and Christianity, 1830–1960*. Basingstoke, U.K.: Palgrave Macmillan, 2011.

Chaudhuri, K. N. *Trade and Civilisation in the Indian Ocean: An Economic History from the Rise of Islam to 1750*. Cambridge: Cambridge University Press, 1985.

Chidzero, B. T. G. *Tanganyika and International Trusteeship*. London: Oxford University Press, 1961.

Chiume, Kanyama. *Autobiography of Kanyama Chiume*. London: Panaf, 1982.

Cliffe, Lionel (ed.). *One Party Democracy: The 1965 Tanzania General Elections*. Nairobi: East African Publishing House, 1967.

Clough, Marshall. 'Review: Kaggia and Kenya's Independence Struggle'. *Africa Today*, 24 (1977), 89–93.

Cmiel, Kenneth. 'Human Rights, Freedom of Information and the Origins of Third-World Solidarity'. In Mark Philip Bradley and Patrice Petro (eds.), *Truth Claims: Representation and Human Rights*. London and New Brunswick, NJ: Rutgers University Press, 2002, pp. 107–130.

Comaroff, John. 'Governmentality, Materiality, Legality, Modernity: On the Colonial State in Africa'. In Jan-Georg Deutsch, Peter Probst and Heike Schmidt (eds.), *African Modernities: Entangled Meanings in Current Debate*. Oxford: James Currey, 2002, pp. 107–134.

Condon, James C. 'Nation Building and Image Building in the Tanzanian Press'. *The Journal of Modern African Studies*, 5 (1967), 335–354.

Conklin, Alice. *A Mission to Civilize: The Republican Idea of Empire in France and West Africa, 1895–1930*. Stanford CA: Stanford University Press, 1997.

Cooper, Frederick. 'Review: The Problem of Slavery in African Societies'. *Journal of African History*, 20 (1979), 103–125.

'Conflict and Connection: Rethinking Colonial African History'. *The American Historical Review*, 99 (1994), 1516–1545.

Cooper, Frederick. *Decolonisation and African Society: The Labour Question in French and British Africa*. Cambridge: Cambridge University Press, 1996.

Cooper, Frederick. 'Review of Citizen and Subject: Contemporary Africa and the Legacy of Late Colonialism by Mahmood Mamdani'. *International Labor and Working Class History*, 52 (1997), 156–160.

Colonialism in Question: Theory, Knowledge, History. Berkeley and London: University of California Press, 2005.

'Possibility and Constraint: African Independence in Historical Perspective'. *Journal of African History*, 49 (2008), 167–196.

Citizenship between Empire and Nation: Remaking France and French Africa, 1945–1960. Princeton, NJ: Princeton University Press, 2014.

Cooper, Frederick and Randall Packard (eds.). *International Development and the Social Sciences: Essays on the History and Politics of Knowledge*. Berkeley: University of California Press, 1997.

Coulson, Andrew. *Tanzania: A Political Economy*. Oxford, Oxford University Press, 1982.

Creech-Jones, Arthur. 'The Place of African Local Administration in Colonial Policy'. *Journal of African Administration*, 1 (1949), 3–6.

Crozon, A. 'Maneno wa siasa, les mots du politique en Tanzanie'. *Politique Africaine*, 64 (1996), 18–30.

Dubow, Saul. *South Africa's Struggle for Human Rights*. Athens, OH: Ohio University Press, 2012.

Dumbuya, Peter. *Tanganyika under International Mandate*. London: University Press of America, 1995.

Dundas, Charles. *African Crossroads*. London: Macmillan and Co., 1955.

Dunn, John. 'Politics of Representation and Good Government'. In Patrick Chabal (ed.), *Political Domination in Africa: Reflections on the Limits of Power*. Cambridge: Cambridge University Press, 1986.

Setting the People Free: The Story of Democracy,. London: Atlantic Books, 2005.

East Africa Commission. *East Africa Royal Commission 1953–1955: Report*. London: HMSO, 1955.

Eckert, Andreas. '"I do not wish to be a tale-teller": Afrikanische Eliten in British-Tanganyika. Das Beispiel Thomas Marealle'. In Andreas Eckert and Gesine Krueger (eds.), *Lesarten eines globalen Prozesses: Quellen und Interpretationen zur geschichte der europaischen Expansion*. Hamburg: Lit, 1998, pp. 172–186.

Eckert, Andreas. '"Useful Instruments of Participation?" Local Government and Co-operatives in Tanzania, 1940s to 1970s'. *International Journal of African Historical Studies*, 40 (2007), 97–118.

Englund, Harri. *Prisoners of Freedom: Human Rights and the African Poor*. Berkeley: University of California Press, 2006.

'Human Rights and Village Headmen in Malawi: Translation beyond Vernacularisation'. In Julia Eckert, Brian Donahoe, Christan Strümpell and Zerrin Özlem Biner (eds.), *Law against the State: Ethnographic Forays into Law's Transformations*. Cambridge: Cambridge University Press, 2012, pp. 70–93.

Englund, Harri (ed.). *Christianity and Public Culture in Africa*. Athens, OH: Ohio University Press, 2011.

Englund, Harri and Francis Nyamnjoh (eds.). *Rights and the Politics of Recognition in Africa*. London: Zed Books, 2004.

Fahmy, Ziad. *Ordinary Egyptians: Creating the Modern Nation through Popular Culture*. Stanford, CA: Stanford University Press, 2011.

Feierman, Steven. *Peasant Intellectuals: Anthropology and History in Tanzania*. Madison, WI: University of Wisconsin Press, 1990.

Ferguson, James. *Expectations of Modernity: Myths and Meanings of Life on the Zambian Copperbelt*. Berkeley: University of California Press, 1999.

Fiedler, Klaus. *Christianity and African Culture: Conservative German Protestant Missionaries in Tanzania, 1900–1940*. Leiden: Brill, 1996.

Finucane, James. *Rural Development and Bureaucracy in Tanzania: The Case of Mwanza Region*. Uppsala: Scandinavian Institute of African Studies, 1974.

Fouéré, Marie-Aude. 'Tanzanie: La nation à l'épreuve du postsocialisme'. *Politique Africaine*, 121 (2011), 69–85.

Frederiksen, Bodil Folke. '"The Present Battle Is the Brain Battle": Writing and Publishing a Kikuyu Newspaper in the Pre-Mau Mau Period in Kenya'. In Karin Barber (ed.), *Africa's Hidden Histories*, pp. 278–313.

Friedland, William H. and Carl G. Rosberg (eds.). *African Socialism*. London: Oxford University Press, 1964.

Fung, Edmund S. K. *In Search of Chinese Democracy: Civil Opposition in Nationalist China, 1929–1949*. Cambridge: Cambridge University Press, 2000.

Geider, Thomas. 'Swahilisprachige Ethnographien (ca. 1890-heute): Produktionsbedingungen und Autreninteressen'. In Heike Behrend and Thomas Geider (eds.), *Afrikaner Schreiben Zurück: Texte und Bilder afrikanischer Ethnographien*. Köln, Rüdiger Koeppe Verlag Köln, 1998, pp. 41–71.

'The Paper Memory of East Africa: Ethnohistories and Biographies Written in Swahili'. In Axel Harneit-Sievers (ed.), *A Place in the World: New Local Historiographies from Africa and South Asia*. Leiden: Brill, 2002, pp. 255–288.

Geiger, Susan. *TANU Women: Gender and Culture in the Making of Tanganyikan Nationalism, 1955–65*. Oxford: James Currey, 1998.

Gershoni, Israel and James Jankowski (eds.). *Rethinking Nationalism in the Arab Middle East*. New York: Columbia University Press, 1997.

Geuss, Raymond. *History and Illusion in Politics*. Cambridge: Cambridge University Press, 2001.

Giblin, James. *A History of the Excluded: Making Family a Refuge from State in Twentieth-century Tanzania*. Oxford: James Currey, 2004.

Glassman, Jonathon. *Feasts and Riot: Revelry, Rebellion, and Popular Consciousness on the Swahili Coast, 1856–1888*. London: James Currey, 1995.

War of Words, War of Stones: Racial Thought and Violence in Colonial Zanzibar. Bloomington: Indiana University Press, 2011.

Glendon, Mary Ann. *A World Made New: Eleanor Roosevelt and the Universal Declaration of Human Rights*. New York: Random House, 2001.

Gluck, Carol. 'Words in Motion'. In Carol Gluck and Anna Lowenhaupt Tsing, *Words in Motion: Toward a Global Lexicon*. London: Duke University Press, 2009, pp. 3–10.

Gluck, Carol and Anna Lowenhaupt Tsing. *Words in Motion: Toward a Global Lexicon*. London: Duke University Press, 2009.

Gordon, David M. *Invisible Agents: Spirits in a Central African History*. Athens, OH: Ohio University Press, 2012.

Government of Tanganyika. *Report of the Committee on Constitutional Development, 1951*. Dar es Salaam: Government Printer, 1951.

Habermas, Jürgen. *The Structural Transformation of the Public Sphere: An Inquiry into a Category of Bourgeois Society*. Cambridge: Polity, 1992.

Hachten, William. *Muffled Drums: The News Media in Africa*. Ames: Iowa State University Press, 1971.

Hampsher-Monk, Iain. 'Speech Acts, Languages or Conceptual History?' In Iain Hampsher-Monk, Karin Tilmans and Frank van Vree, *History of Concepts: Comparative Perspectives*. Amsterdam: Amsterdam University Press, 1998, pp. 37–50.

Harris, José. 'Society and the State in Twentieth-century Britain'. In F. M. L. Thompson (ed.), *The Cambridge Social History of Britain*, Vol. 3, Cambridge: Cambridge University Press, 1990, pp. 63–117.

Havinden, Michael and David Meredith. *Colonialism and Development: Britain and Its Tropical Colonies, 1850–1960*. London: Routledge, 1993.

Held, David. 'Democracy: From City-states to a Cosmopolitan Order?' In David Held (ed.), *Prospects for Democracy, North, South, East, West*, Cambridge: Polity Press, 1993, pp. 13–52.

Hobsbawm, Eric and Terence Ranger. *The Invention of Tradition*. Cambridge: Cambridge University Press, 1992.

Hodgkin, Thomas. *Nationalism in Colonial Africa*. New York: New York University Press, 1957.

Hoffmann, Stefan-Ludwig (ed.). *Human Rights in the Twentieth-Century*, Cambridge: Cambridge University Press, 2011.

Hofmeyr, Isabel, Preben Kaarsholm and Bodil Folke Frederiksen. 'Introduction: Print Cultures, Nationalisms and Publics of the Indian Ocean'. *Africa*, 81 (2011), 1–22.

Hourani, Albert. *Arabic Thought in the Liberal Age, 1798–1939*. Cambridge: Cambridge University Press, 1983.

Howard, M. and A. V. Millard. *Hunger and Shame: Poverty and Child Malnutrition on Mount Kilimanjaro*. New York: Routledge, 1997.

Howe, Stephen. *Anticolonialism in British Politics: The Left and the End of Empire*. Oxford: Oxford University Press, 1993.

Howland, Douglas. *Translating the West: Language and Political Reason in Nineteenth-Century Japan*. Honolulu: University of Hawai'i Press, 2002.

Hunter, Emma. 'Revisiting Ujamaa: Political Legitimacy and the Construction of Community in Post-Colonial Tanzania'. *Journal of Eastern African Studies*, 2 (2008) 471–485.

'"Our Common Humanity": Print, Power and the Colonial Press in Interwar Tanganyika and French Cameroun'. *Journal of Global History* 7 (2012), 279–301.

'Dutiful Subjects, Patriotic Citizens and the Concept of 'Good Citizenship' in Twentieth-Century Tanzania'. *The Historical Journal*, 56 (2013), 257–277.

'A History of *maendeleo*: The Concept of 'Development' in Tanganyika's Late Colonial Public Sphere'. In Joseph M. Hodge, Gerald Hödl and Martina Kopf (eds.), *Developing Africa: Concepts and Practices in Twentieth-Century Colonialism*. Manchester: Manchester University Press, 2014, pp. 87–107.

Huxley, Julian. *Democracy Marches*. London: Chatto and Windus, 1941.

Man in the Modern World. London: Chatto and Windus, 1947.

Hydén, Göran. *Political Development in Rural Tanzania: TANU yajenga nchi*,.Nairobi: East African Publishing House, 1969.

Hydén, Göran. *Beyond Ujamaa in Tanzania: Underdevelopment and an Uncaptured Peasantry*. London: Heinemann, 1980.

Hydén, Göran, Michael Leslie and Folu F. Ogundimu. *Media and Democracy in Africa*. Uppsala: Nordic Africa Institute, 2003.

Iliffe, John. 'The Spokesman: Martin Kayamba'. In John Iliffe, *Modern Tanzanians*, Nairobi: East African Publishing House, 1973, pp. 66–94.

A Modern History of Tanganyika. Cambridge: Cambridge University Press, 1979.

'Breaking the Chain at Its Weakest Link: TANU and the Colonial Office'. In Gregory Maddox and James Giblin (eds.), *In Search of a Nation: Histories of Authority and Dissidence in Tanzania*. Oxford: James Currey, 2005, pp. 168–197.

Irwin, Ryan. *Gordian Knot: Apartheid and the Unmaking of the Liberal World Order*. Oxford: Oxford University Press, 2012.

Ivaska, Andrew. 'Anti-Mini Militants Meet Modern Misses: Urban Style, Gender and the Politics of 'National Culture' in 1960s Dar es Salaam'. *Gender and History*, 14 (2002), 584–607.

Cultured States: Youth, Gender and Modern Style in 1960s Dar es Salaam. Durham, NC: Duke University Press, 2011.

Jaeschke, Ernst. *Bruno Gutmann: His Life, His Thoughts and His Work*. Erlangen: Verlag der Ev.-Luth. Mission, 1985.

Jalal, Ayesha. *The Sole Spokesman: Jinnah, the Muslim League, and the Demand for Pakistan*. Cambridge: Cambridge University Press, 1985.

Jennings, Michael. *Surrogates of the State: NGOs, Development and Ujamaa in Tanzania*. Bloomfield, CT: Kumarian Press, 2008.

Johnson, Frederick. *A Standard English-Swahili Dictionary*. London: Oxford University Press, 1939.

A Standard Swahili-English Dictionary. London: Oxford University Press, 1951.

Joseph, May. *Nomadic Identities: The Performance of Citizenship*. Minneapolis: University of Minnesota Press, 1999.

July, Robert W. *The Origins of Modern African Thought: Its Development in West Africa during the Nineteenth and Twentieth Centuries*. London: Faber and Faber, 1968.

Kahin, George McTurnan. *Nationalism and Revolution in Indonesia*. Ithaca, NY: Cornell University Press, 1952.

Kallmann, Deborah. 'Projected Moralities, Engaged Anxieties: Northern Rhodesia's Reading Publics, 1953–1964'. *The International Journal of African Historical Studies*, 32 (1999), 71–117.

Kandoro, S. A. *Mwito wa Uhuru*. Dar es Salaam: Thakers, 1961.

Karlström, Mikael. 'Imagining Democracy: Political Culture and Democratisation in Buganda'. *Africa*, 66 (1996), 485–505.

Kaviraj, Sudipta. 'Ideas of Freedom in Modern India'. In Robert Taylor (ed.), *The Idea of Freedom in Asia and Africa*. Stanford, CA: Stanford University Press, 2002, pp. 97–142.

Kelsall, Tim. 'Rituals of Verification: Indigenous and Imported Accountability in Northern Tanzania'. *Africa*, 73 (2003), 174–201.

Khan, Yasmin. *The Great Partition: The Making of India and Pakistan*. New Haven, CT: Yale University Press, 2007.

Kimambo, Isaria N. *A Political History of the Pare of Tanzania, c. 1500–1900*. Nairobi: East African Publishing House, 1969.

Penetration and Protest in Tanzania: The Impact of the World Economy on the Pare, 1860–1960. London: James Currey, 1991.

Kopytoff, Igor. 'The Internal African Frontier: The Making of African Political Culture'. In Igor Kopytoff (ed.), *The African Frontier: The Reproduction of Traditional African Societies*. Bloomington: Indiana University Press, 1987, pp. 3–84.

Kopytoff, Igor and Suzanne Miers. 'African 'Slavery' as an Institution of Marginality'. In Suzanne Miers and Igor Kopytoff (eds.), *Slavery in Africa: Historical and Anthropological Perspectives*, Madison, WI: University of Wisconsin Press, 1977, pp. 3–85.

Koselleck, Reinhard. '*Begriffsgeschichte* and Social History'. In Reinhard Koselleck, *Futures Past: On the Semantics of Historical Time*. New York: Columbia University Press, 2004, pp. 75–92.

Krapf, Ludwig. *A Dictionary of the Suahili Language*. London: Truebner and Co., 1882.

Lake, Marilyn. 'Chinese Colonists Assert Their "Common Human Rights"'. *Journal of World History*, 21, 3, 2010, pp. 375–392.

Lal, Priya. 'Militants, Mothers, and the National Family: *Ujamaa*, Gender, and Rural Development in Postcolonial Tanzania', *Journal of African History*, 51 (2010), 1–20.

Lal, Priya. 'Self-reliance and the State: The Multiple Meanings of Development in Early Post-colonial Tanzania'. *Africa*, 82 (2012), 212–234.

Landau, Paul. *Popular Politics in the History of South Africa, 1400–1948*, Cambridge: Cambridge University Press, 2010.

Larmer, Miles. 'Local Conflicts in a Transnational War: The Katangese Gendarmes and the Shaba Wars of 1977–78'. *Cold War History*, 13 (2013), 89–108.

Larmer, Miles (ed.). *The Musakanya Papers: The Autobiographical Writings of Valentine Musakanya*. Lusaka: Lembani Trust, 2010.

Lawrance, Benjamin, Emily Lynn Osborn and Richard L. Roberts. *Intermediaries, Interpreters and Clerks: African Employees in the Making of Colonial Africa*. Madison, WI: University of Wisconsin Press, 2006.

Lee, Christopher J. (ed.). *Making a World after Empire: The Bandung Moment and Its Political Afterlives*. Athens, OH: Ohio University Press, 2010.

Lee, Eugene. *Local Taxation in Tanzania*. Dar es Salaam: Institute of Public Administration, 1965.

Legum, Colin. 'Single-Party Democracy'. *The World Today*, 21 (1965), 526–532.

Lerise, F. S. *Politics in Land and Water Management: Study in Kilimanjaro, Tanzania*. Dar es Salaam: Mkuki wa Nyota, 2005.

Leubuscher, Charlotte. 'Marketing Schemes for Native-Grown Produce in African Territories'. *Africa* 12 (1939), 163–188.

Lewis, Joanna. *Empire State Building: War and Welfare in Kenya 1925–52*. Oxford: James Currey, 2000.

Liebenow, J. Gus. *Colonial Rule and Political Development in Tanzania: The Case of the Makonde*. Evanston, IL: Northwestern University Press, 1971.

Lohrmann, Ullrich. *Voices from Tanganyika: Great Britain, the United Nations and the Decolonization of a Trust Territory, 1946–1961*. Berlin: Lit., 2007.

Lonsdale, John. 'States and Social Processes in Africa: A Historiographical Survey'. *African Studies Review*, 24 (1981), 139–225.

'The Moral Economy of Mau Mau: Wealth, Poverty and Civic Virtue in Kikuyu Political Thought'. In John Lonsdale and Bruce Berman (eds.), *Unhappy Valley: Conflict in Kenya and Africa. Book Two: Violence and Ethnicity*. Oxford: James Currey, 1992, pp. 315–504.

'"Listen while I read": Orality, Literacy and Christianity in the Young Kenyatta's Making of the Kikuyu'. In Louise de la Gorgendière, Kenneth King and Sarah Vaughan (eds.), *Ethnicity in Africa: Roots, Meanings and Implications*. Edinburgh: Centre of African Studies, 1996, pp. 17–53.

'KAU's Cultures', *Journal of African Cultural Studies*, 13 (2000), 107–124.

'Authority, Gender and Violence: The War within Mau Mau's Fight for Land and Freedom'. In John Lonsdale and E. S. Atieno Odhiambo (eds.), *Mau Mau and Nationhood: Arms, Authority and Narration*. Oxford: James Currey, 2003, pp. 46–75.

'"Listen while I read": Patriotic Christianity among the Young Gikuyu'. In Toyin Falola (ed.), *Christianity and Social Change in Africa*, Durham, NC: Carolina Academic Press, 2005, pp. 563–593.

Lovett, Margot. 'On Power and Powerlessness: Marriage and Political Metaphor in Colonial western Tanzania'. *International Journal of African Historical Studies*, 27 (1994), 273–301.

Low, D. A. *Eclipse of Empire*. Cambridge: Cambridge University Press, 1991.

Low, D. A. and J. M. Lonsdale. 'Introduction: Towards the New Order 1945–1963'. In D. A. Low and Alison Smith (eds.), *History of East Africa*, Vol. 3, Oxford: Clarendon Press, 1976, pp. 1–63.

Ludwig, Frieder. *Church and State in Tanzania: Aspects of Changing Relationships, 1961–1994*. Leiden: Brill, 1999.

Lugard, Frederick. *The Dual Mandate in British Tropical Africa*. London: Frank Cass, 1965.

Lydon, Ghislaine. *On Trans-Saharan Trails: Islamic Law, Trade Networks, and Cross-Cultural Exchange in Nineteenth-Century Western Africa*. Cambridge: Cambridge University Press, 2009.

Macola, Giacomo. '"It means as if we are excluded from the good freedom": Thwarted Expectations of Independence in the Luapula Province of Zambia, 1964–1967'. *Journal of African History*, 47 (2006), 43–56.

Madan, A. C. *English-Swahili Dictionary*. Oxford: Clarendon Press, 1902.

Maddox, Gregory. 'African Theology and the Search for the Universal'. In Thomas Spear and Isaria N. Kimambo, *East African Expressions of Christianity*. Oxford: James Currey, 1999a, pp. 25–36.

'The Church and Cigogo: Father Stephen Mlundi and Christianity in Central Tanzania'. In Thomas Spear and Isaria N. Kimambo, *East African Expressions of Christianity*. Oxford: James Currey, 1999b, pp. 150–166.

Maddox, Gregory and James Giblin (eds.). *In Search of a Nation: Histories of Authority and Dissidence in Tanzania*. Oxford: James Currey, 2005.

Maguire, G. Andrew. *Toward 'uhuru' in Tanzania: The Politics of Participation*. Cambridge: Cambridge University Press, 1969.

Mahmood, Saba. *Politics of Piety: The Islamic Revival and the Feminist Subject*. Princeton, NJ: Princeton University Press, 2005.

Malcolm, D. W. *Sukumaland: An African People and Their Country*. London: Oxford University Press, 1953.

Malik, Habib C. *The Challenge of Human Rights: Charles Malik and the Universal Declaration*. Oxford: Charles Malik Foundation, 2000.

Mamdani, Mahmood. *Citizen and Subject: Contemporary Africa and the Legacy of Late Colonialism*. Princeton, NJ: Princeton University Press, 1996.

Mann, Gregory. *Native Sons: West African Veterans and France in the Twentieth Century*. Durham, NC: Duke University Press, 2006.

Marealle, Petro Itosi. *Maisha ya Mchagga Hapa Duniani na Ahera*, Dar es Salaam: Mkuki na Nyota Publishers, 2002 [1947].

Maritain, Jacques. *The Rights of Man and Natural Law*. London: The Centenary Press, 1944.

Maritain, Jacques (ed.). *Human Rights: Comments and Interpretations*. London: Allan Wingate, 1949.

Mason, Horace. 'Pare News and Other Publications of the Pare Mass Literacy and Community Development Scheme'. In UNESCO, *Reports and Papers on Mass Communication: Periodicals for New Literates: Seven Case Histories*, 24 (1957), 19–23.

Matena, Karuna. *Alibis of Empire: Henry Maine and the Ends of Liberal Imperialism*. Princeton, NJ: Princeton University Press, 2010.

Mazower, Mark. *No Enchanted Palace: The End of Empire and the Ideological Origins of the United Nations*. Princeton, N.J.: Princeton University Press, 2009.

'The End of Civilization and the Rise of Human Rights: The Mid-twentieth-century Disjuncture'. In Stefan-Ludwig Hoffmann (ed.), *Human Rights in the Twentieth-Century*, Cambridge: Cambridge University Press, 2010, pp. 29–44.

Governing the World: The History of an Idea. London: Penguin Books, 2012.

Mazrui, Ali. 'Tanzaphilia'. *Transition*, 31 (1967), 20–26.

Mbee, Gicha. 'Letter from Mbugwe, Tanganyika'. *Africa*, 35 (1965), 198–208.

Mboya, Tom. *Freedom and After*. London: André Deutsch, 1963.

McCarthy, Helen. 'Associational Voluntarism in Interwar Britain'. In Matthew Hilton and James McKay (eds.), *The Ages of Voluntarism: How We Got to the Big Society*. Oxford: Oxford University Press, 2011, pp. 47–68.

McHale, Shawn Frederick. *Print and Power: Confucianism, Communism and Buddhism in the Making of Modern Vietnam*. Honolulu: University of Hawai'i Press, 2003.

McHenry, Dean E. *Limited Choices: The Political Struggle for Socialism in Tanzania*. London, Lynne Riener, 1994.

Mehta, Uday Singh. *Liberalism and Empire: A Study in Nineteenth-century British Liberal Thought*. Chicago: The University of Chicago Press, 1999.

Mercer, Claire, Ben Page and Martin Evans. *Development and the African Diaspora: Place and the Politics of Home*. London: Zed Books, 2008.

Mill, J. S. *Utilitarianism, On Liberty, Considerations on Representative Government*. London: J. M. Dent, 1993.

Milner, Anthony. *The Invention of Politics in Colonial Malaya: Contesting Nationalism and the Expansion of the Public Sphere*. Cambridge: Cambridge University Press, 1994.

Misra, Maria. *Vishnu's Crowded Temple: India since the Great Rebellion*. London: Allen Lane, 2007.

Mitter, Rana. 'Modernity, Internationalization and War in the History of Modern China'. *The Historical Journal*, 48 (2005), 523–543.

Moore, Bob (ed.). *Crises of Empire: Decolonization and Europe's Imperial States, 1918–1975*. London: Hodder/Arnold, 2008.

Moore, Sally Falk. 'From Giving and Lending to Selling: Property Transactions Reflecting Historical Changes on Kilimanjaro'. In Kristin Mann and Richard Roberts (eds.), *Law in Colonial Africa*. London: James Currey, 1991, pp. 108–145.

Morgenthau, Ruth Schachter. *Political Parties in French-Speaking West Africa*. Oxford: Clarendon Press, 1964.

Morrison, David R. *Education and Politics in Africa: The Tanzanian Case*. London: C. Hurst, 1976.

Moyn, Samuel. *The Last Utopia: Human Rights in History*. London: Belknap, 2010.

'Personalism, Community and the Origins of Human Rights'. In Stefan-Ludwig Hoffman (ed.), *Human Rights in the Twentieth Century*, pp. 85–106.

Msekwa, Pius. *Towards Party Supremacy*. Kampala: East African Literature Bureau, 1977.

Muoria-Sal, Wangaria, Bodil Folke Frederiksen and John Lonsdale (eds.). *Writing for Kenya: The Life and Works of Henry Muoria*. Leiden: Brill, 2009.

Mustapha, Abdul Raufu and Lindsay Whitfield. *Turning Points in African Democracy*. Oxford: James Currey, 2009.

Mutongi, Kenda. *Worries of the Heart: Widows, Family, and Community in Kenya*. Chicago: University of Chicago Press, 2007.

Mwakikagile, Godfrey. *Life in Tanganyika in the Fifties*. Grand Rapids, MI: Continental Press, 2006.

Newell, Stephanie. 'Entering the Territory of Elites: Literary Activity in Colonial Ghana'. In Karin Barber (ed.), *Africa's Hidden Histories: Everyday Literacy and Making the Self*. Bloomington: Indiana University Press, 2006, pp. 211–235.

'Articulating Empire: Newspaper Readerships in Colonial West Africa'. *New Formations*, 73 (2011), 26–42.

The Power to Name: A History of Anonymity in Colonial West Africa. Athens, OH: Ohio University Press, 2013.

Nkrumah, Kwame. *The Autobiography of Kwame Nkrumah.* Edinburgh: Thomas Nelson and Sons, 1957.

Nugent, Paul. *Africa since Independence: A Comparative History.* Basingstoke, UK: Palgrave Macmillan, 2004.

Nyerere, Julius. *Freedom and Unity: A Selection from Writings and Speeches, 1952–65.* London: Oxford University Press, 1967.

Freedom and Socialism: A Selection from Writings and Speeches, 1965–1967. London: Oxford University Press, 1968.

Ogot, Bethwell A. and William R. Ochieng. *Decolonization and Independence in Kenya, 1940–93.* Oxford: James Currey, 1995.

Parsons, Timothy. *The African Rank-and-File: Social Implications of Colonial Military Service in the King's African Rifles, 1902–1964.* Oxford: James Currey, 1999.

Race, Resistance and the Boy Scout Movement in British Colonial Africa. Athens, OH: Ohio University Press, 2004.

Pedersen, Susan. 'Back to the League of Nations'. *American Historical Review,* 112 (2007), 1091–1117.

Pels, Peter. 'The Pidginization of Luguru Politics: Administrative Ethnography and the Paradoxes of Indirect Rule'. *American Ethnologist,* 23 (1996), 739–761.

'Creolization in Secret: The Birth of Nationalism in Late-Colonial Uluguru, Tanzania'. *Africa,* 72 (2002), 1–28.

Peterson, Derek. *Creative Writing: Translation, Bookkeeping, and the Work of Imagination in Colonial Kenya.* Portsmouth, NH: Heinemann, 2004.

'Language Work and Colonial Politics in Eastern Africa: The Making of Standard Swahili and "School Kikuyu"'. In David L. Hoyt and Karen Oslund (eds.), *The Study of Language and the Politics of Community in Global Context.* Lanham, MD: Lexington Books, 2006, pp. 185–214.

Ethnic Patriotism and the East African Revival: A History of Dissent, c. 1935–1972. Cambridge: Cambridge University Press, 2012.

Peterson, Derek (ed.). *Abolitionism and Imperialism in Britain, Africa, and the Atlantic.* Athens, OH: Ohio University Press, 2010.

Phillipson, G. 'Etude de quelques concepts politiques swahili dans les oeuvres de J. K. Nyerere'. *Cahiers d'Etudes Africaines,* 10 (1970), 530–545.

Porter, Andrew. *Religion versus Empire? British Protestant Missionaries and Overseas Expansion, 1700–1914.* Manchester, U.K.: Manchester University Press, 2004.

Pouwels, Randall L. *Horn and Crescent: Cultural Change and Traditional Islam on the East African Coast, 800–1900.* Cambridge: Cambridge University Press, 1987.

Pratt, Cranford. *The Critical Phase in Tanzania, 1945–1968.* Cambridge: Cambridge University Press, 1976.

Pugliese, Christina. 'Complementary or Contending Nationhoods: Kikuyu Pamphlets and Songs, 1945–52'. In John Lonsdale and Atieno Odhiambo (eds.), *Mau Mau and Nationhood: Arms, Authority and Narration,* Oxford: James Currey, 2003, pp. 97–120.

Rathbone, Richard. 'West Africa: Modernity and Modernization'. In Jan-Georg Deutsch, Peter Probst and Heike Schmidt (eds.), *African Modernities: Entangled Meanings in Current Debate*. Oxford: James Currey, 2002, pp. 18–30.

Reid, Anthony. 'Merdeka: The Concept of Freedom in Indonesia'. In David Kelly and Anthony Reid (eds.), *Asian Freedoms: The Idea of Freedom in East and Southeast Asia*. Cambridge: Cambridge University Press, 1998, pp. 141–160.

Resnick, Idrian N. *Tanzania: Revolution by Education*, Arusha, Longmans, 1968.

Richter, Melvin. *The History of Social and Political Concepts: A Critical Introduction*. Oxford: Oxford University Press, 1995.

Rivers-Smith, Stanley and Frederick Johnson. *Uraia*. London: Macmillan, 1928.

Rugumamu, Severine R., *Lethal Aid: The Illusion of Socialism and Self-Reliance in Tanzania*. Trenton, NJ: Africa World Press, 1997.

Ruhumbika, Gabriel. *Village in Uhuru*. London: Longman Group, 1969.

Runciman, David. *The Confidence Trap: A History of Democracy in Crisis from World War 1 to the Present*. New Haven, CT: Yale University Press, 2013.

Ryan, Alan. 'Newer than What? Older than What?' In Ellen Frankel Paul et al. (eds.), *Liberalism Old and New*. Cambridge: Cambridge University Press, 2007, pp. 1–15.

Said, Mohamed. *The Life and Times of Abdulwahid Sykes: The Untold Story of the Muslim Struggle against British Colonialism in Tanganyika*. London: Minerva Press, 1998.

Sanders, Todd. *Beyond Bodies: Rainmaking and Sense Making in Tanzania*. Toronto and Buffalo: University of Toronto Press, 2008.

Schaffer, Frederick C. *Democracy in Translation: Understanding Politics in an Unfamiliar Culture*. Ithaca, NY and London: Cornell University Press, 1998.

Schatzberg, Michael. *Political Legitimacy in Middle Africa: Father, Family and Food*. Bloomington: Indiana University Press, 2001.

Scheele, Judith. *Smugglers and Saints of the Sahara: Regional Connectivity in the Twentieth Century*. Cambridge: Cambridge University Press, 2012.

Schmidt, Elizabeth. *Mobilizing the Masses: Gender, Ethnicity, and Class in the Nationalist Movement in Guinea, 1939–1958*. Athens, OH: Ohio University Press, 2005.

Schneider, Leander. 'Colonial Legacies and Postcolonial Authoritarianism in Tanzania'. *African Studies Review*, 49 (2006), 93–118.

Scott, James C. *Seeing Like a State: How Certain Schemes to Improve the Human Condition Have Failed*. New Haven, CT: Yale University Press, 1998.

Scotton, C. M. 'Some Swahili Political Words'. *Journal of Modern African Studies*, 3 (1965), 527–541.

Scotton, James F. 'The First African Press in East Africa: Protest and Nationalism in Uganda in the 1920s'. *The International Journal of African Historical Studies*, 6 (1973), 211–228.

'Tanganyika's African Press, 1937–1960: A Nearly Forgotten Pre-independence Forum'. *African Studies Review*, 21 (1978), 1–18.

Shadle, Brett. *"Girl Cases": Marriage and Colonialism in Gusiiland, Kenya, 1890–1970*. Portsmouth, NH: Heinemann, 2006.

Sharkey, Heather. *Living with Colonialism*. Berkeley: University of California, 2003.

Sherwood, Marika. '"There Is No New Deal for the Blackman in San Francisco": African Attempts to Influence the Founding Conference of the United Nations, April-July 1945'. *International Journal of African Historical Studies*, 29 (1996), 71–94.

Shimazu, Naoko. *Japan, Race and Equality: The Racial Equality Proposal of 1919*. London: Routledge, 1998.

Shipway, Martin. *Decolonization and Its Impact: A Comparative Approach to the End of the Colonial Empires*. Oxford: Blackwell, 2008.

Simpson, Alfred B. *Human Rights and the End of Empire: Britain and the Genesis of the European Convention*. Oxford: Oxford University Press, 2001.

Sinha, Mrinalini. *Specters of Mother India: The Global Restructuring of an Empire*. London and Durham, NC: Duke University Press, 2006.

Skinner, Quentin. 'The Empirical Theorists of Democracy and Their Critics: A Plague on Both Their Houses'. *Political Theory*, 1 (1979), 287–306.

Smith, James Howard. *Bewitching Development: Witchcraft and the Reinvention of Development in Neoliberal Kenya*. London: University of Chicago Press, 2008.

Speller, Ian. 'An African Cuba? Britain and the Zanzibar Revolution'. *Journal of Imperial and Commonwealth History*, 35 (2007), 283–302.

Stahl, Kathleen M. *History of the Chagga People of Kilimanjaro*. The Hague: Mouton, 1964.

'The Chagga', in P. Gulliver (ed.), *Tradition and Transition: Studies of the Tribal Element in the Modern Era*. Berkeley: University of California Press, 1969, pp. 209–222.

Sturmer, Martin. *The Media History of Tanzania*. Ndanda: Ndanda Mission Press, 1998.

Suriano, Maria. 'Letters to the Editor and Poems: *Mambo Leo* and Readers' Debates on *Dansi, Ustaarabu*, Respectability, and Modernity in Tanganyika, 1940s-1950s'. *Africa Today*, 57 (2011), 39–55.

Tanganyika National Assembly. *Tanganyika Citizenship, 1961*, Government Paper Number 4, Dar es Salaam: Government of Tanganyika, 1961.

Tilley, Helen. *Africa as a Living Laboratory: Empire, Development and the Problem of Scientific Knowledge*. Chicago: University of Chicago Press, 2011.

Tilley, Helen and Robert Gordon (eds.). *Ordering Africa: Anthropology, European Imperialism and the Politics of Knowledge*. Manchester, U.K.: Manchester University Press, 2007.

Tordoff, William. *Government and Politics in Tanzania*. Nairobi: East African Publishing House, 1967.

Tribe, Keith. 'Translator's Introduction'. In Reinhard Koselleck, *Futures Past: On the Semantics of Historical Time*. New York: Columbia University Press, 2004, pp. vii–xx.

United Nations. *Official Records of the United Nations Trusteeship Council*, First to Twenty-Sixth Sessions.

Vail, Leroy. *The Creation of Tribalism in Southern Africa*. London: James Currey, 1989.

van Hensbroek, Pieter Boele. *Political Discourses in African Thought: 1860 to the Present*. Westport, CT: Praeger, 1999.

Vaughan, Megan. 'Mr Mdala Writes to the Governor: Negotiating Colonial Rule in Nyasaland'. *History Workshop Journal*, 60 (2005), 171–188.

'Africa and the Birth of the Modern World'. *Transactions of the Royal Historical Society*, 16 (2006), 143–162.

Von Eschen, Penny. *Race against Empire: Black Americans and Anticolonialism, 1937–1957*. Ithaca, NY: Cornell University Press, 1997.

Watenpaugh, Keith. *Being Modern in the Middle East: Revolution, Nationalism, Colonialism, and the Arab Middle Class*. Princeton, NJ: Princeton University Press, 2006.

Westcott, N. J. 'An East African Radical: The Life of Erica Fiah'. *Journal of African History*, 22 (1981), 85–101.

Westerlund, David. *Ujamaa na Dini: A Study of Some Aspects of Society and Religion in Tanzania, 1961–1977*. Stockholm: Almquist and Wiksell International, 1980.

Whiteley, W. H. 'Political Concepts and Connotations: Observations on the Use of Some Political Terms in Swahili'. In Kenneth Kirkwood (ed.), *African Affairs*, 1 (St. Antony's Papers, 10). London: Chatto and Windus, 1961, 7–21.

Swahili: The Rise of a National Language. Aldershot: Gregg Revivals, 1993 [1969].

Widner, Jennifer. *Building the Rule of Law: Francis Nyalali and the Road to Judicial Independence in Africa*. New York and London: W. W. Norton, 2001.

Wild-Wood, Emma. *Migration and Christian Identity in Congo (DRC)*. Leiden: Brill, 2008.

Willis, Justin. *Potent Brews: A Social History of Alcohol in East Africa, 1850–1999*. Oxford: James Currey, 2002.

Willis, Justin and George Gona. 'The Mijikenda Union, 1945–1980'. *Comparative Studies in Society and History*, 55 (2013), 448–473.

Winter, J. C. *Bruno Gutmann, 1876–1966: A German Approach to Social Anthropology*. Oxford: Oxford University Press, 1979.

Wraith, Ronald E. *The East African Citizen*. London: Oxford University Press, 1959.

Wright, Marcia. 'Swahili Language Policy, 1890–1940'. *Swahili*, 35 (1965), 40–48.
Strategies of Slaves and Women: Life-stories from East/Central Africa. London: James Currey, 1993.

Zachariah, Benjamin. *Developing India: An Intellectual and Social History c. 1930–50*. Oxford: Oxford University Press, 2005.

Unpublished Theses

Bates, Margaret L. 'Tanganyika under British Administration, 1920–1955'. Unpublished DPhil thesis, University of Oxford, 1957.

Bjerk, Paul, K. 'Julius Nyerere and the Establishment of Sovereignty in Tanganyika'. Unpublished PhD thesis, University of Wisconsin, 2008.

Chalmers, Rhoderick. 'We Nepalis': Language, Literature and the Formation of a Nepali Public Sphere in India, 1914–1940'. Unpublished PhD thesis, SOAS, 2003.

Denault, Leigh. 'Publicising Family in Colonial North India, c. 1780–1930'. Unpublished PhD thesis, University of Cambridge, 2008.

Hunter, Emma. 'Languages of Politics in Twentieth-Century Kilimanjaro'. Unpublished PhD thesis, University of Cambridge, 2008.

James Brennan, Nation, Race and Urbanization in Dar es Salaam, Tanzania, 1916–1976. Unpublished PhD thesis, Northwestern University, 2002.

Lemke, Hilda. 'Die Suaheli-Zeitungen und Zeitschriften in Deutsch-Ostafrika'. Unpublished PhD dissertation, Leipzig University, 1929.

Maro, P. S. 'Population and Land Resources in Northern Tanzania: The Dynamics of Change 1920–1970'. Unpublished PhD thesis, University of Minnesota, 1974.

Rogers, S. G. 'The Search for Political Focus on Kilimanjaro: A History of Chagga Politics, 1916–1952, with Special Reference to the Cooperative Movement and Indirect Rule'. Unpublished PhD thesis, University of Dar es Salaam, 1972.

Scotton, James Francis. 'Growth of the Vernacular Press in Colonial East Africa: Patterns of Government Control'. Unpublished PhD thesis, University of Wisconsin, 1971.

Von Clemm, Michael. 'People of the White Mountain: The Interdependence of Political and Economic Activity amongst the Chagga with Special Reference to Recent Changes'. Unpublished PhD thesis, University of Oxford, 1962.

Westcott, Nicholas J. 'The Impact of the Second World War on Tanganyika, 1939–1949'. Unpublished PhD thesis, University of Cambridge, 1982.

Whyte, Christine. 'Whose Slavery? The Language and Politics of Slavery and Abolition in Siera Leone, 1898–1956'. Unpublished PhD thesis, University of Zurich, 2013.

Index

BOOKS IN THIS SERIES

Lightning Source UK Ltd.
Milton Keynes UK
UKHW01f0459140618
324233UK00001B/68/P

Political Thought and the Public Sphere
in Tanzania

Political Thought and the Public Sphere in Tanzania: Freedom, Democracy and Citizenship in the Era of Decolonization is a study of the interplay of vernacular and global languages of politics in Africa's mid-twentieth century. Decolonization is often understood as a moment when Western forms of political order were imposed on non-Western societies, but this book draws attention instead to debates over universal questions about the nature of politics, the concept of freedom and the meaning of citizenship. These debates generated political narratives that were formed in dialogue with both global discourses and local political arguments. The United Nations Trusteeship Territory of Tanganyika, now mainland Tanzania, serves as a compelling example of these processes. Starting in 1945 and ending with the Arusha Declaration of 1967, Emma Hunter explores political argument in Tanzania's public sphere to show how political narratives succeeded when they managed to combine promises of freedom with new forms of belonging.

Emma Hunter is a Lecturer in History at the University of Edinburgh.